Shipwrecks of Florida

SECOND EDITION

Shipwrecks of Florida

SECOND EDITION

Steven D. Singer

Pineapple Press, Inc.
Sarasota, Florida

To my parents, Morton and Marjorie Singer,
and my daughter, Chelsea

Inquiries should be addressed to:

Pineapple Press, Inc.
P.O. Box 3889
Sarasota, Florida 34230
www.pineapplepress.com

Library of Congress Cataloging-in-Publication Data

Singer, Steven D., 1952–
 Shipwrecks of Florida : a comprehensive listing / by Steven D. Singer. —2nd ed.
  p. cm.
 Includes bibliographical references and index.
 ISBN 1-56164-163-4 (alk. paper)
Shipwrecks—Florida. I. Title.

G525.S556 1998
363.12'32'0916348—dc21   98-20306
                    CIP

Second Edition
10 9 8 7 6 5 4 3 2

Printed in the United States of America

CONTENTS

ACKNOWLEDGMENTS

I would like to thank the following individuals and organizations for their help:

Deborah Crites; Rodney Dillon and the Broward County Historical Commission; the National Archives; the United States Naval Academy Museum; the Naval Historical Center; Jim Dunbar and James Levy of the Florida Bureau of Archaeological Research; Harold E. Brown and the Maine Maritime Museum; the Marine Archaeological Council, Inc.; Thomas Hambright and the Monroe County Public Library at Key West; Jean Haviland; Penobscot Marine Museum; the Steamship Historical Society of America, Inc.; Florida State Archives; Pensacola Historical Society; St. Augustine Historical Society; Mystic Seaport Museum; Peabody Museum; Christie's, New York; Statens Sjohistoriska Museum; Norsk Sjofartsmuseum; Department of Transport, London; Boca Raton Historical Society; Rick Horgan and Oceaneering International, Inc. (Search Division); Dr. Roger Smith, particularly for material supplied for the appendix on "Rights to Wrecks"; Robert Marx for use of his shipwreck research; and the many other people who helped me. The organizations of many of them are listed in the research section. Though all these people helped, any errors are mine alone.

I would also like to mention my fellow divers, without whom I would not have had the opportunity to dive and explore the many shipwrecks off the Florida coast and elsewhere: Bob and Margaret Weller, who have given me the opportunity to actually find treasure; the *Pandion* crew (Don Kree, Bob Luyendyk, Brad Johnson, Carl Ward, Bernie Smith); Ernie Richards; and Jack Pennell (we'll find it yet, Jack!).

Finally, my sincerest thanks go to the late Peter Throckmorton. Known as the "Father of Marine Archaeology," Peter was always willing to share his vast knowledge of maritime history and archaeology with anyone who asked. It was a pleasure to have worked and studied under him. He will be greatly missed.

FOREWORD

Shipwrecks, pirates, sunken gold: these are just a few words that conjure up images of adventure, romance, and mystery. To find a shipwreck, whether 100 or 1,000 years old, is to travel back to another time. To find a gold coin once held by a Spanish conquistador, or a gold medallion once worn by a proud Inca, is a thrilling experience. There is still treasure off Florida's shores, some of it in only a few feet of water.

But treasure is by no means the only lure. It's also exciting to find artifacts, even those with little or no value — especially when you can identify the vessel they once belonged to. Ships can have fascinating stories. Shipwreck, prisoners of war, a drunken captain, fever, starvation, and determination to survive all make for a splendid novel, but they are actually all part of the real story of the ship *L'Athenaise*, which sank off the Florida coast in 1804. This is but one of the many fascinating tales of Florida shipwrecks. I have included six narratives to give an idea of the kinds of stories behind these wrecks.

Ever since I first read about shipwrecks and pirates, I dreamed about finding sunken treasure. I imagined a Spanish galleon sitting on the sandy ocean floor with her torn sails flowing with the current. Little did I know then that a pile of stones, or some anchor or cannon, were all that might be visible of these vessels today and that the real treasure is the history they provide.

I became a certified diver in the cold waters of New Jersey when I was 14 years old and have been hooked ever since. After moving to Florida, I became a scuba instructor and soon discovered some of the wrecks that lie off the Florida coast. My desire to identify these wrecks led me into the research field.

This book is meant to serve as a useful reference for many of the shipwreck sites of Florida. More than 2,100 shipwrecks are listed, from the 16th century to the present. For those wishing to do further research, I've listed additional sources. There are also appendices with some information on what to look for when searching for a wreck, what equipment to use in searching for and excavating a wreck, and how to identify artifacts and wreckage, as well as information on the laws dealing with shipwrecks.

New shipwreck sites are being found all the time, and additional information is provided with each new discovery. Piecing all this together provides an exciting history of shipping along the coast of this New World peninsula.

Shipwrecks of Florida

The *USS Peacock* captures the *HMS Epervier*, April 29, 1814. Illustration by Tomiro.
COURTESY OF MSC – 198, U.S. NAVY. U.S. NAVAL HISTORICAL CENTER.

INTRODUCTION

Galleons, schooners, frigates, steamers...these and many other vessels plied Florida's waters during the last 500 years. Florida's maritime history dates back to the early 1500s. Both the Cantino Map of 1502 and the Nicoli Caveri Map of 1504-1505 show Florida. But it is still uncertain who discovered the peninsula. History has it that the first Spanish landing was made by Juan Ponce de León in 1513. It has been speculated that John Cabot, a Venetian who sailed under a charter for Britain, was the first European to land in Florida, in 1497.

During the Spanish exploitation of the New World, from 1492 until the demise of the Spanish-American colonies in 1815, many ships passed the Florida coast carrying gold and silver back to Spain. Life on these vessels was extremely hard, and many lives were lost due to disease, starvation, pirate attack, and shipwreck.

After St. Augustine was established in 1565, shipping increased between there and Havana. St. Augustine was shipping oranges to the West Indies in the 1730s. In the 18th century, Florida was exporting corn, rice, indigo, and tobacco to the Caribbean. Lumber such as live oak, cypress, and pine was shipped from ports such as St. Augustine and Pensacola. Barrel staves were manufactured in Florida and transported to the West Indies to ship products grown or made there, such as coffee, rum, sugar, and molasses.

As the years passed and new settlements appeared, maritime trade increased. The west coast of Florida became as likely an area for shipwrecks as the east coast. After Key West was established as a major port in the 1820s, shipwrecks in the Keys became more frequent. Because of the wrecking industry, Key West became the wealthiest city (per capita) in the United States during part of the 19th century.

Many other Florida cities became major ports during the 19th century. Florida was a major source of lumber and other goods, and the shipping industry boomed. Cotton from the south was shipped through Florida ports. Coffee, sugar, molasses, rum, and other goods from the Caribbean and South America also made their way through Florida ports. With more lighthouses, better charts and more advanced technology, the shipping trade became safer. Today a shipwreck is a rarity, but many wrecks from earlier times lie off the long Florida coastline.

Types of Ships

What types of ships are likely to be found in the waters of Florida? They can range from a 500-year-old Spanish *caravel* lost in a storm to a 10-year-old yacht scuttled during a drug-running trip. Though not all types of vessels are included here, the most common ones are.

In the early 1500s, Spaniards sailed along the Florida coast in the caravel, a small, fast ship of 35 to 100 tons. A favorite of early explorers, it was the type of ship in which Columbus sailed to America.

11

By the mid-1500s, however, Spain needed larger vessels to carry the growing amount of booty from the New World. *Galleons* (Figure 1) and *naos*, or merchant galleons, became the vessels of choice. Most ranged from 300 to 600 tons, though by the late 1600s they ranged up to 1,200 tons. Early galleons had three or four masts; after about 1650, they were all built with three masts. Galleons also had a high front section (forecastle) and rear section (sterncastle). They were heavily armed with up to 70 cannons. Naos were the same design, but they were not as heavily armed, with maybe ten or twelve cannons, and they were used as merchant vessels. A 16th-century galleon of 400 tons had 34 cubits of keel, 16 of beam, and 11.5 of depth. (A cubit equals 1.828 English feet).

Figure 1: Sketch of a mid-16th-century galleon. AUTHOR.

The Spanish fleets or *flotas* (also called armadas) were organized to safely transport New World treasure back to Spain, whose survival had become dependent on such shipments. Pirates, privateers, and naval vessels of Spain's enemies preyed upon these treasure-laden vessels. To counter these threats, Spain decided in 1564 to send two fleets each year to the New World. One was called the *Nueva España* (New Spain, i.e., Mexican) fleet, and the other was known as the *Tierra Firme* (South American) fleet. Bob Marx has provided me new information that there were actually three fleets which sailed to the New World. The *Armada de la Carrera de Las Indias*, also called "The Galleons," which sailed with the *Tierra Firme* fleet to the New World, was the fleet which carried the treasure back to Spain. All three fleets planned to meet in Havana and return to Spain together.

The *Nueva España* fleet usually would leave Cádiz in the spring and the *Tierra Firme* fleet would leave in August. Each would go south to the Canary Islands and then turn west toward the New World. These fleets carried supplies for the New World and later transported mercury, which was used to refine silver and gold.

It took about two months for the *Nueva España* ships to arrive at Veracruz, Mexico. A celebration was held, and then the trading began. The *Nueva España* fleet carried not only treasure from Mexico but also silk, lacquerware, jewelry, and porcelain from the Far East. Beginning in 1565, these goods were sent from Manila, in the Philippines, to Acapulco on ships called the Manila Galleons. The goods were unloaded at Acapulco and transported overland to Veracruz.

The *Tierra Firme* fleet would arrive at Cartagena, Columbia, to pick up gold and emeralds, then sail to Nombre de Dios, Panama, to load Peruvian silver and other treasures. After 1585 Porto Bello, Panama, replaced Nombre de Dios as the port-of-call because of its better harborage.

For the return to Spain, the two fleets would meet in Havana for repairs and provisions, and then sail home together. The early fleets returned via the "Old Bahama Channel" between the north coast of Cuba and the Bahama Banks. But they soon found it easier to ride the Gulf Stream north between Florida's east coast and the western Bahamas. In this way, they could avoid the many uncharted reefs off the Bahamas and could use Florida's coast to fix their position. Depending on conditions, anywhere from just past Cape Canaveral up to the Carolinas is where the fleets would turn east toward Bermuda, The Azores, and then Spain. This route became known as the "New Bahama Channel."

Sometimes bad weather or other circumstances forced the fleets to return home separately. To avoid the worst of the hurricane season, the treasure fleets tried to leave Havana before August 20. Many vessels never made it home and lie off Florida's coastline.

The Spanish fleets consisted of two to four galleons and a varying number of merchant naos and *pataches*, which had replaced the slower caravels in the late 1500s. The patache, also called an *aviso*, was used as a dispatch boat, but sometimes carried treasure. The lead galleon, or *capitana*, carried the commander of the fleet. Bringing up the rear was a galleon called the *almiranta*. This ship carried the admiral of the fleet, who served under the commander.

With such fleets, Spain retained her hold on the Caribbean until the 17th century. As her power weakened, the English, Dutch, and French colonized and fortified many of the islands in the region. As those three nations vied to become the dominant naval power in the world, illicit trade between them and Spain's New World colonies began to flourish. Also, with the absence of Spain's naval force in the New World in the 17th century, the buccaneers began to prey on the Spanish colonies and ships in the region.

Though the Spaniards continued building their bulky and top-heavy ships until well into the 17th century, other countries began using improved ship designs. For instance, in the late 16th and early 17th centuries, the Dutch reduced the lofty sterncastle of the galleons, making the ships less top heavy.

But it was the French design of the 17th century that other navies eventually copied. The French built bigger and broader hulls to make the ships more stable. They reduced the number of cannon and moved the lower gun ports higher to keep water from getting in.

Galleons—or "men-of-war," as they came to be known—were eventually classed by rate. Rates referred to the ship's size and number of guns. By the mid-17th century, all navies classed their ships from first-rates down to sixth-rates. These were called "ships of the line," a name adopted from the Dutch naval tactic of sailing into battle in a single line. Ships in the front and back part of the line protected the ones in the middle from attack on their bows and sterns, where they were most vulnerable. The first-rates were the pride of the fleet, mounting 100 or more guns. The standard ship of the line was the third-rate, originally with about 50 guns, though it later carried between 70 and 80. The remaining rates were used for day-to-day duties.

The *sloop* of war, called the *corvette* by the French, was developed in the 1600s as a two-masted, square-rigged vessel, but it soon developed into a three-masted vessel carrying 10 to 20 guns. It was next in size to the frigate. The sloop was used for commerce as well as war and was a common merchant ship in America in the early 1700s used in the West Indian and coastal trade. The larger traders were usually 50 to 60 feet long on deck. The bowsprit, a spar extending from the bow, could add 20 feet to the length of the vessel.

During the 17th century, the French also used the *pinasse*, a cargo ship with ten to twelve guns, in the New World trade. The vessel was ship-rigged, which means it had three masts and square sails. The Dutch *pinnace* of the same period was a small, fast vessel used to carry dispatches and personnel. It was considered the prototype of the sloop of war and carried ten to twelve cannon. Many nations used the Dutch *flute* as a merchant vessel during the same period. The pinasse and flute were built as merchantmen.

The *West Indiaman*, developed by England for the New World trade, became popular by the mid-1700s. Though a merchant vessel, it was exceptionally well armed. Ship-rigged and averaging between 150 and 400 tons, it was smaller but faster than the *East Indiaman*, which was used in the Far East trade.

The *frigate*, a sailing warship, was developed in the mid-1700s. Early frigates carried 20 to 30 guns; later ones were larger and carried up to 50 or 60 guns. This frigate is not to be confused with the 16th-century Spanish frigate or *fragata* of no more than 50 tons which was used as a trading vessel in the New World. Another 16th-century Spanish vessel was the *barco de trato* or trading boat of 50 to 100 tons, also used in the New World.

The first large vessels from North America were built in New England in the 1630s. Soon after, ships began to be built in Delaware, Pennsylvania, New Jersey, New York, and the Chesapeake Bay area of Virginia and Maryland. By 1676, 430 vessels of 30 to 250 tons were reported out of Massachusetts. In 1775, the insurance underwriter Lloyds of London listed 2,311 vessels totaling 373,615 tons as having been built in America in the last three years.

By the mid-1700s, ship-rigged vessels were no longer the most common moderate-sized merchantmen: they were being replaced by two-masted *brigs*, *brigantines,* and *schooners*. The early schooner, or scooner, appears to have been developed for small vessels in the Netherlands in the early 17th century. It was introduced in America in the late 17th century and had become the most popular American two-masted rig by the end of the 18th century. It was in demand because the sails could be manned by a much smaller crew than in earlier vessels.

Most of the sailing vessels listed in this book wrecked during the 19th century. Among the most common were:

• *Ship*: Although the term now can mean any large vessel, in the 1800s it referred to square-rigged vessels of three or more masts. These included clippers, packets, and down-easters.

• *Bark* or *barque, barkentine* or *barquentine*: vessels with three or more masts. The bark was square-rigged on the foremast and mainmast, while the barkentine was square-rigged on the foremast only.

• *Brig, brigantine, hermaphrodite brig*: two-masted vessels developed at the beginning of the 18th century. The foremast was square-rigged on all three types. The brig added a sail on the mainmast that stretched from bow to stern (a fore-and-aft sail). The brigantine did away with the square mainsail and replaced it with a fore-and-aft mainsail. The hermaphrodite brig rigged the mainmast with fore-and-aft sails only.

• *Schooner*: There were many different schooner rigs, ranging from those of a few tons to the 7,500-ton, 433-foot, seven-masted *Thomas W. Lawson*, which wrecked off England in 1907. Schooners were used primarily in the coastal and island trade.

• The *steamer* eventually took over the shipping trade. It was not dependent on wind and could deliver goods much faster than sailing vessels.

The first merchant steam vessel, built by John Fitch in 1790, operated out of Philadelphia. Robert Fulton's steamboat, the *North River,* first sailed up the Hudson in 1807. In 1838, the *Sirius* became the first vessel to cross the Atlantic entirely under steam power. Still, all of the early transatlantic steamers also had sails.

Approximately 700 steam vessels were operating in the United States by 1838. These early steamers used a paddlewheel, located either on the side, at the stern, or in the center of the vessel.

The first American screw (propeller) vessel was a 226-ton bark that had been converted to steam in 1841. It used Ericsson's propeller, which was used in Europe starting in 1836.

Although steamers took over the shipping trade, sailing vessels were still used to carry cargoes that steamships would not carry or to go along routes where coaling stations were scarce. An example was the guano and nitrate trade in South America. Schooners, especially the big three-masted ones, competed successfully against steam power along the North American coasts well into the 20th century, mainly because they were more economical to operate. As technology progressed and engines became more efficient, the age of sail came to an end (though the French now have computer-controlled commercial sailing ships).

No one knows exactly how many ships were wrecked in Florida waters. Based on the over 2,000 wrecks listed in this book and the amount of shipping along Florida's coast, I estimate there were between 4,000 and 5,000 Florida shipwrecks since the 1500s.

By comparison, England, one of the largest maritime trading countries, in just one year (1864) lost 1,741 vessels off her coast, along with 516 lives; in 1880, she lost 1,303 vessels and 2,100 lives. The greater number of lives lost was due to the larger number of passengers carried by the increasingly larger steamers.

In 1789, the United States had approximately 3,000 merchant vessels. About 850 new vessels were added annually until 1820, and even more were added each year after 1820. As industry progressed, so did the number of vessels built.

Shipping was the primary means of transporting goods during most of Florida's history. It is possible a shipwreck could lie almost anywhere along the coast. As time goes on, more and more wrecks will be found.

SHIPWRECKS

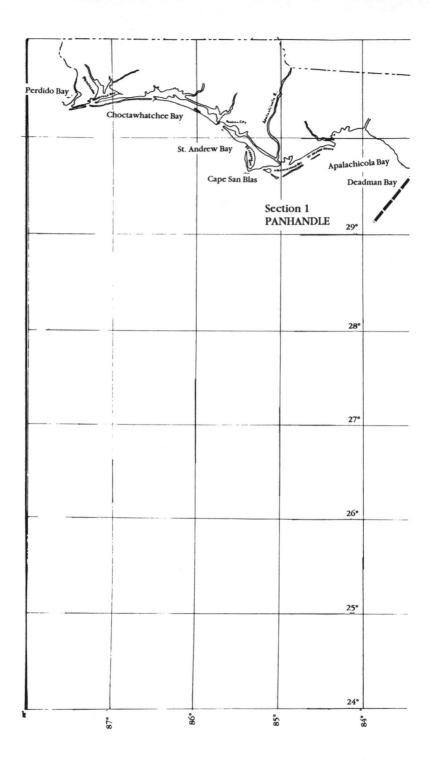

Perdido Bay

Choctawhatchee Bay

St. Andrew Bay

Cape San Blas

Apalachicola Bay

Deadman Bay

Section 1
PANHANDLE

29°

28°

27°

26°

25°

24°

87°   86°   85°   84°

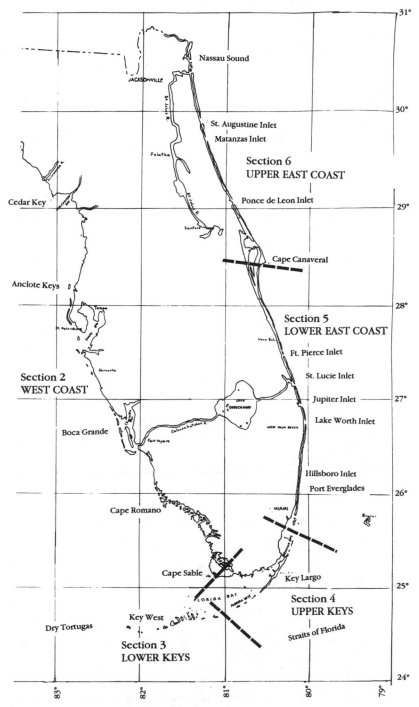

Figure 2: Map of Florida, showing latitude, longitude, and the geographical
sections by which the shipwrecks are organized. AUTHOR.

19

The shipwrecks in this book are listed by area and by the date they wrecked. However, vessels that wrecked during the Civil War and World War II are listed separately in the last two sections.

Section 1, the Panhandle, includes vessels wrecked off Florida's Panhandle up to and including Apalachee Bay.

Section 2, the West Coast, includes vessels wrecked off Florida's west coast from Apalachee Bay to Cape Sable.

Section 3, the Lower Florida Keys, includes vessels wrecked in the lower Florida Keys up to Lower Matecumbe, including the Dry Tortugas.

Section 4, the Upper Florida Keys, includes vessels wrecked from and including Lower Matecumbe up to and including Cape Florida, including Florida Bay.

Section 5, the Lower East Coast, includes vessels wrecked from Cape Florida up to and including Cape Canaveral.

Section 6, the Upper East Coast, includes vessels wrecked from Cape Canaveral up to the Georgia border.

Section 7, Inland Waters, includes vessels wrecked on all inland waterways such as lakes and rivers.

Section 8, Unknown Locations or Dates, includes shipwrecks whose location is not known, possible Florida wrecks, and wrecks whose location is given, but which I cannot find on recent maps.

Section 9, Unidentified Wrecks, includes wreck sites where the identification of the ship is not known.

Section 10, Civil War wrecks.

Section 11, World War II wrecks

Some of the shipwrecks listed give their location as having wrecked by a particular lifesaving station. These stations were built in the later 19th century along our coasts to assist the survivors of the many shipwrecks. Here are the locations of some of these stations, most of which no longer exist:

East Coast Stations

1 (Bethel Creek Station): Approximately ten miles north of Indian River Inlet.

2 (Gilberts Bar Station): On the south end of Hutchinson Island. Now a museum.

3 (Orange Grove Station): Five miles south of the south end of Lake Worth, at present-day Delray Beach.

4 (New River Station): At present-day Hugh Taylor Birch State Park, in Fort Lauderdale. Two stations were built here, the first in 1876, and the second in 1891, not far from the original.

5 (Biscayne Bay Station): On Berrier Ridge, seven miles north of

Norris Cut, near today's 72nd Street and Collins Avenue.

Other Stations

Santa Rosa Station: On Santa Rosa Island, off Pensacola. This station
    was across the street from the present-day park ranger station.
Chester Shoal Station: North of Cape Canaveral.
Mosquito Lagoon Station: North of Chester Shoal Station.

Many of the vessels positions in this book are given by latitude and
longitude. These are all north latitudes and west longitudes.

Some vessels are listed in Section 6 as having wrecked by Mosquito
or Ponce de Leon inlets. These are the same inlet, the name having been
changed from Mosquito Inlet to Ponce de Leon Inlet in the 1920s.

Most of the vessels that wrecked after World War II were motor
vessels. I've used these abbreviations to indicate the type of vessel when
known:

    M/V — motor vessel
    F/V — fishing vessel
    O/V — oil vessel
    G/V — gas vessel
    T/V — towing vessel

I list ship names and place names as they appeared in the source
material. Since there is no way of checking the spelling accuracy of such
sources, I decided to reproduce the names as they originally appeared.

I list ship dimensions in two ways: in feet and tenths of feet, and in
feet and inches. What is used in each case corresponds to how the
measurements appeared in the source material. Please note that the '
mark when applied to measurements means feet.

Section 1: Panhandle

1500

1. Fleet of Spanish ships — Under command of Captain Bartolomé Carreño. Wrecked in the year 1553 off present-day Mobile and the Florida Panhandle. Source: 22.

2. Six Spanish Ships — Under the command of Don Tristan de Luna y Arellano. Lost near Pensacola Bay in a hurricane in 1559. Don Tristan had landed here earlier that year with a band of colonists to settle the area, but the hurricane soon ended those plans. The survivors weren't rescued until 1561. They survived on horse meat and even saddle leather. Source: 43, 67.

1600

3. *Santa Ana María Juncal* — Spanish vessel, under fleet of Captain General Marguis de Cadereyata. Sank off Cabo de Apalachi (believed to be present-day Apalachicola) on June 2, 1611, with several million dollars' worth of treasure. Source: 54.

1700

4. Spanish Frigate — Under Captain Don Joseph Piz. Lost near Pensacola in 1731, with the annual payroll for the garrison there. Source: 54.

5. *Tiger* — Ship, Captain La Couture. The story of this ill-fated voyage is told in detail in the book *The Shipwreck and Adventure of Pierre Viaud*, printed in London in 1771, and more recently in Edward R. Snow's book *Sea Disasters and Inland Catastrophes*, but I will briefly describe her fate.

The *Tiger* left Saint Louis Island, near Cuba, on Jan. 2, 1766, with 16 people on board. She carried a cargo of general merchandise bound for Louisiana, which passengers Pierre Viaud and Monsieur Desclau hoped would bring them a tidy profit.

The voyage seemed doomed from the start. The vessel was becalmed, struck some rocks and developed a leak. To avoid drowning in deep water, the crew attempted to run the ship ashore during a storm. She capsized in the attempt off Cape St. George, on the east end of St. George Island, on Feb. 16, 1766. The story of this shipwreck includes drownings, marooning, murder, and cannibalism.

6. Spanish ship — From the Bay of Campeche bound for Pensacola. Wrecked off Isle of Rosey in 1766, within a few leagues of Pensacola. Vessel a total loss, cargo saved. Source: 54.

7. *Jason* — Ship. Wrecked on the coast of Apalachi, July 28, 1767. Source: 54.

8. *L' Andromaque* — French frigate. Ran aground, April 19, 1778, on the southwest corner of Santa Rosa Island, during the seige of Pensacola. She got off, but 14 of her cannon were thrown overboard, and should still remain. Source: 15.

9. *Sarah & Elizabeth*, the *Mary*, and 12 other vessels — The *Sarah & Elizabeth*, Captain Tovet, British, with lumber bound for Jamaica, and the *Mary*, Captain Blackwell, also British, were sunk along with 12 other large vessels at Pensacola during a hurricane, Oct. 9, 1778. Source: 54.

10. *Francesca* — Spanish frigate, Captain Andromaca, with a large cargo of war materials. Ran aground on a shoal in Pensacola Bay, April 19, 1781. Source: 54.

11. *Mentor* — British naval ship (originally an American ship captured in 1781), 16 guns, Captain Robert Deans. Was burned, May 8, 1781, at Pensacola to avoid capture by the Spanish. Source: 13, 16.

12. *Pallas* — British naval 5th rate, 728 tons, 36 guns, Captain Christopher Parker, 128.5' x 36', built in 1757. Was run ashore on St. Georges Island, March 24, 1783, as unserviceable. Source: 13, 16.

13. *Fox* — British naval schooner, 18 guns (all 18-pounders), 150 tons, purchased in 1799, under command of Lieutenant James

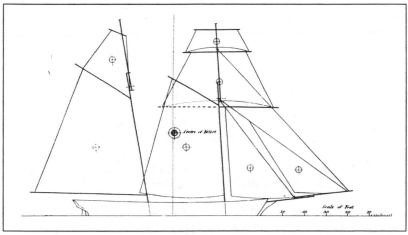

Figure 3: Diagram of a British naval schooner similar to the *Fox*, which wrecked in 1799. FROM JOHN EDYE'S BOOK, *CALCULATIONS RELATING TO THE EQUPMENT, DISPLACEMENT, ETC. OF SHIPS AND VESSELS OF WAR* (SEE BIBLIOGRAPHY).

Woolridge. Ran aground, Sept. 17, 1799, at the entrance of the bay at the east end of St. Georges Island, Lat. 29-44-30, Long. 84-38-35. The *Fox* was returning from Spain via London and the West Indies. She ran aground about three leagues from shore, and fell over and broke up the next day after everyone had abandoned ship. On board was William Augustus Bowles, also known as General Bowles, who had led the Creek Indians. Bowles and the rest of the crew were picked up 33 days later by the schooner *Shark*. They were transferred to the 74-gun *Thunderer*, which took them to Jamaica. (Figure 3 shows a British naval schooner similar to the *Fox*.) Source: 16, 32, 35, 36, research by Carol Andrew.

1800

14. *La Franchise* — Pirate vessel (schooner), five guns. Fought with *U.S. Gunboat #162*, Aug. 7, 1811, off Pensacola, and was set fire by her crew, who then escaped to shore. Reported to have had a very valuable cargo on board. Source: 62.

15. *Earl Bathurst* — British ship, Captain Heron, from Liverpool. Wrecked at Pensacola in 1811. Source: 54.

16. *Intrepido* — Spanish *falacho* (class of vessel), under Alferez de Navio Margues del Moral. Wrecked during a storm in 1814, on a beach at Pensacola. Source: 54.

17. *Volader* or *Volader II* — Spanish schooner, 10 guns, Captain Alferez Viál. Ran aground and broke up, March 25, 1815, near the entrance to Pensacola Harbor. Reported to have had a large cargo of goods, rifles, and money. Source: 54, 67.

18. Several ships — These were lost in Pensacola Bay during a hurricane, Sept. 15, 1821. Source: 54.

19. *American* — Steamer, from Apalachicola bound for New York with cotton. Caught fire while passing over the bar at Apalachicola in 1834. She was run ashore, where she burned to the water's edge. Only the baggage was saved. Source: 103.

20. *Stranger* — Pilot boat. Went ashore during a gale, early December 1835, on St. Vincent Island. Source: 96 (Jan. 4, 1836).

21. *Versailles* — Sidewheel steamer, of Apalachicola, 83 tons, built in 1831 at Cincinnati, bound for St. Joseph with a cargo of cotton. Struck a snag in passing a short angle in the Bayou at Apalachicola, April 1836. Source: 52, 96 (May 9, 1836).

22. *Convoy* — Steamer, from Mobile bound for Tampa with supplies

for the Army in Florida. Sprang a leak, parted in the middle and sank about seven miles from Apalachicola, late September or early October, 1836. Cargo damaged; crew saved. Source: 96 (Nov. 11, 1836).

23. *Henry Crowell* and the *Edwin Forrest* — Both steamers. The *Edwin Forrest* was 27 tons, built in 1834 on the Flint River, Ga., 90' x 14' x 2'6". Both were broken up at Apalachicola by the hurricane of August 31, 1837. Unknown if salvaged. Source: 14, 103.

24. *Lamplighter* — Sidewheel steamer, 186 tons, built in 1835 at Louisville, Ky. Foundered at East Pass, Feb. 13, 1841. Nineteen lives lost. Source: 52.

25. *Augusta* — Sidewheel steamer, 132 tons, built in 1840 at Pittsburgh, Pa. Collided with the *Eufala*, April 15, 1847, at Apalachicola. Source: 52.

26. *Ashlania* — Schooner, 135 tons, from New Orleans bound for Apalachicola. Wrecked at or near Apalachicola, November 1847. Unknown if salvaged. Source: 14, 19.

27. *Mary*(?) (believed to be the *Mary Paul*) — Bark, 198 tons, from New Orleans bound for Apalachicola. Wrecked at or near Aplachicola in May 1848. Unknown if salvaged. Source: 14, 19.

28. *Emily* — Sidewheel steamer, of Apalachicola, 144 tons, built in 1845 at Elizabethtown, Pa. Exploded at Apalachicola, May 27, 1849. Seven lives lost. Source: 52.

29. *Falcon* — Sidewheel steamer, of Apalachicola, 185 tons, built in 1850 at Cincinnati. Stranded at Apalachicola, Aug. 23, 1851. Source: 52.

30. *Ferdinand VII* — Spanish brig. Went aground on Cape San Blas during the summer of 1852. Some cargo salvaged. Source: 104.

31. *Albany* — Sidewheel steamer, of Apalachicola, 168 tons, built in 1846 at Albany, Ga. Stranded off Apalachicola, Oct. 9, 1852. Source: 52.

32. *Palmetto* — Sidewheel steamer, 136 tons, built in 1846 at Brownsville, Pa. Stranded off Apalachicola, Oct. 9, 1852. Source: 52.

33. *Swan* — Bark. Reported in 1856 with seven feet of water in her hold at Lat. 29-00-00, Long. 84-00-00, by Captain Moore of the bark *Corra*, which took off her crew and brought them to New Orleans. Source: 99 (April 23, 1856).

34. *Florida* — Steamer. Blown ashore in St. Joseph's Bay during a hurricane, Aug. 30, 1856. Total loss. Source: 54.

35. *Arabella* — Ship, from Apalachicola bound for Liverpool. Struck by lightning and destroyed in 1857. Captain and crew saved and brought to St. Georges. Source: 99 (April 14, 1857).

36. *Sarah Judkins* — Ship, of Bath, 546 tons, built in 1856 at Hallowell, Maine, 139'8" x 29'2" x 14'7". Reported to have four feet of water in her hold and to be fast settling in the mud, April 3, 1858, at Apalachicola. Two hundred and fifty bales of cotton were saved, though damaged. She then caught fire. A total loss. Source: 6, 19, 99 (April 2, 1858).

37. *South Carolina* — Sidewheel steamer, of Apalachicola, 173 tons, built in 1853 at Brownsville, Pa. Burned at Apalachicola, Jan. 12, 1860. Source: 52.

38. *Gleaner* — Bark. She had loaded 1,370 bales of cotton at Apalachicola (bound for Amsterdam), and had an additional 100 bales on deck, when she caught fire and had to be scuttled in 18 feet of water, Jan. 24, 1860. Source: 99 (Jan. 26, 1860).

39. *Fanny Holmes* — Bark, 673 tons, built by W.H. Webb, of Apalachicola. She was loading cotton at Apalachicola (bound for Antwerp) when, on the night of April 3, 1860, she caught fire and burned to the water's edge. A stevedore was seen with a pipe before he fell asleep, and he was feared killed. The ship and 871 bales of cotton were a total loss. Source: 99 (April 6, 1860).

40. *Switzerland* — Ship, of New York, Captain Trask. Caught fire in Apalachicola Bay and burned to the waterline. A total loss. Source: 99 (May 7, 1860).

41. *A.C. Merryman* — Brig, 231 tons, of Gardiner, Maine, built in 1855 at Pittston, Maine, 106' x 25'2" x 9'7", from Havana, in ballast. Went ashore on Santa Rosa Island, Nov. 14, 1860, well up on the beach. She was not damaged, but it was feared she could not be gotten off, and she was stripped. Source: 6, 19, 99 (Dec. 8, 1860).

See Civil War section for Section 1 wrecks during that period.

42. *Bloomer* — Union 4th-rate sidewheel (one source says sternwheel) steamer, 130 tons, built in 1856 at New Albany, Ind., one 32-pounder, one 12-pounder rifle. Sank in the East Pass off Santa Rosa Island while a tender to the frigate *Potomac*, June 1865. Wreck

was sold on Sept. 27, 1865, for $1,500. Source: 28, 63 (Series II, Vol. 1).

43. *Convoy* — U.S. quartermasters vessel (believed to be a steamer), about 350 tons. Sank in the fall of 1865 after catching fire at Barrancas Wharf, about nine miles below Pensacola, not far from the mouth of the Pensacola Bay. She was cut adrift, and floated down opposite the lighthouse, one-half to one mile further down. Sank in 11 feet of water, where she could be seen for some years later. She had a cargo of lumber and U.S. stores. Her chain and anchor were salvaged. (Note: The steamer *Convoy*, 410 tons, built in 1862 at Williamsburg, N.Y., was sold to the War Department in 1863. Possibly the same vessel). Source: 14, 52.

44. *Hattie* (formerly the *Sophia*) — Steamer (iron), 286 tons, built in 1855 at Wilmington, from New Orleans. Sank in Apalachicola Bay in 1866 with a full cargo of cotton. Though the cargo was damaged, it was reported it would be salvaged. Source: 52, 99 (Nov. 4, 1866).

45. *New Munnerlyn* — Sternwheel steamer, of Apalachicola, 193 tons, built in 1867 at Columbus, Ga. Lost off Apalachicola, May 1, 1867. Source: 52.

46. *Mary Queen* — Norwegian ship. Stranded near Perdido Inlet, December 1869. A partial loss. Source: 14.

47. *Ada* — Spanish ship, 700 tons. Stranded on Pensacola Bar, December 1869 (another source says 1872). A partial loss. Her remains lie in 13 feet of water, near the wreck of the *William Miles*. Source: 14.

48. *William Miles* — British ship, 900 tons. Sank in 1869 in 10 feet of water west of Fort Pickens, in Pensacola Bay. Source: 14.

49. *Barnett* — Sternwheel steamer, of Apalachicola, 311 tons, built in 1865 at Pittsburgh. Collided with a survey schooner, Dec. 1, 1871, at Apalachicola. Source: 52.

50. *Ella May* — Sidewheel steamer, 147 tons, built in 1863 at Malden, N.Y. Burned at Pensacola, July 5, 1872 (one source says March 18, 1875). Source: 14, 52.

51. *Tipposait* — British bark. Stranded on Pensacola Bar, August 1872. A partial loss. Source: 14.

52. *George P. Arnay* — Sloop, from St. Marks bound for Apalachicola. Reported as a total loss from the Dog Island Station, Dec. 28, 1872, on the north bank of St. George Island. Source: 14.

53. *Magnolia* — Steamer, 73 tons, built in 1865 at Berlin, Ohio. Stranded in Perdido Bay, October. 1873. A partial loss. Source: 14, 52.

54. *Grenada* — British bark. Stranded on Pensacola Bar in 1873. A partial loss. Source: 14.

55. *Uncle Sam* — Brig. Wrecked off Pensacola, October 1874. A total loss. Source: 14.

56. *Ferdinand* — Norwegian bark. Burned and sank in 1-1/2 fathoms near the railroad wharf in Pensacola Bay in 1874. Source: 14.

57. *Kele B.* — Schooner, 738 tons, Captain Miller. Drifted and wrecked at Cape San Blas, March 1875, during a storm. Source: 14.

58. *Nettle* — Pilot boat, 34 tons. Sank in 14 feet in Pensacola Bay in 1875. Source: 14.

59. *Minnie Gray* — Ship. Became a partial loss near Rock Island (Apalachee Bay), June 1875. Two lives lost. Source: 14.

60. *J.A. Farley* — Steamer, 606 tons, Captain Thomas, from Apalachicola bound for Pensacola. Sprang a leak and stranded on Cape San Blas Beach, June 18, 1876. A partial loss. Source: 14.

61. *Besluida* — Schooner, 127 tons, built in 1870, from Pensacola bound for Apalachicola. Stranded during a storm on the night of Jan. 31, 1877, on the outside of the beach at Cape San Blas. A total loss. Four lives lost. Source: 14.

62. *Mary E. Oliver* — Schooner, of Georgetown, Maine, 148 tons, built in 1876 at Georgetown, 87.3' x 26.2' x 7.7'. Stranded on Santa Rosa Island, February 1877. A partial loss. Source: 6, 14.

63. *Rebecca* — Schooner. Stranded on St. Vincent Island, October 1877. A partial loss. Source: 14.

64. *George Gilchrest* — Brig, of New York, 438 tons, built in 1863, Captain Urcumm, from Pensacola bound for Greytown, Nicaragua, with yellow and pitch pine lumber. Sprang a leak and foundered 60 miles south of Cape St. George Lighthouse during a storm, Oct. 3, 1877. A total loss. Source: 14.

65. *Three Sisters* — Schooner, 154 tons, built in 1875, from Pensacola bound for Apalachicola. Foundered during a storm the night of Dec. 28, 1877. Two lives lost. Source: 14.

66. *Sallie W. Kay* — Schooner. Collided with another vessel at Pensacola, December 1877. A partial loss. Source: 14.

67. *Mollie Gratz* — Sternwheel steamer, 147 tons, built in 1866 at Madison, Ind. Stranded near Pensacola, December 1877. A total loss. Source: 14, 52.

68. *F.L. Richards* — Schooner. Stranded near Pensacola, December 1877. A partial loss. Source: 14.

69. *Eliza Jane* — Sloop. Stranded at Pensacola, January 1878. A total loss. Source: 14.

70. *Rhoda B. Taylor* — Schooner. Waterlogged and abandoned, she wrecked southeast of Pensacola, December 1878. A total loss. Source: 14.

71. *Monadnock* — Schooner. Wrecked off the Santa Rosa Lighthouse. December 1878. A total loss. Source: 14.

72. *Santa Rosa* — Steamer. Burned at Pensacola, March 1879. A total loss. Source: 14.

73. *Judge* — Schooner, six tons. Lost on the Ochlokonee Bar, Aug. 12, 1880, at 6 a.m. Source: 14.

74. *Mintie* — Sternwheel steamer, of Pensacola, Captain Wilson, no cargo. Sank after her boilers exploded, Jan. 22, 1881, at 3 p.m. approximately three miles east of Minez Ferry, Perdido Bay, killing three. A total loss. Source: 14.

75. *T.J. Mitchell* — Schooner, of Pensacola, 34 tons, Captain Christenson, from Pensacola with lumber. Sank during a storm in Pensacola Bay, Feb. 6, 1881. Some cargo saved. Source: 14.

76. *Jessie Rhnas* — Brig, of Boston, 330 tons, built in 1855, Captain Eaton, from Boston bound for Mobile with ice. Stranded on the East Pensacola Bar, Santa Rosa Island, Feb.19, 1881. Source: 14.

77. *Harry See* — Schooner, of Pensacola, 32 tons, built in 1873, Captain Oliver. Lost (probably near Pensacola), February 1881. Seven lives lost. Source: 14.

78. *Dixie* — Schooner, of Pensacola, 37 tons, built in 1878, Captain Simpson. Stranded on Santa Rosa Island, Oct. 27, 1881, at 9:15 P.M., 30 miles east of the entrance to Pensacola Harbor. A total loss. Source: 14.

79. *Valley City* — Schooner, of Key West, 319 tons, built in 1859, Captain Stewart, from Tampa bound for Pensacola with oranges. Sprang a leak during a storm and sank 40 miles east-southeast off Pensacola (another source says off Cape San Blas), Jan. 23, 1882, at 4:30 P.M. A total loss. Source: 14, 52.

80. *Albatross* — Schooner, of Pensacola, 12 tons, from Pensacola bound for St. Andrews Bay. Drifted into the breakers at St. Andrews after losing her sails during a storm, June 3, 1882. Source: 14.

81. *Mobile American* — River steamboat, of Mobile, 262 tons, built in 1875, from Pensacola bound for Columbus. Was in quarantine at Apalachicola when she was blown ashore 1/2 mile from the west end of James Island in Dog Island Harbor, Sept. 9, 1882, at 9 P.M. A total loss. Source: 14.

82. *Annie Richmond* — Schooner, of Pensacola, 13 tons. Stranded on the outside of Santa Rosa Island, April 30, 1883. Broke up. Source: 14.

83. *City of Manatee* — Vessel, of Pensacola, 88 tons, built in 1881. Sank off the Pensacola Bar, on Pickens Point, Aug. 15, 1885. The machinery was salvaged. Source: 14.

84. *C. Ervlin* — Steam tug, 79 tons, built in 1883, Captain Hill. Sank at the East Pass of Apalachicola Bay, near Cat Point, June 30, 1886, after her cables parted during a hurricane. Two lives lost. She had two barges in tow with lumber on board, and both grounded. Source: 14.

85. *Birgitte* — Norwegian bark, 584 tons, built in 1871, Captain Torgessen. Drifted ashore during a hurricane opposite Dog Island, Apalachicola Bay, June 30, 1886. The cargo of lumber was saved. The vessel, valued at $10,000, sustained a loss of $6,000. Source: 14.

86. *California* — Schooner, 15 tons, built in 1872. Lost at Dog Island Cove during the June 30, 1886 hurricane. Four lives lost. Source: 14.

87. *A.C. Monroe* — Schooner, of Pensacola, 27 tons, built in 1868, from Bay Point with white pine lumber. Collided with the tug *Echo* at 7 P.M., Feb. 10, 1887, in Pensacola Bay. Sank off White Point. A total loss. Source: 14.

88. *Samuel MacManemy* — Schooner. Lost off Apalachicola, March 10, 1887. Source: 9.

89. *Bride of Lorne* — British ship, of Liverpool, 1,324 tons, cargo of timber, Captain Matson. Wrecked four miles west-southwest of Santa Rosa Island Station, April 8, 1887, at Lat. 30-17-30, Long. 87-18-42 (though also listed at Long. 87-13-30). Some cargo saved, but vessel a total loss. Source: 1, 14.

90. *Amanda* — Schooner, of Pensacola, 23 tons, built in 1871, from Pensacola bound for Choctawahatchee Bay. Capsized during a storm at Piney Point, July 26, 1887. Two lives lost. Source: 14.

91. *H.S. Rowe* — Schooner, of Pensacola, 59 tons, 28 years old. Stranded during a storm while fishing, July 27, 1887, at 8:30 A.M., 25 miles east of the East Pass of Santa Rosa Island. A total loss. Source: 14.

92. *Sarah F. Bird* — Schooner, of Rockland, Maine, 381 tons, built in 1873, Captain Grand, from Galveston bound for Pensacola, in ballast. Stranded one mile east of Perdido River during 60 mph winds, Oct. 19, 1887, at 12:15 P.M. A total loss. Source: 14.

93. *Four Brothers* — Two-masted schooner, of Pascagoula, 42 tons, built in 1867, from Pascagoula bound for Key West with lumber. Abandoned at Lat. 29-30-00, Long. 86-00-00, Oct. 19, 1887, at 4 P.M. Source: 14.

94. *Lizzie Ella* — Sloop, 11 tons. Was lost on a fishing trip to Snapper Banks, Dec. 14, 1887. Six lives lost. Source: 14.

95. *H.W. Crawford* — Vessel of New Orleans, 24 tons, built in 1886, Captain Costello, from Mobile bound for Apalachicola. Beached during a storm three miles west of the West Pass of St. Andrews Bar, June 4, 1888, at 4 P.M. A total loss. Source: 14.

96. *Henrietta L* — Schooner, 34 tons, built in 1883, bound for Key West with lumber. Lost on St. George Island, July 16, 1888. A total loss. Source: 14.

97. *Urbano* — Bark. Lost off Pensacola, Jan. 17, 1889. Source: 9.

98. *Advance* — Schooner, of Pensacola, 28 tons, built in 1871, cargo of bricks. Struck a pile of rocks at the southwest corner of the Pensacola Navy Yard, Jan. 17, 1889, at 10 A.M. Some cargo saved. Vessel a total loss. Source: 14.

99. *Bloomer* — Fishing schooner, of Pensacola, 17 tons, built in 1853, Captain Clark. Capsized when hit by a squall, Aug. 4, 1889, at 12:30 A.M., 55 miles east-southeast of Pensacola. Source: 14.

100. *Carl D. Lathrop* — Schooner, 278 tons, built in 1873, from Mobile bound for Cuba with lumber. Sprang a leak and capsized, Oct. 21, 1889, approximately ten miles south-southwest of Cape St. George Lighthouse. A total loss. Source: 14.

101. *Susie* — Steamer, five tons, built in 1886. Burned at Devils Elbow, Apalachicola, Feb. 22, 1890. Source: 14.

102. *John Pew* — Schooner, of Pensacola, 42 tons, 38 years old. Stranded while on a fishing trip, Dec. 3, 1890, at 3:45 A.M., approximately 15 miles east of the East Pass, Santa Rosa Island. A total loss. Source: 14.

103. *Eastern Light* — Ship. Wrecked on Caucus Shoal, Dec. 23, 1890, at Lat. 30-18-54, Long. 87-19-27. Source: 1, 45.

104. *James W. Wherren* — Schooner, of Pensacola, 24 tons, 38 years old, Captain Norton. Stranded on the beach at the point of Barrances Light during a storm while fishing, Jan. 9, 1891. Source: 14.

105. *Hattie G. McFarland* — Bark, of Thomaston, Maine, 546 tons, built in 1873, Captain Dodge, from Havana bound for Pensacola in ballast. Stranded off Santa Rosa Station, Feb. 6, 1891, at 11 P.M., six miles east of the bar, four miles east of Santa Rosa Station at Lat. 30-19.3-00, Long. 87-18.8-00. A total loss. Source: 14.

106. *Aurecus* or *Amicus* — British bark, 516 tons, 36 years old, from Barbados bound for Apalachicola in ballast. Stranded on Flug Island Shoals, near the West Pass of Apalachicola Bay, April 2, 1891, at 4:30 A.M. A total loss. Source: 14.

107. *H.A. DeWitt* — Schooner, of New York, 227 tons, (believed built in 1873 at Bath, 118.3' x 32.1' x 8.6'), cargo of Mexican cedar, Captain Perry. Found stranded and abandoned, four miles east of St. Andrews Bay, August 1891. A total loss. Source: 14.

108. *Ada* — Schooner, of Pensacola, 16 tons. Lost while on a fishing trip, September 1891. Five lives lost. Source: 14.

109. *Maude M. Lane* — Schooner barge (iron), of Pensacola, 573 tons, Captain Bean, from Pensacola bound for Galveston with coal. Foundered approximately 95 miles from Pensacola, southwest by south, Nov. 9, 1891, at 12:15 P.M. Source: 14.

110. *Dexter Clark* — Schooner, of Portland, Maine, 131 tons, built in 1873, Captain Young, from Martinique bound for Apalachicola.

Struck bottom and foundered at Flug Island Shoals, near the west pass of Apalachicola Bay, Dec. 29, 1891, at 7 A.M. A total loss. Source: 14.

111. *J.P. Allen* — Schooner, of Pensacola, 27 tons, 26 years old, Captain Holdridge. Sunk by a whirlwind while on a fishing trip, 55 miles east of the Pensacola Bar, Oct. 26, 1892. Source: 14.

112. *E.W. Monifie* — Barge, of Pensacola, 100 tons, built in 1888. Burned at the railroad wharf, Pensacola, Feb. 2, 1893. A total loss. Source: 14.

113. *Ripple* — Schooner, of Pensacola, 29 tons, built in 1860, Captain Burnham. Stranded while fishing in a fog at Pickens Point, 3-3/4 miles west of Santa Rosa Station, Feb. 13 or 15, 1893. A total loss. Source: 14.

114. *J.A. Bishop* — Steam tug, built in 1883, from Apalachicola bound for Carrabelle. Caught fire and sank at Timber Wharf, Carrabelle, Feb. 19, 1893, at 11 P.M. A total loss. Source: 14.

115. *Kanawha* — Steamer, of New York, 431 tons, built in 1882, from Punta Gorda bound for Mobile with phosphate. Stranded 12 miles east of Pensacola, March 3, 1893, at noon. Eighty tons of phosphate were jettisoned. Unknown if vessel was salvaged. Source: 14.

116. *Octavia A. Dow* — Schooner, of Pensacola, 38 tons, built in 1867, Captain Scalizia. Stranded on Fort Barrancas Bar while fishing, five miles west of the Santa Rosa Station, March 26, 1893, at 1 A.M. A total loss. Source: 14.

117. *Alice N.* — Schooner, of Pensacola, 100 tons, built in 1880. Sank 1,000 yards east of the Beacon at Pensacola, March 16, 1894. A total loss. Note: Another schooner called the *Alice N.*, of Tampa, seven tons, Captain Wilson, was listed as having stranded six miles west-northwest of the Santa Rosa Station, March 17, 1894. Source: 14.

118. *George Jurgens* — Vessel of Key West, 23 tons, approximately 14 years old, Captain Hall, from Cedar Keys bound for Mobile with oranges. Collided with a foreign vessel and was cut in two, Oct. 6, 1894. Four lives lost. Source: 14.

119. *David Mitchell* — Fishing vessel, of Pensacola, 33 tons, built in 1846. Lost in a storm, Oct. 8, 1894. Seven lives lost. Source: 14.

120. *Sea Foam* — Fishing schooner, of Pensacola, 16 tons, 34 years

old, Captain Mitchell. Lost during the Oct. 8, 1894, storm. Four lives lost. Source: 14.

121. *Mary Potter* — Schooner, of Pensacola, 36 tons, cargo of fish, Captain Pratt. Wrecked during the Oct. 8, 1894, storm, 1-1/2 miles east of the Santa Rosa Station. Source: 14.

122. *Mary Potter* — Schooner, of Pensacola, 36 tons, built in 1866, Captain Lanzone. Was fishing when she became waterlogged and beached during a storm, seven miles east of the east pass of St. Andrews Bay, Feb. 5, 1896, at 4 P.M. Note: Possibly the same vessel as #121, which could have been salvaged. Source: 14.

123. *Mabel Taylor* — Vessel of Yarmouth, Nova Scotia, 1,289 tons, Captain Heblard, from Pensacola bound for Rio with lumber. Wrecked five miles southwest of the Santa Rosa Station, Feb. 27, 1896. Vessel and cargo valued at $23,000, with only $8,000 saved. Source: 14.

124. Three schooners — The *Eagle* (20 tons, 17 years old), the *Florence* (22 tons, built in 1880), and the *Leroy*, all of Pensacola. Wrecked during a storm on July 7, 1896. The *Eagle* was at anchor when she sank in Pensacola Bay in seven feet of water, opposite the western part of the city. Some cargo of lumber saved. The *Florence* stranded and sank in the bay, with a cargo of lumber. A total loss. The *Leroy* stranded and broke up on the west shore of Pensacola Bay. A total loss. Source: 14.

125. *Anna Pepina* — Austrian bark, of Fiume, 620 tons, Captain Maruesich, from Loando, Africa, bound for Pensacola. Wrecked three miles west of the Santa Rosa Station, July 19, 1896, at Lat. 30-19-06, Long. 87-18-48. Vessel a total loss. Source: 1, 14.

126. *Red Wing* — Schooner (iron), of Philadelphia, 437 tons, built in 1884 at Philadelphia, 136.4' x 33.2' x 11.7', Captain Carle, from Cuba bound for Pascagoula, in ballast. Foundered after hitting an obstruction, Nov. 22, 1896, at 1 A.M., 60 miles southeast of Pensacola Light. Source: 14.

127. *Amelia* — Sloop, of Pensacola, six tons, built in 1865. Foundered in a storm by the bell buoy, Pensacola Bay, March 28, 1897. Eight of nine on board lost. Source: 14.

128. *Mary Me* — Schooner, 17 tons, built in 1878, from Apalachicola bound for St. George Island. Stranded during a gale, Oct. 7, 1897, at 10 A.M., on the west end of St. George Island. A total loss. Source: 14.

129. *William J. Keyser* — Tug (iron), of Pensacola, 97 tons, built in 1882 at Philadelphia, 92.4' x 19.5' x 8.5', Captain Allen, from Pensacola bound for the Dry Tortugas. Foundered 15 to 20 miles off Point St. Joseph, Aug. 3, 1898, at 1:30 a.m. Four of 13 on board lost. Source: 14.

130. *James Baird* — Schooner, of Philadelphia, 391 tons, built in 1891 at Camden, N.J., 142.7' x 35' x 11.4', Captain Boyer, from Charleston bound for Pensacola with fertilizer. Stranded and then foundered during a storm, Jan. 31, 1899, at 3 a.m., 29 miles east of the entrance to Pensacola Harbor, 24 miles east of Santa Rosa Station. A total loss. Source: 14.

131. *Charles A. Swift* — Schooner, of Pensacola, 24 tons, built in 1885, Captain Calloway, from Perdido bound for Mobile with shingles. Stranded on the west side of the channel off the Perdido Bar, June 10, 1899, at 7 a.m. Half the cargo saved. Vessel a total loss. Source: 14.

132. *Albert Halsey* (or *Haley*) — Fishing schooner, of Pensacola, 47 tons, built in 1846 at Stonington, Conn., 61.6' x 17.1' x 8', Captain Limmick. Blown ashore during a storm after her cable parted, Aug. 1, 1899, at 3:30 P.M., at Carrabelle Harbor. A total loss. Source: 14.

1900

133. *Evelyn* (formerly British ship *Badsworth*) — Steamer (iron), of New York, 1,963 tons, built in 1883 at Southampton, England, 252.8' x 36.3' x 24.5', Captain Ritch, from New York bound for Pensacola with a general cargo. Wrecked 15-1/2 miles west of the Santa Rosa Station, Aug. 15, 1901. Vessel valued at $90,000 and cargo at $25,000, with a loss of $52,000. Source: 14.

134. *Capt. Brainard* — Barge, 211 tons, built in 1876 at Mobile, Captain Butter, from St. Andrews bound for Pensacola with lumber. Wrecked 3-1/4 miles east of the Santa Rosa Station, March 7, 1902. The vessel and cargo valued at $7,000, with a $4,000 loss. Source: 14.

135. *Rosemont* — Schooner barge, of Fall River, Mass., 708 tons, built in 1895 at Bath, 174.3' x 35.4' x 14.2'. Stranded in St. Andrews Bay, Dec. 17, 1902. Source: 14.

136. *Ned* — Barge, 139 tons, built in 1898. Stranded due to an error in navigation while going out over the St. Andrews Bar while in tow, March 31, 1903. Broke up within an hour. Source: 14.

137. *A. Weiskittel* — Schooner, 43 tons, built in 1882 at Madison, Md., 66.5' x 21.6' x 6.3'. Foundered in St. Joseph Bay, Sept. 13, 1903. Source: 14.

138. *Vila Y. Hermano* — Schooner, 327 tons, built in 1891 at Calais, Maine, 131.7' x 31.3' x 10.5'. Collided with the steamer *Mobila*, Sept. 5, 1905, at Lat. 29, Long. 87. Source: 14.

139. *Gus Shammel* — Steamer, 42 tons, built in 1903. Burned in Choctawhatchee Bay, Feb. 28, 1906. Source: 14.

Note: The following 14 vessels all wrecked during the hurricane of Sept. 27, 1906.

140. *Altama* — Schooner, 31 tons, built in 1871 at Cleveland, 58.8' x 17.7' x 6.4'. Stranded in Pensacola Bay. Source: 14.

141. *Angelo* — Sidewheel passenger steamer, of Pensacola, 122 tons, built in 1893 at Pensacola, 88' x 21.4' x 4.3'. Stranded on Pensacola Bar. (See Figure 4). Source: 14, 80.

142. *B.F. Sutter* — Schooner, of Pensacola, 36 tons, built in 1865 at Chelsea, Mass., 66.6' x 19.3' x 7'. Stranded in Pensacola Bay. Source: 14.

143. *Carrie N. Chase* — Schooner, 48 tons, built in 1899. Stranded at Fisherville. Source: 14.

Figure 4: Passenger steamer *Angelo*, wrecked in 1906. PENSACOLA HISTORICAL SOCIETY.

144. *Clara R. Grimes* — Schooner, of Pensacola, 34 tons, built in 1884 at Bristol, Maine, 61' x 17.8' x 6.8'. Stranded in Pensacola Bay. Source: 14.

145. *Francis and Margery* — Schooner, 40 tons, built in 1902. Stranded at Pensacola. Source: 14.

146. *Gloucester* — Steam yacht (formerly the *Corsair, U.S.S. Gloucester*), 786 tons, built in 1891 at Philadelphia, 204' x 27.2' x 12.' Stranded in Pensacola Bay. Listed as sold in 1919 so she was probably salvaged. (See Figure 5). Source: 14, 28, 80, Pensacola Historical Society.

147. *Helen* (formerly U.S. launch *Hawley*) — Steamer, of Pensacola, 20 tons, 63.8' x 12.7' x 4', built in 1884 at Buffalo. Stranded in Pensacola Bay. Source: 14.

148. *Hilary* — Schooner, of Pensacola, 38 (or 22) tons, built in 1893 at Mary Esther, Fla., 43.3' x 20.3' x 4.1'. Stranded at Perdido. Source: 14.

149. *Josie Johnson* — Schooner, 27 tons, built in 1877 at Newburyport, Mass., 56.2' x 18.5' x 5.8'. Stranded in Pensacola Bay. Source: 14.

150. *Minerva* — Schooner, 64 tons, built in 1891 at Essex, Mass., 77.5' x 20.5' x 9.6'. Foundered in Pensacola Bay. Source: 14.

Figure 5: Steam yacht *Gloucester*, wrecked in 1906. PENSACOLA HISTORICAL SOCIETY.

151. *Nelly Keyser* (formerly *Old Glory*) — Steamer (iron), of Pensacola, 42 tons, built in 1885 at New Orleans, 63.7' x 11.9' x 6'. Stranded in Pensacola Bay. Source: 14.

152. *Two Sisters* — Schooner, of Pensacola, 21 tons, built in 1990 at Santa Rosa Sound, 43.8' x 18.5' x 4.1'. Stranded at Bat Point. Source: 14.

153. *William H. Warren* — Schooner, 31 tons, built in 1867. Foundered at St. Joseph Point. All seven on board lost. Source: 14.

Note: End of Sept. 27, 1906, wrecks.

154. *Derrick Barge* — Said to be a Norwegian lumber ship. Wrecked in 1906. The wreck lies 200 yards offshore in 15 to 20 feet of water, at Lat. 30-14-36.7, Long. 87-41-53, scattered over a 100-yard area. Known locally as the "Whiskey" or "Mail Wreck." Source: 1.

155. *Florence Witherbee* — Steamer, 84 tons, built in 1873. Collided with the *Accomac*, Feb. 14, 1907, at Pensacola. Source: 14.

156. *Raymond H.* — Steamer, of Apalachicola, 55 tons, built in 1905. Burned at Janes Landing, Apalachicola, mid-October 1907, at 8 A.M., with a cargo of cotton, cotton seed, and turpentine. A total loss. Source: 14.

157. *Alice* — Steamer, of Pensacola, 25 tons, built in 1889 at Navy Cove, 44' x 11.8' x 3.8'. Struck a pile, Dec. 13, 1907, at Pensacola. Source: 14.

158. *Allen H. Jones* — Schooner, of Tampa, 47 tons, built in 1877 at Essex, Mass., 69.1' x 19.8' x 6.6', Captain Walker, from Apalachicola bound for Tarpon Springs with shingles. Foundered in Apalachicola Bay, Dec. 19, 1907, after being towed over a bar. Half of cargo saved. Source: 14.

159. *Maud Spurling* — Schooner, of Pensacola, 53 tons, built in 1895 at Boothbay, Maine, 70' x 19.9' x 9'. Wrecked while fishing, April 26, 1908, six miles west of Santa Rosa Station. A total loss. Source: 14.

160. *Sun* — Sidewheel steamer, 84 tons, built in 1898 at Hockingport, Ohio, 121' x 21.2' x 4.3'. Stranded off Apalachicola, Feb. 2, 1909. Source: 14.

161. *James C. Clifford* — Schooner, 377 tons, built in 1886 at East Boston, 141.2' x 29.8' x 12.2'. Abandoned 60 miles southeast of Pensacola, April 14, 1909. Source: 14.

162. *Willena* — Sidewheel gas vessel, 50 tons, built in 1907. Stranded on St. Andrews Bar, Jan. 28, 1910. Source: 14.

163. *Triumfo* — Bark, of Santa Cruz, 237 tons, from Havana bound for Pensacola. Wrecked five miles west of Santa Rosa Station, Feb. 17, 1910. Source: 14.

164. *Hjalmar* — Schooner, of Pensacola, 57 tons, built in 1891 at East Bay, Fla., 75.4' x 22.2' x 7'. Foundered near Carrabelle, Dec. 18, 1910. Source: 14.

165. *Herman Oelrichs* — Schooner, 76 tons, built in 1894 at Essex, Mass., 78' x 22' x 9.4'. Stranded on Cape San Blas Shoals, Dec. 22, 1910. Source: 14.

166. *Orona* — Sidewheel steamer, of Apalachicola, 97 tons, built in 1900 at Carrabelle, 100' x 26.8' x 6'. Burned at Apalachicola, March 11, 1911. Source: 14.

167. *Belle* — Sidewheel steamer, of Pensacola, 74 tons, built in 1903 at Vernon, Fla., 84.6' x 20' x 3.9'. Burned in Choctawhatchee Bay, April 26, 1911. Four lives lost. Source: 14.

168. *Frances and Louisa* — Schooner, 27 tons, built in 1874 at Noank, Conn., 51.5' x 17.8' x 6'. Stranded at Crooked Isle, Aug. 11, 1911. Source: 14.

169. *Elzada* — Schooner, of Gulfport, 24 tons, built in 1903, from Apalachicola bound for Gulfport with rosin. Wrecked five miles northwest of Santa Rosa Station, Feb. 14, 1912. A total loss. Source: 14.

170. *Freddie Hencken* — Three-masted schooner, of New York, 500 tons, built in 1892 at Bath, 146.2' x 36' x 12.4'. Stranded on Cape San Blas Shoals, Sept. 12, 1912. Source: 14.

171. *Waul* — Barge, 534 tons, built in 1894. Foundered near St. Andrews Bar, Dec. 24, 1912. Source: 14.

172. *Thomas S. Dennison* — Four-masted schooner, of Thomaston, Maine, 1,491 tons, built in 1900 at Thomaston, 218.2' x 42.7' x 19.7'. Foundered 100 miles south of Pensacola, Jan. 3, 1913. Source: 80.

173. *Carrie B. Welle*s — Schooner, of Pensacola, 41 tons, built in 1891 at Boothbay, Maine, 66.2' x 18.7' x 7.8'. Stranded at Hurricane Island, off St. Andrews Bay, Aug. 9, 1913. Source: 14.

174. *Ned P. Walker* — Schooner, 98 tons, built in 1881 at Jonesboro, Maine, 81.4' x 24.3' x 6.8'. Stranded 80 miles east of Pensacola, Aug. 23, 1913. Source: 14.

175. *Nelly* — Schooner, of Pensacola, 25 tons, built in 1883 at Freeport, Fla., 54' x 20.5' x 4.6'. Foundered at Santa Rosa Island, March 1, 1914. Source: 14.

176. *Priscilla* — Schooner, of Pensacola, 48 tons, built in 1893 at E. Boothbay, Maine, 69.3' x 19.8' x 8.9'. Stranded on Carrabelle Bar, Sept. 24, 1914. Source: 14.

177. *Donna Christina* — Schooner, of Pensacola, 174 tons, built in 1899 at Tampa, 115' x 29.3' x 8.6'. Capsized 60 miles southeast of Cape San Blas, April 9, 1915. All seven on board lost. Source: 14.

178. *John G. Whilldin* — Schooner, 51 tons, built in 1839 at Philadelphia, 78.3' x 18.8' x 6.9'. Foundered near Cape San Blas, Sept. 15, 1915. All nine on board lost. Source: 14.

179. *Alabama* — Schooner, of Pensacola, 51 tons, built in 1893 at Portland, Fla., 61.5' x 23.5' x 5.1'. Foundered in Pensacola Bay, Sept. 30, 1915. Source: 14.

180. *John M. Keen* — Listed as a sloop and schooner, 64 tons, built in 1884 at Essex, Mass., 78.8' x 20' x 8.6'. Stranded near Pensacola, July 5, 1916. Source: 14.

181. *Kathryn B.* — Schooner, 32 tons, built in 1903. Foundered at Pensacola, July 5, 1916. Source: 14.

182. *Cabradroca* — Portuguese steamer, scuttled in Old Navy Cove, Pensacola, sometime between 1910 and 1915. Her remains lie in ten feet of water, with most of the wreck silted over. She was an old steamer, and there remains much coal and machinery scattered over a 100-foot by 50-foot area. Source: 1.

183. *Robert A. Snyder* — Schooner, 375 tons, built in 1891 at Milford, Del., 138.4' x 33.1' x 10'. Stranded on St. Andrews Bar, Sept. 14, 1917. Source: 14.

184. *Annie and Jennie* — Gas vessel, 34 tons, built in 1901. Stranded on St. Andrews Bar, Jan. 7, 1918. Four lives lost. Source: 14.

185. *Emilia Gloria* — Schooner, 59 tons, built in 1903 at Essex, Mass., 76.5' x 20' x 9.2'. Burned in Pensacola Bay, April 7, 1918.

Source: 14.

186. *Wasp* — Steam freighter, of San Francisco, 641 tons, built in 1905 at Fairhaven, Calif., 170.6' x 37.3' x 13.1'. Burned in Pensacola Bay, June 19, 1919. Source: 14.

187. Barge — A barge was located Jan. 17, 1920, 265 degrees, 5.8 miles from Sand Island Lighthouse, 292 degrees, 4.8 miles from Mobile Beacon Light; Lat. 30-11-48, Long. 87-56-30. It was used for decking seaplanes. Source: 1.

188. *Crescent* — Schooner, 463 tons, built in 1883 at New London, Conn., 150.8' x 34.8' x 12.4'. Foundered 150 miles southeast of Pensacola, Jan. 26, 1920. Source: 14.

189. *USS Massachusetts* — Navy first-rate battleship (steel), 10,288 tons, launched in 1893 at Philadelphia, 348' x 69.3' x 24'. Scuttled by Navy off Pensacola Bar, Jan. 6, 1921, at Lat. 30-17-48, Long. 87-18-42, off Pensacola. Fort Pickens used her for bombing practice the next four years. She lies in 30 feet of water, and is a popular dive site. (See Figure 6). Source: 1, 14, 28, 80.

Figure 6: Battleship *USS Massachusetts*, sunk in 1920. NATIONAL ARCHIVES.

190. *Brittannia* — Tug, of Pensacola, 66 tons, built in 1883 at Baltimore, 76.6' x 16.6' x 7.8'. Stolen from her pier at Jersey City, N.J., Oct. 1, 1921. Later found grounded off Pensacola. Source: 14, 80.

191. *Ben* — Barge, of Pensacola, 369 tons, built in 1903 at Pensacola. Sank at Lat. 29-51-00, Long. 84-05-00, Dec. 18, 1921, and was still visible in 1983. Source: 1, 14.

192. *Golden State* (formerly *William F. Garms*) — Schooner, of San Francisco, 1,094 tons, built in 1901 at Everett, Wash., 215.5' x 40.7' x 16'. Burned on Feb. 17, 1922, at Lat. 29-29-00, Long. 85-50-00. Source: 14.

193. *Rollo* — Sidewheel steamer, of Pensacola, 33 tons, built in 1908 at Pinewood, Fla., 67' x 19.8' x 3.3'. Foundered in Choctawhatchee Bay, March 30, 1922. Source: 14.

194. *Ida M. Silva* — Schooner, 55 tons, built in 1903 at Essex, Mass., 70.3' x 19.7' x 9'. Foundered off Pensacola, May 24, 1922. Source: 14.

195. *Colthraps* — Steamer (steel), 5,134 tons, built in 1920, burned at Pensacola, Sept. 5, 1922. One life lost. Source: 14.

196. *Altamaha* — Steamer (steel), 2,667 tons, built in 1908 at Quincy, Mass., 300' x 41' x 25.8'. Stranded at Pensacola, June 26, 1923. Source: 14.

197. *Bronx* — Steamer, 57 tons, built in 1882 at Mystic, Conn., 78.4' x 17.5' x 6.8'. Foundered off Pensacola Bar, Oct. 7, 1923. Source: 14.

198. *Bluefields* (formerly *Andrew Pierce Jr.*) — Schooner, 281 tons, built in 1904 at Noank, Conn., 134.2' x 29.6' x 9.2'. Stranded in Perdido Bay, Oct. 17, 1923. Four lives lost. Source: 14.

199. *Cornelius H. Callaghan* — Schooner, 1,341 tons, built in 1916. Stranded on St. Andrews Bar, Jan. 10, 1924. Source: 14.

200. *Avio* — Schooner barge, of Pensacola, 473 tons, built in 1890 at Nykyoko, Russia, 144.3' x 31.8' x 15.1'. Burned at Port St. Joe, July 6, 1924. Source: 14.

201. *Alpena* — Schooner, 970 tons, built in 1901 at Port Blakeley, Wash., 206' x 40.7' x 16.5'. Foundered in St. Andrews Bay, Dec. 4, 1924. Source: 14.

202. *Thelma* — Schooner, 525 tons, built in 1893 at Rockland, Maine,

157.3' x 35.6' x 13.2'. Burned at Lat. 29-38-00, Long. 85-57-00, May 5, 1925. Source: 1, 14.

203. Sailing Ship — A light tender reported an unknown ship sunk on Aug. 22, 1925, with her masts and rigging protruding 15 feet above the water, at Lat. 29-38-00, Long. 85-49-00. Source: 1.

204. *Marion N. Cobb* — Schooner, of Mobile, 459 tons, built in 1902 at Rockland, Maine, 150.7' x 34.9' x 11.8'. Foundered at Lat. 28-50-00, Long. 87-30-00 (another source says 87-10-00), Nov. 28, 1925. Source: 1, 14.

205. *Robert L. Bean* — Four-masted schooner, of Rockland, Maine, 1,335 tons, built in 1920 at Camden, Maine, 216.6' x 32' x 11.1'. Stranded at Santa Rosa Island, Feb. 17, 1926. Source: 14, 80.

206. *Mattie B.* — Gas vessel, 27 tons, built in 1912. Foundered at Pensacola, June 26, 1926. Source: 14.

207. *J.S. Murrow* — Gas vessel, 28 tons, built in 1904 at Apalachicola, 61.2' x 20.5' x 4.7'. Foundered in Perdido Bay, Sept. 20, 1926. Source: 14.

208. *Leroy* (formerly *U.S. Revenue Cutter Dexter*) — Steamer, 209 tons, built in 1874 at Boston, 129' x 22.8' x 8.8'. Foundered on St. Andrews Bar, Nov. 16, 1926. Source: 14.

Figure 7: Schooner *Santa Rosa,* wrecked in 1928. PENSACOLA HISTORICAL SOCIETY.

209. *Santa Rosa* — Four-masted schooner, of Pensacola, 695 tons, built in 1918 at Milton, Fla., 169.5' x 37.8' x 13.4'. Collided with a submerged derelict, May 7, 1928, believed to be at or near Pensacola. (See Figure 7). Source: 14.

210. *Tecumseh* — Gas vessel (formerly a schooner), 41 tons, built in 1899 at Essex, Mass., 65.8' x 18.8' x 8.8'. Stranded in St. Andrews Bay, Oct. 24, 1929. Source: 14.

211. *E.E. Simpson* — Tug (iron), of Pensacola, 109 tons, built in 1877 at Camden, N.J., 93.4' x 20.1' x 10.8'. Stranded in St. Andrews Bay, Oct. 28, 1930, in shallow water, at Lat. 30-03-18, Long. 85-37-18. Source: 1, 14.

212. *Peter* — Barge, of Pensacola, 453 tons, built in 1902 at Pensacola, 170.8' x 35' x 9.7'. Burned in Pensacola Bay, May 8, 1935. Source: 14.

213. Unknown Wreck — Located in 1935, at Lat. 30-08-25.79, Long. 85-37-59.4, in nine to 16 feet of water. Source: 1.

214. Unknown Wreck — Located in 1935, at Lat. 30-08-43.16, Long. 85-37-54.36, in 12 to 14 feet of water. Source: 1.

215. Unknown Wreck — Located in 1935, at Lat. 30-08-35, Long. 85-37-55.20. Source: 1.

216. Barge — Sank in 1935, at Lat. 30-13-43.40, Long. 85-49-40.5. She would be exposed at low tide. Source: 1.

217. Unknown Wreck — Located in 1935, at Lat. 30-19-12, Long. 87-14-28, and verified in 1976 and again in 1981, when examined from shore. Source: 1.

218. Unknown Wreck — Located in 1935, at Lat. 30-21-56.23, Long. 87-11-30, and verified in 1983, in 13 feet of water. Source: 1.

219. Unknown Wreck — Charted in 1935, verified in 1981, one foot above the sand at West Bay, Pensacola Bay entrance, at Lat. 30-23-36.03, Long. 87-14-43.58. Source: 1.

220. Unknown Wreck — Located in 1935, verified in 1982, at Lat. 30-24-13.5, Long. 87-13-15.05, where a rock shoal believed to be a ballast pile was found. Source: 1.

221. Unknown Wreck — Four boilers and a hulk were found in 1935.

The boilers were verified in 1982, at Lat. 30-24-39.5, Long. 87-12-08.80, and the hulk at Lat. 30-24-41.33, Long. 87-12-07.4. Three other boilers were found at Lat. 30-24-43.20, Long. 87-12-05. Source: 1.

222. *Juno* — Motor vessel, 68 tons, built in 1929. Foundered 10 miles south of St. Georges Light (also listed as having foundered off St. Andrews), April 28, 1938. Source: 14.

223. Unknown Wreck — Located Oct. 3, 1939, in 27 feet of water, at Lat. 30-05-45, Long. 86-56-30. Source: 1.

224. *Grady S.* — Gas vessel, 23 tons, built in 1924. Was in a collision 15 miles west of Fort Walton, Oct. 10, 1939. Source: 14.

225. *Tarpon* — Steam freighter (iron), 449 tons, built in 1887 at Wilmington, 159.9' x 26' x 7.2'. Foundered Sept. 2, 1937, at Lat. 30-05-40.20, Long. 85-56-33, while enroute to Panama from Pensacola, in 90 feet of water. Source: 1, 14.

See World War II section for Section 1 wrecks during that period.

226. *Anaconda* — Barge, 2,217 tons, built in 1921 at Kingston, N.Y., 267.3' x 46' x 23.6'. Foundered Feb. 7, 1946, at Lat. 28-28-00, Long. 86-17-00. Source: 14.

227. *Samuel C. Laveland Jr.* — Steel barge, 1,288 tons, built in 1911 at Camden, N.J., 207.3' x 34.6' x 20.5'. Foundered Nov. 11, 1948, approximately 120 miles northwest of Egmont Key, at approximate Lat. 29-00-00, Long. 84-23-00. Source: 1, 14.

228. Unknown wreck — Charted in the 1940s. Possibly a lumber barge or the Route 79 bridge (which was a floating barge type), at Lat. 30-17-39, Long. 85-51-20. Source: 1.

229. Unknown wreck — Charted in the 1940s (was visible then), at Lat. 30-23-15, Long. 86-46-42, though it is now submerged. Source: 1.

230. *Jolly Roger* — O/V, 37 tons, built in 1953. Stranded in Apalachicola Bay, June 17, 1956. Source: 14.

231. *Eureka* — O/V, 27 tons, built in 1939. Foundered at Apalachicola, May 1957. Source: 14.

232. *Ralph E. Havens* — O/V, 48 tons, built in 1905. Foundered Dec. 9, 1957, approximately 15 miles south-southeast of Carrabelle. Source: 14.

233. *Supertest* — O/V, 51 tons, built in 1942. Stranded on St. George Island, April 2, 1958. Source: 14.

234. *Cracker Boys* — O/V, 33 tons, built in 1950. Wrecked during a storm, April 30, 1960, off Apalachicola. Source: 14.

235. *Islander* — F/V. Wrecked in 1961, at approximate Lat. 28-43-00, Long. 85-06-00, in 12 feet of water. Source: 1.

236. *Tornado* — F/V (oil), 56 tons, built in 1947 at St. Augustine. 57.7' x 20.2' x 6.6'. Foundered in Pensacola Bay, May 18, 1962. Source: 14.

237. *Miss Becky* — O/V (steel), 26 tons, built in 1955. Foundered Oct. 24, 1964, approximately 17 miles south of Destin. Source: 14.

238. *Robert P. Doherty* — T/V (oil), 65 tons, built in 1943 at Houston, 63.7' x 18.2' x 7'. Foundered at South Shores Light, Nov. 17, 1965, off St. Marks. Source: 14.

239. Shrimp boat — Unknown 77-foot shrimper. Sank in 1965. Used as a gunnery target, at Lat. 30-20-32.30, Long. 86-42-39.80 . Source: 1.

240. Tug — Charted in 1967, at Lat. 30-18-50.40, Long. 87-19-27. Source: 1.

241. *PMJ* — O/V, 47 tons, built in 1953. Foundered Oct. 10, 1971, near Cape San Blas. Source: 14.

242. *Captain Bill* — O/V, 85 tons, built in 1968. Foundered June 17, 1972, at Cape St. George Lighthouse. Source: 14.

243. *Point Chicot* — Steel T/V (oil), of Wilmington, 179 tons, built in 1925 at Wilmington, 92.8' x 24.4' x 12.5'. Foundered April 19, 1973, at Lat. 28-00-00, Long. 85-00-00. Source: 14.

244. *Taurus* — 65' yacht. Sank in 1973 in 15 feet of water, at Lat. 30-21-52, Long. 87-03-25. Source: 1.

245. Fishing vessel — 35'. Sank in 1974, at Lat. 30-13-35, Long. 85-41-52. Source: 1.

246. Unknown wreck — Charted in 1975 in shallow water, at Lat. 29-51-14.69, Long. 85-23-53.62. Source: 1.

247. *Yankee Clipper* — Fishing trawler, 49'. Sank in 1975 in 60 feet

of water, at Lat. 30-00-40.03, Long. 85-38-53.40. Source: 1.

248. *Betsy M* — F/V, 55'. Sank in 1975 in 46 feet of water, at Lat. 30-08-00, Long. 87-46-00. Source: 1.

249. *Miss Bessie M* — O/V, 60 tons, built in 1963. Foundered Dec. 9, 1976, at Lat. 30-08-00, Long. 87-46-00. Source: 1.

250. Barge — 60'. Located in 1976, at Lat. 30-06-45.48, Long. 85-42-08.95. Source: 1.

251. *Erma J II* — O/V, 40 tons, built in 1971. Collided with the sunken battleship *USS Massachusetts*, Aug. 18, 1977, in the pass into Pensacola Bay. Source: 14.

252. *Cindy Brent* — Sank in 1977, at approximate Lat. 30-37-00, Long. 84-50-00. Source: 1.

253. *Enjoy* — 40'. Located in 1978 in 15 fathoms, 65 miles sothwest of Apalachicola, at approximate Lat. 28-54-00, Long. 84-01-00. Source: 1.

254. Gravel Barge — 120'. Reported sunk in 1978, at Lat. 31-15-00, Long. 84-55-00. Source: 1.

255. *Lucky Smith* — O/V, 65 tons, built in 1953. Stranded March 30, 1980, in St. Joseph Bay. Source: 14.

256. *Karma* — F/V. Sank in 1980, at Lat. 29-54-18, Long. 84-25-42. Source: 1.

257. *Little Tots* — F/V. Sank in 1981, at Lat. 29-42-20, Long. 84-58-14. Source: 1.

258. *Sandy P* — F/V. Sank in 1981, at Lat. 29-49-00, Long. 84-37-30. Source: 1.

259. Unknown wreck — Visible in 1981, metal hull, at Lat. 29-52-02.13, Long. 85-23-34.50. Source: 1.

260. *Crawfish* — F/V, 35'. Sank June 22, 1981, in 94 feet of water, at approximate Lat. 30-00-00, Long. 87-25-00. Source: 1.

261. *Don't Cha Know* — Sailing vessel. Sank in 1981, at Lat. 29-51-29.50, Long. 85-20-54.95. Source: 1.

262. *Shorty's Boy* — F/V. Sank in 1982, at Lat. 29-37-24, Long. 84-54-06. Source: 1.

263. *Miss Aline* — F/V. Sank in 1982, at Lat. 29-39-02, Long. 84-04-15. Source: 1.

264. *Miss Tammy* — F/V. Sank in 1982, at Lat. 29-49-06, Long. 84-24-18. Source: 1.

265. *Drifter* — F/V. Sank in 1982, at Lat. 29-52-00, Long. 83-59-42. Source: 1.

266. Sport Fishing Hull — Found burned in 1982, at Lat. 30-07-07.25, Long. 85-43-44.59. Source: 1.

267. *Viking IV* — F/V. Sank in 1983, at Lat. 29-24-12, Long. 85-01-00. Source: 1.

268. Unknown wreck — Reported in 1983 in 15 feet of water, at Lat. 29-53-32.12, Long. 85-27-59.42. Source: 1.

269. *Davy's Navy* — F/V. Sank in 1984, at Lat. 29-23-42, Long. 84-57-30. Source: 1.

270. Cluster of wrecks — Reported in 1984 in 17 to 25 feet of water, at Lat. 30-07-01.49, Long. 85-42-15.08. Source: 1.

271. Hopper barge — Reported in 1986 in 62 feet of water, at Lat. 30-13-03.54, Long. 87-19-24.85. Wreck measured 120' x 40' x 15'. Source: 1.

Figure 7A: Tin-lined copper pitcher from the Emanuel Point Ship (1559). FLORIDA BUREAU OF ARCHEOLOGICAL RESEARCH.

Section 2: West Coast

1500

1. Spanish ship — On April 4, 1528, Pánfilo de Narváez landed at a place he called Santa Cruz (believed to be Sarasota Bay). He and his men went inland, leaving his four ships under the command of Lieutenant Caraballo, who was ordered to look for a harbor while they went on their expedition. Soon after, one of the ships was wrecked on the coast. Caraballo sailed up and down the coast for a year looking for Narváez, but never found him. Source: 7.

2. Spanish fleet — Barcia's narrative mentions that a Juan Muñoz was found in 1549 near a bay which Hernando de Soto named "Espirito Santa Bay" (Bay of the Holy Spirit). Most academics believe it was Tampa Bay. Muñoz was thought to have been one of de Soto's soldiers, or a survivor of a Spanish fleet which wrecked on this coast 14 years before (1535). Source: 7.

3. Two Spanish ships — Part of a fleet under Pedro Menéndez de Avilés. They were lost in 1563 on the west coast of Florida near Charlotte Harbor. Source: 22.

1800

4. Pirate ship of José Gaspar — There has been much speculation as to whether José Gaspar and his ship, the *Doña Rosalia,* really existed. Some say that real estate developers made him up, to give the area a colorful history. Old Spanish coins do turn up along the beaches of Charlotte Harbor, and some believe a treasure ship did sink off the southwest tip off of Boca Grande.

The book *The Pirates Who's Who*, by Phillip Gosse, published in 1924, says José Gaspar, alias Gasparilla or Richard Cœur de Lion, was an officer in the Spanish Navy until 1782, when he turned pirate. He supposedly settled at Charlotte Harbor and built a fort. In 1821 his ship alledgedly engaged an American man-of-war. When defeated, he wrapped himself in an anchor chain and jumped overboard.

A book on local history says that the *Doña Rosalia* was sunk by the *USS Enterprise*, under command of Lieutenant Lawrence Kearny, on Nov. 5, 1821. Another book, *Lawrence Kearny, Sailor Diplomat*, by Carol Alden, published in 1936, has a report by Kearny, dated Nov. 12, 1821. In it, he says he had captured some pirate vessels off the coast of Cuba on Oct. 16, 1821, with no mention of any engagements off Florida at this time.

Another book, *Our Navy and the West Indian Pirates*, by G. Allen, published in 1929, makes no mention of a pirate stronghold at Charlotte Harbor, but does mention Commodore Aury's pirate stronghold on Amelia Island. It also describes an incident in which the ship

Orleans was involved. Pirates robbed her of more than $40,000 in goods when she was off the Abacos in the Bahamas in September 1821. The head of the pirates gave a note to a U.S. officer, who happened to be a passenger on board. It stated, "Between buccaneers no ceremony. I take your dry goods and in return I send you pimento; therefore we are now even — I entertain no resentement... The goods of this world belong to the brave and valiant." It was signed "Richard Cœur de Lion."

Somehow Richard Cœur de Lion and the fictitious José Gaspar became one and the same. The Tampa Bay area still holds an annual pirate festival in Gaspar's honor.

5. *Exchange* — Schooner, of Frankfort, Maine. Went ashore during a storm at Tampa Bay, Jan. 31, 1836. She had no cargo. Sails and rigging saved and taken to Key West. Source: 96 (Feb. 26, 1836).

6. *Marion* — Steamer. Reported ashore between Apalachicola and Tampa, November 1836. Source: 96 (Nov. 30, 1836).

7. *Isis* — Sidewheel steamer, 130 tons, built in 1837 at New York. Burned at Tampa, Jan. 5, 1842. Source: 52.

8. *George P. Sloate* — Ship, from Pensacola bound for Key West with bricks. Wrecked at Charlotte Harbor, Dec. 22, 1855. Vessel lost. Wreckers awarded $798. Source: 37.

9. *Ostervald* — Ship, believed to be 902 tons. Reported on fire, nearly burned to the waterline, by the ship *Milton*, at Lat. 25-00-00, Long. 85-20-00, May 8, 1858. Believed to be the *Ostervald*. Source: 19, 99 (May 25, 1858).

10. *Heidelberg* — Ship, of the New Orleans-Liverpool Line, 1,053 tons, from New Orleans bound for Europe with cotton and $31,000 in specie (coins). Went ashore 12 miles north of Cape Florida during the storm of November 1859. Her cargo was saved. She was brought to Key West by wreckers.

She left Key West for New Orleans on Dec. 18, 1859, with a number of pumps on board. She started leaking badly and the pumps could no longer keep out the water. On Dec. 12, Captain Rodewald decided to abandon ship at about Lat. 27-23-00, Long. 86-08-00. He and the crew were picked up later. Source: 19, 99 (Jan. 12, 1860).

See Civil War section for Section 2 wrecks during that period.

11. *USS Narcissus* (formerly *Mary Cook*, sold to the U.S. Navy, September 1863) — Steamer 4th-rate, tug-rigged, 115 tons (also listed at

101 tons), built in 1863 at East Albany, N.Y., 81'6" x 18'9" x 8', one 20-pounder parrot, one heavy 12-pounder. Left Pensacola on New Year's Day. Sank off Egmont Key, Jan. 4, 1866, with all hands. Source: 28, 52, 63 (Series II, Vol. 1).

12. *Suwanee* (formerly the *Pompero*) — Sidewheel steamer, 379 tons, built in 1850 in Baltimore. Foundered off Cape Romano, Dec. 4, 1866. Source: 52, 60.

13. *Idonia* — Schooner. Wrecked in Tampa Bay, December 1869. Source: 14.

14. *Flying Fish* — Schooner. Wrecked in Tampa Bay, December 1869. Source: 14.

15. *Rosa* — Schooner. Wrecked in Tampa Bay, December 1869. Source: 14.

16. *Louisburg* — Sidewheel steamer, 894 tons, built in 1863 at New York. Burned at Cedar Keys, April 24, 1870. Source: 52.

17. *Sea Drift* — Schooner. Wrecked at Cedar Keys, December 1871. Source: 14.

18. *Rusa* — Schooner, from Key West bound for Manatee with a light cargo. Wrecked on Palusa Sola Key, April 7, 1872, at 10 p.m., reported from the Egmont Key Station. A total loss. Source: 14.

19. *Louisburg* — Steamer. Burned at Cedar Keys, August 1872. (Possibly same vessel as #16). Source: 14.

20. *Evening Star* — Schooner. Wrecked at Clearwater, August 1872. Source: 14.

21. *Sarah Gormas* — Schooner. Stranded at Cedar Keys, August 1872. A partial loss. Source: 14.

22. *Eagle* — Sloop. Wrecked at Cedar Keys, August 1872. Source: 14.

23. *Huntress* — Steamer, 38 tons, Captain Mason, on her first voyage from Cedar Keys bound for Charlotte Harbor with building materials. Was swamped and sank during a storm, Oct. 6, 1873 (possibly 1874), off Sanibel Island. Vessel valued at $4,500 ($4,000 loss), cargo at $2,500 ($2,000 loss). Source: 14.

24. *Chief* — Fishing schooner, of Key West, 36 tons, Captain Gonzales.

51

Sprang a leak and sank, May 5, 1874, at the mouth of the Manatee River. Sails and rigging saved. Source: 14.

25. *Ocean Queen* — Schooner, of Key West, 35 tons, built in 1852, Captain Allen, from Key West bound for Havana in ballast. Stranded at the mouth of Charlotte Harbor, Aug. 14, 1877. A total loss. Source: 14.

26. *Antarctic* — Sloop, of Key West, 24 tons, built in 1840, Captain Thompson. Stranded on Perico Shoal, Tampa Bay, Dec. 8, 1877. Source: 14.

27. *Florida* — Schooner, of Key West, 61 tons, Captain Nelson, from Punta Rassa bound for Key West with cattle and hogs. Stranded in Northwest Bay, Dec. 29, 1877. A total loss. Source: 14.

28. *Rosita* — Sloop, 142 tons, built in 1866, from Cedar Keys bound for Fort Myers. Stranded at Cape Romano, Sept. 10, 1878, at 10 P.M., during a hurricane. Source: 14.

29. *Henry Mearn* — Schooner, 129 tons, built in 1866, from Mobile bound for Kingston with lumber. Sprang a leak and foundered, Dec. 9, 1878, at 10 A.M., at Lat. 25-00, Long. 84-05. Source: 14.

30. *Sea Bird* — Schooner, of Key West, 21 tons, built in 1865. Foundered at Punta Rassa, Aug. 29, 1880. A total loss. Source: 14.

31. *Lucy M* — Schooner, 19 tons. Foundered at sea, Oct. 2, 1881, at 2 p.m., 50 miles northwest of Key West, after springing a leak. She was an old vessel. Source: 14.

32. *Chimborazo* — British bark, of New Castle, 850 tons, built in 1851, Captain Ford, from Mobile bound for Southampton with pitch pine timber. Wrecked 30 miles south of Egmont Key, Feb. 9, 1882, at 11 A.M. A total loss. Source: 14.

33. *Martha M. Heath* — Schooner, of New York, 207 tons, built in 1871, Captain Jordan, from New York bound for Sanibel Island with coal and lighthouse fixtures. Stranded on Sanibel Shoal, May 5, 1884, 2-1/2 miles from East Point. Vessel a total loss. Cargo valued at $100,000; some saved. Source: 14.

34. *Dictator* — Sidewheel steamer, of Key West, 582 or 623 tons, built in 1863 at Brooklyn, N.Y., Captain McKay, from Key West bound for Manatee. Wrecked at the mouth of the Hillsborough River, Dec. 26, 1884, at 5 A.M. Valued at $40,000; a total loss. Source: 14, 52.

35. *Millie Wales* — Steamer, of Pensacola, 85 tons, built in 1875. Caught fire in Tampa Bay, while fishing, June 4, 1885, at 3 P.M. A total loss. Source: 14.

36. *Freddie L. Porter* — Three-masted schooner, of Boston, 346 tons, built in 1866, Captain Russel, from Galveston bound for Mobile with fertilizer. Sank off Sarasota Pass, Jan. 20, 1887, at 4:15 P.M., in 6-1/2 fathoms, approximately 15 miles south of Egmont Key. Source: 14.

37. *Mary Ellen* — Schooner, 69 tons, built in 1867, cargo of lumber, Captain Webb. Capsized in a sudden gale, May 3, 1890, at 3 A.M., at Lat. 27-10-00, Long. 85-00-00. Two lives lost. Source: 14.

38. *Watulla* — Schooner, of Tampa, 14 tons, built in 1885, Captain Walker. Went ashore and bilged, Jan. 4, 1891, on the south side of Egmont Key Channel, on Passage Key Shoal. A total loss. Source: 14.

39. *City of Athens* — Sternwheel steamer, 23 tons, built in 1892, Captain Gilbert. Burned at wharf in Tampa, Jan. 30, 1893, at 8:30 P.M. Source: 14.

40. Schooner — Of Tampa, 19 tons, built in 1885, Captain Fogarty. Stranded in Little Sarasota Bay, Feb. 19, 1893, at 8 A.M. A total loss. Source: 14.

41. *Silver Spray* — Schooner, of Tampa, 24 tons, built in 1873. Burned while anchored in port, Aug. 16, 1893. Source: 14.

42. Tug — 28 tons, built in 1891, Captain Cassidy. Caught fire at Long Dock, Punta Gorda, April 24, 1894. A total loss. Source: 14.

43. *Rambler* — Schooner, of Tampa, 29 tons, built in 1881, Captain Fogarty. Sank at the dock, Dec. 15, 1894. A total loss. Source: 14.

44. *Scotia* — Schooner, of New York, 406 tons, built in 1883 at Belfast, Maine, 138.3' x 33' x 12', Captain Perry, from Mobile bound for Havana with lumber. Foundered 100 miles northwest of Tortuga, Dec. 31, 1895, at 12 P.M. A total loss. Source: 14.

45. *Henry Stanbury* — Schooner, of Tampa, 59 tons, built in 1868 at Essex, Mass, 70.2' x 20.8' x 7.4', Captain Baker. Capsized and sank during a squall, July 5, 1898, while in port off Gadsen Point. Cargo of structural iron salvaged. Source: 14.

46. *Glad Tidings* — Schooner, of Tampa, 18 tons, built in 1896, from Fort Myers bound for Tampa with tobacco and corn. Beached during

a storm, Aug. 16, 1899, one mile south of Little Sarasota Pass. A total loss. Source: 14.

1900

47. *Belle* — Two-masted schooner (pilot boat), of Tampa, 23 tons, built in 1872 at Savannah, 52' x 16.5' x 7', Captain Fitzgerald. Went ashore in a fog, Feb. 8, 1900, on the south end of Egmont Key. A total loss. Source: 14.

48. *Augusta E. Herrick* — Schooner, of Tampa, 99 tons, built in 1877 at Gloucester, 90.6' x 24.7' x 7.6', cargo of lumber, Captain Alley. Foundered on Jerovedances Reef, March 6, 1900, west by southwest of Hog Island. Source: 14.

49. *John Smart* — Schooner, of Tampa, 17 tons, built in 1887, Captain Dolphin, wrecked on Mullet Key Shoal while fishing, Oct. 3, 1900, approximately 1-1/2 miles northwest of Egmont Key Light. A total loss. Source: 14.

50. *Lula Frances* — Schooner, of Tampa, 15 tons, built in 1894 at Choctawhatchee, Captain Thompson, from Tampa bound for Fort Myers with lumber and grain. Stranded on Sarasota Bar, Oct. 13, 1900. A total loss. Source: 14.

51. *Marion* — Vessel of Tampa, 16 tons (believed to be the schooner *Marion*, 17 tons, built in 1885 at New Smyrna, 41.4' x 13.5' x 3.7'), from Tampa bound for Caseys Pass with lumber, shingles, and bricks. Stranded at Caseys Pass, North Point Pass, Feb. 11, 1901. Cargo saved. Source: 14.

52. *Caroline Kage* — Schooner, of Apalachicola, 20 tons, built in 1875 at Pensacola, 43.7' x 14.4' x 5.3'. Stranded in Tampa Bay, January 1902. Source: 14.

53. *Sammy Lee* — Schooner, of Tampa, 20 tons, built in 1893 at Tampa, 51.2' x 14.2' x 4.7', Captain Donaldson. Collided with the dock at St. Petersburg, Feb. 24, 1902. A total loss. Source: 14.

54. *Mary Blue* — Sidewheel steamer, of Key West, 113 tons, built in 1892 at Hull, Fla., 76.2' x 19.7' x 3'. Burned at Charlotte Harbor, July 29, 1902. Source: 14.

55. *Nineveh* — Barkentine, of New York, 494 tons, built in 1874 at Boston, 126.2' x 30.5' x 17'. Foundered at Cape Romano, Jan. 20, 1903. Source: 14.

56. *Bassinger* — Sidewheel steamer, 87 tons, built in 1899. Burned at

Charlotte Harbor, March 2, 1903. Source: 14.

57. *Lewis* — Sidewheel steamer, 127 tons, built in 1901. Burned at Tampa, Oct. 11, 1903. Source: 14.

58. *G.L. Daboll* — Schooner, of Pensacola, 49 tons, built in 1872 at Noank, Conn., 64' x 19.7' x 7.7'. Stranded at Egmont Key, April 17, 1906. Source: 14.

59. *Vandalia* — Schooner, of Tampa, 41 tons, built in 1898 at Fogarty-ville, Fla., 71' x 18.4' x 4.6'. Foundered off Cape Romano, May 8, 1906. Four lives lost. Source: 14.

60. *Emma L. Cottingham* — Schooner, of New Bedford, 522 tons, built in 1875 at Somers Point, N.J., 139.4' x 34' x 10.2', Captain Phiney, from Mobile bound for Knights Key with gravel. Foundered approximately 135 miles west-southwest of Egmont Key, June 10, 1905, at Lat. 26-58-00, Long. 85-10-00. Of the seven on board, five were lost and one was left on the wreck. Source: 14.

61. *Withlacoochee No. 9* — Barge, 119 tons, built in 1901. Foundered off Port Inglis, June 12, 1906. Source: 14.

62. *Dandaha* — Schooner, of Tampa, 41 tons, built in 1894, Captain Fogarty, from Key West bound for Manatee River. Capsized off Cape Romano, July 1906. Four lives lost. Source: 14.

63. *Ardell* — Schooner, of Tampa, 50 tons, built in 1885 at Key West, 52.2' x 16.3' x 5', Captain Wick, from Bradenton bound for Tampa. Capsized in a whirlwind, Aug. 20, 1906, at 5 P.M., one mile south of Pinellas Point. Source: 14.

64. *A.A. Rowe* — Schooner, of New York, 45 tons, built in 1859 at Mystic, 63' x 18.6' x 8', Captain Kemp, from Tarpon Springs bound for Tampa. Foundered on a sand bar near Egmont Key, Oct. 19, 1906, at 7 A.M. A total loss. Source: 14.

65. *Eugene Batty* — Schooner, of Tampa, 19 tons, built in 1884 at Cedar Keys, 54' x 15.7' x 3.8', from Clearwater bound for Tampa with empty casks and bottles and dried apples. Collided with a steamer, Jan. 30, 1908, between the second and third lights at the cut leading into the Hillsborough River. A total loss. Source: 14.

66. *Addie F. Cole* — Schooner, of Tampa, 76 tons, built in 1867 at Essex, Mass., 78' x 23' x 8', Captain Tsolinas, from Tampa bound for Tarpon Springs, no cargo. Foundered near the middle buoy of North

Anclote Channel, April 15, 1908, after springing a leak. Source: 14.

67. *Wave* — Schooner, 67 tons, built in 1883 at Rockyhill, Conn., 73' x 24.2' x 6'. Burned at Tampa, Nov. 3, 1908. Source: 14.

68. *Davy Crockett* — Schooner, of Pensacola, 85 tons, built in 1876 at Bath, 80.7' x 27.7' x 8'. Stranded at the South Pass, Tampa Bay, July 8, 1909. Source: 14.

69. *Jimmie* — Schooner, of Key West, 18 tons, built in 1878 at Port Jefferson, N.Y., Captain Knowles, from Key West bound for Tampa with oil, gas, and turpentine. Exploded at Tampa, July 10, 1909. Source: 14.

70. *Ira* — Schooner, of Pensacola, 75 tons, built in 1908 at Boggy, Fla., 65' x 25.2' x 6.3'. Foundered near Cedar Keys, Oct. 24, 1909. Source: 14.

71. *Ellen M. Adams* — Schooner, of Tampa, 90 tons, built in 1876 at Boothbay, Maine, 81' x 22.5' x 8', Captain Johnson. Foundered while on a sponging trip, Dec. 20, 1909, by the middle buoy, North Anclote Channel. Source: 14.

72. *Lily White* — Schooner, of Key West, 55 tons, built in 1883 at Maddisonville, La., 70.8' x 22.4' x 5.8'. Burned at Tampa, Dec. 23, 1910. Three lives lost. Source: 14.

73. *Olga* — Three-masted schooner, of Mobile, 308 tons, built in 1881 at Manitowoc, Wis., 137' x 30.4' x 10', from Mobile bound for Havana, no cargo. Sank 150 miles southwest of Egmont Key, April 26, 1911, at 11 P.M. Crew saved. Another source says she sank 53 miles south of Egmont Key. Source: 14.

74. *Ruth A* — Schooner, of Tampa, 34 tons, built in 1901, Captain Roberts, from Punta Gorda bound for Tampa. Burned to the water line and sank, May 31, 1911, five miles north of Boca Grande, off Gasparilla Island. Also listed as a gas vessel, 31 tons, built in 1900, which burned at same place, June 1, 1911. Source: 14.

75. *Gertrude Summers* — Schooner, of Tampa, 64 tons, built in 1871 at Boothbay, 75.2' x 22' x 7.4', Captain Castaros, from Tarpon Springs on a sponging trip. Foundered during a storm at midnight, June 8, 1912, 80 miles west by north of Anclote Light, in 13-1/2 fathoms. Source: 14.

76. *Iola* — Steam tug, of Tampa, 72 tons, built in 1908 at Scranton,

Miss., 89' x 21.9' x 7.4', Captain Lache. Caught fire and sank, July 6, 1912, at 10:30 A.M., approximately one mile north of Longboat Key, off Bradenton. Source: 14.

77. *Vaudalia* — Gas vessel, of Tampa, 109 tons, built in 1898, from Tampa bound for St. Petersburg with general merchandise. Caught fire when a galley lantern exploded, Jan. 27, 1913, at 11:30 P.M., at the St. Petersburg wharf. One life lost. Source: 14.

78. *Mary B. Franklin* — Gas vessel, 25 tons, built in 1905. Burned in Tampa Bay, Aug. 2, 1913. Source: 14.

79. *Thomas A. Edison* — Sidewheel steamer, of Key West, 33 tons, built in 1901 at Apalachicola, 80' x 20.5' x 3.7'. Burned at Fort Myers, Jan. 30, 1914. Source: 14.

80. *Mildred* (formerly *City of Haverhill*) — Steamer, 343 tons, built in 1902 at Boston, 121.7' x 24' x 10.7'. Collided with the schooner *Brazos*, Nov. 1914, seven miles south of Egmont Key. Source: 14.

81. *Theodore Weems* (formerly *East Side*) — Steamer (iron), 926 tons, built in 1884 at Philadelphia, 204.3' x 37.6' x 16.2'. Collided with the *S.S. Heridia*, March 27, 1915, in Tampa Bay. Source: 14.

82. *Hereward* — Schooner, 90 tons, built in 1874 at Essex, Mass., 81' x 22.3' x 8.5'. Foundered at Stump Pass, Dec. 9, 1917. Source: 14.

83. *Bessie Whiting* — Schooner, 559 tons, built in 1882 at Port Jefferson, N.Y., 149.8' x 32.1' x 16.8'. Stranded by Perico Island (off Bradenton), Jan. 11, 1918. Source: 14.

84. *Maggie Todd* — Schooner, 136 tons, built in 1873 at Calais, Maine, 103' x 26.8' x 8.3'. Foundered 100 miles northwest of Egmont Key, Aug. 22, 1918. Source: 14.

85. *Mylu* — Gas yacht, 27 tons, built in 1892 at Grand Rapids, Mich., 59.4' x 11' x 4.9'. Burned in Tampa Bay, Aug. 29, 1918. Source: 14.

86. *Pride* — Schooner, 22 tons, built in 1858, 56' x 15.6' x 5.5'. Stranded off Anclote Light, Sept. 28, 1918. Source: 14.

87. *Millie R. Bohannan* — Schooner, 686 tons, built in 1891 at Milford, Del., 162.5' x 36.9' x 13.2'. Foundered on Feb. 17, 1919, at Lat. 28-35-00, Long. 83-40-00. Source: 14.

88. *John Francis* — Schooner, 322 tons, built in 1897 at Tottenville,

N.Y., 126' x 32.2' x 9'. Stranded by Egmont Key, May 29, 1919. Source: 14.

89. *Shamrock* — Schooner, of Key West, 25 tons, built in 1887 at Biloxi, Miss., 50.5' x 19' x 4.5'. Burned at Tarpon Springs, Oct. 7, 1919. Source: 14.

90. *City of Philadelphia* — Steamer, 542 tons, built in 1896 at Wilmington, 140' x 26.7' x 10'. Burned near Punta Rassa, Oct. 14, 1919. Source: 14, 80.

91. *City of Sarasota* — Steamer, 125 tons, built in 1911 at Tampa, 76.2' x 20' x 4'. Foundered near Tampa, Nov. 5, 1919. Source: 14.

92. *Yarrow* — Gas yacht, 29 tons, built in 1913 at Chicago, 60' x 12.4' x 5.2'. Stranded off Cortez, March 8, 1920. Source: 14.

93. *Holliswood* — Barge (formerly a barque), 1,141 tons, built in 1893 at East Boston (possibly the last square rigger from this yard), 185.8' x 38' x 19.2' (originally 176' x 38' x 19.5'). Foundered approximately 110 miles southeast of Cape San Blas, June 30, 1920, in 114 feet of water, at Lat. 28-29-30, Long. 84-01-00. She was a vessel which had been in trouble before, having been badly dismasted on two other occassions. After her first dismasting in 1903, she was refitted as a barquentine, but was dismasted on her next voyage and was re-rigged again as a three-masted schooner. At the time of her loss she was listed as a barge. Source: 1, 14, 51.

94. *City of Tampa* — Steamer, 88 or 125 tons, built in 1887 at Mason City, W.V., 91.3' x 20' x 3'. Burned near Bay Point Light, June 29, 1921. Source: 14.

95. *Thomas B. Garland* — Three-masted schooner, 319 tons, built in 1881 at Bath, 126.6' x 32' x 11.4'. Stranded at Tampa, Oct. 27, 1921. Source: 14.

96. *Iris* — Gas yacht (formerly a schooner), 32 tons, built in 1900 at Bayport, N.Y., 54' x 20.5' x 4.7'. Burned in Tampa Bay, Jan. 22, 1922. Source: 14.

97. *Sunoco Jr.* — Gas vessel, 29 tons, built in 1915. Burned at Tampa, Sept. 23, 1925. Two lives lost. Source: 14.

98. *Gwalia* — Steamer (steel), 415 tons, built in 1907 at Philadelphia, 130' x 27.5' x 15.5'. Foundered at Egmont Key, Dec. 4, 1925. Source: 14.

99. *Robert B. Burney* — Freight vessel (gas), 38 tons, built in 1906 at Dover Bluff, Ga., 55.5' x 18.2' x 5.8'. Stranded at Boca Grande, Jan. 10, 1926. Source: 14.

100. *Eclectic* — Gas vessel, 21 tons, built in 1908. Stranded at Boca Grande, Sept. 18, 1926. Source: 14.

101. *Thomas Clooney* — Barge, of Pensacola, 574 tons, built in 1905 at Lake Chales, La. Foundered at Bayport, Feb. 15, 1927. Source: 14.

102. *Javelin* — Gas vessel, 57 tons, built in 1907. Burned at Dunedin, Sept. 8, 1927. Source: 14.

103. *Stranger* (formerly *Hilda M. Stark*) — Schooner, 595 tons, built in 1918 at Annapolis Royal, Nova Scotia, 171.5' x 35' x 13.2'. Burned at Tampa, Sept. 15, 1927. Source: 14.

104. *Josephine* — Gas yacht, 32 tons, built in 1905 at New Orleans, 70.9' x 12.6' x 5.6'. Foundered at St. Petersburg, Oct. 21, 1927. Source: 14.

105. *Pawnee* — Freight vessel (gas), of New York, 36 tons, built in 1922 at Brooklyn, N.Y., 56' x 19.6' x 6.2.'. Stranded at Crescent Beach, Dec. 26, 1927. Source: 14.

106. *Chase* — Freight vessel (gas), of Tampa, 40 tons, built in 1898 at Tampa, 65' x 16' x 4.2'. Stranded on Sanibel Shoals, Jan. 10, 1928. Source: 14.

107. *City of Everglades* — Freight vessel (gas), of Tampa, 93 tons, built in 1921 at Fort Myers, 82.1' x 20.5' x 5.6'. Burned at Collier City, May 17, 1928. Source: 14.

108. *Wallace A. McDonald* — Gas vessel, 20 tons, built in 1909. Foundered in Tampa Bay, Sept. 17, 1928. Source: 14.

109. *A.H. Daughdrill* — Oil vessel, of Tampa, 35 tons, built in 1920 at Fish River, Ala., to carry freight, 53.7' x 18.6' x 4.6'. Burned at Fort Myers, May 1, 1929. Source: 14.

110. *Zalophus* — Gas yacht (steel), 300 tons, built in 1922 at New York, 119.4' x 21.4' x 11.4'. Stranded off Sarasota, Feb. 4, 1930, at Lat. 27-21-00, Long. 82-38-00. Still visible in 1983. Source: 1, 14.

111. *Silver City* — Towing vessel (gas), of Tampa, 21 tons, built in 1921 at Tampa, 47.8' x 14.2' x 3.3'. Burned in Clearwater Bay, March 30, 1930. Source: 14.

112. Dredge — Used for pipeline installation. Sank March 26, 1936, at Lat. 26-20-50, Long. 82-07-50. Source: 1.

113. *Belmont* — Schooner barge (steel), formerly a bark, of Mobile, 1,491 tons, built in 1891 at Port Glasgow, 236.4' x 38.1' x 21.8'. Foundered at the entrance to Tampa Bay, Jan. 25 or 31, 1940, at approximate Lat. 27-37-30, Long. 82-52-00. Four lives lost. Source: 1, 14, 80.

See World War II section for Section 2 wrecks during that period.

114. *Eagle* — M/V, 188 tons. Sank in 1945, at approximate Lat. 25-52-00, Long. 82-20-00. Source: 1.

115. Unknown wreck — Sank in 1945, at Lat. 28-13-00, Long. 83-43-00. This wreck was verified in 1983. Source: 1.

116. *Okeechobee* — Dredge, 116 tons, built in 1925. Foundered two miles east of Gadsen Point, Tampa Bay, Sept. 23, 1947. Source: 14.

117. *Nandoma* — G/V, 51 tons, built in 1910. Burned on Feb. 2, 1948, at Anclote Anchorage. Source: 14.

118. *Seawave* — O/V, 46 tons, built in 1924. Burned at Everglades, Fla., Sept. 15, 1950. Source: 14.

119. *Desire* — M/V, 82 tons, built in 1913. Burned six miles off Venice, Fla., March 9, 1951. Source: 14.

120. *Blackthorn* — Coast Guard cutter (Cactus Class), 936 tons, built in 1944 at Duluth, 180' x 37' x 12'. Scuttled off Tampa in 1951 after a collision. Now a popular dive site. Source: 44, 101 (September 1990, Florida pull-out map).

121. *Miss Nancy* — O/V, 39 tons, built in 1944. Foundered 70 miles southeast of Tampa Inlet, Aug. 2, 1952. Source: 14.

122. *Pentrel 14* — Patrol craft, 320 tons. Sunk by marine casualty, July 21, 1953, at approximate Lat. 25-56-48, Long. 82-52-30. Source: 1.

123. *USS PC 463* — Patrol craft, 280 tons, 173'8" x 23' x 6'6". Sank in 1953, at Lat. 25-56-48, Long. 82-52-30. Most likely collided with *Pentrel 14.* Source: 1, 44.

124. *Cayo Hueso* — O/V, 41 tons, built in 1950. Foundered 73 miles southwest of Egmont Bar, Tampa, Oct. 8, 1953. Source: 14.

125. *Blue Stack # 79* — Barge (steel), 669 tons, built in 1951. Foundered 13 miles west of Egmont Key, Nov. 1, 1954, at Lat. 27-35-00, Long. 83-06-00. Still visible in 1983. Source: 1, 14.

126. *Rosie II* — M/V, 54 tons, built in 1943. Foundered approximately 90 miles due north of Dry Tortugas, April 11, 1954. Source: 14

127. *Kim Too* — O/V, 63 tons, built in 1953. Stranded one mile northwest of Anna Maria, Jan. 18, 1955. Source: 14.

128. *No. B-29* — Barge (steel), 344 tons, built in 1918. Foundered in Tampa Bay, Sept. 18, 1955. Source: 14.

129. *Fillete* — 80'. Sank in 1957 at Lat. 28-37-00, Long. 82-47-00. Source: 1.

130. *Dania* — Dredge, 242 tons, built in 1925. Foundered approximately 1,500 feet east of Cut "F" in the channel of Tampa Bay, Feb. 15, 1958. Source: 14.

131. *Capt. Grumpy* — O/V/, 48 tons, built in 1948. Burned off Fort Myers, May 2, 1958. Source: 14.

132. Unknown wreck and pilings — Visible in 1958 and 1981, at Lat. 26-55-46, Long. 82-03-47. Source: 1.

133. Unknown wreck — Visible in 1958 and 1981, at Lat. 26-57-53.56, Long. 81-59-34.21. Source: 1.

134. *Pamela Ann* — O/V, 55 tons, built in 1950. Burned March 23, 1959, approximately 10 miles, 190 degrees from Black Can Buoy, Fort Myers Beach. Source: 14.

135. *Virginia Ann* — O/V, 48 tons, built in 1951. Burned off Naples, June 4, 1959. Source: 14.

136. *Louanna* — O/V, 74 tons, built in 1953. Foundered Dec. 10, 1959, near Tampa, at approximate Lat. 27-15-00, Long. 82-28-00. Source: 14.

137. *Valintine* — G/V, 20 tons, built in 1949. Exploded off Cedar Keys, Dec. 19, 1960. Source: 14.

138. *Mary E* — G/V, 25 tons. Stranded Feb. 8, 1961, at John's Pass, Madeira Beach. Source: 14.

139. *Miss Margie* — O/V, 40 tons, built in 1957. Burned April 26, 1961, at Lat. 27-07, Long. 82-42. Source: 14.

140. *Santa Maria* — O/V, 26 tons, built in 1929. Foundered off Sanibel Island, Aug. 10, 1961. Source: 14.

141. *Jordan Girls* — O/V, 42 tons, built in 1946. Foundered 60 miles southwest of Egmont Key, Nov. 18, 1961. Source: 14.

142. *Rampart* — O/V, 38 tons, built in 1903. Burned June 30, 1961, approximately one mile off Davis Island, Tampa Bay. Source: 14.

143. *Madam Queen II* — O/V, 67 tons, built in 1961. Burned Dec. 17, 1961, off Fort Myers Beach. Source: 14.

144. *Miss Powerama* — F/V (oil), 64 tons, built in 1955 at St. Augustine, 61.6' x 18.4' x 8.5'. Stranded Jan. 31, 1962, off Passage Key, Tampa Bay. Source: 14.

145. *David B* — F/V (oil), 57 tons, built in 1949 at St. Augustine, 59.5' x 17.9' x 7.7'. Foundered May 6, 1963, approximately 35 miles northwest of Tampa Sea Buoy, Lat. 28-03, Long. 83-00. Source: 14.

146. Unknown vessel — Reported sunk in 1963, at Lat. 25-25-30, Long. 82-55-00. Source: 1.

147. *Bellatrix* — F/V (oil), 63 tons, built in 1952 at St. Augustine, 58.7' x 18.5' x 8.2'. Foundered Jan. 16, 1964, at Lat. 26-15-00, Long. 82-08-00. Source: 14.

148. *Independence* — F/V (oil), 65 tons, built in 1953 at St. Augustine, 61.6' x 18.4' x 8.7'. Burned approximately 17 miles west of Tarpon Springs, Dec. 10, 1964. Source: 14.

149. *Campeche* — F/V (oil), 31 tons, built in 1926 at Pascagoula, 49' x 15.5' x 5.4'. Stranded at Southwest Pass, Egmont Key, March 7, 1965. Source: 14.

150. *Leslie Ann* — F/V (oil), 38 tons, built 1959 at Tarpon Springs, 49.7' x 16.5' x 7.5'. Foundered off St. Petersburg, Oct. 14, 1965. Source: 14.

151. *Cindy* — Tug. Wrecked in 1965, approximately 1-1/2 miles, 196 degrees from Egmont Key Light, at Lat. 27-34-36, Long. 84-42-06. Protruded 10 to 15 feet above the water. Source: 1.

152. *Candice* — O/V, 25 tons, built in 1965. Foundered in Clearwater Pass, Sept. 29, 1966. Source: 14.

153. *Tinsley* — O/V, 145 tons, built in 1943 at West Atlantic, N.J.,

99.9' x 19.6' x 11.4'. Burned Dec. 3, 1966, at Lat. 28-04-00, Long. 82-56-00. Source: 14.

154. *Mark E. Singleton* — O/V, 99 tons, built in 1965. Burned Aug. 1, 1967, off Egmont Key, at approximate Lat. 27-36-00, Long. 82-45-00. Source: 14.

155. *Empress Ann* — M/V. Wrecked in 1967, at approximate Lat. 28-08-00, Long. 82-51-00. Source: 1.

156. *Silver Star* — F/V (oil), 75 tons, built in 1954 at St. Augustine, 68.4' x 18.8' x 8.5'. Collided with a submerged object, March 3, 1969, southwest of the sea buoy off Fort Myers. Source: 14.

157. *Go Go Girl* — F/V (oil), 49 tons, built in 1954. Burned approximately six miles west of Tarpon Springs, May 17, 1969. Source: 14.

158. *Miss Tyla* — F/V (oil), 74 tons, built in 1965 at St. Augustine, 60.1' x 19.7' x 7.4'. Stranded off Gordon Drive, Gordon Pass, Naples, Oct. 1, 1969. Source: 14.

159. *Marie* — O/V, 37 tons, built in 1950. Foundered approximately 6.5 miles northwest of Boca Grande Key, Jan. 31, 1970. Source: 14.

160. *118* — Barge, 212 tons, built in 1948. Foundered 60 miles west of St. Petersburg, Aug. 18, 1970. Source: 14.

161. *Topsy* — O/V, 42 tons, built in 1926 at Salisbury, Md., 53.2' x 22.2' x 6.5'. Foundered 6.5 miles west of sea buoy #2, Homosassa Bay, June 1, 1972. Source: 14.

162. *Sandy Belle* — F/V (oil), 79 tons, built in 1964 in Alabama, 64.3' x 22.2' x 6.9'. Foundered approximately three miles west of Clearwater, June 19, 1972. Source: 14.

163. *Athenian* — F/V, 83 tons, built in 1966. Burned 30 miles off Fort Myers, May 26, 1973. Source: 14.

164. *Gemini* — O/V, 101 tons, built in 1973. Stranded at Egmont Key, Dec. 20, 1973. Source: 14.

165. *YSD 71* — Pile driver (oil), Navy seaplane wrecking derrick in WWII, 138 tons, built in 1943. Foundered in 1973 off St. Petersburg. Source: 14, 44.

166. *American Team* — F/V (oil), 40 tons, built in 1954. Stranded off

Boca Grande, June 1, 1974, in the channel. Source: 14.

167. *Broward II* — Dredge, 358 tons, built in 1924 at Baltimore, 125' x 40' x 5.9'. Burned off Gadsen Point, Cut C, July 26, 1974, in Tampa Bay. Source: 14.

168. *Anna Marie* — F/V (oil), 21 tons, built in 1937. Foundered off Fort Myers Beach, Aug. 21, 1974. Source: 14.

169. *Coral Sea* — F/V, 68'. Sank in 1975, at Lat. 25-56-12, Long. 82-06-12. Source: 1.

170. *Restless* — Yacht. Sank in four feet of water in 1975, at Lat. 27-40-00, Long. 82-44-10. Source: 1.

171. *Sundowner* — O/V, 100 tons, built in 1974. Stranded one mile, 305 degrees true from Bell Buoy 8, Egmont Channel, May 18, 1976. Source: 14.

172. Unknown wreck — M/V, 41'. Sank in 1976 in 40 feet of water, at Lat. 27-40-51, Long. 82-57-08. Verified in 1983. Source: 1.

173. Unknown wreck — 41' vessel. Located in 1976 in five feet of water, at Lat. 27-58-05, Long. 82-50-05. Source: 1.

174. *Nona Gale* — F/V, 40'. Sank in 1976 at Lat. 28-17-54, Long. 83-18-06. Source: 1.

175. *Queen RV* — M/V (Chris Craft), 34'. Burned and sank in 1977 in 14 feet of water, at Lat. 26-53-18, Long. 82-07-54. Source: 1.

176. *Gunsmoke* — F/V, 70'. Scuttled by her crew in 1977 while being chased by the U.S. Coast Guard, with a cargo of marijuana, in 80 feet of water at Lat. 27-33-31.94, Long. 83-05-05.41. Now a popular dive site. Source: 1, 101 (September 1990, Florida pull-out map).

177. *Nellie* — Barge, 75'. Sank in 1978 at Lat. 26-55-46, Long. 82-03-47. Visible above the water. Source: 1.

178. *Escape Machine* — M/V, 40'. Sank in 1979, at Lat. 25-10-18, Long. 81-30-00. Source: 1.

179. *Jackie M* — M/V. Sank in 1979, at Lat. 28-41-30, Long. 83-00-00. Source: 1.

Section 3: Lower Keys

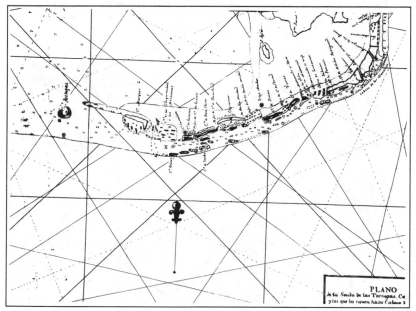

Figure 8: 1777 Spanish map of the Florida Keys. PHILLIP MASTERS.

1600

1. Spanish patache — From Vera Cruz bound for Spain with mail. Capsized by a large wave about three leagues off the Dry Tortugas in 1621. Thirty people drowned. The rest reached one of the cays and were soon rescued along with the mail bags they had saved. Source: 54.

2. 1622 Spanish Plate Fleet — On Sept. 4, 1622, twenty-eight ships left Havana for Spain. On Sept. 5, a hurricane hit the fleet near the Florida Keys. The *Nuestra Señora de la Consolacion* was the first to sink, after capsizing in deep water. The lead ship, the *Nuestra Señora de Candelaria*, and 20 other ships passed west of the Dry Tortugas and rode out the storm in the Gulf of Mexico.

The others weren't as lucky. The galleons *Nuestra Señora de Atocha* and the *Santa Margarita* wrecked west of the Marquesas Keys. The galleon *Nuestra Señora del Rosario* wrecked at Loggerhead Key in the Dry Tortugas, and a patache wrecked nearby.

Within a week, salvage efforts were made. The *Atocha* was found near the last Key of Matecumbe. Her mizzenmast was protruding above water, but she was in 55 feet of water — too deep for divers. Salvors failed to find the *Margarita*, but did locate and salvage the *Rosario.*

In June 1626, a new salvage group found and salvaged the *Margarita.* The *Atocha* remained lost until July 16, 1985, when Mel Fisher's salvage company found the motherlode.

Different sources say that from eight to ten vessels were lost from

Figure 9: An 80-pound silver bar along with a gold finger bar, both recovered from the wreck of the *Atocha* (1622). AUTHOR.

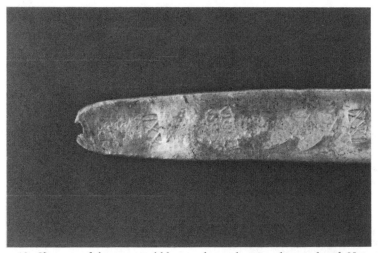

Figure 10: Close-up of the same gold bar as above showing the royal seal. Note the assayer's "byte" (his payment for services rendered) on the end of the bar. AUTHOR.

this fleet. One of the merchant naos, the *Jesus y Nuestra Señora del Rosario*, was listed as lost in the Florida Keys. Just a couple of years ago, a salvage group advertised a search for the *Candelaria*, but my research indicates she survived the storm. In 1989, a group from Tampa called Seahawk found a wreck they believe to be the *Nuestra Señora de la Merced* of this fleet. She lies off the Tortugas in 1,500 feet of water. A bell and a number of gold bars dating from this time have been recovered. Source: 54, 55, 67.

3. Spanish galleon — One of two galleons sent to protect the salvage operation of the *Margarita* of the 1622 fleet. Sank four leagues to windward of the wreck of the *Atocha* in the spring of 1623. All her bronze cannon were soon salvaged. Source: 54.

4. Three Spanish ships — The almirante and two other ships of the fleet of the Marquis of Cadereyta were lost on the Keys of Matecumbe in 1634. Source: 57.

5. Spanish frigate — From Mexico bound for Puerto Rico with 200 soldiers and 11,000 pesos. Wrecked on a coral reef at the Dry Tortugas in 1649. Sixty men drowned and all the money was lost. Source: 10.

6. Dutch ship — In May of 1677, the governor of Cuba sent a frigate to salvage cannon from a Dutch ship which sank at Key West the previous year. Source: 54.

1700

7. *Henrietta Marie* — British merchant-slaver. Left London in September, 1699, sailing for Africa, where she traded her cargo for slaves and brought them to Jamaica. She was bound home in June 1700, with a cargo of sugar, indigo, cotton, and logwood, when she wrecked just south of the Marquesas Keys. She was found in 1972 by Mel Fisher's salvage company. In 1984, a bell was found with the ship's name inscribed on it. Source: 92 (Moore, David. *Henrietta Marie*. pp.199-205).

8. 1733 Spanish Plate Fleet — See Section 4 (Upper Florida Keys).

9. *HMS Tiger* — British naval ship, 50 guns, built in 1647, 457 tons, rebuilt for the third time in 1722 to 712 tons, Captain Edward Herbert. Lost on a key near Tortuga, Jan. 12, 1742 (another source says 1743). The crew got ashore with some stores and provisions, and built a fortification with 20 of the ship's guns. This proved a wise move, since after hearing of the wreck, the Spanish sent a warship to capture the crew. The warship wrecked in the attempt. After two months on the island, the crew captured a sloop with their small gunboats, and reached Jamaica. (Note: There is an island of Tortuga off Haiti, which

could also be the wreck site, though Marx states she wrecked on "the cayos," which was the Spanish name for the Florida Keys.) Source: 13, 16, 54.

10. *Fuerte* — Spanish naval ship, 60 guns. Sent to capture the crew of the *HMS Tiger*. Wrecked near the *Tiger* while attempting to do so. Source: 13, 54.

11. *HMS Looe* and Spanish vessel — British naval frigate, 5th rate, 44 guns (believed to have had 20 18-pounders, 20 9-pounders, and four 6-pounders), 685 tons, built in 1741, 124.5' x 36', Captain Ashby Utting. Wrecked on what is now called Looe Reef, along with a captured Spanish vessel, Feb. 5, 1744, at 1:30 A.M. All hands were saved. Utting ordered his vessel destroyed. Source: 16, 65.

12. *Grenville Packet* — British ship, Captain Curlett, from Falmouth bound for Pensacola with mail. Ran ashore on the Dry Tortugas, Feb. 27, 1765. Crew saved. Total loss. Source: 54.

13. *San Antonio* — Spanish ship, Captain Font, from Havana. Wrecked on a reef near Key West, Jan. 22, 1768. The crew and passengers survived 22 days on the reef until they were rescued by a turtling sloop and taken to Havana. Source: 54.

1800

14. *Maria* — Ship, Captain Rundle, from Jamaica bound for Halifax. Wrecked on the Dry Tortugas in 1806. Source: 54.

15. *Sir John Sherbroke* — Ship, Captain Kennedy, from Jamaica bound for New York with a general cargo and $60,000 in specie. Wrecked in 1816 on a reef off the Dry Tortugas and broke up. Crew and specie saved. Source: 54.

16. *Acasta* — British merchantman, Captain Parkin, from Jamaica bound for Liverpool. Wrecked sometime before Dec. 5, 1818, on the Dry Tortugas. Crew and most cargo saved. Source: 54.

17. *Swift* — Ship, Captain Miller, from Havana with sugar, indigo, and cochineal. Wrecked on Long Island in 1824. Wreckers saved 900 boxes of sugar and all the other cargo. Source: 54.

18. *Ceres* — Ship, from New Orleans. Wrecked on Dry Tortugas in 1824. Crew saved and taken to Havana. Source: 54.

19. *Vineyard* — Brig. Lost off Long Key, 1830. Source: 9

20. *William Tell* — Brig, believed to be 207 tons, Captain Riley, from

Figure 11, 12 and 13: Prints from a story on wrecking in the Florida Keys in the 1800s, from *Harper's Magazine*. From upper left, clockwise, divers salvaging a wreck, wreckers at work on a vessel, and shipwrecked sailors on a raft. BROWARD COUNTY HISTORICAL COMMISSION.

New York bound for New Orleans with dry goods, cutlery, and other cargo. Grounded on Bird Key near the Tortugas Light, April 11, 1831. Some cargo saved. Source: 19, 95 (Diddle, Albert W. "The Adjudication of Shipwrecking in Florida in 1831." No. VI, 1946, pp. 44-49).

21. *Exertion* — Bark, of Eden, Captain John Thomas, from Providence, R.I. bound for New Orleans with cotton. Reported in newspaper, May 4, 1831. Wrecked on rocks near the Tortugas and bilged. Some cargo and rigging saved. Source: 37, 95 (Ibid).

22. *Concord* — Brig, Captain M'Known, from New York bound for Mobile with $15,000 worth of groceries, dry goods, and other cargo. Wrecked on Tortugas Reef, Oct. 2, 1831. Some cargo saved. Source: 95 (Ibid).

23. *Florence* — Ship, Captain Blacker, from Boston bound for New Orleans. Wrecked on the Tortugas, Nov. 22, 1831. Source: 95 (Ibid).

24. *Dumfries* — Ship. Reported in newspaper, Nov. 23, 1831, to have wrecked on the Tortugas. Cargo saved. Source: 37, 97 (Hammond,

E.A.. "Wreckers and Wrecking on the Florida Reef, 1829-1832." Vol. XLI, January 1963, No. 3, pp. 239-273).

25. *Leo* — Brig. Reported in newspaper, Dec. 7, 1831, to have wrecked on the Tortugas. Unknown if salvaged. Source: 37.

26. *Splendid* — Ship. Reported in newspaper, Feb. 15, 1832, to have wrecked on Marquesas Key. Unknown if salvaged. Source: 37.

27. *Pulaski* — Ship, of the Center Line, New York, 468 tons, Master Ezra Post. Wrecked on the Tortugas, February 1832. Possible that Pulaski Shoal was named after this vessel. Source: 19.

28. *Othello* — Bark. Reported in newspaper, March 14, 1832, to have wrecked on Collins Patch (likely Coffins Patch). Unknown if salvaged. Source: 37.

29. *Eliza Plummer* — Ship. Reported in newspaper, Aug. 29, 1832, to have wrecked, probably in the lower Keys. Unknown if salvaged. Source: 37.

30. *Tennessee* — Ship. Reported in newspaper, Sept. 8, 1832, to have wrecked on Long Key. Unknown if salvaged. Source: 37.

31. *Sea Flower* — Brig. Reported in newspaper, Nov. 15, 1834, to have wrecked on southwest Tortugas. Unknown if salvaged. Source: 37.

32. *United States* — Schooner. Reported in newspaper, June 1835, to have wrecked on the Quicksands. Unknown if salvaged. Source: 37.

33. *Courier* — Brig, believed to be 148 tons. Reported in newspaper, Feb. 27, 1836, to have gone ashore on Knights Key. Unknown if salvaged. Source: 19, 37.

34. *Belle* — Brig. Reported in newspaper, Feb. 27, 1836, to have gone ashore at Sugarloaf Key. Unknown if salvaged. Source: 37.

35. *Stranger* — Brig, believed to be 133 tons. Reported in newspaper, March 5, 1836, to have wrecked on Western Dry Rocks. Unknown if salvaged. Source: 19, 37.

36. *Eleanor* — Bark. Reported in newspaper, June 4, 1836, to have gone ashore on the Tortugas. Unknown if salvaged. Source: 37.

37. *America* — Ship, of the Packet Line of E.D. Hurlburt & Co., of New York, Captain Aiken, from New York bound for Mobile with a

general cargo and 30 passengers. Wrecked off the Dry Tortugas, Nov. 7, 1836. Crew and cargo saved. Source: 70, 96 (Nov. 30, 1836).

38. *Sarah Ann* — Schooner, from Charleston bound for Mobile. Wrecked on Sombrero Reef, Sept. 6, 1837. Vessel lost. Wreckers were awarded $574. Source: 37.

39. *Hyder Alley* — Schooner, from Havana bound for New Orleans with coffee, sugar, and cigars. Wrecked on Marquesas Key Shoals, Sept. 15, 1838. Vessel lost. Wreckers were awarded $3,000. Source: 37.

40. *Forrest* — Schooner, of Lubec, Maine, with a cargo of live oak. Struck a reef and sank, Sept. 18, 1838, one day after leaving Key West. Crew returned to Key West in her boats. Source: 86 (Summer/Fall 1986, reprinted from "Niles National Register," Vol. 55-56, Oct. 13, 1838, p. 103).

41. *Ella Hand* — Bark, of the Hand's Line, New York, 383 tons. Lost on Stirrup Key, October 1838. Source: 19.

42. *Mary Howland* — Ship, 576 tons, of the Merchant's Line, from New York bound for New Orleans with assorted cargo. Wrecked on Delta Shoal, Oct. 11, 1839. Vessel lost. Wreckers awarded $9,860. Source: 19, 37.

43. *Orion* — Wrecking schooner. Reported in newspaper, Nov. 10, 1839, to have been lost at Sand Key. Unknown if salvaged. Source: 37.

44. *Poacher* — Bark, 219 tons, built at Warren, Maine. Wrecked at Dry Tortugas, Oct. 27, 1840. Source: Harold E. Brown, curator of the Maine Maritime Museum.

45. *Columbia* — Schooner, from Boston bound for Mobile with assorted cargo. Wrecked at Crayfish Key, Key West, Oct. 20, 1841. Vessel lost. Wreckers awarded $2,558. Source: 37.

46. *Pequot* — Schooner, believed to be 149 tons, from New Orleans bound for Charleston with tobacco, beef, and pork. Wrecked on Washerwoman Shoal, Jan. 21, 1842. Vessel lost. Wreckers awarded $442. Source: 19, 37.

47. *New York* — Schooner, from Trinidad de Cuba bound for New York with molasses. Wrecked on the Northwest Reef, Tortugas, May 4, 1842. Vessel lost. Wreckers awarded $929. Source: 37.

48. *North America* — Ship, from New York bound for Mobile with

dry goods and furniture. Wrecked on Delta Shoals, Nov. 25, 1842. Vessel lost. Wreckers awarded $2,257. Source: 37.

49. *Francis Ashby* — Brig, 125 tons, of the Hurlburt Line, from Mantanzas bound for New York with coffee, honey, and tobacco. Wrecked at Loggerhead Key (American Shoals), Jan. 20, 1843. Vessel lost. Wreckers awarded $573. Source: 19, 37.

50. *Rudolph Groning* — Brig, from New York bound for Apalachicola with an assorted cargo. Wrecked on the Southwest Reef, Tortugas, June 1, 1843. Vessel lost. Wreckers awarded $9,530. Source: 19, 37.

51. *Pilgrim* — Brig, from New Orleans bound for New York with lard, whiskey, molasses, and lead. Wrecked on Bush Key Reef, Tortugas, Nov. 17, 1843. Vessel lost. Wreckers awarded $6,149. Source: 37.

52. *Conservative* — Type unknown, from Galveston bound for Liverpool with cotton and tallow. Wrecked on Long Key Reef, Nov. 26, 1844. Vessel lost. Wreckers awarded $6,278. Source: 37.

53. *Zotoff* — Ship, from New Orleans bound for Boston with cotton, flour, lead, sugar, and hides. Wrecked at Loggerhead Key, Dec. 15, 1844. Vessel lost. Wreckers awarded $6,224. Source: 37.

54. *Oconee* — Ship, of the Holmes Line, New York, 461 tons, built in 1839, Master W.S. Lyons. Lost on Stirrup Key, March 1845. Source: 19.

55. *Exchange* — Vessel, type unknown, of Portland, Maine, from Portland bound for Havana with a general cargo. Wrecked near Key West during the hurricane of Oct. 11, 1846. Valued at $16,000. Sold as she lay on the reef. Source: 14.

56. *Commissary* — Vessel, type unknown, of and from Havana with a general cargo. Wrecked near Key West during the October 1846 hurricane. Valued at $10,000. Sold as she lay on the reef. Source: 14

57. *Iris* — Believed to be a bark, of Bath, 330 tons, built in 1841 at Topsham, Maine, 70'7" x 21' x 6'10", from New Orleans bound for Cork with provisions. Went ashore, probably in the lower Keys, during the October 1846 hurricane. Valued at $45,000, the vessel was a total loss, though wreckers saved the cargo. Source: 6, 14.

58. *Eben Preble* — Type unknown, of Boston, from Liverpool bound for New York with salt. Went ashore, probably in the lower Keys, during the October 1846 hurricane. Valued at $22,000, she was to be broken up. Source: 14.

59. *La Reunion* — French vessel, type unknown, from New Orleans bound for Marseilles with tobacco. Went ashore, probably in the lower Keys, during the October 1846 hurricane. Valued at $5,000, ship and cargo were nearly a total loss. Source: 14.

60. *Villaneuva* — Spanish vessel, type unknown, from Cuba bound for Havana. Went ashore, probably in the lower Keys, during the October 1846 hurricane. Valued at $20,000. A total loss. Source: 14

61. *Navigator* — Vessel, type unknown, of New York, from St. Marks bound for New York with cotton. Went ashore, probably in the lower Keys, during the October 1846 hurricane. Valued at $20,000. A total loss. Source: 14

62. *Olive and Eliza* — Ship, of Portsmouth (Regular Line), 386 tons, from New Orleans bound for Cadiz with staves. Went ashore, probably in the lower Keys, during the October 1846 hurricane. Ship and cargo condemned and sold. Source: 14, 19.

63. *Platina* — Ship, of Bath, 380 tons, built in 1832 at Bath, 116'11" x 26'9" x 13', from New Orleans bound for France with staves. Went ashore, probably in the lower Keys, during the October 1846 hurricane. Ship and cargo condemned and sold. Source: 6, 14.

64. *Cutter Morris* — Type unknown. Went ashore at Key West during the October 1846 hurricane. Condemned and sold. Source: 14.

65. *Napoleon* — Vessel, type unknown, of New York, (possibly the 539-ton ship of Fourth or Swallowtail Line), from Havana bound for Cardenas with a general cargo. Went ashore near Key West during the October 1846 hurricane. Condemned and sold. Source: 14, 19.

66. *Warsaw* — Ship, of Charleston, 342 tons, from Mobile bound for France with spars. Went ashore on a reef, probably in the lower keys, during the October 1846 hurricane. Condemned and sold. Source: 14, 19.

Note: Nearly every wrecking vessel on the reef was lost or damaged during the October 1846 hurricane. Sand Key was also swept away during this storm.

67. *St. Mary's* — Schooner, 135 tons, from Baltimore bound for Pensacola. Wrecked on the Sambos, Aug. 9, 1847. Unknown if salvaged. Source: 14.

68. *Millinoclat* — Brig, 185 tons, from Havana bound for New York.

Wrecked on American Shoal, Dec. 11, 1847. Unknown if salvaged. Source: 14.

69. *Rudolph Groning* — Brig, of New York, 195 tons, Captain Besling, from Mobile bound for Tortugas. Wrecked on N'th Key, Tortugas, December 1847. Vessel and cargo valued at $7,000. A total loss. Source: 14.

70. *Mortoun* — Ship, of Belfast, Captain Hamilton, from New Orleans bound for Liverpool. Went ashore near Key Vaca, February 1848, and was sold. Vessel and cargo valued at $90,000. Wreckers awarded $16,400. Source: 14.

71. *Flora* — Barque, of Newport, 293 tons, from Boston bound for New Orleans. Wrecked on Dry Rocks, June 9, 1848, and was condemned and sold. Wreckers awarded $6,000. Source: 14.

72. *Hudson* — Schooner, 116 tons, from New York bound for Port La Vaca in ballast. Wrecked on Little Sand Key, June 10, 1848, and was condemned. Wreckers awarded $192. Source: 14.

73. *Benjamin Litchfield* — Brig, 190 tons, of and from Thomaston bound for Mobile with lime. Wrecked near the Lightship at Sand Key, June 30, 1848. Caught fire and burned. A total loss. Wreckers awarded $320. Source: 14.

74. *Henry* — Bark, from Salem bound for the Pacific Ocean. Wrecked and was plundered on the Marquesas in 1848. Crew saved. Source: 14.

75. *Canton* — Ship, of Bath, Captain Silsby, from New Orleans bound for Liverpool with cotton and flour. Wrecked on Garden Key, Tortugas, Nov. 3, 1848. Vessel lost. Wreckers awarded $6,286. Source: 14, 37.

76. *Nancy W. Stevens* — Ship, from New York bound for New Orleans with an assorted cargo. Wrecked on Loggerhead Key, Sept. 12, 1849. Vessel lost. Wreckers awarded $13,761. Source: 37.

77. *Maryland* — Ship, from Baltimore bound for New Orleans with an assorted cargo. Wrecked on Washerwoman Shoal, Dec. 11, 1849. Vessel lost. Wreckers awarded $18,468. Source: 37.

78. *Ganymede* — Brig, from Jamaica bound for New York with pimento, coffee, rum, and other cargo. Wrecked on Matecumbe Bar, Jan. 20, 1850. Vessel lost. Wreckers awarded $3,558. Source: 37.

79. *Sylphide* — Brig, from New Orleans bound for Trieste with cotton.

Wrecked on Loggerhead Key, Dec. 21, 1850. Vessel lost. Wreckers awarded $7,311. Source: 37.

80. *Mars* — Brig, believed to be a British brig of 322 tons, from Cardenas bound for Halifax with molasses. Wrecked on Dry Rocks, Feb. 25, 1851. Vessel lost. Wreckers awarded $1,010. Source: 19, 37.

81. Eight vessels — Type unknown. Reported ashore near Sand Key between May 1850 and August 1851, with a total valued loss of $425,000. Source: 24.

82. *Tilamon* — Ship, from New York bound for New Orleans with an assorted cargo. Wrecked on Delta Shoals, Jan. 12, 1852. Vessel lost. Wreckers awarded $14,323. Source: 37.

83. *Grace Clark* — Bark, of St. Mary's, Captain Crosby. Wrecked at Grand Key during a norther, Sept. 24, 1852. Source: 99 (Oct. 28, 1852).

84. *Fanny A. Everett* — Bark, from Baltimore bound for New Orleans with an assorted cargo. Wrecked on American Shoals, Jan. 8, 1853. Vessel lost. Wreckers awarded $9,995. Source: 37, 99 (Feb. 24, 1853).

85. *Nathaniel Kimball* — Ship, of Gardiner, Maine, 784 tons, built in 1848 at Bath, 156'3" x 33' x 16'6", Captain Howe, from New Orleans bound for Liverpool with 2,550 bales cotton. Grounded on Eastern Dry Rocks and bilged, Jan. 17, 1853. 1,500 bales of cotton saved. Wreckers awarded $19,657. Source: 6, 8, 37, 99 (Feb. 16, 1853).

86. *Edgar* — Bark, of Boston, Captain Pendelton, from New Orleans bound for Norfolk with a cargo of molasses, whisky, and sugar. Ran ashore on North Key Reef, Tortugas, during a gale, Jan. 24, 1853. Some cargo saved. Source: 99 (Feb. 16, 1853).

87. *Colony* — British bark, of Newcastle, 470 tons, Captain Weatherburn, from New Orleans bound for London with a cargo of oil cake. Ran ashore on Culbins Patches during a heavy gale, Feb. 2, 18 53. A total loss. Source: Ibid.

88. *E.G. Willard* — Schooner, from New Orleans bound for Charleston with bacon, hams, beef, pork, lard, and other cargo. Wrecked at Long Key, March 9, 1853. Vessel lost. Wreckers awarded $5,530. Source: 37.

89. *Cimbrus* — Brig, believed to be 200 tons, of the Merchant's Line, from Philadelphia bound for New Orleans with a locomotive engine and assorted cargo. Wrecked on Western Dry Rocks, March 17, 1853.

Vessel lost. Wreckers awarded $8,135. Source: 19, 37.

90. *Robert Morris* — Bark, from Cienfuegos bound for Philadelphia with sugar. Wrecked on Pelican Shoal, July 21, 1853. Vessel lost. Wreckers awarded $2,531. Source: 37.

91. *Harriet & Martha* — Bark, 189 tons, from Charleston bound for New Orleans. Wrecked on Jarden Key Shoal (most likely Garden Key), Jan. 13, 1854. Source: 19, 99 (Jan. 26, 1854).

92. *Athalia* — Schooner, from New York bound for Apalachicola with an assorted cargo. Wrecked on Western Dry Rocks, Sept. 10, 1854. Vessel lost. Some cargo saved. Wreckers awarded $11,992. Source: 37, 99 (Sept. 30, 1854).

93. *L.W. Maxwell* — Brig, of Wells, Maine, from Santa Cruz bound for Liverpool with mahogany and cedar. Struck on Eastern Dry Rocks and bilged, Sept. 24, 1854. Cargo saved. Vessel a total loss. Wreckers awarded $1,510. Source: 37, 99 (Sept. 30, 1854).

94. *Tartar* — Brig, from Charleston bound for New Orleans with rice. Wrecked on East Key Reef, Tortugas, Jan. 4, 1855. Vessel lost. Wreckers awarded $1,649. Source: 37.

95. *Brig* — A derelict brig. Found deserted 13 miles south of Sand Key, April 22, 1855. Wreckers awarded $389. Source: 37.

96. *Eliza W. Dalton* — Brig, from Port au Prince bound for New York. Struck on Bird Key, April 25, 1855, and sprang a leak. Went to Long Cay, where her cargo of logwood and coffee was taken off. Vessel condemned. Source: 99 (May 16, 1855).

97. Unknown ship — Brig *Piumas* reported a ship on fire and burned to the waterline at Great Stirrup Key (possibly Stirrup Key, Bahamas). Source: Ibid.

98. *Rainbow* — Bark, from England bound for Havana with coal. Wrecked at Thomas Harbour Key, Aug. 29, 1855. Vessel lost. Wreckers awarded $310. Source: 37.

99. *Concoridia* — Ship, from Mobile bound for Liverpool with cotton. Burned at Key Vaca, Nov. 24, 1855. Vessel lost. Wreckers awarded $190. Source: 37.

100. *Levinia Adams* — Ship, 883 tons, built in 1854 at Bowdoinham, Maine, 165'6" x 34' x 17'. Reported in newspaper, Nov. 24, 1855, to

have wrecked at Looe Key. Unknown if salvaged. Source: 6, 37.

101. *W. Empire* — Vessel, type unknown. Reported in newspaper, November 1855, to have wrecked at Tortugas. Unknown if salvaged. Source: 37.

102. *Mary London* — Bark, from Honduras bound for London with mahogany. Went aground on Looe Key, Dec. 7, 1855. Source: 99 (Dec. 15, 1855).

103. *Northern Light* — Schooner, of Rockland, Maine, Captain Doyle, from New York. Went ashore on Grand Key, Dec. 7, 1855. Cargo and crew saved. Vessel a total loss. Source: 99 (Dec. 31, 1855).

104. *Isabella* — Brig, of Apalachicola, from Mobile bound for New York with a cargo of cotton. Ran ashore at Bahia Honda Key, Dec. 8, 1855. Wreckers were at the scene. Source: 99 (Dec. 15, 1855).

105. Unknown ship — Ship *Atlantic* reported a large ship ashore at Lat. 24-27-00, Long. 81-30-00, Dec. 13, 1855, and reported seeing her again on the 15th, being stripped by wreckers, during a gale. Source: 99 (Dec. 31, 1855).

106. *Francis* — Ship, of Portland, from Boston bound for Havana with ice. Wrecked on Dry Rocks, April 3, 1856. Wreckers awarded $461. Source: 37, 99 (April 15, 1856).

107. *Isaac Allerton* — Ship, from New York bound for New Orleans with an assorted cargo. Wrecked off Key West, Aug. 28, 1856. Though the vessel could not be saved, more than 400 wreckers worked on salvaging the valuable cargo. She was one of the richest wrecks worked by the wreckers, who were awarded $43,852.58 for their efforts. She was found during the 1980s, and many artifacts were salvaged. Source: 37, 38, 99 (Oct. 14, 1856).

108. *Garden Pike* and the *Excell* — The stern frames, one from the *Pike* (a ship from New York), and another from a large vessel (supposedly the *Excell*), were reported in the newspaper, Oct. 14, 1856, to have come ashore at Sugar Loaf Key. Source: 99 (Oct. 14, 1856).

109. Unknown vessel — A vessel from New York bound for Port au Prince. Reported ashore at Sand Key by the brig *Princess Royal.* Captain and crew were taken to the Turks Islands. Source: 99 (March 24, 1857).

110. *William T. Dugan* — Brig, believed to be 144 tons. Wrecked at Sandy Key in 1857. Possibly the ship mentioned in #109. Crew

taken off by the brig *Winena*. Source: 19, 99 (April 3, 1857).

111. *Pacific* — Bark, believed to be 274 tons, of the Hurlburt Line, from New York bound for Mobile with an assorted cargo. Wrecked on East Key, Tortugas, July 24, 1857. Vessel lost. Wreckers awarded $9,937. Source: 19, 37.

112. Unknown bark — A bark, built in 1854, from Rockland bound for New Orleans with a cargo of lime. Reported from Key West on fire at Stirrup Key. Wreckers saved some rigging. Source: 99 (Sept. 1, 1857).

113. *Phoenix* — Coast Survey schooner. Went ashore, Nov. 4, 1857, at Key Vaca. A total loss. Source: 99 (Nov. 18, 1857).

114. *Ostean* — Ship, 1,200 tons, had on board 1,200 bales of cotton from the ship *Sultan,* which had wrecked May 18 and was condemned at Key West. The *Ostean* was to bring the cargo to Boston, but caught fire at 2 a.m., July 26, 1858, and was scuttled in four fathoms at Navy Harbor, Key West, where she burned to the waterline. Source: 99 (Aug. 26, 1858).

115. *Caraquena* — French bark, from Minititian bound for Havre with mahogany, logwood, and hides. Went ashore on the Sandbornes or West Sambos, near Key West, Nov. 5 or 6, 1858. Vessel lost. Cargo and materials later sold at auction at Key West. Wreckers awarded $1,723. Source: 37, 99 (Nov. 16 & 30, 1858).

116. *Ann Harley* — British bark, enroute to Hull, England, with lumber. Lost the night of Nov. 30, 1858, at Loggerhead Shoal. Cargo saved. Source: 99 (Dec. 13 and 16, 1858).

117. *Martha Gilchrist* — Bark, from Pensacola bound for Tortugas with bricks. Wrecked at North Key, Tortugas, Dec. 18, 1858. Vessel lost. Wreckers awarded $225. Note: A brig *Martha Gilen*, of St. George, Maine, from Pensacola with bricks, was listed in the *N.Y. Times* to have wrecked on the northeast shoal off Fort Jefferson, Jan. 1, 1859. A total loss. Most likely same vessel. Source: 37, 99 (Feb. 24, 1859).

118. *Martha Regan* — Hermaphrodite brig (slaver), about 250 tons, eastern built, four years old. On March 3, 1859, the schooner *Hermitage* brought the officers and crew of the wrecked brig to Key West. Had been wrecked on the Marquesas Shoal to destroy evidence of a successful slave trip. She had a slave deck, and many casks of water and provisions. The slaves had been dropped off in Cuba. Source: 99 (March 16, 1859).

119. *Mulhouse* — Ship, of New Orleans, bound for Havre, Captain Wilner, with 2,700 bales of cotton and $25,000 in coins. Went ashore on the quicksands near the Tortugas, March 26, 1859. The schooner *Tortugas* fell in with her on the 27th, and informed the wreckers. Passengers, coins, and 1,200 bales of cotton saved. Wreckers awarded $27,849. Source: 37, 99 (April 16, 1859).

120. *William Chesnut* — Wrecking schooner, of Key West. Lost in July 1859. Source: 99 (Aug. 2, 1859).

121. *Holems* — Ship. Reported in newspaper, Dec. 10, 1859, to have wrecked on East Key, Tortugas. Unknown if salvaged. Source: 37.

122. *C. C. Fowler* (believed to be the *Charles C. Fowler*, 521 tons) — Bark. Reported in newspaper in 1859 to have wrecked on Washerwoman Shoal. Unknown if salvaged. Source: 37.

123. *Tiger* — Brig, from New Orleans bound for Baltimore with molasses. Wrecked on Eastern Sandbornes, Feb. 18, 1860. Vessel lost. Wreckers awarded $2,704. Source: 37.

124. *William Jarvis* — Ship, believed to be 670 tons. Reported from Key West, Sept. 17, 1860, to have wrecked on Marquesas Key. Most of the cargo saved. Source: 19, 99 (Sept. 25, 1860).

125. *Fernandia* — Bark, 238 tons. Wrecked on Elbow Key, September 1860. Materials from wreck sold and half given to wreckers. Source: 19, 99 (Ibid).

126. *Cerro Gordo* — Ship, 577 tons, of the Pelican Line, Captain J. L. Randall, from New Orleans bound for Queenstown with 710 bales of cotton. Wrecked on Loggerhead Reef, Oct. 13, 1860. Vessel lost. Wreckers saved all but 11 bales and were awarded $1,733. Source: 19, 37, 99 (Nov. 13, 1860).

127. *Cordelis* — Bark, of Boston. Reported ashore, Nov. 4, 1860, on Loo Choo Key, with bottom breaking up. Wreckers were trying to save cargo and rigging. Source: 99 (Nov. 13, 1860).

See Civil War section for Section 3 wrecks during that period.

128. *Ringgold* — Schooner, from Chasahowika bound for New York with red cedar. Wrecked in the Northwest Channel, Key West, Oct. 23, 1865. Vessel lost. Wreckers awarded $1,750. Source: 37.

129. *James W. Lawrence* — Schooner, from New York bound for Galveston

with an assorted cargo. Wrecked on Middle Sandbornes, Nov. 11, 1865. Vessel lost. Wreckers awarded $3,146. Source: 37.

130. *Sea Lark* — Brig. Wrecked at Spanish Harbor, Nov. 11, 1865. Wreckers awarded $1,841. Source: 37.

131. *Oswingo* — Ship, from Liverpool with coal. Wrecked 3/4 miles from Key West, Nov. 11, 1865. Vessel lost. Wreckers awarded $739. Source: 37.

132. *Dwight* — Schooner, from Tabasco bound for New York with mahogany and hides. Wrecked on Eastern Dry Rocks, Dec. 13, 1865. Vessel lost. Wreckers awarded $1,638. Source: 37.

133. *Angela* — Brig. Wrecked on Agamemnon Reef, southeast of Key West, Jan. 7, 1866, with a cargo of cotton, hides, dywood, and other goods. Vessel lost. Wreckers awarded $5,276. Source: 37.

134. *Rebecca Barton* — Steamer, 353 tons, built in 1864 at Wilmington. Foundered off Key West, March 17, 1866. Source: 52.

135. *Omaha* — Brig. Reported from Key West to have capsized, May 1, 1869. Source: 99 (May 11, 1869).

136. *Golconda* — British ship, from Pensacola bound for Liverpool. Went ashore 30 miles east of Key West, May 18, 1869. Wreckers thought she might be gotten off. Unknown if salvaged. Source: 99 (May 20, 1869).

137. *Muller* — North German bark, Captain Schultz, from Pensacola bound for West Hartepool, England. Reported from Key West, Dec. 28, 1869, to have gone ashore ashore and bilged on Sugar Loaf Reef. Source: 99 (Dec. 29, 1869).

138. *Governor Marvin* (formerly *USS Honduras,*) — Sidewheel steamer, 376 tons, 150' x 27' x 10,' built in 1861 at New York. Stranded at Key West in 1870. (See Figure 14). Source: 52.

139. *Star* — Bark, from Key Francis bound for Queenstown with sugar. Wrecked at Conch Key, March 20, 1870. Vessel lost. Note: This vessel is also listed as having wrecked on Conch Reef (See Section 4, #155). Source: 37.

140. *Maria Ferguson* — British brig, from Mobile bound for Liverpool with cotton. Went ashore on the Tortugas, January 1871. Cargo saved. Source: 99 (Jan. 23, 1871).

Figure 14: *Governor Marvin* (formerly *USS Honduras* – picture taken then), stranded in 1870. U.S. NAVY HISTORICAL CENTER.

141. *St. James* — Ship, from Cardiff bound for Mobile with railroad iron. Wrecked at Conch Key, Nov. 16, 1871. Vessel lost. Wreckers awarded $16,210. Source: 37.

142. *E.K. Brown* — British schooner, from St. Andrews. Reported from Key West, Dec. 18, 1871, to have wrecked on Riding Rocks. A total loss. Captain died. Source: 99 (Dec. 20, 1871).

143. *Amazon* — Norwegian bark, built in 1868 at Grimstad, from Galveston bound for Liverpool. Went ashore on Canny's Foot Reef (Dry Rocks) and bilged, March 14, 1872, at 2 a.m. Cargo of cotton saved. Wreckers awarded $10,673. Source: 37, 99 (March 17, 1872).

144. *S.S. George Cromwell* — Steamer, Captain Clapp, from New York bound for New Orleans with bagging. Reported from the Loggerhead Key Station to have wrecked, July 26, 1872. Unknown if salvaged (another *George Cromwell* is listed as wrecked in 1877). Source: 14.

145. *Restless* — Bark, from Mobile bound for Boston with lumber. Reported from the Loggerhead Key Station to have wrecked, Sept. 20, 1872, at 9 p.m. Source: 14.

146. *Matawa* — British ship, of Glasgow. Went ashore near Key West, Nov. 14, 1872. Cargo of salt was jettisoned in hopes of lightening the ship. Unknown if salvaged. Source: 99 (Nov. 15, 1872).

147. *Leone* — French ship, from New Orleans bound for Bordeaux with cotton. Wrecked at Key West, Dec. 18, 1872, while entering the port. Source: 99 (Dec. 18, 1872).

148. *Sonara* (or *Senora*) — Schooner, from Apalachicola bound for Cardenas with lumber. Wrecked and bilged on Pulaski Reef, Tortugas, Dec. 22, 1872. Some cargo saved. Wreckers awarded $738. Source: 37, 99 (Dec. 28, 1872).

149. *Thomas P. Barklow* — Schooner, of Key West, 67 tons, Captain King, from Cedar Keys bound for Key West with yellow pine lumber. Foundered in Florida Bay, Feb. 8, 1874. A total loss. Source: 14.

150. *Eveline* — Schooner. Stranded near Key West, November 1874. A partial loss. Source: 14.

151. *S.S. Lee* — Schooner. Foundered off the Tortugas, November 1874. A total loss. Source: 14.

152. *Mountain Home* — Schooner. Lost north of Key West, January 1875. A total loss. Source: 14.

153. *Prairie Bird* — Bark. Burned in Key West Harbor, with cotton, June 16, 1875. Loss of $17,000. Wreckers awarded $14,000. Source: 14, 37.

154. *Nordkyn* — Norwegian bark, of Tonberg, 550 tons, built in 1840, Captain Anderson, from St. Anna, Mexico bound for Queenstown with mahogany. Stranded on Coffin Patches (one source says Vacas Key), Sept. 14 or 16, 1875. Half of cargo saved. Wreckers awarded $463. Source: 14.

155. *Sparkling Water* — Brig. Wrecked northwest of the Tortugas in the fall of 1875. A partial loss. Source: 14.

156. *Athenaise* — British ship, 984 tons, of St. John, New Brunswick, built in 1875, Captain Jones, from Pensacola bound for Liverpool with lumber and pitch pine. Stranded on the southwest point of the Quicksands, March 7, 1876, at 3:30 P.M. Wreckers awarded $284. Source: 14, 37.

157. *Abbie Carson* — Schooner. Wrecked off Key West, March 1876, after springing a leak. A partial loss. Source: 14.

158. *Jalapo* — German brig, 218 tons, built in 1850, from Laguna bound for Hamburg with logwood. Stranded five miles east of the Marquesas, July 7, 1876, at 4 A.M. Cargo saved. Source: 14.

159. *Yole* — Brig. Reported in newspaper, May 13, 1876, to have burned at Looe Key. Source: 37.

160. *Prairie Rose* — Brig, 314 tons, built in 1864 at Harpswell, Maine, 114' x 28'1" x 9'7". Stranded on Marquesas Keys, September 1876. A partial loss. Source: 6, 14.

161. *City of Houston* — Steamer. Grounded on the shoals near Saddle Bunches, Oct. 19, 1876, approximately 12 miles from Key West. Source: 11.

162. *Galveston* — Bark. Wrecked at Duck Key during the 1876 hurricane. A partial loss. Source: 14.

163. *Mollie Emma* — Schooner. Capsized during the October 1876 hurricane, 30 miles east of Key West. A partial loss. Source: 14.

164. Unknown Schooner — Bound for Galveston with railroad iron. Lost in the channel near Western Dry Rocks at the entrance to Key West Harbor, during the second hurricane of 1876. Source: 61.

165. *Emilie* — Steamer, of Cedar Keys, 370 tons, built in 1841, Captain Leppert, from Cedar Keys bound for Key West with assorted cargo. Foundered eight miles south-southwest of the Northwest Light, Jan. 2, 1877. Four of 17 on board lost. Source: 14.

166. *William M. Jones* — Three-masted schooner, of Port Jefferson, N.Y., 374 tons, built in 1872, Captain Davis, from New Orleans bound for New York with sugar, molasses, and rice. Stranded on Pulaski Shoal, Jan. 24, 1877, ten miles west-southwest of Loggerhead Light, five miles south-southwest of East Key, Tortugas. Vessel a total loss, though 30% of the cargo saved. Wreckers awarded $7,537. Source: 14, 37.

167. *Henry J. May* — Three-masted schooner, 392 tons, built in 1874, Captain Blackman, from Somers Point bound for New York with sugar and molasses. Stranded on the southwest end of Loggerhead Reef, Feb. 12, 1877, at 4:30 a.m. Vessel a total loss, but some cargo saved. Wreckers awarded $6,599. Source: 14, 37.

168. *Meggie* — British brig, of Guernsey, Captain Ellis, from Pensacola bound for London with lumber. Stranded on the southwest point of Loggerhead Reef, Sept. 21, 1877. A total loss. Source: 14.

169. *R.E. Lee* — Schooner, of Key West, 15 tons, cargo of wood, Captain Roberts. Ran on a shoal, Dec. 22, 1877. A total loss. Source: 14.

170. *Edith* — Schooner. Wrecked west of Key West, December 1877. A total loss. Source: 14.

171. *George Peabody* — Ship, of Boston, 1,562 tons, built in 1854, Captain Clark, from Liverpool bound for Key West with 400 tons of salt. Stranded on American Shoals (25 miles northeast of Key West), April 20, 1878. A *George Peabody*, 1397 tons, built in 1853 at Boston, is listed as condemned in 1881. Likely the same vessel. Source: 14, 105.

172. *Lewis J. Stocker* — Bark. Damaged at Key West during the 1878 hurricane. Source: 14.

173. *Thomas R. Pillsbury* — Schooner. Sprang a leak off the Tortugas, November 1878. A partial loss. Source: 14.

174. *Aurora* — Dutch bark, 368 tons, built in 1868, Captain Smit, from Pensacola bound for Harlingen, Holland, with lumber. Stranded on the Southwest Reef of the Tortugas, Feb. 2, 1879. A total loss. Wreckers awarded $18.95. Source: 14, 37.

175. *Folomer* — Bark. Wrecked on the Southwest Reef, Tortugas, March 2, 1881, with cargo of cotton. Vessel lost. Wreckers awarded $6,384. Source: 37.

176. *R.B. Gove* — Brig, of Camden, Maine, 463 tons, built in 1865, Captain Hodgman, from Pensacola bound for New Haven with yellow pine lumber. Stranded on Pulaski Shoal, Tortugas, Jan. 4, 1882. A total loss. Source: 14.

177. *Island Home* — British bark, of Windsor, Nova Scotia, 750 tons, built in 1860, Captain McKinlay, from Pensacola bound for Greencock, Scotland, with pitch pine lumber, and deals (fir or pine planks). Wrecked near Sand Key Light (one source says Marquesas Key), Jan. 25, 1882, at 3:45 P.M. A total loss. Wreckers awarded $808. Source: 14, 37.

178. *Luisa A* — Schooner, of Boston, 122 tons, built in 1863, Captain Atkins, from Pascagoula bound for Boston with lumber. Stranded at Loggerhead Key, Sept. 6, 1882, at 4:30 P.M. A total loss. Source: 14.

179. *William S. Fearwell* — Schooner, of Rockland, Maine, 146 tons, built in 1873, Captain Hunt, from Cedar Keys bound for New York with lumber. Wrecked on Miller Reef, on bank of Tortugas, Sept. 5, 1882, at 3 p.m. Four of the six in the longboat were lost. Some of the vessel and cargo saved. Source: 14.

180. *Dolcouth* — British schooner, of Cardiff, 1,171 tons, three

months old, from New Orleans bound for Antwerp with cotton and grain. Stranded on the North Key Spit, Tortugas, March 31, 1883. Unknown if salvaged. Source: 14.

181. *Lalia* — British bark, of Nova Scotia, 390 tons, 16 years old, Captain Rogers, from Pesacola bound for Nova Scotia with lumber. Stranded on Southwest Reef near Tortugas, June 17, 1883. Vessel valued at $1,000 ($500 loss), cargo at $1,000 ($750 loss). Source: 14.

182. *Marcia Reynolds* — Schooner, of New Jersey, 294 tons, Captain Holmes, from Philadelphia bound for Galveston. Foundered 20 miles northwest by west of Sombrero Light, May 24, 1884, at 9:40 A.M. Crew escaped in a yawl and arrived at Fernandina, June 14, 1884. Source: 14.

183. *Gutenberg* — German bark, of Bremen, 654 tons, built in 1861, from New Orleans bound for Bremen with cotton, staves, and oil meal. Stranded on Bird Key Reef, Tortugas, Dec. 15, 1884, at 4 A.M. Vessel a total loss. Some cargo saved. Wreckers awarded $26,702. Source: 14, 37.

184. *Elenora* — Ship, from Pensacola bound for London with lumber. Wrecked on the Southwest Reef, Tortugas, July 2, 1885. Vessel lost. Wreckers awarded $217. Source: 37.

185. *Cetewajo* — British schooner, of Nova Scotia, 141 tons, built in 1879, from Port Williams, Nova Scotia, bound for Havana with potatoes and lumber. Stranded on Bird Key Reef, Dry Tortugas, Dec. 27, 1885. Vessel a total loss. Some cargo saved. Source: 14.

186. *Rask* — Norwegian brig, 198 tons, Captain Olsen. Stranded on the Quicksands, Nov. 18, 1886. Unknown if salvaged. Source: 14.

187. *E.J. Watte* — Schooner, from New York bound for Galveston with iron. Wrecked on Little Pelican Shoals, June 7, 1886. Vessel lost. Wreckers awarded $10,948. Source: 37.

188. *Vidette* — Schooner-rigged steamer, of Boston, 429 tons, built in 1881, Captain Kelly, from New York bound for Mobile with general merchandise. Foundered 90 miles southeast of Sand Island Light, June 13, 1887, at 7:30 P.M. A total loss. Source: 14.

189. *Joshua H. Marvell* — Schooner. Wrecked on the Tortugas, July 25, 1887. Source: 9.

190. *Arthur* — Barge. Abandoned near Tortugas, July 26, 1887. Source: 9.

191. *Sebulow* — Norwegian bark, 327 tons, built in 1884, Captain Svenson, from Central America bound for Ireland with mahogany and cedar. Stranded on the Southwest Reef, Tortugas, Nov. 30, 1887 (one source says 1888). Vessel lost. Wreckers awarded $3,000. Source: 14, 37.

192. *Sabino* — Nowegian bark, 1,225 tons, 26 years old, cargo of lumber, Captain Bergenson. Stranded on Pulaski Shoal on the Southwest Reef, Tortugas, Jan. 27, 1888. It is unknown if salvaged. Source: 14.

193. *Prince Umbito* (or *Umberto*) — British bark, of Liverpool, 1,400 tons, built in 1873, Captain Mulgram, from Pensacola bound for Greenwich with timber. Stranded on Coffin Patches, Oct. 30, 1888, at 4:40 P.M. A total loss. Source: 14.

194. *Petrie* — Schooner, of Key West, 22 tons, built in 1878, Captain Thompson. Stranded on Washerwoman Shoal, Dec. 9, 1888. A total loss. Source: 14.

195. *True Briton* — British ship, of Liverpool, 1,364 tons, built in 1865, from Pensacola bound for Glasgow with timber. Stranded on Rebecca Shoal at the Quicksands, Jan. 29, 1889, at 7 A.M. A total loss. Source: 14.

196. *Adelaide Baker* — Bark. Wrecked on Coffin Patches, Jan. 30, 1889. Unknown if salvaged. Source: 9.

197. *Cav. Ivanissiveck* — Bark. Lost on the Quicksands, Jan. 31, 1889. Vessel lost. Wreckers awarded $234. Source: 37.

198. *Bridesmaid* — British barkentine, 497 tons, built in 1875, Captain Davies, from Pensacola bound for Rotterdam with lumber. Stranded on Tennessee Reef, Jan. 20, 1890, at 9 A.M. Unknown if salvaged. Source: 14.

199. *Bell Hooper* — Vessel, of Boston, 451 tons, built in 1875, from Pensacola bound for Philadelphia with lumber. Ran aground on the Southwest Reef, Tortugas, Jan. 28, 1890, at 5:40 P.M. Some cargo saved. Note: *Bell Hooper*, of the same tonnage, is listed as having wrecked July of 1897. Possibly it was salvaged. Source: 14.

200. *Joseph Baker* (or *Barker*) — Barkentine, of Bangor, 379 tons, built in 1873, Captain Eaton, from New Orleans bound for Baltimore with molasses and rice. Stranded on North Cay Flat, Tortugas,

Jan. 13, 1891, at 6 A.M. Vessel a total loss, one-third of cargo saved. Wreckers awarded $6,104. Source: 14, 37.

201. *Lone Star* — Schooner, of Key West, 39 tons, built in 1871, Captain Fabal, from Havana bound for Key West, in ballast. Stranded on North Dry Rocks, March 6, 1891. A total loss. Source: 14.

202. *Mabel* — British bark, 619 tons, built in 1874, Captain Davies, from Charlotte bound for London with phosphate rock. Stranded on Pulaski Shoals Flat Reef, Tortugas, Sept. 14, 1891, at 3 A.M. Unknown if salvaged. Source: 14.

Figure 15: Brig *Shannon*, wrecked in 1892. PENOBSCOT MARINE MUSEUM.

203. *Mexico* — Schooner barge, of Pensacola, 906 tons, Captain Loring, from Pensacola bound for Havana with coal. Stranded and broke up, Dec. 9, 1891, at 5 P.M. on the shoals of the Tortugas. A total loss. Source: 14.

204. *Shannon* — Brig, of Bangor, 374 tons, built in 1867, from Mobile bound for Mantanzas with lumber. Stranded on Pulaski Shoals Flat Reef, March 11, 1892. A total loss. Wreckers awarded $199. (See Figure 15). Source: 14.

205. *London* — Scottish bark (iron), 1,115 tons, built in 1863, Captain Ewan, from Pensacola bound for Rio with lumber and deals. Stranded on Rebecca Shoal, Dec. 27, 1892, at noon. A total loss. Wreckers awarded $524. Source: 14, 37.

206. *Arcadia* — British brig, of Nova Scotia, 241 tons, built in 1876, from Apalachicola bound for Cuba with lumber. Stranded on North Flats, Tortugas, April 18, 1893. Some cargo saved. Source: 14.

207. *Benjamin Hale* — Three-masted schooner, of Newburyport, Mass., 567 tons, built in 1882 at Newburyport, 162' x 32.7' x 16.2', Captain Hall, from Boston bound for Texas with barbed wire. Stranded on Bird Key Shoals, April 19, 1893, at 11 P.M. A total loss. Source: 14, 80.

208. *Carmelita* (or *Carmalita*) — British bark (composite built), of Falmouth, 537 tons, built in 1865, Captain Austin. Stranded on East Key Shoal, in ballast, Oct. 16, 1893, at 8 A.M., at Lat. 24-39.5, Long. 82-48. Vessel lost. Wreckers awarded $446. Source: 14.

209. *Curler* — British bark, of St. Johns, Newfoundland, 807 tons, built in 1890. Stranded on Southwest Key in the Marquesas, Feb. 15, 1894, with deals. Unknown if salvaged. Source: 14.

210. *Ida C. Southard* — Schooner, of New York, 778 tons, built in 1883, Captain Southard. Was in a collision off Sombrero Light, March 7, 1894, at 9 P.M., bearing west approximately 20 miles. Cargo of sugar saved. Source: 14.

211. *Nada* — German barkentine, of Hamburg, 387 tons, built in 1878, Captain Rulei, from New Orleans bound for Lisbon with staves and flour. Stranded during a storm, Sept. 28, 1894, at 5 A.M., on the inside of Tennessee Reef off Long Key. Some cargo saved. Wreckers awarded $2,694. Source: 14, 37.

212. *R. Bowers* — Schooner, of Boston, 413 tons, built in 1880,

Captain Wilson, from Apalachicola bound for Boston with yellow pine. Stranded on Southwest Reef, Dry Tortugas, April 13, 1895, at 1:30 A.M. Unknown if salvaged. Note: A schooner *R. Bowers* of 435 tons, built in 1879, is listed in service in 1899. Possibly the same vessel. Source: 14.

213. *Walter D. Walleth(?)* — British ship, of Liverpool, 1,416 tons, built in 1876, Captain Price, from Mobile bound for Belfast with lumber. Stranded off Loggerhead Light bearing east by northeast, April 13, 1895. Ship was valued at $10,000 ($7,000 loss), cargo at $12,000 ($5,000 loss). Source: 14.

214. *Harry B. Ritter* — Schooner, 611 tons, built in 1868, Captain Peterson, from New York bound for Charlotte Harbor with railroad iron. Stranded on the Southwest Reef, Tortugas, June 1, 1895, at 2:30 A.M. Vessel valued at $16,000 ($14,000 loss), cargo at $11,000 ($6,000 loss). Source: 14.

215. *Beatrice M. Leau* — British schooner, of St. John, New Brunswick, 249 tons, built in 1890, Captain Gerrard, from Mobile bound for San Domingo City with lumber. Stranded on the Southwest Reef, Tortugas, Nov. 20, 1895, at 10 P.M. Some cargo saved. Source: 14.

216. Schooner — Of Key West, 22 tons. Bilged on the jetty at the northwest entrance to Key West, Feb. 10, 1896, at 7 P.M. A total loss. Source: 14.

217. *Shelter Island* — Iron paddlewheel steamer, 648 tons, built in 1886 at Harlan & Hollingsworth's Delaware River Shipyard, 176' x 31' x 10'. Chartered from the Montauk Steamboat Co. by the Florida East Coast Steamship Co. for the Miami to Key West run. Approximately 50 staterooms on board.

She left New York, Feb. 13, 1896, and arrived at Jacksonville on the 16th. She left Miami bound for Key West on Feb. 20 for her first and last trip for the Florida East Coast Steamship Co. More than 200 citizens of Key West and many more from Jacksonville were on board for this first passage. Only two hours out she struck some rocks. She got free and continued for Key West with her pumps on. Her pumps eventually failed, and the water rose and put her fires out. She settled to the bottom only 19 miles from Key West. No casualties. Vessel a total loss. Most of cargo saved. Source: 95 (Mueller, Edward. "The Florida East Coast Steamship Company." No. XXXVI, 1976, pp. 43-53).

218. *Riverside* — Norwegian ship, of Stavenger, 1,160 tons, built in 1868, Captain Neilson, from Mobile bound for Belfast with lumber.

Stranded on the Quicksands, Nov. 7, 1896, at 7:15 A.M., east by north-east of Rebecca Shoal Light. Cargo saved. Note: The Norwegian Maritime Museum has no record of this ship, and believes this to be the *Riverside*, which left Mobile on March 19, 1899, with pitchpine and was later reported lost. Possibly the *Riverside* was salvaged in 1896 and is the same as lost in 1899. Source: 14.

219. *Apphia & Amelia* — Schooner, of Portland, Maine, 250 tons, built in 1884 at Yarmouth, Maine, 128.3' x 31' x 9.3', Captain Millard, from Pascagoula bound for New York with lumber. Caught fire at American Shoals, June 15, 1897, at 12:10 P.M. A total loss. Source: 14.

220. *Lily White* — Schooner, of Key West, 55 tons, built in 1883 at Madisonville, La., 70.8' x 22.4' x 5.8', Captain Griffin, from Key West bound for Punta Rassa. Capsized 30 miles northwest of Key West, July 30, 1897. One life lost. Source: 14.

221. *Mathilda* — Norwegian ship, formerly the *Northern Light*, 1,748 tons, built in the United States in 1873, Captain Gram, from Mobile bound for Newcastle on Tyne, England, with timber and deals. Stranded on the Quicksands, Aug. 13, 1897, at 10:30 A.M. Vessel a total loss. Source: 14, Norsk Sjofartsmuseum.

222. *Speedwell* — Schooner, of Key West, 25 tons, built in 1896 at Marco, Fla., 51.5' x 17' x 4.8', Captain Collier (founder of Collier County). During a squall off the Marquesas in 1899, she capsized 18 miles from Key West. Nine of the crew drowned, including three of the captain's sons caught inside the schooner. The captain and three others survived. Source: 76, 80.

1900

223. Unknown Vessel — Lost or abandoned in 1903, by the Northwest Passage Lighthouse, Lat. 24-37-06.61, Long. 81-53-57.57. Source: 1.

224. *Sylph* — Schooner, 68 tons, built in 1889 at Port Jefferson, N.Y., 72.6' x 22.5' x 8.9'. Stranded on the Sambo, Jan. 28, 1904. Source: 14.

225. *Sweetheart* — Schooner, of Tampa, 21 tons, built in 1899, Captain Taylor, from Miami with fish. Burned off Long Key, Dec. 1, 1904. A total loss. Source: 14.

226. *Volunteer* — Schooner, of Key West 26 tons, built in 1888 at Key West, 49.2' x 17.4' x 5.5'. Foundered at Sand Key, Jan. 16, 1905. Source: 14.

227. *Glamo* — Bark, from New Orleans bound for Portugal. Wrecked on Marquesas Reef and bilged, June 1, 1905. Vessel lost. Wreckers

awarded $7,696. Source: 37.

228. *S.O. Co. No. 90* — Schooner, 2,019 tons, built in 1900. Foundered off the Tortugas, Sept. 26, 1906. All nine on board lost. Source: 14.

229. *Race* — Schooner, of Key West, 28 tons, built in 1875 at Indian Key, 56' x 19.4' x 5'. Stranded at Knights Key, Oct. 18, 1906. Source: 14.

230. *Adam W. Spies* — Schooner (formerly a barque), 1,235 tons, built in 1884 at Newburyport, Mass., 185' x 38.4' x 22.8'. Stranded 40 miles west of Stirrup Key, Dec. 1, 1906. She was an extremely fast vessel, and in 1888 had made the Newcastle to Hong Kong run in 31 days, a record beaten only by the famous tea clipper *Thermopylae*. Source: 14, 51.

231. *Anna M. Stammer* — Three-masted schooner, 419 tons, built in 1890 at Bath, 142.3' x 34.1' x 10.8'. Wrecked at Duck Key with lumber, Dec. 6, 1906. Vessel lost. Wreckers awarded $1,418. Source: 14, 37.

232. *Haroldine* — Four-masted schooner with stone for the Key West extension. Wrecked off Bear's Cut in 1906 and soon broke up in a gale. Source: 61.

233. *Irene* — Schooner, of Key West, 33 tons, built in 1885 at Key West, 50.5' x 19.2' x 6.5'. Stranded at Hospital Key, Tortugas, Feb. 17, 1907. Source: 14.

234. *Manatee* — Schooner, of Key West, 31 tons, built in 1887 at Titusville, 58.9' x 14.6' x 5.5'. Burned at Key West, July 16, 1907. Source: 14.

235. Unknown Wreck — 30', found in 1908, at Lat. 24-35-02.64, Long. 81-40-09.63. Source: 1.

236. Unknown Wreck — Found in 1908, at Lat. 24-35-32.01, Long. 81-47-58.65. Source: 1.

237. *Emma Eliza* — Schooner, 22 tons, built in 1901. Foundered at Cudjoe Key, Sept. 28, 1909. Source: 14.

238. *Medford* — Four-masted schooner, of Boston, 1,351 tons, built in 1900 at Bath, 201.7' x 40' x 18.6', with cargo of 2,000 tons of sand and gravel for the Pen Bridge Co. Was blown five miles towards Sand Key from Key West during the storm of Oct. 11, 1909. She sank. One life lost. Source: 11, 14.

239. *Peerless* — Sidewheel steamer, of St. Augustine, 50 tons, built in 1903 at Morgantown, Ky., 100' x 20' x 4'. Foundered by Boot Key during the storm of Oct. 11, 1909. Source: 14.

240. *Freddie W. Alton* — Schooner, 86 tons, built in 1867 at Provincetown, Mass., 77' x 22.7' x 8.2'. Struck the dock at Key West and sank during the storm of Oct. 11, 1909. Source: 14.

241. *Impulse* — Schooner, of Key West, 21 tons, built in 1894 at Key West, 46' x 16.7' 4.9'. Foundered at Key West during the storm of Oct. 11, 1909. Source: 14.

242. *Florida* — Gas vessel, 48 tons, built in 1886. Stranded at Key West during the storm of Oct. 11, 1909. Source: 14.

243. *S.R. Mallory* — Schooner, of Cedar Keys, 34 tons, built in 1895 at Cedar Keys, 54.4' x 18' x 6'. Stranded at Key West during the storm of Oct. 11, 1909. Source: 14.

244. *Braganza* — Schooner, 95 tons, built in 1892 at Essex, Mass., 86.6' x 23.2' x 9.2'. Foundered near Key West during the storm of Oct. 11, 1909. Source: 14.

245. *Nannie C. Bohlin* — Two-masted schooner, of Tampa, 130 tons, built in 1890 at Gloucester, Mass., 110.2' x 23.5' x 11.2', Captain Bordeu, from Tampa bound for Bahia Honda with lumber. Became waterlogged and beached during a gale, Oct. 18, 1909, at 9 A.M., 200 yards northeast of Garden Key, Tortugas, and sank in 40 feet of water. A total loss. Source: 14, 80.

246. *Triton* — Schooner, of Tampa, 39 tons, built in 1871 at Bristol, R.I., 65.3' x 18.6' x 6.5', Captain Lightburn. Caught fire in Key West Harbor while on a sponging trip, Oct. 27, 1909, at 9 P.M., 300 yards from the dock. A total loss. Source: 14.

247. *Magnolia* — Schooner, of Key West, 46 tons, built in 1893 at Key West, 64.9' x 20.3' x 5.1'. Foundered at Key West, September 1910. Source: 14.

248. *Louisiana* — French vessel, type unknown. Wrecked off Sombrero Reef, Oct. 17, 1910. Source: 8.

249. *Virginia* — Sidewheel steamer, of St. Augustine, 79 tons, built in 1905 at Wabasha, Minn., 104.5' x 23.5' x 4'. Foundered at Boca Chica, Oct. 17, 1910. Source: 14.

250. *Edward T. Stotesbury* — Schooner, 1,446 tons, built in 1900 at Verona, Maine, 210' x 41.6' x 21.6'. Stranded at Knights Key, Oct. 17, 1910. One life lost. Source: 14.

251. *Pendleton Brothers* — Four-masted schooner, of New York, 970 tons, built in 1903 at Belfast, Maine, 194.8' x 38.8' x 19.4'. Stranded on the Tortugas, March 17, 1913. (See Figure 16). Source: 14, 80.

252. *Clifford N. Carver* — Four-masted schooner, of New York, 1,101 tons, built in 1900 at Bath, 188.9' x 39.5' x 18.6'. Stranded on Tennessee Reef, April 2, 1913. Source: 14, 80.

Figure 16: Schooner *Pendelton Brothers*, wrecked in 1913. MAINE MARITIME MUSEUM.

253. *Amelia* — Schooner, 23 tons, built in 1866 in Louisiana, 50.8' x 17.3' x 4.3'. Burned three miles from Key West, May 22, 1914. Source: 14.

254. *Edna Louise* — Schooner, of Tampa, 45 tons, built in 1902 at Key West, 60.8' x 20.1' x 5.8', from Tarpon Springs on a sponging trip. Was set fire by unknown parties, May 26, 1914, 30 miles from Key West. Source: 14.

255. *Brazos* — Schooner, 226 tons, built in 1902 at Baltimore, 131.5' x 26.5' x 8.6'. Stranded on the Tortugas, Nov. 3, 1917. Source: 14.

256. *F.A. Kilburn* — Steamer, 997 tons (also listed at 728 tons), built in 1904. Burned near American Shoal Light, June 14, 1918. Source: 14.

257. *Lake City* (formerly *Sidi Msbrouk*) — Freighter (steel), of New York, 2,485 tons, built in 1917 at Ashtabula, Ohio, 253' x 43.5' x 27.5'. Sank off Key West, Oct. 3, 1918, at approximate Lat. 24-30-00, Long. 81-29-00. One source says she was torpedoed with more than 30 lives lost, while another says she collided with the steamer *James McGee,* with no casualties. Source: 1, 14.

258. *Robert* — Barge, of New Orleans, 278 tons, built in 1917 at Harrisburg, Texas. Foundered near Key West, Oct. 9, 1918. Source: 14.

259. *Louis H* (formerly Swedish bark *Verdandi*) — Barge of Savannah, 323 tons, built in 1884 at Sikea, Sweden. Burned by Sombrero Key Light, May 2, 1919. Source: 14.

260. *Santa Cristina* — Freighter (gas vessel), of Seattle, 2,119 tons, built in 1917 at Aberdeen, Wash., 224.5' x 42.6' x 25.9'. Burned 25 miles off Key West, July 8, 1919. Source: 14.

261. *Bayronto* — British steamer. Abandoned and foundered during a hurricane off Key West, Sept. 11, 1919. All passengers saved. Source: 99 (Sept. 17, 1919).

262. *Valbanera* — See Shipwreck Narratives.

263. *Hugh De Payens* — Three-masted schooner, of New Orleans, 416 tons, built in 1910. Abandoned off the Dry Tortugas during the

Figure 17: *Lewis H. Goward* (at her launching), wrecked in 1921. MAINE MARITIME MUSEUM.

September 1919 hurricane. Crew picked up by a Cuban steamer. She was later seen drifting upside down in the Florida Channel, between Sal Key and Key West. Note: *Merchant Vessels of the U.S.* states she foundered off Cardenas, Cuba, Sept. 9, 1919. Source: 14, 98 (Sept. 22 and 27, 1919).

Figure 18: Schooner *Herbert May*, wrecked in 1922. MAINE MARITIME MUSEUM.

264. *Priscilla R. Ray* (formerly *Henry L. Peckham*) — Schooner (steel), 712 tons, built in 1891 at East Boston, 183' x 37.5' x 14'. Stranded in the Northwest Passage, Key West, Feb. 16, 1920. Source: 14.

265. *Lewis H. Goward* — Four-masted schooner, 1,199 tons, built in 1895 at Bath, 205.6' x 39.4' x 19.6'. Burned near Key West, April 1, 1921. (See Figure 17). Source: 14.

266. *C.W. Mills* — Schooner, 371 tons, built in 1904 at Granville, Nova Scotia, 141' x 31.8' x 11.4'. Burned south of Tortugas, May 1, 1921. Source: 14.

267. *Planter* — Schooner (formerly a barkentine), 524 tons, built in 1886 at Port Ludlow, Wash., 158.7' x 37.5' x 13.5'. Foundered at Lat. 24-18-00, Long. 81-08-00, Aug. 15, 1921. Source: 1, 14.

268. *Agnes Belle* — Schooner, of Tampa, 29 tons, built in 1877 at Millbridge, Maine, 58.4' x 18.3', 6.6'. Foundered at Dry Tortugas, Oct. 25, 1921. Seven lives lost. Source: 14.

269. *Herbert May* — Three-masted schooner, 384 tons, built in 1906 at Phippsburg, Maine, 140' x 33.4' x 10.4'. Stranded at the Marquesas, Feb. 7, 1922. (See Figure 18). Source: 14.

270. *Caldwell H. Colt* — Schooner, 64 tons, built in 1887 at Greenpoint, N.Y., 79' x 21.5' x 9.1'. Stranded at the Tortugas, Feb. 16, 1922. Seven lives lost. Source: 14.

271. *Carrie S. Allen* — Schooner, of Tampa, 24 tons, built in 1871 at Harpswell, Maine, 47.9' x 16.4' x 5.8'. Burned at Key West, April 25, 1923. Source: 14.

272. *Robin Hood* — Schooner, 1,983 tons, built 1918. Burned at Lat. 24-00-00, Long. 82-48-00, June 25, 1924. Source: 14.

273. *Fannie & Fay* — Three-masted schooner, of New London, 233 tons, built in 1885 at New London, 117.5' x 30.8' x 8.8'. Foundered near Dry Tortugas, June 29, 1925. Source: 14, 80.

274. *Island Belle* — Steamer, of Newport, 132 tons, built in 1892 at Bath, 95.6' x 23.1' x 7.5'. Stranded at Key West, March 25, 1926. (See Figure 19). Source: 14.

275. *John Henry Sherman* — Motor vessel, 77 tons, built in 1924. Stranded at Garden Key, Tortugas, Sept. 17, 1926, during a hurricane. Source: 14.

276. *Serafina C.* — Schooner, 44 tons, built in 1890 at Baypoint, Fla., 66.2' x 20.7' x 5.6'. Foundered at Key West, Oct. 20, 1926. Source: 14.

277. *Thendara* (formerly *Jessie P. Logie)* — Steamer, 58 tons, built in

Figure 19: Steamer *Island Belle*, wrecked in 1926. MAINE MARITIME MUSEUM.

1886 at Boston, 85.9' x 15' x 8.3'. Foundered at Key West, Oct. 20, 1926. Source: 14.

278. *Rose Murphy* (formerly *Lake Indian*) — Steamer (steel), of Boston, 1,991 tons, built in 1918 at Duluth, Minn., 251' x 43.6' x 18.1'. Foundered at Sand Key Light, Jan. 25, 1927. Source: 14.

279. *Cynthiana* — Gas vessel, 25 tons, built in 1910. Foundered at Key West, Nov. 11, 1927. Source: 14.

280. *Monroe County* — Oil vessel, 129 tons, built in 1927. Burned at Key West, Sept. 15, 1928. Source: 14.

281. *Arago* — Tug (gas), 109 tons, built in 1905 at Portland, Ore., 84' x 18.7' x 8.8'. Stranded at East Sambo Key, Oct. 3, 1928. Source: 14.

282. *Rosemary* — Four-masted schooner, of New Orleans, 901 tons, built in 1917 at Handsboro, Miss., 184' x 38' x 16.2'. Burned at Key West, Nov. 7, 1930. Source: 14, 80.

283. *W.J. Colle* — Schooner, of Gulfport, 450 tons, built in 1922 at Pascagoula, Miss., 155' x 35.1' x 13.9'. Foundered near Key West, Dec. 21, 1930. Source: 14.

284. *Elizabeth* (formerly *Macomet)* — Steam freighter (steel), of New York, 3,482 tons, built in 1919 at Wilmington, 328' x 46.2' x 22.9'. Sank at Lat. 24-48-36, Long. 80-05-09, Nov. 4, 1935. Source: 1, 14.

285. *Marie J. Thompson* — Schooner, approximately 75 meters by ten meters. Sank in 1935, at Lat. 24-35-08.75, Long. 81-48-32.17. Source: 1.

286. *Nor Wester* — Ship, from New Orleans bound for Liverpool with cotton. Caught fire in Key West Harbor, Feb. 23, 1938. Vessel lost. Wreckers awarded $26,837. Source: 37.

287. *E.J. Bullock* (formerly *William H. Doheny*) — Steamer (steel), of Wilmington, 6,630 tons, built in 1920 at San Francisco, 435' x 56.2' x 33.6'. Foundered off southwest Dry Tortugas, Dec. 2, 1938, at Lat. 24-30-00, Long. 83-00-00. Three lives lost. Source: 1, 14.

288. Sponge boat — Approximately 30'. Sank in the 1930s, at Lat. 24-34-55.25, Long. 81-48-42.90. Source: 1.

289. *Erickson* — Fishing smack, 20 meters by three meters. Sank in the 1930s, at Lat. 24-35-11.08, Long. 81-48-35.54. Source: 1.

See World War II section for Section 3 wrecks during that period.

290. Landing Craft — 1,000 tons. A notice to mariners listed this on May 16, 1948, at approximate Lat. 24-34-30, Long. 82-14-00. Source: 1.

291. Landing Craft — Sank in 1948, at approximate Lat. 24-38-00, Long. 83-08-00. Source: 1.

292. *USS Eagle Boat* — Vessel of 800 tons. Sank in 1948, at Lat. 24-38-25, Long. 82-06-30 (accurate within one mile). Note: Eagle Class Patrol Boats are listed at 430 tons, 200' long. Source: 1.

293. *U 2513* — Ex-German U-Boat. Was one of the new Type 21 subs constructed toward the end of WWII, 1,621 tons, 251'9" x 21'9" x 20'3", capable of 16 knots. She surrendered to the Allies at Horten, Norway, in May 1945, after the Nazi collapse. The U.S. Navy took possession of her, and she was in service from 1946 until 1949 on the East Coast. She ended up at Key West Naval Base. On Sept. 2, 1951, the order was given to sink her by gunfire, and it was carried out soon after at approximate Lat. 24-52-00, Long. 83-19-00. (See Figure 20). Source: 1, Naval Historical Center.

Figure 20: Ex-German U-boat *U 2513*, sunk in 1951. NATIONAL ARCHIVES.

294. *Dayco* — O/V, built in 1950. Foundered off Dry Tortugas, November 1951. Source: 14.

295. *Joan C* — O/V, 23 tons, built in 1941. Stranded 12 miles northeast of New Ground Shoal, near Key West, June 29, 1951. Source: 14.

296. Unknown wreck — Located in 1951, seven feet from the surface in 95 to 105 feet of water, at Lat. 26-45-49.25, Long. 82-50-46.90. Demolished to 65 feet of water. Source: 1.

297. *Merry Sea* — O/V, 37 tons, built in 1950. Burned between Rebecca Shoals and Pulaski Light, Feb. 29, 1952. Source: 14.

298. *Sa-La* — O/V, 55 tons, built in 1947. Burned between New Ground and Rebecca Light, June 4, 1952. Source: 14.

299. *F.W. Scheper* — O/V, 32 tons, built in 1941. Foundered 30 miles north of Tortugas, April 7, 1953. Source: 14.

300. *Elliot* — O/V, 48 tons, built in 1925. Stranded on a reef, Jan. 31, 1954, 15 miles northwest of Key West. Source: 14.

301. *Barbara II* — O/V, 27 tons, built in 1946. Foundered approximately 55 miles west of Key West, Feb. 18, 1954. Source: 14.

302. *Spot Jack* — M/V, 147 tons, built in 1941. Sank April 28, 1954, at Lat. 24-56-30, Long. 82-46-30. Source: 1.

303. *Ramos* — O/V, 27 tons, built in 1927. Burned eight miles off Key West, May 19, 1954. Source: 14.

304. *Markie Singleton* — O/V, 47 tons, built in 1948. Burned Sept. 24, 1954, at Lat. 24-47-00, Long. 82-12-00. Source: 14.

305. *YMS 319* — Navy minesweeper, 215 tons (also listed at 320 tons), launched in 1943, 136' x 24'6" x 6'1". Sunk by a Navy mine in 1954, at approximate Lat. 24-38-00, Long. 82-10-00. Source: 1, 28, 44.

306. *Blue Bonnet* — O/V, 46 tons, built in 1948. Burned 50 miles northeast of Dry Tortugas, May 2, 1955. Source: 14.

307. *Caterpillar* — Trawler. Sank in 1955, at approximate Lat. 24-46-06, Long. 82-04-30. Source: 1.

308. *Goloenk* — F/V. Sank in 1956, at Lat. 24-30-40, Long. 81-48-28, six to eight feet from the surface. Source: 1.

309. *Miss Columbia* — O/V, 37 tons, built in 1946. Burned off Key West, June 12, 1957. Source: 14.

310. *Santa Barbara* — O/V, 44 tons, built in 1948. Stranded off Key West, Oct. 15, 1957. Source: 14.

311. *Evening Star* — O/V, 74 tons, built in 1947. Burned 20 miles west of Key West, Jan. 31, 1958. Source: 14.

312. *Flying Ace* — O/V, 30 tons, built in 1939. Foundered at Dry Tortugas, Aug. 18, 1958. Source: 14.

313. *Cathie* — Steel vessel, 36 tons, built in 1947. Foundered approximately 10 to 12 miles north of Loggerhead Light, Dec. 9, 1958. Source: 14.

314. *Emily A* — O/V, 37 tons, built in 1957. Burned approximately 3.5 miles off Dry Tortugas, Feb. 25, 1960. Source: 14.

315. *Cape Lookout* — O/V, 35 tons, built in 1952. Burned approximately 35 miles northwest of Key West, Dec. 28, 1960. Source: 14.

316. *Lainee K* — O/V, 35 tons, built in 1955. Foundered approximately 600 yards east of White St. Pier, off Hawkes Channel, Key West, Dec. 24, 1961. Source: 14.

317. *Buddy Lynn* — O/V, 64 tons, built in 1958. Foundered approximately 15 miles south of Rebecca Shoals Light, approximately 45 miles west of Key West, Feb. 11, 1961. Source: 14.

318. *Joe Rizzo* — F/V (oil), 38 tons, built in 1941. Burned approximately 16 miles northwest of Key West, Jan. 11, 1962. Source: 14.

319. *Grand Mar* — F/V (oil), 35 tons, built in 1954. Foundered northwest of Key West, Feb. 12, 1962. Source: 14.

320. *Danny Boy* — F/V (oil), 30 tons, built in 1953. Foundered approximately 35 miles southwest of Key West, April 25, 1962. Source: 14.

321. *Miss Sarah* — F/V (oil), 64 tons, built in 1954. Burned at East Key, Dec. 1, 1962, approximately 50 miles southwest of Key West. Source: 14.

322. *William R* — F/V (oil), 57 tons, built in 1951. Collided with a trawler, Dec. 8, 1962, off Dry Tortugas. Source: 14.

323. *Comanche* — O/V, 63 tons, built in 1952. Burned Jan. 6, 1963, at Lat. 25-02-00, Long. 82-52-00. Source: 14.

324. *Helen Lee* — F/V (oil), 64 tons, built in 1954 at St. Augustine, 61.4' x 18.4' x 8.5'. Foundered off Key West, Feb. 29, 1964, at Lat. 24-11-00, Long. 84-18-00. Source: 14.

325. *Yellow Jacket* — F/V, (oil), 29 tons, built in 1949. Foundered approximately 20 miles west by northwest of Key West, Sept. 11, 1964. Source: 14.

326. *Gulf Maid* — F/V (oil), 44 tons, built in 1950. Foundered approximately 45 miles north by northeast of Pulaski Light, Dry Tortugas, Dec. 7, 1965. Source: 14.

327. *Celeste Joan* — F/V (oil), 57 tons, built in 1951 at St. Augustine, 59.5' x 17.9' x 7.7'. Stranded approximately 1000 yards west of Fort Jefferson, Dry Tortugas, Jan. 29, 1966. Source: 14.

328. *Debby D* — F/V (oil), 64 tons, built in 1954 at St. Augustine, 61.4' x 18.4' x 8.5'. Foundered near Key West, Oct. 10, 1966. Source: 14.

329. *Two Brothers* — Wrecking oil vessel (steel), 67 tons, built in 1916 at Baltimore, 80.7' x 16.8' x 4.6'. Foundered at Key West, March 1967. Source: 14.

330. *Coral Isle* — F/V (oil), 69 tons, built in 1950 at Biloxi, 62.5' x 21' x 8.7'. Collided with a submerged object, Jan. 18, 1968, northeast of Loggerhead Light, Tortugas. Source: 14.

331. *Miss Lorraine* — F/V (oil), 45 tons, built in 1957. Foundered on jetty in Northwest Channel, Key West, Nov. 16, 1968. Source: 14.

332. *Nanu* — F/V (oil), 59 tons, built in 1953 at St. Augustine, 62.2' x 18.8' x 7.6'. Foundered in the Gulf off Key West, Sept. 4, 1969. Source: 14.

333. Unknown wreck — Located in 1970, at Lat. 24-32-04, Long. 81-50-42. Source: 1.

334. *Good Luck* — F/V and shrimp boat. Wrecked high and dry in 1970, at Lat. 24-36-15, Long. 81-53-21. Source: 1.

335. *Alexander* — Navy destroyer-escort, 300'. Sank in 1970, four miles west-northwest of Cotrell Key, and lies on her side in 40 feet of water. Note: I can't find a navy vessel named *Alexander* that fits this description. Source: 25.

336. *Springtime* — F/V (oil), 76 tons, built in 1959 at St. Augustine, 63.2' x 19.1' x 9.1'. Collided with a submerged object, Jan. 31, 1971, northwest of Loggerhead Light. Source: 14.

337. *King Conch* — F/V (oil), 63 tons, built in 1952 at St. Augustine, 58.7' x 18.5' x 8.2'. Foundered three miles north of Old Towne, Dry Tortugas, Feb. 3, 1971. Source: 14.

338. *USS Wilkes-Barre* — Navy cruiser (Cleveland-Vincennes Class), 10,000 tons, 608'4" x 63' x 20', launched Dec. 24, 1943, at New York. Part of the Pacific Fleet in WWII. Later used for underwater explosives tests by the Navy. Sank off Key West, May 12, 1972, in 320 feet of water after her hull broke in two. The top of the deck lies at 210 feet and the top of the wreck at 140 feet. Some Key West dive shops offer trips to this site, but only the experienced wreck diver should attempt this dive. (See Figure 21). Source: 28, 44.

Figure 21: *USS Wilkes Barre*, sunk in 1972. NATIONAL ARCHIVES.

339. *DC 715* — Barge, 3,086 tons, built in 1970. Foundered near Dry Tortugas, July 31, 1973. Source: 14.

340. *Miss Five Eleven* — F/V (oil), 64 tons, built in 1954. Foundered at Stock Island, Key West, Jan. 3, 1974. Source: 14.

341. *Capt. Buck* — O/V, 99 tons, built in 1966. Foundered off Key West, July 1974. Source: 14.

342. Barge — 225'. Located in 1977 on her port side in 25 feet of water, at Lat. 24-32-33.55, Long. 81-49-34.03. Source: 1.

343. *Susan H* — F/V (oil), 99 tons, built in 1966 at St. Augustine, 67' x 20.5' x 9.5'. Foundered off the jetties near Key West, Jan. 4, 1978. Source: 14.

344. Sailing vessel — 40-50'. Reported in 1980, in 30 feet of water, at Lat. 24-57-00, Long. 81-30-00. Source: 1.

345. Yacht — 34'. Located in 1982, at Lat. 24-33-13.90, Long. 81-48-28.40, in 13 feet of water. Source: 1.

346. Chris Craft — 34'. Located in 1982, at Lat. 24-33-19.64, Long. 81-48-29.33, in 38 feet of water. Source: 1.

347. 2,000-pound anchor — Reported by divers in 32 feet of water, at Lat. 24-33-06.05, Long. 81-48-57.77. Source: 1.

Figure 21A: Bronze bell from the wreck of the *Henrietta Marie* (1700) inscribed with her name and date built. AUTHOR.

Section 4: Upper Keys

1500

1. Three Spanish vessels — In 1549, three vessels from New Spain (Mexico), bound for Spain, wrecked in the Florida Keys at Los Martires (Key Largo area). Most people survived, but endured extreme hardship afterwards. Source: 7.

2. Spanish ship — Wrecked on *"Los Cayos de los Martires,"* during a storm, Dec. 2, 1551. Only 17 survived to reach St. Augustine. Source: 54.

3. Two Spanish vessels — From Havana, wrecked off the head of *Los Martires* (Upper Keys), August 1577. All but two were killed by the Indians. Source: 54.

4. Spanish nao — From Havana bound for Spain. Lost at the head of the Florida Keys, probably on Key Largo, in 1579. Source: 54.

1600

5. Two Spanish galleons — From Havana bound for St. Augustine with supplies, under Maestre de Campo Antonio de Oteyca. Wrecked at the head of the Florida Keys in 1630. Crew and 56 cannon were saved. Source: 54.

6. *Kinsdale* — British ship, Captain D. Dent. Wrecked during a storm, April 18, 1638, on a sand bar near Cape Florida. A total loss. Source: 54.

7. English warship — Under command of D. Jacob Jackson. Sank within sight of land in the Florida Straits in 1644. Source: 57.

8. *Santa Anna Maria* — Spanish merchant ship. Wrecked on Key Largo, Feb. 15, 1665. Unknown if salvaged. Source: 54.

9. *Nuestra Señora de Concepción y San Josefe* — Spanish frigate. Lost at Key Largo in 1689. Source: 54.

10. *HMS Winchester* — British 4th-rate ship of the line, 60 guns, Captain John Soule, 933 tons, built in 1693, 146.5' x 38'. Sank on Carysfort Reef Sept. 14 or 24, 1695, after separating from her consorts during a storm. Found and salvaged in 1939 by Charles Brookfield. Some iron cannon salvaged and melted down for new weapons during WWII. Source: 16, 24.

1700

11. 1733 Spanish Plate Fleet — Some of this fleet sank in the area covered in the Lower Florida Keys section, but the majority sank in the

Upper Keys area. On July 13, 1733, 21 or 22 ships left Havana bound for Spain loaded with treasure from the New World. On the 14th, a hurricane hit the fleet off the Florida Keys. By nightfall most, if not all, the ships wrecked or were stranded. Within weeks, the Spaniards had recovered all the registered treasure as well as some unregistered or smuggled treasure, and some ships were refloated.

However some treasure did remain, and modern-day salvors such as the late Art McKee have recovered valuable treasure from these wrecks (See Figures 22 and 23). Many dive shops in the upper Keys offer trips to some of these wrecks. Coins and other artifacts are still being found. Some wrecks are still actively worked under a government lease, and some are being considered for designation as a state park.

The names of these vessels can become confusing, since many went by more than one name. One which most commonly goes by the name of the *San Jose*, also goes by the names *San José de las Animas, San José y las Animas, St. Joseph, El Conde,* and the *Africa.* Here is a list of the other ships that wrecked, by their most common name.

Almiranta, *Gallo*	*Angustias*
Capitana, *El Rubí*	*Chaves*
El Aviso	*El Infante*
El Lerri	*El Populo*
El Sueco	*Herrera*
La Valandra	*Murguia*
Poder	*San Fernando*
San Francisco	*San Ignacio*
San Pedro	*Tres Puentes*

Most of these vessels have been found, and their positions are listed on charts sold at local dive shops. Many lie close to each other. You could dive on the *Almiranta*, the *San Francisco*, and the *El Lerri* in one day. The ballast piles of many of these wrecks are still visible. The ballast of the *Almiranta* is appoximately 100 feet long and six feet high, and piles of cannon balls can still be found. Some of the wreck's hull structures are also partially intact, buried under sand or ballast but sometimes exposed by the shifting sand. For someone who has never seen an ancient wreck site, I'd recommend taking a trip to one of the popular sites, such as the *El Infante*. They are a good example of what a wreck looks like after a few hundred years. And there's still the chance you might find some Spanish treasure! Source: 54, 56, 67.

12. *HMS Fowey* — British warship, 20 guns (Colledge says a 5th-rate, 44 guns, 709 tons, built 1744), Captain Francis Drake. Wrecked June 26, 1748. She wrecked on a reef and was later lifted off by the tide, and she drifted five miles north to Legare Anchorage. A captured Spanish vessel also wrecked at the same time. The crews and all treasure

Figure 22: Treasure and artifacts from the *San Pedro* (1733). BOB WELLER.

were saved and brought to shore. Fowey Rocks were named after this vessel. Gerald Klien found her in 1979 in Biscayne National Park, and a legal battle ensued over the rights to the wreck. The National Park Service ended up with all rights. Source: 16, 54, 78.

13. *Dolphin* — British ship, Captain Bagat, bound for North Carolina. Had been captured by the Spanish but soon after wrecked near Cape Florida in 1748. Source: 54.

14. *Howlet* — Merchant vessel of Boston. Went ashore near Cape Florida in 1748. All except one slave were killed by the Indians. Source: 54.

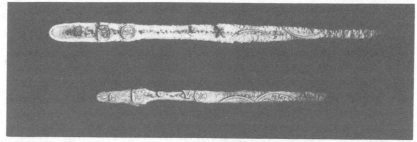

Figure 23: Two gold finger bars recovered from 1733 Plate Fleet wrecks. The one on the left is 6 ¾" long, is dated 1659, and shows the Mexican mint mark. The one on the right is 9¾" long and also has the Mexican mint mark. CHRISTIE'S, NEW YORK.

15. *Alexander* — British merchantman, Captain Johnson, from Jamaica bound for London. Lost on the Masters, west of Cape Florida, in 1763. Source: 54.

16. *Ledbury* — British snow (a snow and a brig are basically the same), Captain John Lorain, from Jamaica bound for Bristol. Lost near Elliot Key, either Aug. 30 or Oct. 29, 1769. Ledbury Reef was named after this vessel. Source: 57, 54.

17. *HMS Carysford* or *Carysfort* — British naval frigate, 20 guns. Ran aground, Oct. 23, 1770, on a reef now known as Carysfort Reef. There was an *HMS Carysfort* listed at this time (6th-rate, 28 guns), but she remained in service until sold in 1813. Most likely the *Carysfort* ran aground, but was later gotten off and continued to sail for many years. Source: 16, 24.

18. *El Nauva Victoriosa* — Spanish nao, Captain Joseph Varán, had left Cadiz, Nov. 3, 1770, bound for Vera Cruz, wrecked in 1771, at the head of the Florida Keys. She hit a reef in ten feet of water. The crew, most of the treasure, and the small arms were taken off the next day by another ship of the fleet. She eventually came off the reef and settled in the sand to the west of the reef. She now lies in a sand pocket, in 25 feet of water, southeast of Caesars Creek at about Lat. 25-19-30, Long. 80-10-30. There is a shallow reef here, and the sand pocket is on the southwest corner of a shoal, just northeast of the reef. This wreck was salvaged in the 1960s and 1970s, and became known as the "Pillar Dollar Wreck." Pillar dollars dated 1770 can still be found. Source: 54, 56, 100 (Frederick, Carl. "New Clues to the Pillar Dollar Wreck," July 1977).

19. *Maria Beckford* — British merchantman, Captain Boyd. Wrecked at Cape Florida in 1772. A total loss. Source: 54.

20. *Mill* — Ship, Captain Hays, from Jamaica bound for Boston in

ballast. A vessel reported seeing a ship ashore at Cape Florida without her main and mizzen mast, April 23, 1774, and believed it was the *Mill*. Unknown if salvaged. Source: 54.

21. *Montague* — British merchantman, Captain Pickles, from Jamaica bound for Liverpool. Wrecked at Cape Florida in 1774. Crew and 30 hogsheads of sugar saved. Source: 54.

22. *Diana* — British ship, Captain Buckley, from Jamaica bound for Rhode Island. Wrecked at Cape Florida in 1774. Crew saved. Ship and cargo a total loss. Source: 54.

23. *Earl of Bute* — British naval ship, 26 guns, Commander Benjamin Hill. Foundered in the Gulf of Florida, early 1777. Source: 13 (Vol. 4).

24. *Mary* — British ship, Captain Hoincastte, from Jamaica bound for London. Lost off Cape Florida, December 1778, while being chased by two American privateers. Source: 54.

25. *Noble Bounty* — British ship, Captain Herbert, from Jamaica bound for London. Wrecked on Cape Florida Reef in 1787. Crew saved by the vessel *Friendship*. Source: 54.

26. *Hazard* — British merchantman, Captain New, from Honduras bound for London. Wrecked near Cape Florida in 1789. Crew saved. A total loss. Source: 54.

27. *Apollo* — Ship, Captain Cragg. Was seen wrecked at Cape Florida on Aug. 10, 1790. Unknown if salvaged. Source: 54.

28. *Edmund & George* — Ship, Captain Rainy. Was seen wrecked at Cape Florida at the same time as the *Apollo*, Aug. 19, 1790. Source: 54.

29. Unknown ship — The ship *Trelawney Planter* reported seeing a ship on Carysfort Reef, Aug. 14, 1792, with several wrecking vessels nearby. Source: 54.

30. *Speedwell* — British merchantman, Captain Brownlow, from Honduras bound for Charleston. Wrecked on Carysfort Reef, Aug. 28, 1796. Crew and ship's materials saved. Source: 54.

31. *Bermuda* — British naval brig-sloop, 14 12-pounder carronades, 170 tons, built in 1795, 80' x 24', Commander Thomas Maxtone. Foundered in the Gulf of Florida, September 1796. All hands lost. Source: 16, 35, 36.

32. *Hope* — Brig, Captain West, from Havana bound for America. Lost near Cape Florida in 1796. Source: 54.

33. Spanish sloop — This sloop had been captured by a New Providence privateer. Wrecked on Nov. 12, 1799, one hour from Key Largo. Crew taken off by a privateer under Captain Watkins. Source: 32.

1800

34. *Fly* — British naval sloop, 18 guns (believe six-pounders), 369 tons, built in 1804, 106' x 28' Captain Pownole Pellew. Wrecked on Carysfort Reef, March 2, 1805, due to an error on the chart. All 121 on board saved. Source: 16, 35, 36.

35. *Rattler* — British merchantman, Captain Balmond, from Honduras bound for London. Wrecked on Carysfort Reef in 1805. Very little cargo saved. Source: 54.

36. *Ohio* — American merchantman, Captain Hall, from Jamaica bound for New York. Wrecked near Cape Florida, Jan. 15, 1808. Crew and most of the cargo saved. Source: 54.

37. *Araucana* — Spanish ship, Captain Benito de la Rigada, from Havana bound for Spain with mail. Wrecked on Elliot Key during a hurricane, Oct. 26, 1811. Crew got ashore on the key and were later saved. Source: 54.

38. *Highlander* — British merchantman, Captain Cuthbert, from Jamaica bound for London. Wrecked on Carysfort Reef, July 15, 1812. Crew saved by ship *Hopewell*. Source: 54.

39. *Juno* — American ship, Captain Pratt, from New Orleans bound for Boston. Wrecked on Carysfort Reef, June 16, 1812. Source: 54.

40. *Racer* — British naval schooner (formerly the *Independence,* an American privateer captured in 1812), twelve 12-pounder carronades and two six-pounder, 250 tons, 93.5' x 25'. Under the command of Lieutenant H.F.Y. Pogson. Wrecked in the Gulf of Florida, Oct. 10, 1814. All 178 on board saved. Source: 16, 35, 36.

41. Unknown ship — Reported aground on Carysfort Reef, Dec. 6, 1815. Unknown if salvaged. Source: 54.

42. *Martha Brae* — From Jamaica bound for Whitehaven, Captain Farish. Wrecked near Cape Florida in 1816. Total loss. Two lives lost. Source: 54.

43. *Three Sisters* — Ship, of New York, Captain Arnington, from New

York bound for New Orleans. Wrecked on Carysfort Reef, Aug. 30, 1816. Crew saved. Source: 54.

44. *Three Sisters* — British ship, of Nassau, from New York bound for Nassau. Wrecked on Carysfort Reef in 1816. Possibly the same vessel as above. Source: 54.

45. Ship and a brig — The ship *Brandt* arrived at New York, June 3, 1817, and reported seeing a ship and a brig aground on Carysfort Reef, with eight wrecking vessels around them. Source: 54.

46. *Despatch* — American merchantman, Captain Field, from Havana bound for Charleston. Wrecked on Carysfort Reef, June 15, 1817. Crew and cargo saved. Source: 54.

47. *Unity* — British ship, Captain Lambourn, from Jamaica bound for London. Wrecked on Carysfort Reef, Aug. 13, 1817. She previously saved a crew from a wrecked ship and both crews were picked up by a passing ship. Source: 54.

48. *Eliza* — Ship, Captain Murphey, from Jamaica bound for Philadelphia. Wrecked on Carysfort Reef in 1818. Crew and six boxes of dollars saved. Source: 54.

49. *Modeste* — French ship, Captain D'Barron. Wrecked at Key Largo, May 21, 1819. Source: 54.

50. Unknown vessel — Reported seen aground on Carysfort Reef, Aug. 12, 1819, with wreckers nearby. Source: 54.

51. *General Jackson* — American ship, Captain Taylor, from New Orleans bound for Rotterdam. Wrecked on Cape Florida in 1819. Most cargo saved. Source: 54.

52. Unknown ship — At the end of February, 1821, a ship was seen on Carysfort Reef wrecked and dismasted. Source: 54.

53. *Pearl* — British merchantman, Captain Johnson, from Havana bound for Gibraltar. Lost near Cape Florida, March 8, 1821. Some lives lost. Source: 54.

54. Three vessels — On April 25, 1822, a full-rigged brig was reported wrecked on Carysfort Reef. Two other brigs were also reported wrecked on Ledbury Reef with wreckers assisting. Source: 54.

55. Unknown ship — A ship with plain yellow sides was reported

wrecked on Carysfort Reef, May 19, 1822. Source: 54.

56. *USS Alligator* — Naval schooner, 12 guns (six-pounders), 198 tons, 86' x 24'7" x 10'4", built in 1820 at Boston Navy Yard. Wrecked on what is now called Alligator Reef, Nov. 19, 1822, only a few hundred feet from the current lighthouse. She was returning from a recent battle with pirates in a bay 40 to 50 miles from Mantanzas, Cuba, in which her commander, Lieutenant Allen, was killed. After three days on the reef, she was ordered by her new commander, Lieutenant J.M. Dale, to be blown up. The crew left in the brig *Ann Maria*. Key West was originally called "Allentown" in honor of Allen. (See Figure 24). Source: 14, 24, 28, 67.

Figure 24: U.S. schooner *Alligator*, wrecked in 1822. U.S. NAVAL HISTORICAL CENTER.

57. *George III* — British merchantman, Captain Danning, from Honduras bound for Dublin. Wrecked on Carysfort Reef, Feb. 24, 1824. Crew saved. Total loss. Source: 54.

58. Unknown vessel — A long black vessel was reported wrecked on a reef, with her masts cut down, March 26, 1824, near Caesar Creek. Source: 54.

59. American brig — A brig, deeply laden, was seen on Aug. 5, 1824, wrecked on the southwest end of Carysfort Reef, with wreckers alongside her. Source: 54.

60. *Point-a-Petre* — French ship, from New Orleans bound for Bordeaux. Wrecked on Carysfort Reef, Feb. 7, 1825. Crew and cargo saved. Source: 54, 97 (Dodd, Dorothy, "The Wrecking Business on the

Florida Reef, 1822-1860." Vol. XXII, April 1944, No.4, pp. 171-199).

61. *Revenge* — French brig, from Campeche bound for France with cochineal and logwood. Went on a reef approximately three miles from Caesars Creek and bilged, early September 1825. Crew abandoned her. Jacob Houseman, one of Florida's early settlers, salvaged her and sold the goods at St. Augustine. He was later accused of illegally salvaging the vessel, and the issue went to court. Source: 95 (Schene, Michael G., "Indian Key." No. XXXVI, 1976, pp. 3-21).

62. *Orleans* — Ship, of the Heron's Line, 219 tons, Master J. Grover, from Santiago de Cuba bound for Philadelphia. Lost on Carysfort Reef, May 5, 1826. Source: 19.

63. *Ellen* — Ship, 266 tons, from Havana bound for Philadelphia. Lost on the Florida Reef, Dec. 6, 1826. Source: 19.

64. *Guerrero* — Spanish brig (slaver), 18 guns. Chased onto Carysfort Reef by the British schooner *Nimble*, Dec. 20, 1827. On board were 561 slaves and a crew of 90. Three wrecking vessels arrived to help. Two were seized by the Spanish and forced to sail to Havana with 250 of the slaves. The wrecking vessel *Splendid* rescued 121 slaves and took them to Key West. Of the remaining slaves, 163 lost their lives. Source: 38, 77.

65. *Correrro* (one source says *Curreo No. 1*) — Spanish brig, Captain Qureau, bound for Spain. Wrecked on Carysfort Reef and bilged, April 2, 1829. Crew and cargo of treasure saved. Source: 70, 97 (Hammond, E.A., "Wreckers and Wrecking on the Florida Reef, 1829-1832." Vol. XLI No. 3, Jan. 1963, pp. 239-273).

66. *Marcella* or *Marcelly* — British brig, Captain Monroe, from New Orleans bound for Greenock, Scotland, with cotton. Wrecked near Cape Florida, Feb. 15, 1831. Vessel lost. Crew and cargo saved. Source: 70, 97 (Ibid).

67. *Amulet* — Ship, Captain Winsor, from Boston bound for New Orleans with furniture, dry goods, shoes, fish, and other cargo. Wrecked on Pickles Reef, March 22, 1831. Vessel lost. Some cargo saved. Source: 37, 70.

68. *Waverly* — Schooner, of New York, Captain Sellers, from New Iberia bound for New York with sugar. Wrecked near Cape Florida Light, March 24 or 27, 1831. Cargo saved. Source: 70, 97 (Hammond, E.A."Wreckers and Wrecking on the Florida Reef, 1829-1832." Vol. XLI No. 3, January 1963, pp. 239-273.

69. *Doris* — Brig, from Matanzas bound for Portland, Maine with 300 hogshead of molasses. Wrecked on Carysfort Reef, Nov. 16, 1831. Though damaged, most cargo saved. Wreckers awarded $2,145. Source: 95 (Diddle, Albert W. "The Adjudication of Shipwrecking in Florida in 1831." Vol.VI, 1946, pp 44-49).

70. *Lavinia* — Ship, one of the Collins packets, 310 tons, from Vera Cruz. Wrecked on Colorado's Reef, February 1832. Note: I've seen mention of a reef near Cape Florida called Colorado Reef during the 19th century, though the Coloradoes, where the *Lavinia* possibly wrecked, is off Cuba. Source: 19.

71. *Kentucky* — Ship, of the Holmes Line, New York, 418 tons, Captain E.S. Dennison. Lost on the Florida Reef, Oct. 29, 1832. Three lives lost. Source: 19.

72. *Bahama* — Schooner. Reported in newspaper, Jan. 8, 1835, to have gone ashore on Carysfort Reef. Unknown if salvaged. Source: 37.

73. *Seadrift* — American brig, Captain Hoyt, from New York bound for Mobile with an assorted cargo. Wrecked on Carysfort Reef during a hurricane, Sept. 15, 1835, and later washed ashore on Key Largo, high and dry. Source: 54.

74. *Laura* — Schooner. Reported in newspaper, Sept. 18, 1835, as having wrecked on Carysfort Reef. Unknown if salvaged. Source: 37.

75. *Maria* — Ship. Reported in newspaper, Oct. 3, 1835, as having wrecked on Carysfort Reef. Unknown if salvaged. Source: 37.

76. *Grecian* — Bark. Reported in newspaper, Feb. 27, 1836, as having gone ashore on Carysfort Reef. Unknown if salvaged. Source: 37.

77. *Olive Branch* — Schooner. Reported in newspaper, Feb. 27, 1836, to have been lost off Cape Florida. Source: 37.

78. *Theophilus* — Schooner. Reported in newspaper, Feb. 27, 1836, to have wrecked on Alligator Reef. Unknown if salvaged. Source: 37.

79. *Norman* — Ship. Reported in newspaper, May 7, 1836, to have gone ashore on Conch Reef. Unknown if salvaged. Source: 37.

80. *Agenora* — Brig, from Mobile bound for Liverpool with cotton. Abandoned in April 1836 with eight feet of water in her hold on Carysfort Reef. Source: 96 (April 28, 1836).

81. *Dorothy Foster* — British barque, Captain Lilly or Tilly, from Old Harbor, Jamaica, bound for London with rum, sugar, and coffee. Lost on Pickles Reef, Aug. 9, 1836. Thirty hogsheads of sugar and 180 of rum were saved. Source: 96 (Sept. 13, 1836).

82. *Mary* — Schooner, of Key Vaccas, 15 tons. Attacked by Indians while at anchor in Key Tavernier Creek, Oct. 8, 1836. Crew escaped in a small boat to Indian Key, while dodging bullets, and Indians burned the schooner. Source: 96 (Nov. 11, 1836).

83. *Louisiana* — Brig, eight days out from New Orleans bound for Norfolk. Wrecked on the south point of Carysfort Reef, Nov. 2, 1836. Source: 96 (Nov. 1836).

84. *Ajax* — Ship, Captain Charles Hein (believed to be Captain Charles A. Heirn), 627 tons, built in 1826 at Kensington, Pa., 132.8' x 32', from New York bound for Mobile with an assorted cargo. Struck on Carysfort Reef, Nov. 14, 1836, and could not be gotten off. Jacob Houseman, one of the salvors, was accused by Captain Hein of stealing his cargo. Source: 95 (Schene, Michael. "Indian Key." No. XXXVI, 1976, pp. 3-21), 97 (Dodd, Dorothy. "The Wrecking Business on the Florida Reef, 1822-1860," Vol. XXII, April 1944, No.4, pp. 171-199), 105.

85. *Lowell* — Brig, from Charleston bound for New Orleans. Wrecked on the Florida Reef, November 1836. Crew saved. Source: 96 (Nov. 30, 1836).

86. Schooner — Found capsized in Gulf Stream, April 3, 1837, off Cape Florida. Vessel lost. Wreckers awarded $1,705. Source: 37.

87. *Rosalina* — Bark, from Jamaica bound for London with rum, sugar, and mahogany. Wrecked on Pickles Reef, June 28, 1837. Vessel lost. Wreckers awarded $2,577. Source: 37.

88. *Pee Dee* — Schooner. Wrecked on Biscayne Key, Nov. 4, 1837, with a cargo of iron and coffee. Vessel lost. Wreckers awarded $1,384. Source: 37.

89. *Hebrus* — Brig, from Havana bound for Isle of Guernsey with coffee and sugar. Wrecked on Pickles Reef, March 10, 1838. Vessel lost. Wreckers awarded $1,404. Source: 37.

90. *Export* (brig) and Unknown ship — The *Export* (believed to be 246 tons, of Salem, built in 1824 at Bath, 90'9" x 24'10" x 12'5"), from Mantanzas bound for Boston with sugar. Both these vessels wrecked during the hurricane of Sept. 7, 1838, off Caesars Creek.

Approximately 300 boxes of sugar were saved from the *Export*. Wreckers awarded $1,990. Source: 6, 37, 86 (Summer/Fall 1986, reprinted from Niles National Register, Vol. 55-56, Oct. 13, 1838, p. 103).

91. *Caroline* — Schooner, of Key West. Sank during the hurricane of Sept. 7, 1838. She was at anchor at Caesars Creek when her lines parted and she hit a reef, killing Captain Williams and all seven of the crew. Source: 86 (Ibid).

92. Unknown ship (possibly the *Thracian*) — Wrecked during the September 1838 hurricane (believed to be near the *Caroline*). The wreck was investigated by the revenue cutter *Madison*, which concluded she was a new Boston-built ship. The cargo included a locomotive engine named *Camden*, directed to Hyde & Comstock, New Orleans. Also on board were assorted goods, bar, tire iron, a carriage, saddles and harness, rails and machinery. Source: 86 (Ibid).

93. *Caledonia* — Schooner, from Havana bound for New Orleans with sugar, coffee, and cigars. Became a total loss on the Colorados (near Cape Florida), Sept. 8, 1838. All hands feared lost. Source: 86 (Ibid).

94. *Wilmington* — Sidewheel steamer, 229 tons, built in 1829 at Philadelphia, Captain John Gallagher, from Mobile bound for Philadelphia. Stranded in Biscayne Bay, Dec. 10, 1838. (Cutler says she wrecked on Nov. 10, 1838, 60 miles north of Cape Florida.) Source: 19, 52.

95. *Claudine* — Bark. Wrecked on the Florida Reef, March 3, 1841. Vessel lost. Wreckers awarded $351. Source: 37.

96. *Manchester* — Ship. Lost on Florida Reef, April 3, 1841. Wreckers awarded $575. Source: 37.

97. *Herald* — Ship, from Vera Cruz, believed to have a cargo of copper. Wrecked on Ledbury Reef, Dec. 6, 1842. Vessel lost. Wreckers awarded 1/3 of the cargo. Source: 37.

98. *Charles Fifth* — Brig, from Havana bound for Antwerp with sugar, cigars, tobacco, and other cargo. Wrecked on Carysfort Reef, Dec. 7, 1842. Vessel lost. Wreckers awarded $2,396. Source: 37.

99. *Hayne* — Brig, from Charleston bound for Havana with rice. Wrecked five miles south-southeast of Cape Florida, March 15, 1845. Vessel lost. Wreckers awarded $1,000. Source: 37.

100. *Rienzi* — Ship, of the Post Line, New York, 327 tons, Master S.

Clark, from New York bound for New Orleans with an assorted cargo. Wrecked on Carysfort Reef (one source says Pickles Reef), May 15, 1845. Vessel lost. Wreckers awarded $617. Source: 19. 37.

101. *Newark* — Ship, from Mobile bound for New York with cotton. Wrecked on Pickles Reef, June 6, 1845. Vessel lost. Wreckers awarded $4,604. Source: 37.

102. *Feronia* — Bark, from Jamaica bound for London with sugar and rum. Wrecked on Conch Reef, Sept. 8, 1845. Vessel lost. Wreckers awarded $3,200. Source: 37.

103. *Telumah* — Ship, believed to be 346 tons, from Liverpool bound for Havana with iron in bars, crockery, hardware, sugar boilers, machinery, and other cargo. Wrecked on Biscayne Reef on Nov. 18, 1845. Vessel lost. Wreckers awarded $11,931. Source: 37, 70.

104. *Samuel Young* — Type unknown, of Bangor, from Jacksonville bound for Texas with lumber. Went ashore on the Florida Reef, January 1846. Valued at $87,000. Unknown if salvaged. Source: 14.

105. *York* — Scottish vessel, type unknown, of Glasgow, from New Orleans bound for Liverpool with cotton and other goods. Went ashore on Carysfort Reef, March 1846. Valued at $95,000. Salvage amount $13,500. Source: 14.

106. *Frances* — Type unknown, from Jamaica bound for New York with pimento. Went ashore on Alligator Reef, March 1846. Unknown if salvaged. Source: 14.

107. *Linedora* — Spanish vessel, type unknown, from Havana. Went ashore on Carysfort Reef, October 1846. Valued at $80,000. Wreckers assisted, but the vessel was lost. Source: 14.

108. *Yucatan* — Bark, from New Orleans bound for Liverpool with cotton, lard, pork, flour, and other cargo. Wrecked on French Reef, April 20, 1847. Vessel lost. Wreckers awarded $17,521. Source: 37.

109. *Elizabeth* — Schooner, from Manzanillo bound for Quebec with sugar, honey, and lignumvitae. Wrecked on Florida Reef, June 12, 1847. Vessel lost. Wreckers awarded $984. Source: 37.

110. *Minerva* — Schooner, from Jacksonville bound for Newport. Went ashore on Carysfort Reef, Aug. 16, 1847. Source: 14.

111. *Gilbert Hatfield* — Brig, 200 tons, from New York bound for

Mobile. Wrecked on the Florida Reef, Oct. 29, 1847. Unknown if salvaged. Source: 14.

112. *Samuel Roberts* — Schooner, 95 tons, from Attakapsas bound for New York. Wrecked on the Florida Reef, Nov. 1, 1847. Unknown if salvaged. Source: 14.

113. *Brewster* — Ship, of Boston, 696 tons, Captain Thatcher, from New Orleans bound for Boston with cotton, hemp, lard, and sugar. Wrecked on Fowey Rocks, March 6 or 16, 1848. Vessel lost. Wreckers awarded $4,098 (one source says $17,600, the value of ship and cargo $100,000). Source: 14, 37.

114. *Mandarin* — Schooner, from Richmond bound for New Orleans. Wrecked on Elbow Reef, March 7, 1848. Unknown if salvaged. Source: 14.

115. *Brutus* — Ship, from New Orleans bound for Boston. Went ashore on the Florida Reef, March 25, 1848. Unknown if salvaged. Source: 14.

116. *Taglioni* — Ship, of Boston, 798 tons, Captain Rodgers, from Havre bound for New Orleans with 28 passengers and an assorted cargo. Wrecked on Carysfort Reef, three miles from the Lightship, April 7, 1848. Some cargo saved. Wreckers awarded $4,798. Vessel and cargo valued at $60,000. Source: 14, 37.

117. *Kestrel* — Irish ship, of Belfast, Captain Turner, from New Orleans bound for Liverpool. Went ashore at Cape Florida, August 1848, and was condemned. Vessel and cargo valued at $80,000. Wreckers awarded $13,800. Source: 14.

118. *Petrus* — French brig, Captain Lamartine, from Cuba bound for France. Lost near Cape Florida, September 1848. Vessel and cargo valued at $20,000. Wreckers awarded $943. Source: 14.

119. *Isabella Reed* — Brig, believed to be 159 tons, from New Orleans bound for Savannah with molasses, whiskey, sugar, and rope. Wrecked on Conch Reef, Feb. 14, 1850. Vessel lost. Wreckers awarded $2,980. Source: 19, 37.

120. *Pilita* — Brig, with a cargo of sugar, cigars, and other goods. Found wrecked on Carysfort Reef with no crew, May 2, 1851. Wreckers awarded $2,492. Source: 37.

121. *Merchant* — U.S. mail schooner, from Charleston bound for Key

West and Havana. Wrecked on Pacific Shoal, Nov. 28, 1851. Cargo and $8,000 in coins were saved. Wreckers awarded $827. Source: 99 (Dec. 19, 1851).

122. *Matthew Von Bree* — Belgian bark, from Havana bound for New York with 2,500 boxes of sugar. Wrecked on Yucatan Reef (a small shoal near the east end of Alligator Reef), July 2, 1852. Wreckers saved 900 to 1000 boxes and were awarded $7,235. Source: 37, 99 (July 19, 1852).

123. *Woodside* — Ship, from Mobile bound for Rochefort with spars and other timber. Wrecked on Ledbury Reef, Dec. 31, 1852. Vessel lost. Wreckers awarded $649. Source: 37.

124. *Palo Alto* — Brig, of Charleston, bound for Mantanzas with molasses. Sunk by the French bark *Nevstine* between Cape Florida and Gun Key, Dec. 4, 1853. Source: 99 (Dec. 17, 1853).

125. *Elizabeth Bruce* — Ship, 586 tons, from Liverpool bound for Mobile with crockery, ironware, and other cargo. Wrecked on Elbow Reef (one source says near Carysfort Light), Jan. 11 or 16, 1854. Some cargo saved. Wreckers awarded $3,387. Source: 37, 99 (Jan. 26, 1854).

126. *Meteor* — Brig, of St. John, N.B., from Cienfuegos. Wrecked on Pickles Reef, Jan. 25, 1854. A total loss. Vessel valued at $20,000 and cargo at $25,000. Source: 99 (Feb. 13, 1854).

127. *Pauline* — Schooner, from Attakapar bound for New York with sugar and molasses. Wrecked on Pickles Reef, April 5, 1854. A total loss. Crew saved. Source: 99 (April 26 and May 1, 1854).

128. *Sterling* — Brig, of Boston, from Mantanzas bound for Montreal. Went ashore on Conch Reef, May 10, 1854. A total loss. Source: 99 (May 27, 1854).

129. Unknown full rigged ship — Reported ashore on Carysfort Reef by the schooner *Albatross*. She was not salvageable, and wreckers were nearby. Source: 99 (Sept. 7, 1854).

130. *Mayflower* — Ship. Reported in newspaper, Nov. 6, 1855, to have wrecked on Carysfort Reef. Unknown if salvaged. Source: 37.

131. *Mariner* — Ship, of Boston, from Liverpool bound for New Orleans with salt. Wrecked on French Reef (one source says Pickles Reef), March 12 or 19, 1856. Vessel lost. Wreckers awarded $3,651.

Source: 37, 99 (March 29, 1856).

132. *Emigrant* — Bark, from New Orleans bound for Liverpool with cotton and oak plank. Wrecked on Alligator Reef, Aug. 22, 1856. Vessel lost. Wreckers awarded $13,863. Source: 37.

133. *Crown* — British ship, from New Orleans bound for Liverpool with 2,916 bales of cotton, corn, and wheat. Went aground on Ajax Reef, Jan. 22, 1857. Vessel lost. A wrecking vessel caught fire and sank attempting to salvage her cargo. Wreckers awarded $23,050. Source: 24, 37, 99 (Jan. 28, 1857).

134. *Helen E. Booker* — Ship, of Georgetown, Maine, 898 tons, built in 1856 at Georgetown, 167'3" x 34'1" x 34'1", Captain Olis, from Cardiff bound for New Orleans with 1,105 tons of railroad iron. Struck on Elbow Key (one source says Carysfort Reef), May 1, 1857, at 4 p.m. Some cargo saved. Wreckers awarded $21,050. Source: 6, 37, 99 (May 18, 1857).

135. *Cynasure* — Brig, of Boston, from Rockland with lime. Went ashore near Elliot Key, and had been on fire since May 12, 1857. Source: 99 (June 11, 1857).

136. *Riversmith* — Ship, from Liverpool bound for New Orleans with salt. Went ashore and bilged at Caesars Creek (one source says Carysfort Reef), Feb. 9, 1858. Wreckers awarded $1,046. Source: 37, 99 (Feb. 24, 1858).

137. *Agamemnon* — British ship, of Liverpool, from New Orleans bound for Liverpool with flour, lard, and staves. Ran ashore on Grecian Shoals (one source says Yucatan Reef), Feb. 12, 1858. 3,000 barrels of flour were saved, and the rest, though wet, were also to be saved. Wreckers awarded $10,872. Source: 37, 99 (March 2, 1858).

138. *Malcolm* — Scottish bark, Captain Brockbank, from Rio de la Hache bound for Columbia with divi-divi and fustic (types of dyewood.) Ran ashore on French Reef and bilged, Sept. 11, 1858. Some cargo saved. Source: 99 (Oct. 4, 1858).

139. *Mini* — German bark, of Bremen, from Galveston bound for Amsterdam with cotton. Went aground on Pickles Reef and bilged, Jan. 28 or 29, 1859. Key West reported 725 bales saved, though 600 were damaged. Wreckers awarded $13,420. Source: 37, 99 (Feb. 15 and March 1, 1859).

140. *Nathan Hanan* — Ship, of Boston, from Boston bound for New

Orleans with ice, furniture, boots, and shoes. Wrecked on Brewster Reef (one source says she ran ashore at Cape Florida and bilged), Feb. 21 or March 2, 1859. Some furniture, boots, and shoes saved. Wreckers awarded $1,801. Source: 37, 99 (March 14 and 15, 1859).

141. *Indian Hunter* — Ship, of Newcastle, Maine, Captain Austin, from Mobile bound for Liverpool with 3,700 bales of cotton. Ran onto French Reef and bilged, June 25, 1859. Most cargo saved. Wreckers awarded $33,852. Source: 37, 99 (July 13, 1859).

142. *Ney* — Schooner. Reported in newspaper, July 16, 1859, to have wrecked on Pickles Reef. Unknown if salvaged. Source: 37.

143. *Samuel Lawrence* — Believed to be a ship of 1,050 tons. Reported in newspaper, Jan. 7, 1860, to have wrecked on Grecian Shoal. Unknown if salvaged. Source: 37.

144. *J.W. Rowland* — Brig. Reported in newspaper, January 1860, to have wrecked on Pickles Reef. Unknown if salvaged. Source: 37.

145. *Horace* — Bark, from Pensacola bound for Montevideo with lumber. Wrecked on Pickles Reef, Dec. 2, 1860. Vessel lost. Wreckers awarded $576. Source: 37.

See Civil War section for Section 4 wrecks during that period.

146. *Dahlia* — Bark, from Jamaica bound for London with rum, ginger, hides, and pimento. Wrecked on Pickles Reef, May 11, 1865. Vessel lost. Wreckers awarded $3,210. Source: 37.

147. *Waltham* — Bark, (believed to be 466 tons, built in 1851 at Richmond, Maine, 130'4" x 27'11" x 13'11"), from New Orleans bound for Boston with cotton, wool, and hides. Wrecked at Matecumbe Key, Oct. 23, 1865. Vessel lost. Wreckers awarded $18,196. Source: 6, 37.

148. *Caroline Nesmith* — Ship, (believed to be 832 tons, built in 1848 at Bath, 157'3" x 34' x 17'), from Mobile bound for Liverpool with 2,500 bales of cotton. Wrecked on Carysfort Reef, Oct. 23, 1865. Vessel lost. Wreckers awarded $60,565. Source: 6, 37.

149. *Isabel* — Bark. Wrecked on Triumph Reef, March 11, 1866, with a cargo of rum, sugar, ginger, hides, and other goods. Vessel lost. Wreckers awarded $7,561. Source: 37.

150. *Tonawanda* (formerly *USS Arkansas*) — Steamer, 752 tons, built in 1863 at Philadelphia, from Boston bound for Havana.

Stranded on Grecian Shoals (one source says Elbow Reef), March 28, 1866. Vessel lost. Wreckers awarded $5,166. Source: 37, 52.

151. *Joseph A. Davis* — Bark, Captain Wild, from Cienfuegos bound for New York or Boston with sugar. Wrecked on Grecian Shoals, July 5, 1866. Vessel lost. Some cargo saved. Wreckers awarded $5,200. Source: 37, 99 (Aug. 1, 1866).

152. *Scandinavia* — Brig, from Pensacola bound for Queenstown with timber. Wrecked on Conch Reef, March 18, 1867. Vessel lost. Wreckers awarded $1,281. Source: 37.

153. *Letter Be* — Brig, from St. Johns, New Brunswick, bound for Havana with nails. Wrecked at Ceasars Creek, Oct. 26, 1867. Vessel lost. Wreckers awarded $791. Source: 37.

154. *Oracle* — Bark, from Mexico bound for Liverpool with mahogany. Wrecked on Conch Reef, July 4, 186?. Vessel lost. Wreckers awarded $1,391. Source: 37.

155. *Star* — British bark, from Calabrian bound for Falmouth with sugar. Went ashore and bilged on Conch Reef, March 20, 1870. Note: This vessel is also listed as wrecked at Conch Key (see Section 3 #139). Source: 37, 99 (March 24, 1870).

156. *Tomas de Resa* — Bark, from New Orleans bound for Barcelona with staves. Wrecked on Turtle Reef, Oct. 6, 1870. Vessel lost. Wreckers awarded $490. Source: 37.

157. *Three Sisters* — Brig, of New Brunswick, Nova Scotia, from Nova Scotia bound for Cuba with lumber. Wrecked off Virginia Key in Bear Cut, Oct. 21, 1870 (one source says Oct. 13). Vessel lost. Wreckers awarded $94. She was later burned. Source: 37, 95 (Parks, Ava. "The Wreck of the Three Sisters." No. XXXI, 1971, pp. 19-28).

158. *Patriarca San José* — Brig, from Havana bound for Barcelona with furniture, hides, and coffee. Wrecked on Pickles Reef, Nov. 11, 1870. Vessel lost. Wreckers awarded $1,816. Source: 37.

159. *Aquillo* — Brig, from Havana with sugar. Wrecked at French Reef, March 16, 1871. Vessel lost. Wreckers awarded $4,197. Source: 37.

160. *Hermanos* — Spanish brig, from Havana with sugar. Reported from the Carysfort Reef Station to have wrecked, Aug. 4, 1872, at 1 A.M. Some cargo saved. Source: 14.

161. *Cornwall* — British bark, of London, 389 tons, Captain Coghlan, from Belize bound for London with mahogany, cedar, and 6,000 coconuts. Stranded on Ajax Reef, Dec. 30 or 31, 1873. Spars, rigging, and 75% of her cargo saved. Wreckers awarded $2,474. Source: 14, 37.

162. *Mississippi* — British ship (one source says a steamer), 1,370 tons, Captain Wrake, from Liverpool bound for New Orleans with general merchandise. Stranded on Brewsters Reef (one source says Fowey Rocks), April 20, 1874, between Cape Florida and Carysfort Reef, seven miles southeast by south of Cape Florida. 75% of cargo saved. Wreckers awarded $9,114. Source: 14, 37.

163. *Governor Troup* — Bark, 474 tons, Captain Langdon. Stranded on Davis Shoals, July 12, 1874. Cargo saved. Another source says she wrecked on Little Conch Reef, and was gotten off on the 14th, after her cargo was removed, which is more likely since she is listed in service after this time. Believed to formerly be a ship-rigged whaler of New Bedford, which was sold in 1872 to Boston interests and became a merchantman. Source: 14, 33.

164. *Evandale* — British ship, of Glasgow, 1,305 tons, built in 1863, Captain Hillhouse, from Pensacola bound for Liverpool with sawed timber and deals. Stranded on Carysfort Reef (one source says French Reef), Feb. 19, 1875. Sails and rigging saved. Wreckers awarded $880. Source: 14, 37.

165. *Florence Rogers* — Three-masted schooner, Captain Horton, from Milk River, Jamaica, bound for New York with logwood. Ran ashore Sept. 14, 1875, three miles west of Alligator Reef Light Station, on a bank near Indian Key, after losing all her sails during a storm Sept. 13. Unknown if salvaged. Source: 14.

166. *Zodiac* — Schooner. Burned off Elbow Cay, September 1875. A total loss. Source: 14.

167. *Isabella* — Schooner. Stranded on French Reef, September 1875. A partial loss. Source: 14.

168. *Deodueus* — British bark, Captain Peters, from Havana bound for Falmouth. Went ashore on Molasses Reef, Feb. 28, 1876, at 1:30 a.m., after mistaking that light for Carysfort Light. Source: 14.

169. *Charles A. Coulcoumb* — Schooner. Lost in the Florida Straits, April 1876. One life lost. Source: 14.

170. *Witch Hazel* — Schooner, (believed to be a three-masted schooner,

251 tons, built 1872 at Bath, 118.2' x 32.1' x 8.15'). Sprang a leak in the Florida Straits, July 1876. A partial loss. Source: 6, 14.

171. *Georges* — French brig, of Marseilles, 248 tons, built in 1861, Captain Napoleoni, from Carmen, Mexico, bound for Marseilles with logwood. Stranded on Molasses Reef, Oct. 5, 1876, at 11:45 A.M., approximately 14 miles east of the Alligator Reef Light Station. Sank in three fathoms, having mistaken the Alligator Reef Light for Carysfort Light. A total loss. Source: 14.

172. *W.R. Knighton* — Schooner, of New York, 157 tons, built in 1870, Captain Hagemon, from Roatan bound for New York with coconuts. Stranded 1-1/2 miles from Cape Florida Light during a storm, Oct. 18, 1876. Vessel valued at $8,000 ($5,040 loss), cargo at $5,000 ($3,150 loss). Source: 14.

173. *Godfrey Keebler* — Steamer. Wrecked on the Florida Reef (usually referred to as the area between Cape Florida and Carysfort Light), October 1876. A total loss. Source: 14.

174. *David Nichols* — Schooner. Wrecked on Fowey Rocks, October 1876. A total loss. Source: 14.

175. *Arakanapka* — Steamer. Wrecked only a few yards northeast of the Fowey Rock Lighthouse, in 1876. Workmen who were building the light watched in disbelief as the steamer's lights headed right for them. Source: 24.

176. *Vengern* — Swedish bark, from Pensacola bound for Europe with timber. Ran ashore on Pickles Reef, Feb. 11, 1877, at 11 P.M. On the 19th, she broke in two. A total loss. Source: 14.

177. *Suerige* — Swedish bark, of Gothenburg, 1,271 tons, built in 1859, Captain Wettersburg, from Pensacola bound for Liverpool with sawed timber. Stranded on Pickles Reef, Feb. 17, 1877. A total loss. Source: 14.

178. *Neto* — Schooner, 393 tons. Wrecked on the Florida Reef, March 1877. Note: A schooner *Veto*, Captain Kriel, from Pensacola with timber ran ashore on Conch Reef, March 27, 1877, around 2 A.M., and was gotten off on the 28th. It is likely the same vessel. Source: 14.

179. *Memphis* — Brig, of Madison, Nova Scotia, 167 tons, built in 1866, Captain Reynolds, from Mantanzas bound for Falmouth with sugar. Stranded on Conch Reef, April 15, 1877, at 5 P.M. Cargo saved. Note: An American brigantine *Memphis,* Captain Smith, from Cuba

bound for Falmouth with sugar, was listed as run ashore on Parkland Shoal near Alligator Light, April 4, 1877, at 5 P.M., and was gotten off the next day. Possibly repairs were made but the vessel wrecked again. Source: 14.

180. *Halcyon* — Bark, 625 tons, built in 1865 at Bath, 135.2' x 31.2' x 19.1'. Wrecked on the Florida Reef, July 1877. Cargo saved. Source: 6, 14.

181. *General Grant* — Schooner, 89 tons. Wrecked on the Florida Reef, August 1877. Source: 14.

182. *Merrie England* — British bark, of Whitly, 444 tons, from Havana bound for Falmouth with lumber. Stranded on Pickles Reef, Dec. 15, 1877, just southwest of the lighthouse. A total loss. Source: 14.

183. *Energia* — Bark, from New Orleans bound for Europe with grain. Wrecked on Molasses Reef, Dec. 30, 1877. Vessel lost. Wreckers awarded $799. Source: 37.

184. *Samuel H. Crawford* — Bark. Stranded near Pickles Reef, December 1877. A partial loss. Source: 14.

185. *Merri England* — Bark, with mahogany. Wrecked on French Reef, Jan. 16, 1878. Vessel lost. Wreckers awarded $239. Note: Possibly the same wreck as #182. Source: 37.

186. *Arratoon Apcar* — British steamer, of London, 1,500 tons, built in 1862, Captain Pottinger, from Liverpool bound for Havana with coal and iron. Stranded on Fowey Rocks, Feb. 17, 1878, 15 miles south of Lifesaving Station #5. A total loss. Source: 14.

187. *Bennington* — Schooner. Sprang a leak and stranded near Cape Florida, September 1878. A partial loss. Source: 14.

188. *Hope* — British bark, of London, 371 tons, built in 1868, Captain Scott, from Belize bound for Falmouth with mahogany and coconuts. Stranded on Pickles Reef, Oct. 22, 1878. Some cargo saved. Source: 14.

189. *Mary E. Riggs* — Ship, of Bath, 1,124 tons, built in 1864 at Phippsburg, Maine, 185' x 36'2" x 18'1", Captain Langdon, from New Orleans bound for Bremen with cotton. Stranded inside French Reef during a storm, April 23, 1879 at 10 P.M. Vessel lost. Wreckers awarded $44,371. Source: 6, 14, 37.

190. *Excelsior* — Bark, of Boston, 594 tons, built in 1864, Captain

Eddy, from Mantanzas bound for New York with sugar. Ran ashore on Grecian Shoals, May 23, 1879 (one source says 1880), bearing north-east one-half degree north of Carysfort Light, ten miles distant. Small amount of cargo saved. Wreckers awarded $1,386. Source: 14, 37.

191. *O.M. Remington* — Schooner, of Portland, Maine, 154 tons, built in 1870, Captain Pierce, from Roatan bound for Philadelphia with coconuts. Wrecked on Colorado Reef, Oct. 8, 1882, at 8 P.M. Source: 14.

192. *Northampton* — Ship, of Bath, 1,073 tons (also listed at 983 tons), built in 1852 at Bath, 175'6" x 34'9" x 17'4", Captain Gakan, from New Orleans bound for Liverpool with cotton and staves. Wrecked on Molasses Reef and bilged, May 24, 1883, at 8:20 P.M. Cargo valued at $86,000 ($38,000 loss). Vessel a total loss. Wreckers awarded $19,285. (See Figure 25). Source: 6, 14, 37.

Figure 25: Ship *Northampton*, wrecked in 1883. MAINE MARITIME MUSEUM.

193. *Slabdova* — Ship, from New Orleans with cotton. Wrecked on French Reef, March 16, 1887. Vessel lost. Wreckers awarded $52,882. Source: 37.

194. *Hannibal* — British ship, 1,142 tons, built in 1862, Captain Griffith, from Pensacola bound for Holland with lumber. Stranded on Elbow Reef, March 4, 1890, at 9:30 P.M. Unknown if salvaged. Source: 14.

195. *Edda* — Bark. Lost in the Florida Straits, May 10, 1891. Source: 9.

196. *Erl King* — Steamer, from Bremen bound for New Orleans with assorted cargo. Wrecked on Long Reef, Dec. 15, 1891. Vessel lost. Wreckers awarded $2,831. Later, much of her steel plate was salvaged during the war. Source: 37, 56.

197. *Oxford* — British steamer (iron), of Bristol, 1,892 tons, built in 1877, Captain James, from Mantanzas bound for Philadelphia with sugar. Stranded on Pickles Reef, Feb. 11, 1894, at 5:20 A.M., bearing northeast by north of Carysfort Light. She suffered extensive damage. Unknown if salvaged. Source: 14.

198. *Adelaide* — Schooner, of Key West, 10 tons, built in 1881, Captain Roberts. Capsized on Pickles Reef, Feb. 16, 1894. A total loss. Source: 14.

199. *Moonstone* — British steamer, from Portland bound for Tampico, Mexico, with coke. Wrecked near Carysfort Reef, Aug. 14, 1894, in daylight. Source: 24.

200. *Wandering Chief* — British bark, of Bariff, 418 tons, built in 1876, Captain Richards, from Belize bound for Havre with logwood. Stranded during a storm on Elbow Reef, Sept. 24, 1894, at 6:30 P.M. Vessel lost. Nine of 11 lives lost. Wreckers awarded $1,597. Source: 14, 37.

201. *Ingrid* — Norwegian bark, of Oslo, 1,312 tons, built in 1877, Captain Olsen, from Pensacola bound for Rio with lumber. Stranded on Fowey Rocks just north of the light, April 18, 1895, at 4:45 A.M. Vessel lost. She carried one million feet of lumber; 200,000 feet was salvaged soon after. The wreck was then sold for $1, and the salvor was able to remove three-fourths of the remaining 800,000 feet of lumber. Source: 14, 61.

202. *Clyde* — Steamer (iron), of Key West, 96 tons, built in 1862 at Chester, Pa., no cargo. Caught fire at Hawks Channel near Tavernier, Oct. 14, 1897. A total loss. Source: 14, 52.

1900

203. *South American* — Bark, with a cargo of mahogany. Wrecked on French Reef, Sept. 5, 1900. Vessel lost. Wreckers awarded $11,925. Source: 37.

204. *Veteran* — Schooner, of St. Augustine, 15 tons, built in 1894 at Georgiana, Fla., 51' x 14' x 5.9'. Foundered off Key Largo, Feb. 14, 1903. Source: 14.

205. *Sweetheart* — Schooner, 21 tons, built in 1899. Burned at Long Key, Dec. 1, 1904. Source: 14.

206. *Pargo* — Schooner, 25 tons, built in 1902. Burned at Cape Sable, Nov. 25, 1905. Source: 14.

207. *Mount Pleasant* — Gas vessel, 20 tons, built in 1902. Burned at Plantation Key, Dec. 12, 1905. Source: 14.

208. *Alicia* — Spanish steamer (steel), of Bilbao, built in 1883 at Glasgow, 334.5' x 37.7' x 25.9', from Liverpool bound for Havana. Wrecked on Ajax Reef, April 25, 1905, with a cargo of silks, laces, wines, liquors, household furnishings, pianos, and provisions. Wreckers from both Key West and the Bahamas (known as the Black Fleet) arrived at the scene. Tensions grew between both sides, and to avoid any bloodshed, a line was drawn down the middle of the ship, with one group working one side and the other the opposite side. Both sides helped themselves to the rum that was on board, and work slowed down considerably. The wreckers were awarded $17,690.80. She lies at approximate Lat. 25-24-50, Long. 80-07-45, in 25 feet of water, and many artifacts, especially bottles, have been found here. Source: 37, 38, 56, 80.

209. *St. Lucie* — Sidewheel steamer (steel), 165 tons, built in 1888 at Wilmington, 122' x 24' x 4.2', Captain Bravo. Foundered during a storm, Oct. 18, 1906, off Elliot Key. 21 lives lost. She was a famous Indian River steamer. Source: 14, 29.

210. *Joseph B. Thomas* — Four-masted schooner, of Thomaston, Maine, 1,564 tons, built in 1900 at Thomaston, 220' x 42.3' x 20.4', carrying 2,500 tons of gravel for the Key West railroad. Stranded on Fowey Rocks and bilged, March 21, 1909. Source: 14, 61, 80.

211. *Wanderer* — Sidewheel steamer, 84 tons, built in 1897 at Clinton, Iowa, 100' x 21' x 3.6'. Foundered at Money Key in Florida Bay, March 24, 1909. Source: 14.

212. *Alexander Jones* — St. Johns riverboat steamer (iron), 134 tons, built in 1877 at Baltimore, 106' x 23' x 11.2'. Stranded on Fowey Rocks, Oct. 14, 1910. Source: 14, 20.

213. *Star of the Sea* (formerly *Katie J. Barrett*) — Schooner, 967 tons, built in 1887 at Bath, 191.2' x 38' x 19'. Stranded on the Florida Reef, Oct. 26, 1911. Source: 14.

214. *Willie Wallace* — Schooner, of Jacksonville, 22 tons, built in 1879 at New Berlin, Fla., 51' x 17.3' x 6.1'. Stranded on the Florida Reef, Oct. 28, 1911. Source: 14.

215. *Isaac Collins* — Schooner, 98 tons, built in 1889 at Essex, Mass., 89' x 23.5' x 9.8'. Stranded in Biscayne Bay, Nov. 21, 1911. Source: 14.

216. *William R. Wilson* — Four-masted schooner, of Bath, 1,385 tons, built in 1908 at Bath, 214.3' x 41.2' x 21.8'. Stranded on Pickles Reef, Jan. 13, 1912. (See Figure 26). Source: 14, 80.

Figure 26: Schooner *William R. Wilson*, wrecked in 1912. MAINE MARITIME MUSEUM.

217. *Lugano* (or *Liguana*) — British steamer, (believed to be the 3,788-ton, 12-knot *Lugana*, built in 1882 at Barrow, England, of the Atlantic and Eastern Steamship Co. Ltd.), from either Liverpool or Glasgow bound for Havana with a general cargo including silks, wines, and other high-grade items. Wrecked on Long Reef, March 9, 1913, during a storm. The tug *Rescue* saved 116 passengers and crew. The British steamer *Howth Head* also wrecked at Long Reef at the same time, but was gotten off. Over 75 wrecking vessels worked on her for more than a month. Most cargo saved. Source: 14, 90 (March 22, 1913), 98 (March 10, 1913).

218. *Venture* — Dutch schooner. Abandoned during the March 1913 storm, probably in the upper Keys area. Crew picked up by British steamer *Reliance*. Source: 90 (March 22, 1913).

219. *Samuel T. Beacham* — Schooner, 185 tons, built in 1898 at Baltimore, 121' x 23.7' x 8.2'. Collided with the British steamer *Teodoro De Larrinaga*, in the Florida Straits, March 30, 1913. Source: 14.

220. *City of Washington* — Steamship (iron), single screw, two masts and one funnel, of the Ward Line, 2,683 tons, built in 1877 at Chester, Pa., 300.5' x 38.4' 19.2'. Stranded on Elbow Reef, July 10, 1917. Note: Became a barge carrier in 1911. Source: 14, 73.

221. *Evadne* — See Section 5, #134.

222. *Quoque* — Steam freighter, 2,540 tons, built in 1918 at Astoria, Ore., 266.8' x 46.1' x 23.8'. Stranded six miles off Carysfort Light, Jan. 12, 1920. Source: 14.

223. *J. Frank Seavy* — Three-masted schooner, 413 tons, built in 1888 at Bath, 144' x 33.9' 10.2'. Foundered in the Florida Straits, March 3, 1920. Source: 14.

224. *Nancy Hanks* — Four-masted schooner, of Philadelphia, 1,162 tons, built in 1917 at Thomaston, Maine, 204' x 41' x 19.2'. Stranded on the Florida Reef, Jan. 10, 1926. (See Figure 27). Source: 14, 80.

225. *Alecia* — Gas vessel, 32 tons, built in 1911. Burned at Turkey Point, May 25, 1926. Source: 14.

Figure 27: Schooner *Nancy Hanks*, stranded in 1926. PENOBSCOT MARINE MUSEUM.

226. *Jemina F. III* — Gas yacht (steel), 149 tons, built in 1908 at New York, 98.8' x 21' 8.1'. Foundered in Biscayne Bay during a hurricane, Sept. 18, 1926. Source: 14.

227. *Francis E* — Freighter. Sank in Biscayne Bay during the September 1926 hurricane. Source: 64.

228. *Massachusetts* — Dredge, of Miami, 472 tons, built in 1914 at Albany, 132.4' x 39.4' 8.4'. Foundered at Fowey Rock Light, April 10, 1928. Source: 14.

229. *Northern Light* — Schooner barge (steel), formerly a steamer, 2,351 tons, built in 1888 at Cleveland, 299.5' x 40.8' x 21.6'. Foundered at Lat. 25-03-00, Long. 80-13-00, Nov. 11, 1930. Five lives lost. Source: 1, 14.

230. *Eureka II* — Gas vessel, 81 tons, built in 1921. Burned at Cape Florida, Dec. 14, 1930. Three of 133 on board lost. Source: 14.

231. *Nepenthe* — Gas yacht, 84 tons, built in 1917 at Camden, N.J., 75.6' x 17.3' x 8.4'. Burned at Tavernier Key, Jan. 24, 1932. Source: 14.

232. *Hilton* — Motor vessel, 53 tons, built in 1925. Stranded one mile southwest of Carysfort Light, Dec. 18, 1937. Source: 14.

233. *Alyce B.* — Oil vessel, 27 tons, built in 1917. Burned at Fowey Rock Light, April 12, 1939. Source: 14.

See World War II section for Section 4 wrecks during that period.

234. *Old River* — O/V, 299 tons, built in 1928. Burned at Lower Matecumbe Key, Nov. 28, 1947. Source: 14.

235. Barge — Sank March 3, 1949, at Lat. 25-20-30, Long. 80-09-54. Source: 1.

236. *Sunshine* — G/V, 64 tons, built in 1917. Burned at Cross Key, Dec. 25, 1949, 50 miles south of Miami. Source: 14.

237. *Corky C* — G/V, 28 tons, built in 1924. Burned at the north point of Fishers Island, Biscayne Bay, Feb. 14, 1956. Source: 14.

238. *Chimaera* — O/V, 44 tons, built in 1954. Collided with a floating object, April 8, 1959, approximately 12 miles off Fowey Rock Light. Source: 14.

239. *Rosalie* — F/V (oil), 130 tons, built in 1942 at Detroit, 108.4' x 18.3' x 10.4.' Burned off Plantation Key, Jan. 25, 1964. Source: 14.

240. Barge — 85' x 22'. Grounded in 1966, at Lat. 25-39-14.67, Long. 80-10-40.39, in six feet of water. Source: 1.

241. *Mandalay* — Steel sailing vessel (belonged to the Windjammer Fleet), 128'. Wrecked in 1966 on Long Reef, off Homestead. Picked clean. Masts salvaged to re-create a Spanish galleon replica, the *Golden Doubloon*. Source: 56.

242. *Enchantress III* — O/V, 26 tons, built in 1951. Stranded on Carysfort Reef, Jan. 23, 1971. Source: 14.

243. *Island City* — F/V (oil), 48 tons, built in 1950 at St. Augustine, 53.6' x 18.4' x 6.4'. Foundered north of Fowey Rock Light, Dec. 23, 1971. Source: 14.

244. *Geja* — M/V, 122'. Sank in 1975, at Lat. 25-42-13, Long. 80-00-39. Source: 1.

245. Unknown wreck — 60'. Charted and visible in 1977, at Lat. 25-38-44.16, Long. 80-10-30.36. Source: 1.

246. Barge — 60' x 20'. Located in 1977 with a load of concrete slabs, at Lat. 25-38-45.24, Long. 80-10-28.36. Source: 1.

247. Dredging barge — 60' x 20'. Remains were located in 1977, at Lat. 25-38-47.11, Long. 80-10-45.75, four feet from the surface. Source: 1.

248. Unknown wreck — 55' x 15'. Located and visible in 1977, at Lat. 25-38-47.73, Long. 80-10-40.52. Source: 1.

249. Two wrecks — One wooden, 70' x 20', and one wooden barge, 75' x 25'. Located in 1979, at Lat. 25-41-10.03, Long. 80-10-49.74. Source: 1.

250. Unknown wreck — A 70' steel vessel was sunk in 110 feet of water, five miles off the south end of Islamorada, in the late 1970s. Her cargo consisted of marijuana, and local divers have dubbed her the "Cannabis Cruiser."

251. Unknown wreck — Located in 1980, at Lat. 25-38-10.11, Long. 80-08-21.06, in five feet of water. Source: 1.

252. Fuel barge — 120' x 40'. Visible in 1980, at Lat. 25-38-49.12,

Long. 80-09-47.14. Source: 1.

253. Two visible wrecks — Located in 1980, one at Lat. 25-39-15.46, Long. 80-09-51.91, and the other, consisting of ribs of a barge-like vessel, at Lat. 25-39-15.78, Long. 80-09-50.82. Source: 1.

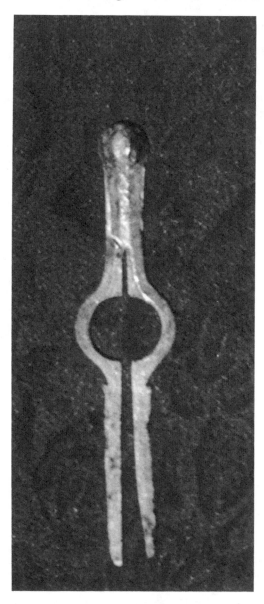

Figure 27A: Brass dividers from the HMS *Winchester* (1695). AUTHOR.

Section 5: Lower East Coast

1500

1. *San Nicolás* and unknown vessel — Spanish ship, Captain Juan Christóval, and a vessel of the Vizcaino. Wrecked near Ais (area off Indian River) in 1551. Fontaneda also mentions a ship under Captain Hernando de Andino that also wrecked in 1551. Source: 22.

2. Three Spanish ships — Three ships carrying treasure were reported wrecked near Rio Palmas at Lat. 26-30, in 1554. These are possibly the *Santa María del Camino*, 350 tons, Captain Diaz, of the Tierra Firme Flota, or the *San Esteva*, 200 tons, Captain Mercerno, and the *Santa María de Yciar*, 200 tons, Captain Ozosi, both coming from Mexico. All these were reported wrecked in 1554 and most of the treasure was salvaged by the Spanish and the Indians of Ais. Source:54.

3. *La Madelena* — Spanish galleon, 250 tons, Captain Cristobel Rodríquez, from Veracruz bound for Spain with a large load of treasure. Wrecked on a shoal during a storm in 1563, near Cape Canaveral. Only 16 of the 300 on board survived. Source: 54.

4. *Vizcayo* (nao) and the *Urca El Mulato* — Both vessels were lost off Indian River, with treasure, in 1568. Source: 67.

5. Two Spanish tenders — On Dec. 20, 1572, Pedro Menéndez de Avilés left St. Augustine for Havana in two small tenders and a bark. A storm hit the vessels and both tenders wrecked, one near Ais and the other with Menéndez near Cape Canaveral. Source: 50.

6. Spanish ship — Lost 48 leagues south of St. Augustine near Ais, November 1582. Source: 54.

7. Spanish nao — From Mexico bound for Spain. Lost off Cape Canaveral in 1582. Source: 54.

8. Spanish ship — A ship of the fleet under command of Martín Pérez de Olesbal. Wrecked at Cape Canaveral during a storm in 1589. Forty of her crew were rescued. Source: 53.

9. Spanish frigate — From Havana bound for St. Augustine. Wrecked near Cape Canaveral, October 1592. All but one were killed by the Indians. Total loss. Source: 54.

1600

10. *San Martin (Almiranta of Honduras)* and a nao — Spanish vessel, 300 tons. Wrecked in 1618 off present day Wabasso, in front of Sea Grapes Park, known locally as the "Green Cabin Site." She left the port of Trujillo with a cargo of indigo, cochineal, hides, and a small quantity of gold and silver. After a quick stop in Havana, she joined the Tierra Firme Fleet for Spain in early September 1618. There were only 53 survivors. The Spanish did not salvage her. At first this wreck was thought to be part of the 1715 Fleet, since some of the *San Roman's* (1715) coins were found on the wreck site. But the amount of earlier dated coins and bronze cannon found at the site identified her as the *San Martin*. She is now actively worked under a state lease. A smaller nao also sank nearby at the same time. Source: 54, 67, 91, 92.

11. *Espiritu Santo el Mayor* — Spanish galleon, 400 tons. Sank in a hurricane with all her treasure near Ais in 1623. Only 50 of 300 on board survived. The *Satissima Trinidad*, 600 tons, sank slowly during the same storm. All was saved. Marx says she most likely sank in deep water. Source: 54, 42.

12. *Almiranta de Honduras* and a frigate — From Havana bound for Spain. Believed to have wrecked near present-day Miami, the night of April 2, 1632. The frigate carried cocoa from Maracaibo. Source: 54.

13. English vessel — Carrying supplies to Alxacan. Wrecked 70 leagues south of St. Augustine in 1633. Forty reached shore. All but three (who were captured by the Spanish, Nov. 10) were killed by the Indians. Source: 54.

14. *San Francisco y San Antonio* — Spanish aviso. Wrecked on the Florida coast at Gega (present-day Jupiter) in 1659. Indians rescued 33 survivors. Source: Research by Dr. Eugene Lyon (noted Spanish historian).

15. *San Miguel de Archangel* — From Cartagena bound for Spain with thousands of coins meant to show the king of Spain the quality of the coinage from the new mint at Lima, which opened in 1656. Wrecked in January, 1660, near present-day Jupiter. This is believed to be the treasure wreck being salvaged today just south of the Jupiter Inlet. Source: 54, *The Palm Beach Post* (Oct. 21, 1991).

16. *Reformation* — Bark. Wrecked in a storm off Hobe Sound, Sept. 23, 1696, approximately five miles north of Jupiter Inlet. On board were Jonathan Dickinson and 24 others. Source: 27.

17. *Burrough* or *Smith* and the *Nantwitch* — British merchantmen,

from Bristol bound for Port Royal. The *Burrough* (or *Smith*) wrecked north of Jupiter Inlet, Sept. 23, 1696, the same time as the *Reformation*. The bark *Nanwitch* wrecked south of Ft. Pierce Inlet, about one-third the distance between Fort Pierce and St. Lucie Inlets. Source: 54.

1700

18. The 1715 Spanish Plate Fleet — From 1701 to 1713, Spain was at war, and the maritime trade from the New World nearly stopped. In 1715, a fleet left Havana on July 27 with more than 14,000,000 pesos in silver and a large consignment of gold, eagerly awaited by Spain. On July 31, 1715, a hurricane swept across the east coast of Florida, hitting 12 ships of the 1715 Plate Fleet. Only one survived. The Spanish soon set up a salvage camp on the site of the present-day McLarty Museum and salvaged what they could, but much treasure remained. Privateers also raided the salvage camp and took much of the salvaged treasure.

It wasn't until Kip Wagner began the salvage of these vessels in the early 1960s that this fleet attracted the attention of would-be treasure hunters, and Florida's treasure fever began. Six ships of the fleet have been found, and salvage work continues after more than 20 years. Since 1987, Mo Molinar has found thousands of gold and silver coins on one wreck alone.

Of the wrecks that have been found, the *Nuestra Señora de las Nieves* is the southernmost. By car, take A1A south from Fort Pierce Inlet, about four miles. There's a park there called John Brooks Park. Take the access road to the beach, and you are opposite the wreck site, which is scattered to the north.

The *Santissima Trinidad y Nuestra Señora de la Concepción*, also called the *Urca de Lima*, or "Wedge Wreck," lies some 200 yards off the north end of Pepper Park in Fort Pierce just north of the inlet. The wreck has been designated a state park, and is now open to the public.

The *Nuestra Señora del Rosario*, or "Sandy Point Wreck," lies just north of the *Urca de Lima* off Sandy Point. Much of her treasure has yet to be found. The state salvaged six cannons off this site and relocated them to John Pennekamp Underwater State Park.

The *Nuestra Señora del Carmen*, or "Rio Mar Wreck," lies approximately 900 feet off the first green of the Rio Mar Golf Course.

The *Santo Cristo de San Roman*, or "Corrigans Wreck," lies just north of the *Carmen*, just south of Wabasso. It is off Turtle Trail Beach, where parking is available. The main part of the wreck is just south of the park, though she scattered a good distance to the north. This wreck is a favorite of beach hunters, and has produced many coins.

The *Nuestra Señora de la Regla*, or "Cabin Wreck," is the northernmost of the 1715 wrecks that have been found. She lies approximately

1-1/4 miles south of Sebastian Inlet. A few cannon still remain.

Beach hunters have found coins from Chuck's Steak House, just north of Sebastion Inlet, to approximately four miles south of Fort Pierce Inlet. The best time for beach hunting is after storms that blow in from the northeast, usually in the fall. These storms wash the beach away, exposing coins that have been buried for more than 200 years.

The other wrecks from the 1715 Fleet have yet to be found. Two supposedly sank in deep water, and one supposedly wrecked on the beach and was completely salvaged. Another supposedly wrecked off Cape Canaveral. Where the others wrecked remains a mystery. Coins from this period reportedly have been found near Nassau Sound, just south of Fernandina. Coins and a cannon from this period have been found off Pompano Beach near Hillsboro Inlet, and coins from this period also have been found off Jupiter, south of the Inlet. (See Figures 28 - 35). Source: 54, 67, 83.

19. *Liberty* — Schooner, Captain John Hunt, from Mississippi. Was overset at sea and conducted into Rio d'Ais in 1773. Source: 54.

20. Unknown brig — Reported ashore north of Cape Florida being stripped by the wreckers in 1774. Source: 54.

21. *Otter* — British naval sloop, 10 or 14 guns, 302 tons, 95' x 27', Lieutenant John Wright (Commander). Stranded and lost off Cape Canaveral, Aug. 25 or 30, 1778. Source: 13 (Vol. 4), 16, 72 (Vol. 1).

22. *Fanny* — British ship, Captain Farquar, from Jamaica bound for Liverpool. Ran aground north of Cape Florida and broke up, March 7, 1782. Crew and some cargo saved. Source: 54.

23. Spanish troopship — During July of 1784, British emigres reported a wreck of a Spanish ship 200 miles south of St. Augustine. They rescued an officer of the Asturias Infantry Regiment, who said the ship had left Havana on June 1, and had wrecked on June 5, 1784. Source: 75.

24. *Amaranthe* — British naval brig-sloop (formerly French *Amarante*, captured in 1796), 14 guns, 290 tons, built in 1796, 86' x 28', Captain George Blake. Wrecked approximately 22 leagues south of Cape Canaveral, Oct. 25, 1799. Twenty-four of 86 men died of starvation. The Captain was blamed for having sailed too fast without using a sounding lead. Source: 16, 36, 36.

1800

25. *L'Athenaise* — See Shipwreck Narratives.

26. *Triton* — Schooner, Captain Hand, from Havana bound for Richmond.

Figures 28 and 29: Two views of gold two-handed cup, recovered in 1985 from what is believed to be the *San Roman* (1715 Fleet). CHRISTIE'S, NEW YORK.

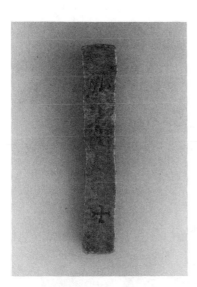
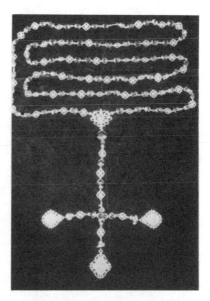

Figure 30 (left): Rare silver finger bar from a 1715 Fleet wreck. ERNIE RICHARDS.
Figure 31 (right): A 9" x 6" gold cross with five feet of gold chain recovered from the wreck of the *Nieves* (1715) found by Bob Weller and Whitey Keevan. ERNIE RICHARDS.

Figure 32: Author and treasure hunter Bob Weller with a day's gold find on the wreck of the *Nieves*. AUTHOR.

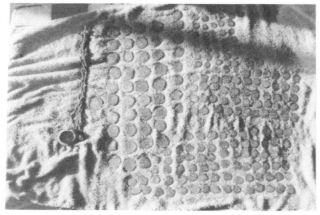

Figure 33: A gold "relicarios," with 9' of gold chain, along with gold escudos found on the wreck of the *Nieves* (1715) site in 1988, by Mo Molinar's and Harold Holden's salvage crews. Note the far left coin, a "Royale 8 Escudo," some of which have sold for over $60,000 each. JOHN dEBRY.

Figure 34: Author up from the bottom with silver ½'s, 1's, 2's, 4's, and an eight real, from the *Nieves* site. AUTHOR.

Figure 35: Photos of some silver cob coins from the wrecks of the 1715 Fleet. AUTHOR.

Wrecked on Florida's east coast, Oct. 19, 1810, at approximate Lat. 27. Source: 54 and information from a Charleston newspaper provided by treasure hunters John Brandon and Harold Holden.

27. *Caroline* — Ship, Captain Curtis, from New Orleans bound for Liverpool with cotton. Was ashore near the *Triton*, Oct. 25, 1810. Source: Ibid.

28. *Union* — Spanish ship from Havana bound for London with logwood. Wrecked near the *Caroline*, Oct. 25, 1810. Source: Ibid.

29. *African* — Spanish brig, Captain Garcia, from Havana bound for New York. Wrecked near the *Union*, Oct. 25, 1810. Source: Ibid.

30. *Spring of Whitby* — British merchantman, built in 1801 in the Whitby Shipyard. Wrecked off Wabasso near the wreck of the *San Martin* (1618). Her bell, dated 1801 and with her name inscribed on it, was found on the site. Pillar dollars have been found here dating 1807-1809, so she likely wrecked in 1809 or 1810. Source: 91 (Weller, Bob. "Wabasso's 'Mystery' Wreck." Vol. 5, No. 1 and 2, 1987).

31. *Epervier* — British naval brig, 477 tons, Captain Wales. She engaged the U. S. sloop of war *Peacock*, 505 tons, under Captain Warrington on April 29, 1814, off Cape Canaveral. The *Peacock* captured the *Epervier* after only 42 minutes of battle, along with $118,000 in specie found on board, and the *Epervier* later joined the U.S. Naval Fleet. More coins may have been thrown overboard to prevent their seizure. Source: 14, 16, 35, 36, 62.

32. *Supply* — Ship, from Jamaica bound for the Cape Verde Islands, Captain Fisher. Wrecked during a heavy gale, Jan. 26, 1821, at Lat. 26-20-00. Source: 23.

33. *Gil Blas* — Spanish brig, 200 tons, from Havana bound for Santo Andero, Spain, with sugar and cigars. Went aground during a storm, nine miles north of the New River (near Hillsboro Inlet) in September 1835. Many other vessels wrecked along the Florida coast during this storm. On Jan. 6, 1836, while local settlers continued to salvage the wreck, their families were attacked by Indians. The Second Seminole War was being fought at this time. The remaining settlers fled the area for the Cape Florida Lighthouse, then Indian Key, leaving Broward County unsettled for another 50 years. Some returned to the brig shortly after, and salvaged two brass cannons to help defend Indian Key from the Indians. Later, the Navy was sent to burn the brig to prevent the Indians from retrieving six tons of lead on board. Source: 23.

34. *James* — Ship, of Portsmouth, N.H., Captain John Plase from Mobile

bound for Cowes, England with 1,081 bales of cotton. Wrecked during a storm about 50 miles northwest of Cape Florida, March 27, 1836. 519 bales of cotton saved and brought to Key West. Source: 96 (April 26, 1836), 97 (Dodd, Dorothy. "The Wrecking Business on the Florida Reef, 1822-1860." Vol. XXII No. 4, April 1944, pp. 171-199).

35. *Cyrus Butler* — Bark, 360 tons, with the Regular Line in 1835, from New Orleans bound for Liverpool with cotton. Wrecked at Hillsboro Inlet, Aug. 11, 1837. Vessel lost. Wreckers awarded $3,465. Source: 37.

36. *Industry* — Schooner, from Montego Bay bound for Quebec with sugar. Wrecked 45 miles north of Cape Florida, Sept. 13, 1837. Vessel lost. Wreckers awarded $5,408. Source: 37.

37. *Alna* — See Shipwreck Narratives.

38. *Courier de Tampico* — French brig, Captain Jule Julian, from Havana bound for Bordeaux with sugar and cigars. Wrecked during the same storm as the *Alna,* Sept. 7, 1838, about 12 miles north of Cape Florida Light (one source says she wrecked on Aug. 30, 1838, on French Shoals with a cargo of logwood, cigars, and cochineal, and the wreckers were awarded $3,000.). Seven out of 16 survived. Source: 25, 37, 86 (Summer/Fall 1986, reprinted from Niles National Register, Vol. 55-56, Oct. 13, 1838, p.103).

39. *Alabama* (Captain Parks, 42'), *Dread* (44'), both of Mystic, Conn., and the *Caution* (Captain Helmes, 45 tons, built in 1838, 46.1' x 17.1' x 6.8', of Mystic) — All were sloops, and all wrecked during the Sept. 7, 1838, hurricane, near the *Courier de Tampico*. All three were bound for Key West. More than 20 lives were lost in the storm, and all but one of the survivors were killed by Indians. The one survivor, Joseph Noble, fell in with the survivors of the *Courier de Tampico* and, passing himself off as a Frenchman, was spared by the Indians. Source: 66, 86 (Ibid).

40. *Muscogee* — Sidewheel steamer, of Apalachicola, 117 tons, built in 1837 at Pittsburgh. Foundered 40 miles north of Cape Florida, May 23, 1838. Three lives lost. Source: 52.

41. *Delaware* — Steamer. Went ashore during a gale at Cape Florida in 1838. A total loss. Source: 14.

42. *Tennfaute* — Brig. Wrecked 70 miles north of Cape Florida, Feb. 18, 1839, off Boca Raton with cotton and cigars. Vessel lost. Wreckers awarded $5,015. Source: 37.

43. Pilot Boat — Capsized in November 1841 on her way to the steamer *William Gaston*, on the Indian River Bar. 11 on board were lost. The steamer sent a boat to help, but it also capsized, drowning three of the four on board. Source: 14.

44. *Formento* — Spanish brig, Captain Garcia, from Havana bound for Vigo, Spain, with sugar, liquor, and money. Wrecked on March 8, 1848, near present-day Pompano Beach. The wrecker *Lavinia* recovered an iron chest which, when opened, contained $3,000 in pesetas, and also found $90 in pesetas on the bottom in five feet of water. Vessel and cargo valued at $40,000. Source: 14, 23.

45. *Cushnoc* — Brig, from Cardenas bound for New York with sugar. Wrecked northwest of Cape Florida, June 2, 1853. Vessel lost. Wreckers awarded $943. Source: 37.

46. *Saxony* — Ship, of Boston, from Mantanzas bound for Liverpool. Went ashore at Hillsboro Inlet, April 8, 1854. Reported 12' of water in her hold (one source says she was from Halifax bound for Mantanzas, with white pine, and wrecked 50 miles north of Cape Florida). The crew arrived at Key West on April 26, and reported the ship could not be freed. Approximately 55% of cargo salvaged, amounting to $1,952. Wreckers awarded $921. Source: 37, 99 (April 22 and June 14, 1854).

47. *E.S. Rudderrow* — Vessel, type unknown, 87 tons, Captain Chadwick, from Charleston bound for Indian River with oats and hay for U.S. troops. Wrecked on the bar at Indian River Inlet, Dec. 14, 1857. Crew was saved, along with some cargo and rigging. Source: 99 (Jan. 5 and 8, 1858).

48. *Admiral Saultzemann* — Dutch ship, of Rotterdam, Captain Vantazack, from Holland bound for Havana. Lost off Hillsboro Inlet, March 16, 1858. Crew rescued by the steamer *Daniel Webster*, March 24, and taken to Havana. Cargo taken to Key West and sold by wreckers. Source: 99 (May 17, 1858).

49. *Elizabeth Ellen* — Ship, from New Orleans bound for Breeman with cotton and tobacco. Wrecked 45 miles north of Cape Florida, Dec. 3, 1858 (believe this date should be 1859; see *Elizabeth Allen*, #190 in Section 8. Vessel lost. Wreckers awarded $14,525. Source: 37.

50. *Thales* — Bark, believed to be 234 tons, Captain Marsh, from New Orleans bound for Africa (reported by one source as a slaver). Ran ashore near Hillsboro Inlet and bilged, Jan. 11, 1859. She was driven high on the beach near the Hillsboro Inlet Bar. The revenue cutter *John Appleton* saved the crew. The Indians took much of the cargo of flour,

bread, cheese, and ale, though wreckers saved some, and were awarded $1,052. Source: 19, 23, 37, 99 (Jan. 31 and Feb. 1, 1859).

51. *Enterprise* — See Shipwreck Narratives.

Note: The following seven vessels all wrecked during the same storm in early November 1859. Most were reported on July 13 by the steamer *Isabel* from Charleston.

52. *Eliza Mallory* — Ship, of the Hurlburt Line, New York, 649 tons, built in 1851 at Mystic, 130' x 33'6", Master J. Williams, from New Orleans bound for San Blas with 4,923 bales of cotton valued at $136,000. Went ashore 65 miles north of Cape Florida and bilged, Nov. 4, 1859. Only 1,800 bales were saved (one source says all cargo salvaged). Wreckers awarded $16,788. Source: 19, 37, 99 (Nov. 14 and 15, 1859, Dec. 14, 1859), 105.

53. *North* — Brig, believed to be 297 tons, from Galveston bound for New York with 1,021 bales of cotton. Went ashore and bilged north of Jupiter Inlet (one source says 65 miles north of Cape Florida), Nov. 4, 1859. Some cargo saved. Wreckers awarded $1,515. Source: 19, 37, 99 (Ibid).

54. *Mary Coe* — Bark, 563 tons, from Mobile bound for Havre with 1,172 bales of cotton. Went ashore and bilged north of Jupiter Inlet (one source says 77 miles north of Cape Florida), Nov. 4, 1859. Some cargo saved. Wreckers awarded $6,583. Source: 19, 37, 99 (Ibid).

55. *Charles Crocker* (or Crooker) — Ship, believed to be 960 tons, from New Orleans bound for Liverpool with 3,150 bales of cotton and 50 hogsheads of tobacco, valued at $186,000. Went ashore on the beach, Nov. 7, 1859, about 25 miles north of Cape Florida (one source says 40 miles north of Cape Florida). Most cargo saved. Wreckers awarded $19,286. Source: 19, 37, 99 (Nov. 14 and 15, Dec. 14, 1859).

56. *Jupiter* — Ship. Went ashore and bilged. Source: 99 (Ibid)

57. *Juliet* — Ship. Went ashore and bilged. Source: 99 (Ibid)

58. *Margaret* — Brig. Wrecked. Cargo saved. Source: 99 (Ibid)

See Civil War section for Section 5 wrecks during that period.

59. *Jane M. Harward* — Bark, 578 tons, built in 1864 at Bowdoinham, Maine, 140'11 x 30' x 15', from New Orleans bound for Havre with cotton. Wrecked 12 miles north of Cape Florida, Oct.

143

31, 1865. Vessel lost. Wreckers awarded $33,848. Source: 6, 37.

60. *John Wesley* — Bark, from New Orleans bound for Liverpool with 1,460 bales of cotton. Wrecked 20 miles north of Cape Florida, Nov. 3, 1865. Vessel lost. Wreckers awarded $34,684. Source: 37.

61. *Daniel Webster* — Sidewheel steamer, 1,035 tons, built in 1851 at New York, 223.4' x 31' x 18.6'. Left New York bound for Havana on Sept. 27, 1866, with 44 passengers and crew. Encountered a hurricane off Cape Canaveral and foundered approximately 80 miles off Cape Canaveral on Oct. 3. All passengers and crew were picked up by the vessel *George Cromwell.* Note: "Merchant Steam Vessels of the U.S." (the Lytle Holdcamper List) says she foundered 180 miles off Tybee Island, Ga. Source: 40 (Vol. 5, 1967).

62. *Sebastopol* — Ship, Captain Savin, from Sagua, Cuba, bound for New York. Abandoned in a sinking state, Oct. 9, 1866. Had run into a heavy gale on Oct. 1, at Lat. 26-39, Long. 79-38, and by the 4th was sinking, with 18 feet of water in her hold. Abandoned on the 9th. Crew rescued by the steamer *Mississippi.* Source: 99 (Oct. 1866).

63. *June Ross* — Bark, from Cardenas bound for New York with sugar, molasses, and asphaltum (asphalt). Wrecked 45 miles north of Cape Florida, Dec. 5, 1867. Vessel lost. Wreckers awarded $2,352. Source: 37.

64. *Lewis W. Alexander* — Schooner. Driven ashore north of Indian River Inlet, August 1869. A partial loss. Source: 14.

65. *E.A. Carver* — Brig. Collided with an unknown vessel, south of Cape Canaveral, December 1869. A partial loss. Source: 14.

66. *Sampson* — Steamer. Stranded during a gale, February 1870, 13 miles south of Indian River Inlet. Three lives lost. Note: This may have been the ex-Confederate sidewheeler *Samson*, 313 tons, built 1856 at Savannah, listed as lost in 1870. Source: 14, 52.

67. *Merino* — British brig. Stranded during a gale, February 1870, nine miles south of Jupiter Light. A partial loss. Source: 14.

68. *Minerva* — Schooner. Stranded nine miles south of Jupiter Light, February 1870. One life lost. A total loss. Source: 14.

69. *Mattie Richmond* — Schooner. Stranded 20 miles south of Jupiter Inlet, February 1870. A partial loss. Source: 14.

70. *Rafborn* — Ship. Stranded the same place as the *Mattie Richmond*, February 1870. A partial loss. Source: 14.

71. *Varuna* — Steamer, 670 tons, 200' x 27.6' x 17', built in 1869 by Charles Mallory, Mystic, Conn., Captain Joseph T. Sencer, from New York bound for Galveston. Foundered at sea during a hurricane, the night of Oct. 20, 1870, approximately 35 miles east by north of Jupiter Inlet. Loss of 52 lives, 36 of which were passengers. Only the second mate and four seamen survived. Vessel valued at $35,000 and cargo at $300,000 (one source says $400,000). Source: 29, 66.

72. *Col. J.T. Sprague* — Schooner. Wrecked near Cape Canaveral, October 1870. A total loss. Source: 14.

73. *Mississippi* — Steamer. Wrecked 70 miles above Cape Florida, 20 miles south of Jupiter Light, August 1871. A total loss. Source: 14, 99 (Sept. 1, 1871).

74. *Pomona* — Brig, (believed to be 422 tons, built in 1866 at Richmond, Maine, 125.6' x 31' x 15.8'). Stranded 12 miles south of Cape Canaveral during a storm, August 1871. A total loss. Source: 6, 14.

75. *S.W. Walsh* — Brig. Stranded same place as the *Pomona* during the same storm. A total loss. Source: 14.

76. *H. Burg* — Brig. Stranded same place as the *Pomona* and the *S.W. Walsh*, during the same storm. Three lives lost. A total loss. Source: 14.

77. *Schooner* — From Central America bound for Boston with mahogany. Wrecked near Hillsboro Inlet in 1871. Dennis O'Neill, a passenger, told how he rode ashore on a mahogany log through a school of sharks. Source: 23.

78. *Victor* — Mallory Line steamer, 1,339 tons, built in 1864 at Mystic, 205.5' x 36' x 19', Captain Gates, from New York bound for New Orleans with a valuable cargo of general merchandise. Wrecked off Jupiter Inlet, Oct. 20, 1872, exactly two years after the *Varuna* (another Mallory Line steamer). The *Victor* wrecked a few hundred yards offshore, south of Jupiter Inlet. Unlike the *Varuna*, all passengers and crew landed safely on shore. Her rusty boilers now mark her grave. Local divers have brought up many artifacts from the wreck in recent years. Source: 29, 52, 66.

79. Ship — Wrecked near present-day Hollywood during a storm, October 1873. It was weeks before the starving survivors were found. Source: 23.

80. *J.W. Coffin* — Schooner. Wrecked off Port Jupiter, August 1875. A partial loss. Source: 14.

81. *Western Empire* — Ship. Found abandoned Nov. 3, 1875, at Indian River. Wreckers awarded $344. Source: 37.

82. *Louisa A.* — Schooner. Capsized in the Gulf Stream off Cape Canaveral, September 1876. A partial loss. Source: 14.

83. *Protector* (formerly the *Mazeppa*) — Norwegian ship, of Stavenger, 799 tons, 162'7" x 32'7" x 23'2", built in 1858 at Richmond, Maine, by H. Springer, Captain H. Falch, from Pensacola bound for Norway with rosin and deals. Wrecked Feb. 11, 1877, just offshore at the border of present-day Deerfield Beach and Boca Raton. She lies a few hundred feet offshore, just inside the first reef. Her windlass with chain lies approximately 50 feet inside the reef in sand, though it is not always exposed. When the sand washes away, her ballast and other wreckage can be seen just on the inside of the reef. Spikes, deadeyes, and other artifacts have been found at this site. (See Figure 36). Source: 23.

84. *Providencia* — Spanish brig or schooner (most likely a brig), of Barcelona, 130 tons, from Carmen, Mexico, bound for Barcelona, Captain Paules, with hides, logwood, and coconuts. Stranded Jan. 9, 1878, on the beach 17 miles north of Lifesaving Station #3. Cargo saved. It's said that the thousands of palm trees planted from the

Figure 36: This windlass is all that remains visible of the ship *Protector*, wrecked off Florida in 1877. AUTHOR.

salvaged coconuts are what attracted Henry Flagler to Palm Beach.
Source: 14, 29.

85. *Alexander Nickels* — Hermaphrodite brig, of New York, 271
tons, built in 1863 in Maine, 110' x 26'9", Captain Peacock, from
Cienfuegos bound for Boston with sugar. Stranded during a hurricane, Sept. 7, 1878, 1-1/2 miles south of New River, Ft. Lauderdale.
One life lost. Source: 23.

86. *Sevre* — French brig, 400 tons, Captain Trocher, from Tampico
bound for Havre with corn and jute. Wrecked during the September
1878 hurricane, 16 miles north of Lifesaving Station #1. One life lost.
Source: 14.

87. *Virgin de las Nieves* — Bark, 366 tons, from Havana bound for
New York. Wrecked Oct. 23, 1878, 2-1/2 miles south of Station #3.
Source: 14.

88. *Norina* — Austrian bark, of Trieste, 579 tons, Captain Sutora,
from New Orleans bound for Gibraltar with corn and lumber.
Wrecked March 31, 1879, ten miles north of Station #2. A total loss.
Source: 14.

89. *Triunfo* — Spanish brig, of Barcelona, 153 tons, Captain
Guardiola, from Cuba bound for Savannah. Wrecked Nov. 2, 1883,
nine miles north of Station #3. Source: 14.

90. *Giovanni* — Bark, of Malta, 265 tons, Captain Mantindis, from
Black River, Jamaica, bound for Trieste with logwood. Wrecked Nov.
9, 1884, 7-1/4 miles north of Station #3. A total loss. Source: 14.

91. *America* — Steamer, of New York, 782 tons, Captain Miller, from
Cardenas bound for Boston with sugar. Wrecked 8-1/2 miles north of
Gilberts Bar Station (#2), Feb. 11, 1885, on the St. Lucie Rocks. A
total loss. Source: 14.

92. *J.H. Lane* — Brig, of Searsport, Maine, 391 tons, Captain Alonzo
Shute, from Mantanzas bound for Philadelphia with molasses. Ran
into a storm, April 16, 1886, approximately 5-1/2 miles southeast of
Gilberts Bar Station. She put her anchors out, hoping to ride it out.
On the 19th at 1:30 A.M., her lines parted and she went aground, approximately 3/4 mile from shore. At daybreak, the crew took to the
lifeboat. It capsized, drowning one man. The others clung to the
boat, which made its way to shore, approximately 7-1/2 miles from
the station. The station keeper helped them and they all made it
safely to the station. The vessel broke up that evening, and casks of
molasses washed ashore. Source: 14, 29.

93. *Ilo* — Schooner (iron), of Jacksonville, 33 tons, built in 1874, from Jacksonville bound for Lake Worth with lumber. Parted her chain and beached at Lake Worth Inlet, Nov. 16, 1886, at 7 A.M. Vessel a total loss. Cargo saved. Source: 14.

94. *Saragossa* (formerly *Thomas A. Scott*) — Steamer, 1,052 tons, built in 1863 at Philadelphia. Foundered 200 miles off Cape Canaveral, March 23, 1887. Source: 52.

95. *Queen* — Schooner, of St. Augustine, 15 tons, Captain McFadden, from Melbourne bound for Abaco with lumber. Wrecked eight miles south of the Orange Grove Station, Sept. 14, 1891. Cargo saved. Source: 14.

96. *Red Wing* — Schooner. Lost near Indian River Inlet, Oct. 22, 1891. Source: 9.

97. *Bijou* — Sloop, of Cocoa, Fla., from Cocoa bound for Coconut Grove with a miscellaneous cargo. Wrecked eight miles north of Biscayne Bay Station, Nov. 2, 1891. A total loss. Source: 14.

98. *Orrie V. Drisco* — Schooner. Lost off Cape Canaveral, Dec. 22, 1891. Source: 9.

99. *Mattie S* — Sloop, of Lake Worth, from Lake Worth bound for Titusville. Wrecked 2-1/2 miles south of Gilberts Bar Station, Jan. 22, 1894. Source: 14.

100. *Breaconshire* or *Breconshire* — British steamer, of London, 2,544 tons, Captain Taylor, from New York bound for Tampa. Foundered one mile south-southeast of Bethel Creek Station, April 30, 1894, in 20 feet of water, at Lat. 27-39-06, Long. 80-20-54. A total loss. She is now a popular site for beach diving. She lies just offshore between Holiday Inn and the Ocean Grill Restaurant at Vero Beach. One boiler is still visible at low tide. Source: 1, 14.

101. *Georgie* — British bark, Captain Paul LeBlanc. Went ashore two miles north of Hillsboro Inlet during a storm, Oct. 10, 1894. A total loss. Source: 23.

102. *Janet* — Sloop, of Ft. Pierce. Wrecked one mile north of Jupiter Inlet, March 26, 1895. Source: 14.

103. *Nathan Cleaves* — Schooner, of Portland, Maine, 80 tons, Captain Varrey, from Indian River Inlet bound for Jacksonville. Wrecked 1/2 mile north of Indian River Inlet Station, April 20, 1895.

A total loss. Source: 14.

104. *Phoenix* — Schooner, of St. Augustine, 24 tons, Captain Baird, from Jacksonville bound for Lemon City with lumber. Wrecked 9-1/2 miles north of Jupiter Inlet Station, Oct. 11, 1895. Most cargo saved. Source: 14.

105. *Oh Kim Soon* — British bark, of Digsby, Nova Scotia, 336 tons, built in 1891 at Centreville, Nova Scotia, 145' x 36.5' x 13', Captain L.D. Morton, from Las Palmas, Canary Islands, bound for Fernandina, in ballast. Wrecked just off Lantana Beach, either Jan. 30 or Feb. 3, 1897, at 10:30 P.M. Rigging was saved. Remains can be seen just off the Lantana public beach, when the sand gets washed away. Source: 14, 29.

106. *Biscayne* — Dredge. Broke her lines while being towed during a storm, October 1897, and broke up on the rocks near Jupiter Inlet. Source: 29.

1900

107. *Auchenblac* — British steamer. On Jan. 12, 1900, the observer at Jupiter Light reported a mast sticking out of the water about six feet, lying east-southeast of Jupiter Light, approximately two miles offshore. The British Admiralty reported the steamer wrecked approximately six miles southeast of Jupiter Light in 36 feet of water. This wreck was taken off the charts in 1917. Source: 29.

108. *Copenhagen* — British steamer, of Glasgow, 3,297 tons, built in 1898 at Sunderland, by J. Priestman & Co., 325' x 47' x 25.5', Captain Jones, from Philadelphia bound for Havana with coal. Ran aground on a reef off Pompano Beach, May 26, 1900. Cargo was jettisoned, and three pumps employed. Crew left the ship on June 1, and on July 17, after more than a month of salvage efforts, she was abandoned, a total wreck. Her mahogany saloon table was salvaged and was used as the board table at the Biscayne Yacht Club. Remains lie on the outside of the second reef, just north of the Sea Watch Restaurant, Pompano Beach, in 20 to 35 feet of water. It is a popular dive site, since most of her superstructure is still intact. She was used for target practice by Navy fighter planes during WWII, and 50 caliber bullets can be found at the site. (See Figure 37). Source: 23.

109. *Paul* — Danish bark, 126.8' x 25.4' x 15.3', from Cuba bound for New York with cedar and wine. Wrecked just north of the Hildebrand place in Hobe Sound, Sept. 6, 1900. Source: 29.

110. *Mary E. Morse* — Three-masted schooner, of Bath, 644 tons,

Figure 37: British steamer *Copenhagen,* aground on reef off present-day Pompano Beach, 1900. ST. AUGUSTINE HISTORICAL SOCIETY.

built in 1881 at Bath, 169.7' x 36.4' x 13.5', Captain Newburg, from Pascagoula bound for New York with lumber. Wrecked 14 miles north of the Bethel Creek Station, Sept. 9, 1900. Vessel and cargo valued at $40,000 ($19,000 loss). Source: 14.

111. *Plunger* — Schooner, 24 tons, built in 1897. Stranded at Jupiter Inlet, July 20, 1902. Source: 14.

112. *La Barbara* — 37-ton vessel, type unknown. Stranded below Palm Beach, Jan. 29, 1903. Source: 14.

113. *Inchulva* — British steamer, 400' x 48', built in 1891 at Ulva Isle for the Inch Line. Sailed from Cardiff for Galveston, where she loaded a cargo of 7,000 tons of wheat, 150 tons of lumber, 18 bales of cotton, and some cotton seed meal. Left Galveston under Captain G.W. Davis, Sept. 6, 1903. A storm hit when she was off Fowey Rocks, and her cargo began to shift. On Sept. 11 around 5 P.M., she ran aground off Linton (now Delray Beach), and fired a distress signal. An hour or two later she began to break up. The stern toppled over, carrying five men with it. Help did not arrive until the next

morning. Nine men lost their lives. They were buried on a ridge by the beach where they were found. I have heard that they came ashore at Lantana and that their graves can still be seen there. Remains of the ship lie only a few hundred feet off the southernmost end of Delray Beach's public beach. The site is one of the most popular dive sites in the area. Her boilers rise to only a few feet below the surface, and other wreckage is scattered close by. Check before attempting a beach dive, since I have heard that the city no longer allows scuba diving from the public beach. However, it is also a good spot to snorkel. Source: 47.

114. *Martha T. Thomas* — Three-masted schooner, 789 tons, built in 1891 at Thomastom, Maine, 174.3' x 37.2' x 18', from Apalachicola bound for Boston with lumber. Wrecked Sept. 11, 1903, off Hobe Sound in a 90-mph gale, the same storm that wrecked the *Inchulva*. Source: 14, 29, 80.

115. *Zion* (formerly the *Robert Dixon*) — German bark, of Emden, 1,366 tons, built in 1873 in Maine, 194.9' x 38.7' x 24.3', Captain A. Hemmes Jr., from Pensacola bound for London with 902,000 feet of lumber. On Oct. 14. 1904, she ran into a storm and weathered it for three days, wrecking on the 17th at midnight on a reef off Fort Lauderdale. The next morning the crew launched a boat, but it was smashed to pieces. All 12 men managed to reach shore by nightfall by riding on planks. The ship broke up and some cargo washed ashore. The crew's personal belongings and the ship's goods were stolen from the beach by local residents. Source: 23.

116. *James Judge* — Four-masted schooner, of Philadelphia, 680 tons, 159.2' x 36.6' x 13.4', built in 1890 at Wilmington, Captain Davidson, from Cardenas bound for Jacksonville, in ballast. Wrecked during a storm, Oct. 16, 1904, when she drove up on the beach at Palm Beach, in front of the property owned by Richard Crocker. (See Figure 38). Source: 14, 29, 80.

117. *Georges Valentine* — Italian bark, of Camagoli, 767 tons, built in 1874, Captain M. Prospero, from Pensacola bound for Buenos Aires with lumber. Wrecked during a severe storm, Oct. 16, 1904, at 8:20 P.M., approximately 500 yards east of the Gilberts Bar Station. A total loss. One man was killed by a falling mast. Four others died while attempting to swim to shore, killed either by hitting floating lumber or by striking the rocks. One man rode the floating lumber to shore and walked to the station cold, hungry, and naked. He helped rescue the remaining six men, who suffered from exposure and injury, and could not stand when rescued. (See Figure 39). Source: 14, 29.

118. *Cosme Colzado* — Spanish ship, of Barcelona, 1,246 tons, built

Figure 38: Remains of the schooner *James Judge*, wrecked at Palm Beach in 1904.
BOCA RATON HISTORICAL SOCIETY.

in 1870, from Gloucester, Mass., bound for Brunswick, Ga., in ballast. Wrecked during the same storm as the *Georges Valentine*, Oct. 17, 1904, around noon, three miles north of Gilberts Bar Station, 300 yards offshore. One of the crew fastened a line to himself and swam to shore. He hauled in the three-inch line, which 14 others used to reach shore. One man drowned after getting tangled in the ship's lines. Crew escaped serious injury, since they wrecked off a sandy beach, not a rocky beach like the *Valentine's* crew. Source: 14, 29.

119. *Edith L. Allen* — Four-masted schooner, of Philadelphia, 969 tons, built in 1890 at Richmond, Maine, 185'3" x 39'1" x 18'4", Captain P. LeBlanc, from Baltimore bound for Port Arthur with steel rails. Foundered June 17, 1906, at Lat. 26-10-00, Long. 79-38-00. Source: 23.

120. *Norna* — Schooner, of St. Augustine, 23 tons, built in 1893 at Eau Gallie, Fla., 52' x 18' x 7'. Foundered at Lake Worth, Oct. 28, 1906. Source: 14.

121. *Grace Deering* — Barge (formerly a bark), 627 tons (originally 733 tons), built in 1877 at Cape Elizabeth, Maine, 151.8' x 33.1' x 18.3' (dimensions in 1877). Foundered off Miami, Nov. 1, 1906. Source: 14.

122. *Anna F* — Schooner, 21 tons, built in 1901. Foundered off Fort Lauderdale, Feb. 24, 1907. Source: 14.

123. *Mollie S. Look* — Three-masted schooner, of Maine, 572 tons, built in 1904 at Machias, Maine, 159' x 36'2" x 12'8", Captain O. Look, from Norfolk bound for Carrabelle with 800 tons of coal. Ran aground off the beach, Feb. 14, 1908, 1-1/2 miles above New River Inlet (Fort Lauderdale).

Figure 39: Wreck of the *Georges Valentine*, wrecked in 1904. FLORIDA STATE ARCHIVES.

Crew took to the rigging and were saved the next day. Some rigging was saved. Vessel a total loss. (See Figure 40). Source: 23.

124. *Melrose* — Schooner, built in 1880. Recorded as wrecked ten miles south of Okranoke Inlet, N.C., Feb. 15, 1908. Remains were found off Hobe Sound Beach, buried in the sand. Source: 29, 80.

125. *Harry T. Hayward* — Four-masted schooner, of Thomaston, Maine, 1,203 tons, built in 1902 at Thomaston, 190' x 40' x 19.4', Captain Nash, from Boston with a cargo of gravel for the Florida East Coast Railroad extension. Wrecked 1/2 mile off False Boca Raton, Oct. 18, 1910, at 4 A.M. Three lives lost. She sank eight feet from the surface, with her bow in sight. Source: 14, 80, 90 (Oct. 18, 19 ,22, 1910).

126. *Stella* — Steamer, of Puerta Perlos, Nicaragua, 36 tons, from New York bound for Nicaragua. Wrecked 1-1/4 miles north of Indian River Station, Feb. 17, 1911. Note: Possibly the 36-ton *Stella*, built in 1876 at Brooklyn. Source: 14.

127. *Edithanna* — Gas vessel, 20 tons, built in 1904. Foundered 20 miles northeast of Jupiter Inlet, March 16, 1911. Source: 14.

128. *Harold J. McCarthy* — Schooner, 312 tons, built in 1893 at Bath, 133.1' x 31.8' x 9.1'. Stranded near Lake Worth, March 25, 1911. One life lost. Source: 14.

129. *Huntress* — Gas vessel, 76 tons, built in 1906. Burned at Cape Canaveral, Jan. 6, 1913. Three lives lost. Source: 14.

130. *Alice Holbrook* — Four-masted schooner, of New York, 722

tons, built in 1890 at Camden, Maine, 170.2' x 35.9' x 18.3', Captain Ellis, from Baltimore bound for Mantazas, Cuba, with crossties. Ran aground on a reef, April 19, 1913, eight miles north-northeast of Fort Lauderdale Station #4. Source: 23.

131. *Frances* — Gas vessel, 20 tons, built in 1892. Stranded at Miami, Jan. 2, 1915. Source: 14.

132. *St. Paul* — Barkentine, of Chicago, 471 tons, built in 1890 at Newport, Nova Scotia, 134.9' x 33' x 15', Captain M.J. Marcial, from Chrome, N.J., bound for Mantazas with sulphate ammonia. Dismasted at sea during a storm. Stranded abreast of Jensen Beach, Nov. 8, 1916, at 4 A.M., about one mile offshore, approximately four miles north of Gilberts Bar Station. Vessel valued at $30,000 and cargo at $56,000. A total loss. Source: 14.

133. *Helen T* — Barge, 436 tons, built in 1916. Stranded off Jupiter Light, Dec. 27, 1917. Source: 14.

134. *Evadne* — British three-masted schooner, of Pictou, Nova Scotia, 405 tons, built in 1900 at River John, Nova Scotia, 129.2' x 34' x 12.10', Captain Walters. Pressed into service during WWI. Sprang a leak and had to be abandoned with a cargo of lumber in 1917. The top half of the vessel, along with the lumber, came ashore at Caesar's Creek, at the southern end of Biscayne Bay, during a storm that year.

Figure 40: Schooner *Mollie S. Look*, wrecked off Ft. Lauderdale in 1906. PENOBSCOT MARINE MUSEUM.

Harry DuBois found the hull of the *Evadne*, along with the captain's cabin, washed up on a sand bar south of Jupiter Inlet, approximately 100 miles from the rest of the wreck. The ship's wheel was found by a diver in 1963 at Carlin Park, and is now set in concrete there. Source: 29, 80.

135. Curtis Seaplane #A-2300 — U.S. Navy plane, on patrol from Port Sewall, made a forced landing and washed ashore on the beach, June 19, 1918, five miles northwest of Gilberts Bar Station. The pilot, Ensign Schmidt, was not injured. Prop and engine were later salvaged. Source: 14.

136. *Sanibel* — Gas yacht, 44 tons, built in 1890 at Brooklyn. Burned at Miami, March 1919. Source: 14.

137. *Jaxshipco No. 4* — Barge, 75 tons, built in 1920. Foundered off Miami, April 1, 1920. Source: 14.

138. *Emma M. Robinson* — Schooner, 63 tons, built in 1881 at Milford, Del., 76.5' x 23.6' x 5.8'. Stranded at Jensen, May 16, 1920. Source: 14.

139. *Thomas B. Cator* — Schooner, 46 tons, built in 1883 at Taylor Island, Md., 69.2' x 23.6' x 5.2'. Stranded off Fort Pierce, May 16, 1920. Source: 14.

140. *Osiris* — Gas yacht, 137 tons, built in 1911 at New York, 109'. Burned at Miami, Feb. 12, 1921. Source: 14.

141. *Coniscliffe* — Three-masted schooner, of Bangor, 444 tons, built in 1891 at Buckport, Maine, 149.5' x 33.1' x 12'. Burned off Stuart, April 7, 1921, at Lat. 27-21-00, Long. 79-31-00. Source: 1, 14, 80.

142. *Thames* (formerly *Yuma*) — Steamer, of Wilmington, 447 tons, built in 1889 at Philadelphia, 160.5' x 23' x 8.3.' Foundered north of Jupiter Light, Oct. 22, 1921. Source: 14.

143. *Shuttle* — Steamer, 33 tons, built in 1906. Burned at Miami, April 1923. Source: 14.

144. *Fides* — Motor vessel, 61 tons, built in 1921. Burned at Jupiter, March 21, 1924. Source: 14.

145. *Adeline* — Steamer, of New York, 70 tons, built in 1903 at New York, 110' x 14' x 7.3'. Burned at Ft. Pierce, May 12, 1924. Source: 14.

146. *Mohican* — Steam freighter (steel), of New York, 2,255 tons, owned by the Clyde Steamship Co., built in 1904 at Philadelphia, 237.9' x 40.1' x 19.5'. Burned off the Cape Canaveral Light, either May 10 or Sept. 5, 1925 (another source says 1934), at Lat. 28-23-54, Long. 80-32-12. Demolished in 1944 in 30 feet of water. Source: 1, 14, 80.

147. *Amazon* — Barkentine, 1,167 tons, built in 1902 at Beicia, Calif., 209' x 42.5' x 19'. Burned at Lat. 27-25-00, Long. 79-30-00, July 4, 1925. Source: 14.

148. *Wilbert S. Bartlett* — Four-masted schooner, of New York, 741 tons, built in 1918 at Millbridge, Maine, 183.1' x 37.5' x 14'. Stranded off Jupiter, Dec. 19, 1925. Source: 14, 80.

149. *Gulfsprite* — Gas vessel, 47 tons, built in 1916. Burned at Miami Beach, Jan. 5, 1926. Three lives lost. Source: 14.

150. *Simmons* — Schooner, 62 tons, built in 1890 at Cambridge, Md., 76.5' x 23' x 6.2.' Foundered off Hollywood, Jan. 29, 1926. Source: 14.

151. *Tifton* — Four-masted schooner, 594 tons, built in 1905 at Mystic, 173' x 36.2' x 13.8', from Boston bound for Miami with building supplies. Swamped during a storm, Jan. 29, 1926, off Boca Raton. Two lives lost. Crew took to the boats; rescued by the steamer *America*.
    There is a hull of a wreck known locally as the "Lumber Wreck" off Red Reef Park in Boca. It is exposed sometimes in 15 to 20 feet of water. This wreck could be the *Tifton*, since mounds of iron spikes and copper nails were found nearby. Source: 14, 89 (Jan. 30, 1926).

152. *Endurance* — Tug. Foundered six miles off Boca Raton during the same storm as the *Tifton*, Jan. 29, 1926. All 11 on board took to the lifeboat and were saved. Source: 89 (Ibid).

153. *Lynn* — Barge, 441 tons, built in 1914. Stranded at Lake Worth Inlet, Feb. 16, 1926. Source: 14.

154. *Satisfaction* — Oil vessel, 30 tons, built in 1924. Foundered at Fort Pierce, April 27, 1926. Source: 14.

155. *Brooklyn* — Barge, of New York, 154 tons, built in 1887 at South Brooklyn. Stranded at Lake Worth Inlet, May 10, 1926. Source: 14.

156. *Algemac* — Gas vessel, 36 tons, built in 1924. Stranded at Lake Worth, July 26, 1926. Source: 14.

157. *Patricia* — Motor vessel, 73 tons, built in 1922. Foundered off Fort Lauderdale, Aug. 18, 1926. Source: 14.

158. *Prins Valdemar* — Bark (steel), 1,338 tons, 241', built in 1892. This vessel is unique in that she contributed to the collapse of the real estate boom in South Florida during the 1920s. She tried entering Miami Harbor in the fall of 1926 at the height of the building boom, grounding at the entrance to the turning basin. A northeaster struck soon after, turning her over on her starboard side and preventing more than 100 vessels carrying lumber and building supplies from entering the harbor.

The schooner *City of Portland* tried to right her to no avail, and the Army Corps of Engineers ended up cutting her masts and building a channel around her. No sooner were they completed when a steamer ran aground, preventing the channel from being used. Soon after that two barges blocked the channel. Not long after the channel was cleared, the Sept. 17, 1926 hurricane hit, ending what little was left of the building boom. Ironically, the only vessel which rode out the storm was the refloated *Prins Valdemar*. (See Figure 41). Source: 14, *Fort Lauderdale News* (article by Stuart McIver in the Sunshine supplement).

Figure 41: The *City of Portland* attempts to right the schooner *Prins Valdemar* in Miami Harbor, 1926. FLORIDA STATE ARCHIVES.

159. *Delta* (formerly schooner barge *Jeanie*) — Schooner, of Gulfport, 317 tons, built in 1892 at Cheverie, Nova Scotia, 118.3' x 30.5' x 11.9'. Stranded at Delray Beach, Sept. 18, 1926, during the hurricane. One life lost. Source: 14.

160. *Esmeralda* — Steam yacht (steel), 219 tons, built in 1897 at New York, 147.1' x 21.1' x 11.4'. Foundered off Miami, Sept. 18, 1926, during the hurricane. Source: 14.

161. *Fleetwood III* — Motor vessel, 55 tons. Stranded at Miami, Sept. 18, 1926, during the hurricane. Source: 14.

162. *Kemah* — Motor vessel, 59 tons, built in 1907. Foundered at Miami, Sept. 18, 1926, during the hurricane. Source: 14.

163. *Millie* — Barge, 153 tons, built in 1889 at Tomkins Cove, N.Y. Foundered at Miami, Sept. 18, 1926, during the hurricane. Source: 14.

164. *Altomary* — Gas vessel, 37 tons, built in 1913. Collided with an unknown barge at Miami, Sept. 18, 1926, during the hurricane. Source: 14.

165. *Delphin* — Gas vessel, 35 tons, built in 1913. Foundered at Miami, Sept. 18, 1926, during the hurricane. Source: 14.

166. *Seafoam* — Gas vessel, 46 tons, built in 1904. Stranded at Miami, Sept. 18, 1926, during the hurricane. Source: 14.

167. *Sumida* — Gas vessel, 22 tons, built in 1908. Foundered at Miami, Sept. 18, 1926, during the hurricane. Source: 14.

168. *Relief #5* — Barge, of New York, 87 tons. Foundered off Miami, Sept. 18, 1926, during the hurricane. Source: 14.

169. *Rose Mahoney* — Five-masted schooner, of San Francisco, 2,051 tons, built at Benicia, Calif., 260.7' x 48.3' x 22.4'. Blown on shore at the south end of Miami's municipal docks during the September 1926 hurricane. She remained there until November 1928, when a salvage contract was awarded. Source: 14, 102 (Peterson, Susan B.. Vol. 7, Issue 11, February 1991).

170. *Richmond* — Mills & Mills three-masted schooner, of Miami, 288 tons, built in 1909 at Sharptown, Md., Captain Morton. Went aground high on the beach at Fort Lauderdale, Sept. 22, 1926, during the hurricane. Remains lie under the Point of Americas condominium. (See Figure 42). Source: 23.

Figure 42: Schooner *Richmond,* wrecked high on the beach at Ft. Lauderdale, 1926.
HOLLYWOOD HISTORICAL SOCIETY.

171. *Jacksonville* — Four-masted schooner, of Providence, R.I., 620 tons, built in 1906 at Jacksonville, 197.4' x 36.2' x 13.8'. Wrecked at Miami, Sept. 22, 1926. Source: 80.

172. *Lilian L.* — Gas yacht, 29 tons, built in 1906 in Ohio, 63.5' x 10.8' x 5.1'. Foundered at Palm Beach, Nov. 19, 1926. Source: 14.

173. *Sea Bird* — Motor vessel, 81 tons, built in 1918. Foundered, May 22, 1927, at Lat. 28-24-00, Long. 80-35-00. Source: 14.

174. *Kingfisher* — Gas vessel, 36 tons, built in 1909. Foundered off West Palm Beach, Dec. 18, 1927. All six on board lost. Source: 14.

175. *Olga* — Freight vessel (gas), of Key West, 42 tons, built in 1903 at Biloxi, Miss., 60' x 18.2' x 4.4'. Stranded at North Jupiter Light, Jan. 5, 1929. Source: 14.

176. *Captain Bartlett* — Dredge, 194 tons, built in 1925. Burned at Miami, Jan. 21, 1930. Source: 14.

177. *Dunham Wheeler* — Five-masted schooner, of New York, 1,926 tons, built in 1917 at Bath, 254.5' x 44.2' x 23'. Foundered off Melbourne in 60 feet of water, Nov. 15, 1930, at Lat. 28-11-10, Long. 80-19-40. (See Figure 43) Source: 1, 14, 80.

Figure 43: Schooner *Dunham Wheeler*, wrecked in 1930. MAINE MARITIME MUSEUM.

178. *Wonder* — Gas vessel, 25 tons, built in 1929. Burned at Fort Pierce, Nov. 22, 1930. Source: 14.

179. *Half Moon* — Sailing yacht (steel). Sank during a storm in 1930, at Lat. 25-43-36.24, Long. 80-08-05.13, in three feet of water. Wreck still visible in 1980. Source: 1.

180. *Cumberland* — U.S. Army Corps of Engineers hopper dredge, 1,870 tons, built in 1906 at Belfast, Maine, 200' x 40'8" x 20'. The last of the wooden-hulled, self-propelled, steam-class vessels in use by the Army Corps of Engineers. Left Savannah June 22, 1931, under Captain J. Lavell, bound for Mobile via Key West, where she was to stop for fuel. On the 24th, she grounded on a pile of cement that had been jettisoned by another vessel a few years earlier off Fort Lauderdale. Coast Guard vessels attempted to pull her off, but rough seas prevented them from doing so. Fifty of the crew were taken off the next day.

A Navy tug arrived the next day from Key West to pull her off, but was unable to. Since she was an old vessel, and her bottom was breaking up, it was decided not to make any more attempts at salvage. Remains lie off the Ocean Manor condominium on Galt Ocean Mile, Fort Lauderdale, in ten feet of water. Navy fighter planes used the wreck for target practice during WWII. Her bronze nameplate was recovered in the 1960s. The wreck is not visible today. (See Figures 44 and 45). Source: 23.

Figures 44 and 45: U.S. Army Corps of Engineers hopper dredge *Cumberland,* wrecked in 1931. WALTER SCHAAF (U.S. ARMY CORPS OF ENGINEERS).

181. *Salvor II* — Scow, 53 tons, built in 1920. Foundered at approximate Lat. 26-00-00, Sept. 27, 1931, 26 miles off the coast. Source: 14.

182. *Walter* — Schooner, 100 tons, built in 1875 at Churchcreek, Md., 96' x 25.5' x 6.2'. Collided with the steamer *Eleanor Boling*, Oct. 21, 1932, off Fort Pierce. Source: 14.

183. *W.W. Miller* — Gas vessel, 29 tons, built in 1918. Foundered at Sebastian Inlet, Nov. 23, 1933. Source: 14.

184. *Emily Sears* — Fishing schooner (gas), of Apalachicola, 44 tons, built in 1906 at Gloucester, Mass., 63.6' x 18.1' x 8.3'. Foundered at St. Lucie Inlet, Sept. 7, 1934. Source: 14.

185. *Comet* — Vessel, type unknown, 59 tons, built in 1905. Burned at the foot of 24th Avenue, Miami, Aug. 9, 1935. Source: 14.

186. *Elizabeth* — Steam freighter (steel), of the Bull Line, 3,482 tons, built in 1919 at Wilmington, 334' x 46' x 22,' Captain C.F. Grant, from Tampa bound for New York with 4,800 tons of phosphate rock. Stranded Nov. 4, 1935, 2-1/2 miles north of the Miami sea buoy, 500 yards off Miami Beach's Roney Plaza Hotel. She cracked in two at #4 hold. Salvage was abandoned on Nov. 16; 60% loss. Sources: 14, 98 (Nov. 7 and 16, 1935).

187. *Hallie K.* — Gas vessel (formerly a schooner), 23 tons, built in 1891 at Solomons, Md., 53' x 15.6' x 4'. Foundered 30 miles northeast of Jupiter Light, Dec. 13, 1935. Source: 14.

188. *Eunice M.* — Gas vessel, 49 tons, built in 1906. Burned 10 miles off Jensen, March 17, 1938. Source: 14.

189. *Messenger* — Gas vessel, of Galveston, 77 tons, built in 1918 at New Orleans, 108.6' x 15' x 7'. Stranded one mile south of Jupiter Light, Oct. 14, 1940. Source: 14.

See World War II section for Section 5 wrecks during that period.

190. *Mary DeCosta* — Freighter, of Baltimore, 147 tons, built in 1909 at Gloucester, 88.6' x 22.8' x 10.4'. Foundered at Lucretia Light, Dec. 22, 1945, ten miles east of Miami. Source: 14.

191. *Emma* — G/V (composite built), 43 tons, built 1940. Foundered three miles south of Fort Pierce, Sept. 26, 1947. Source: 14.

192. *George C. Bell* — O/V, 88 tons, built in 1929. Collided with USS

YP 629, Jan. 1, 1948, at the east end of the main channel in Miami Harbor. Source: 14.

193. *Vahadah* — G/V, 52 tons, built in 1921. Foundered off Palm Beach in 1948. Source: 14.

194. *Jackie Faye* — O/V (steel), 20 tons, built in 1947. Foundered two miles offshore, five miles north of Melbourne, April 5, 1952. Source: 14.

195. *Helen C* — O/V, 28 tons, built in 1937. Burned off Cocoa, Sept. 15, 1952. Source: 14.

196. Barge — Sank in 1952, at approximate Lat. 27-28-48, Long. 80-16-44, in 27 feet of water. Source: 1.

197. *Maggie II* — O/V, 25 tons, built in 1943. Foundered 2-1/2 miles east of Port Everglades sea buoy, Nov. 11, 1956. Source: 14.

198. *Dragoon* — G/V, 70 tons, built in 1926. Collided with a floating object, March 7, 1957, off Port Everglades. Source: 14.

199. *Capt. Tap* — O/V, 41 tons, built in 1952. Foundered off Cape Canaveral, March 7, 1959. Source: 14.

200. *Yankee Girl II* — O/V, 30 tons, built in 1928. Foundered off Miami, Nov. 28, 1959. Source: 14.

201. *Ruxton #2* — O/V, 97 tons, built in 1934. Foundered approximately six miles east of Port Everglades, Dec. 28, 1960. Source: 14.

202. *Arizona Sword* — Barge (steel), 3,161 tons, built in 1946. Foundered approximately ten miles off West Palm Beach, Jan. 13, 1961. Source: 14.

203. *Antonio* — O/V, 68 tons, built in 1932. Burned approximately 13 miles off West Palm Beach, June 4, 1961. Source: 14.

204. *Leonie* — G/V, 164 tons, built in 1917. Burned at Miami, Sept. 1, 1961. Source: 14.

205. *Samay* — G/V, 56 tons, built in 1926. Burned at Miami Beach, Oct. 21, 1961. Source: 14.

206. *Whereaway* — G/V, 70 tons, built in 1918. Foundered at Coyler Island, off Lake Park, Dec. 5, 1962. Source: 14.

207. *Knockout* — F/V (oil), 32 tons, built in 1954 at St. Augustine, 46.3' x 16.8' x 6.1'. Foundered approximately ten miles north of Port Everglades, Jan. 27, 1963. Source: 14.

208. *Savannah* — F/V (oil), 26 tons, built in 1942. Stranded one mile north of Sebastian Inlet, Oct. 23, 1964. Source: 14.

209. *Gradco Pioneer* — F/V (oil), 70 tons, built in 1944. Burned approximately one mile north of the sea buoy, off Miami Beach, June 20, 1965. Source: 14.

210. *Amaryllis* — Greek freighter. Beached on Singer Island during a hurricane, Sept. 9, 1965. She was removed in pieces, and her remains became an artificial reef off Singer Island in 90 feet of water. Source: 29.

211. *Southwind II* — G/V, 26 tons, built in 1953. Foundered off Palm Beach, Aug. 12, 1967. Source: 14.

212. *Skylark II* — O/V, 49 tons, built in 1932. Burned five miles off Lake Worth, June 22, 1968. Source: 14.

213. *Scotchie* — O/V, 35 tons, built in 1949. Foundered off Fort Lauderdale, March 1969. Source: 14.

214. *Ask Me* — O/V, 29 tons, built in 1959. Foundered off Fort Lauderdale, Aug. 17, 1969. Source: 14.

215. Steel vessel — 97'. Sank in 1973, in 66 feet of water, at approximate Lat. 28-25-00, Long. 80-23-00. Source: 1.

216. *Cindy Lee* — O/V, 30 tons, built in 1951. Foundered off Jupiter Beach, Feb. 16, 1974. Source: 14.

217. *Dallas Neal* — O/V, 63 tons, built in 1952. Foundered approximately five miles east of Melbourne, Oct. 19, 1974. Source: 14.

218. *Tegra* — 60'. Sank in 1974, in 12 feet of water, at Lat. 26-54-08, Long. 80-03-25. Source: 1.

219. *Calico* — F/V (converted minesweeper), 234 tons, 124'9", wood hull. Sank on Dec. 29, 1974, at Lat. 28-18-30, Long. 80-20-00. Source: 1.

220. *Viking* — G/V, 26 tons, built in 1963. Foundered off Boca Raton, Aug. 13, 1975. Source: 14.

221. *Miss Eileen* — O/V, 64 tons, built in 1958. Foundered off Cape Canaveral, Feb. 10, 1977. Source: 14.

222. *Erica of Exuma* — Landing craft, 114'. Sank in 1977, in 600 feet of water, at approximate Lat. 27-40-00, Long. 79-53-00. Source: 1.

223. *Tomador* — O/V, 78 tons, built in 1959. Burned off Fort Lauderdale, May 1978. Source: 14.

224. Unknown wreck — Visible wreck located in 1979 along shore, at Lat. 27-08-01, Long. 80-15-55. Source: 1.

225. *Captain Furnie* — F/V (oil), 51 tons, built in 1979. Foundered off Vero Beach, April 29, 1980. Source: 14.

226. *North Easter* — F/V (oil), 64 tons, built in 1956. Foundered approximately 37 miles south of Ponce De Leon Inlet, Canaveral National Seashore Park, in 1980. Source: 14.

227. Iron Barge — Visible in 1981, at Lat. 27-07-46, Long. 80-16-05. Source: 1.

228. *Hydro Atlantic* — Dredge, 4,327 tons, built in 1905 at Sparrows Point, Md., 315.5' x 64.1' x 20.9'. Scuttled during a storm in 1987, while being towed to Texas to be scrapped. Lies in 162 feet of water, 1.2 miles off Boca Raton, Loran #62083.0/14284.1. Valued at $500,000. Source: 14, 89 (June 18, 1989).

229. Sport fishing boat — The wreck of a twin diesel drug boat lies just off the southeast end of the Deerfield Beach Pier. Sank in the mid-1980s.

230. *Raychel* — Honduran freighter, 164', cargo of construction materials. Capsized and sank after her load shifted, approximately 2-1/2 miles east of Miami Beach near the Miami sea buoy, Oct. 18, 1990, shortly after midnight. She sank in 43 feet of water. Source: 89 (Oct. 19, 1990).

231. *Jesulla II* — Honduran freighter, 185'. Cargo of rice, flour, sugar, clothing, cars, and bicycles. Loaded on the Miami River, and was bound for Gonaives, Haiti, when a fire started in the forward hatch and soon spread, March 28, 1991, around 6 A.M., ten miles east of Elliot Key and 26 miles south of Miami Harbor. Crew rescued by the *Seabulk Challenger*. Coast Guard soon on the scene. The vessel began to drift north toward Biscayne Park's sensitive reefs. Fighting the fire and rough seas, the Coast Guard eventually attached a steel

165

hawser and towed the ship six miles east of Miami. She was sunk by 50-caliber machine gun shells fired by the Coast Guard cutter *Dauntless*, in 650 feet of water, 23 miles north of where she first caught fire. Source: 98 (March 29, 1991).

Figure 45A: Author's sketch of the wreck of the bark *Georgie* (1894) near Hillsboro Inlet.

Section 6: Upper East Coast

1500

1. French Fleet of Jean Ribaut — Jean Ribaut's fleet left Fort Caroline in September 1565 to engage the Spanish forces under Pedro Menendez de Avilés at St. Augustine. On Sept. 12, 1565, a storm hit the fleet off St. Augustine and drove Ribaut's ships south. The Spanish took advantage of the situation, and Fort Caroline fell on Sept. 20. Two or three of Ribaut's ships wrecked on Sept. 28, about five leagues south of Mantanzas Inlet. Three ships wrecked 20 to 25 leagues south of St. Augustine, near the Ormond-Daytona Beach area. The *Trinity* ran aground five leagues south of the above wrecks, at an area called Dead Lake, about 15 miles south of Mantanzas Inlet. Ribaut and his men surrendered, but were killed by Menendez. Source:17.

The following is a list of the vessels of the French fleet:
Trinity - Flagship, 32 guns, Captain LeBlanc.
Emérillon - Captain Nicolas d Ornano (Vice Admiral).
Pearl - Vessel of ten guns, Captain Jacques Ribaut (Jean's son).
Leuriere - Vessel of ten guns, Captain Vivien Maillard.
Emérillon - Second vessel of the same name, 29 guns, Captain Vincent Collas.
Shoulder of Mutton - Captain Machonville.
Trout - No information.

2. Three Spanish naos — These were part of a combined fleet which left Havana on Sept. 9, 1589, bound for Spain. A storm hit and three naos, the *Santa Catalina*, 350 tons, Captain Domingo Ianez Ome, the *Jesus María*, 400 tons, Captain Francisco Salvago, and an unknown nao, all sank in thirty fathoms at about Lat. 30 degrees. The almiranta had sunk previously at the mouth of the Bahama Channel with much treasure. Source: 54.

1600

3. Spanish frigate — From Havana bound for St. Augustine with salaries and supplies for the fort. Went aground on the bar at the entrance to St. Augustine in 1626. A total loss. Source: 54.

4. Spanish frigate — From Vera Cruz bound for St. Augustine, with supplies and money to replace those lost in the above frigate since soldiers at the garrison were threatening mutiny if not paid. She wrecked in 1627 on the same bar as the other frigate, though the crew and 12,000 pesos in silver were saved. Only 11 of the 200 barrels of flour were salvaged and two iron cannon. Source:54.

5. Five ships of the Nueva España Flota — On Sept. 27, 1641, a

hurricane hit the fleet, wrecking five ships (four naos and one patache), on the Florida coast at Lat. 30. The almiranta, the *Nuestra Señora de la Concepción*, survived and headed for Puerto Rico, but she wrecked on Silver Shoals, north of the Dominican Republic. William Phipps, in 1687, and more recently Burt Webber, in the late 1970s, have salvaged most of her treasure. Source: 54.

1700

6. Eight British ships — Set on fire by Commodore Moore in St. Augustine harbor, November 1702, while two Spanish warships sat outside the harbor. Source: 5.

7. *Santo Cristo de Maracaibo* — Spanish ship. Sank eight leagues southeast of St. Augustine, sometime before Jan. 31, 1706, during a storm. Source: 54.

8. *Nuestra Señora del Rosario y San Cristobal* — Spanish nao, from Havana bound for Spain. Lost on the Florida coast at Lat. 30-20-00 in 1711. Source: 54.

9. Spanish nao — From Havana bound for Spain. Wrecked near the mouth of the St. Johns in 1731. Source: 54.

10. *Charming Sally* (schooner) and two French sloops — One of the sloops wrecked at St. Augustine and the other two vessels a few miles down the coast from St. Augustine in late October 1763. Source: 97 (Siebert, Wilbur H. "The Port of St. Augustine During the British Regime." Vol. XXIV No. 4, April 1946, pp. 248-265).

11. *Industry* — British ship, Captain Lawrence. Wrecked trying to enter St. Augustine Harbor, May 6, 1764. Crew saved along with a few items and six boxes of money for the troops. Source: 54, 97 (Ibid).

12. *Nelly* — Ship, Captain Smith, from Philadelphia bound for St. Augustine. Lost on the bar at St. Augustine in 1766. Crew and some cargo saved. Source: 54.

13. *Prince George* — British ship, from London bound for St. Augustine. Lost going into St. Augustine in 1769. Source: 54.

14. Unknown wreck — Listed on Bernard Roman's chart as wreck 1769, indicating the year it sank, at Mount Tucker, north of Cape Canaveral. Source: 54.

15. *Sally* — Ship, Captain Mathews, from Lisbon bound for South Carolina. Wrecked during a snow storm near St. Augustine,

Feb. 22, 1773. Everyone but the mate was lost. Source: 54.

16. *East Florida Merchant* — British merchantman, Captain Lost-house, from London bound for St. Augustine. Lost on the bar at St. Augustine in 1773. Two-thirds of cargo saved. Source: 54.

17. *Nuestra Señora del Carmen* — Spanish ship, from New Orleans bound for the Canaries. Wrecked on Anastasia Island in 1778. Source: 85.

18. Unknown privateer — Wrecked above New Smyrna in 1779. Fifty crewmen taken prisoner and brought to St. Augustine. Source: 85.

19. A sloop — Wrecked on St. Augustine Bar, October 1782. Source: 72 (Vol. II).

20. *Rattlesnake* (galley), two provision ships, and six private vessels — These vessels were part of a squadron bringing Loyalists to St. Augustine. Wrecked on the bar at St. Augustine, December 1782. Four lives lost. Source: 72 (Vol. 1).

21. *Mary* — British ship, Captain Stafford, from St. Augustine bound for London. Lost on the St. Augustine Bar, April 19, 1783. Source: 54.

22. *Tony* — British merchantman, Captain Welsh, from Charleston bound for St. Augustine and then London. Lost on the St. Augustine Bar in 1783. Source: 54.

23. *La Esclavitud* and two supply vessels— Spanish brigantine. Left Havana along with a schooner, and both were seen off St. Augustine on May 3, 1786. *La Esclavitud* carried $40,000 in silver pesos eagerly awaited by the debt-ridden town. A storm hit, preventing the vessels from entering St. Augustine. Five days later, the schooner returned and reported she had lost sight of *La Esclavitud,* which was never heard from again. Another supply ship was lost near Cape Canaveral on Nov. 4, 1786, and another wrecked in daylight on the shoals north of Cape Canaveral on Dec. 11. Source: 75.

24. *Betsey* — British ship, Captain Grant, from Nassau bound for Florida. Lost on Mosquito Bar in 1788. Source: 54.

25. *Santa Marie* — Ship, Captain Wicks, from St. Augustine bound for Havana. Lost on the St. Augustine Bar in 1790. Source: 54.

1800

26. *Phoebus* — American schooner, Captain Dominique, from Norfolk. Lost on the St. Augustine Bar in 1802 or 1803. Source: 54.

27. *Susan* — British merchantman, Captain Beard, from Amelia Island bound for Clyde. Lost on Amelia Island in 1810. Crew and cargo saved. Source: 54.

28. *Hanover* and the *George* — Both British merchantmen, Captain Baxter and Captain Decone, from Liverpool bound for Amelia Island. Lost on Amelia Island, Oct. 20, 1810. Source: 54.

29. American schooner — Captain Fowler, from St. Mary's bound for Savannah with salt and cotton. Wrecked at St. Augustine in 1810. Source: 54.

30. *Minerva* — British merchantman, Captain McNelly, from London bound for Amelia Island. Lost on Amelia Island, March 2, 1811. Crew saved. Source: 54.

31. *North Star* — Ship. Reported wrecked at Amelia Island in May 1811. Source: 54.

32. *Lady Provost* — British merchantman, Captain Clary. Wrecked on a bar after leaving Amelia Island, May 9, 1811. Source: 54.

33. *Horatio* — Ship, Captain Turner. Reported wrecked at Amelia Island in June 1811. A total loss. Source: 54.

34. *Windsor* and the *Maria* — Both British merchantmen. The *Windsor*, Captain Low, from Savannah bound for Amelia Island, and the *Maria*, Captain Forster, from London bound for Amelia Island. Both reported in June 1811. The *Windsor* wrecked on Amelia Bar and the *Maria* blew up at Amelia Island. Source: 54.

35. *Eagle* — British vessel of London. Lost on the Amelia Island Bar, October 1811. Source: 54.

36. *Fair Weather* — Ship, from Amelia Island bound for England. Reported lost on the Amelia Island Bar, December 1811. Source: 54.

37. *Betsey* — British ship, Captain Telly, from St. Vincent. Reported wrecked at Amelia Island, August 1812. A total loss. Source: 54.

38. *Flor de Guadiana* — Spanish merchantman, with eight to nine hundred bags of cotton. Went ashore during a storm, Sept. 13, 1813, on Amelia Island and broke up. Source: 54.

39. *Santa Rosa* — Ship, from Liverpool. Reported lost on the Amelia Island Bar in October 1814. Source: 54.

40. *Oscar* — Ship, bound for Liverpool. Reported burned at Amelia Island, October 1814. Source: 54.

41. *Nicholas Adolph* — Ship, Captain Hoas. Lost on the Amelia Island Bar, Nov. 10, 1814. Some cargo saved. Source: 54.

42. *Empecinada* — Spanish vessel, six guns, under Captain Villacencio, from Havana with four other ships. Wrecked on Amelia Island Bar during a storm, Jan. 8, 1815, while trying to enter the port. Crew and cargo saved. Source: 54.

43. *Santa Anna* — Ship, from Bermuda. Lost off Amelia Island, March 7, 1815. Source: 54.

44. *Huron, Due Bill*, and the *Water Witch* — The *Huron*, a ship, Captain Snow, from Charleston bound for St. Mary's, and the other two schooners, of Savannah. All wrecked near St. Augustine in early June 1816. Source: 54.

45. *Amiable Antoinetta* — Ship, from Charleston. Wrecked near St. Augustine, Dec. 26, 1816. Crew and cargo saved. Source: 54.

46. *Frolic* — American merchantman, Captain Kennedy, from Havana bound for Charleston. Reported wrecked on Anastasia Island in December 1816. Crew and cargo saved. Source: 54.

47. *Neptune* — British merchantman, Captain Conolly, from Amelia Island bound for Jamaica. Wrecked on Amelia Island Bar in 1816. Source: 54.

48. Ship — Captain Patterson, from St. Ubes bound for Savannah. Wrecked 12 miles south of St. Augustine around March 12, 1817. Crew saved, cargo lost. Source: 54.

49. *Julian* — Ship, from St. Ubes bound for Savannah. Lost at Anastasia Island, March 15, 1817. Crew and some cargo saved. Source: 54.

50. *Sarah* — British brig, Captain Rowe, with logwood and mahogony. Wrecked eight miles from St. John's Bar in 1824. Source: 54.

51. *Lyon* — Schooner, from St. Johns River bound for St. Augustine. Went ashore on the north breakers of St. Augustine, early July 1836. Crew saved. Source: 96 (July 22, 1836).

52. *Saluda* — Schooner. Driven past the St. Johns Bar during a storm in July 1836, and ended up beached nine miles north of Mosquito

Bar. She was sold for $5. Source: 96 (July 29, 1836).

53. *Dolphin* — Two-masted steam schooner, 133 tons, built in 1935 at New York, 115' x 16' x 7', Captain Rudolph. On Dec 19, 1836, her boiler exploded off the St. Johns Bar, killing 15 people. The rest of the passengers were rescued by the vessel *Santee.*

The *Dolphin* was one of the first pioneer steamers in Florida. Her fares in 1836 were: Charleston to Havana, $40; Charleston to St. Augustine, $15; St. Augustine to Key West, $20; St. Augustine to Havana, $30.10. Source: 97 (Dec. 23, 1836), 97 (Mueller, Edward A. "East Coast Florida Steamboating, 1831-1861." Vol. XXXX No. 3, January 1962, pp. 241-260,).

54. *John McLean* — Steamer, of Charleston, 133 tons, built in 1837 at Charleston, Captain A.S. Adams, 120' x 27'6" x 7'4." She left St. Augustine on Nov. 15, 1838, bound for New Smyrna, laden with government stores and also carrying a company of United States troops (Company H. Fourth Artillery, of Fort Mellon). The troops were to establish a new military post at New Smyrna to help in the Second Seminole War. She arrived safely off Mosquito Bar about 3 P.M. the same day.

After passing near the breakers a few times looking for the passage, the two pilots on board concluded that the channel had shifted. Night was approaching and the seas were becoming rough. Captain Adams consulted with the pilots and the commanding officers of the troops. He decided to try to pass over the bar where the seas broke the least, rather than risk remaining outside the bar under the threatening weather conditions. In the attempt, the steamboat struck, bilged in a few minutes, and was lost.

There was no loss of life, but most of the stores, which included arms and ammunition, went to the bottom. The original road from New Smyrna to Lake Monroe was cut getting supplies to the survivors. The *John Mclean* was under contract with the U.S. government at $4,000 per month. Source: 14, 52.

55. *Mutual Safety* — Sidewheel steamer, 420 tons, built in 1842 at New York. Stranded on the St. Johns Bar, Oct. 11, 1846. Source: 52.

56. *Narragansett* — Sidewheel steamer, 576 tons, built in 1836 at New York, from New York bound for New Orleans with passengers and freight. Wrecked some distance above the Ponce De Leon Lighthouse, on the North Beach, Oct. 28, 1847. Years later, a portion of the hull floated into the inlet at Port Orange, and into the Halifax River. The copper sheathing was salvaged. Source: 14 (article by Captain Charles A. Coe), 52.

57. *Roxanna* and the *Ocean* — About the same time the *Narragansett*

wrecked, the *Roxanna* wrecked north of Mosquito Inlet, and the *Ocean* grounded inside the inlet on a sand bar. Source: 14 (Ibid).

58. *Frank* — Brig, of Boston. Went ashore on Amelia Beach after parting her chains, Nov. 8, 1851. She had no cargo, and it was believed she would be a total loss. Source: 99 (Nov. 12, 1851).

59. *Robert Morris* — Bark, believed to be 241 tons, of Philadelphia, Captain Downs, from Cienfuegos bound for Philadelphia. Went ashore on Pelican Shoal, near Fernandina, and bilged, Jan. 21, 1853. Source: 8, 19.

60. *Crawford* — Brig, Captain Chillon. Found by the brig *Amesbury*, dismasted and hove to, Oct. 9, 1853, at Lat. 29-57-00, Long. 79-19-00. The *Amesbury* took off the crew and left the *Crawford* to her fate. Source: 99 (Nov. 2, 1853).

61. *Bloomer* — Schooner, of Frankfort, Maine, from Mayport Mills bound for Martinique with lumber. Sprang a leak, Dec. 11, 1853, and on the 12th she beached 25 miles south of the St. Johns Bar. A total loss. Source: 99 (Dec. 23, 1853).

62. *Enterprise* — Brig, from Boston bound for Jacksonville. Went ashore between mouth of the St. Johns and St. Augustine, Jan. 27, 1854. Source: 99 (Feb. 18, 1854).

63. *Montague Doyle* — Brig, from Wareham bound for Jacksonville. Wrecked on the St. John Bar, ten miles from Jacksonville, Sept. 30, 1855. Crew saved after spending 24 hours on the wreck. Source: 99 (Oct. 8, 1855).

64. *Welaka* — Sidewheel steamer, 256 tons, built in 1851 at Savannah, 137' x 25' x 8', Captain McNelty, left Jacksonville bound for Savannah, Dec. 3, 1857, with cotton. On Dec. 4 at 1 A.M., her machinery gave way while she was crossing the St. Johns Bar. She grounded in the breakers and broke in two. Crew and 100 bales saved by the steamer *Everglades*. Source: 52, 99 (Dec. 12, 1857), 97 (Mueller, Edward. "East Coast Florida Steamboating, 1831-1861." Vol. XL No. 3, January 1962, pp. 241-260).

65. *Pee Dee* — Sidewheel steamer, 138 tons, built in 1845 at Charleston. Wrecked on the St. Augustine Bar, Jan. 27, 1858, while bringing stores and troops to Florida. Source: 52, 99 (Feb. 4, 1858).

66. *Dido* — Brig, of Jacksonville, from Jacksonville with lumber.

Sprang a leak about 100 miles off the coast, and headed back toward Florida. On Jan. 1, 1858, she made either Mantanzas or Mosquito Inlet and anchored just inside the outer bar, her bow under water. Captain Edwards drowned, and it was reported she would likely go to pieces. Source: 99 (Jan. 10 and Feb. 1859).

67. *John Howard* — Schooner, from Boston bound for Smyrna. Struck the bar at St. Augustine, Jan. 20, 1859. A total loss. She sold for $405.00. Source: 99 (Feb. 2, 1859).

68. *Manfred* — Schooner, Captain Guion. Reported from St. Augustine Nov. 13, 1860, as a total loss at New Smyrna. Source: 99 (Nov. 23, 1860).

See Civil War section for Section 6 wrecks during that period.

69. *Villanfranco* — Bark, Captain Waters, from Zasa bound for New York with sugar and molasses. Sprang a leak and foundered, August 1865, at approximate Lat. 29-00-00, Long. 80-00-00. All hands saved. Source: 99 (Aug. 27, 1865).

70. *Taminend* — Sidewheel steamer (formerly the *Miantonomi*), 245 tons, built in 1850 at Providence, R.I., rebuilt in 1853, 255 tons, 170' x 24' x 6.6', from St. Augustine bound for Jacksonville. Grounded on passing the St. Johns Bar, June 10, 1867, at 8:30 P.M., in a full gale. Broke up by 10 P.M. Passengers and crew saved, though some had to spend the night on the wreck. Source: 40 (Vol. 3, 1965), 52.

71. *Crocket* — Steamer. Stranded during a gale near St. Augustine Light, July 1869. A partial loss. Source: 14.

72. *Luella* — Vessel, type unknown, of Boston, Captain Bugess. Wrecked after discharging her cargo of machinery, in the late 1860s, on the outside of Ponce de Leon Inlet. Source: 14.

73. *Martha* — Sloop. Capsized off Ponce DeLeon Inlet during a squall, in late 1860s, and drifted onto south beach. Some cargo of salt saved. One source says the cargo of salt mullet was salvaged. Two lives lost. Source: 14, 97 (Strickland, Alice. "Ponce De Leon Inlet." Vol. XLIII No.3, January 1965, pp. 244-261).

74. *Wilton* — Schooner. Hit by a storm off Mosquito Inlet, and let her anchors out. They parted and she drifted onto the beach approximately four miles south of the inlet, in late 1860s. Source: 14.

75. *Martha* — Schooner. Stranded eight miles north of Mosquito Inlet, February 1870. A total loss. Source: 14.

76. *Lodona* (or *Sodona*) — Steamer. Sank in August 1870. Twenty-one lives lost. One source says she wrecked off Jacksonville, with her bow exposed above the water, and that her cargo was strewn for 30 miles. Another source says she wrecked six miles north of Cape Canaveral. Source: 14, 99 (Aug. 30, 1871).

77. *Hulda* — Bark. Ran ashore five miles southeast of St. Augustine Light, August 1871, during a gale. A total loss. Source: 14.

78. *Nellie Burgess* — Schooner. Driven ashore on the bar at Mosquito Inlet, November 1871, during a gale. A total loss. Source: 14.

79. *Enterprise* — Schooner. Run onto the Mosquito Inlet Bar by the pilot, December 1871. A total loss. Source: 14.

80. *Elizabeth Fry* — British ship, Captain Mickle, from New Orleans bound for Liverpool with 3,100 bales of cotton. Burned to the water-line, Feb. 5, 1872, 200 miles southeast of Savannah. Crew saved. Source: 99 (Feb. 8, 1872).

81. *E.A. Baizley* — Schooner. Stranded at Fernandina, October 1874. A partial loss. Source: 14.

82. *L.A. Danenhower* — Schooner. Wrecked on the St. Johns Bar, May 1875. A partial loss. Source: 14.

83. *Henry C. Shepherd* — Schooner. Wrecked off Fernandina, September 1875. A partial loss. Source: 14.

84. *Lizzie Baker* — Steamer, of Savannah, built in 1860, Captain LaRose, from Jacksonville bound for Savannah with cotton, cotton-seed, and general merchandise. Struck the wreck of the *Welaka* (wrecked 1857), Dec. 11, 1875, on the St. John's River Bar. Some cargo saved. Total loss $75,275. Source: 14.

85. *Catherine Thomas* — Schooner. Stranded at Mosquito Bar, March 1876. A total loss. Source: 14.

86. *Roseadale Turo* — Spanish bark, of Malaga, 612 tons, built in 1866, from St. Marys, Ga., bound for Malaga with pitch pine lumber. Wrecked on the southwest side of the light on Pelican Shoals (Fernandina), May 21, 1876, at 5:30 P.M., after her lines parted from the tug that was towing her. A total loss. Source: 14.

87. *Ann Dole* — Schooner. Stranded on the St. Johns Bar, July 1876. A partial loss. Source: 14.

88. *Katie Ranger* — Schooner. Stranded on the St. Augustine Bar, August 1876. A partial loss. Source: 14.

89. *Frank E. Stone* — Schooner, Captain Charles Fossard or Fozzard. Capsized while trying to get over the bar at Ponce De Leon Inlet during a storm, with a lack of ballast, June 28, 1877. Three lives lost. Source: 14.

90. *J.G. Stover* — Schooner. Stranded on Jacksonville Bar, November 1877. A partial loss. Source: 14.

91. *T.H. Livingston* — Schooner. Driven ashore on the St. Johns Bar, March 1878. A partial loss. Source: 14.

92. *Florida* — Schooner. Stranded on the St. Johns Bar, March 1878. A partial loss. Source: 14.

93. *Agnes* — Steamer, 583 tons, built in 1865 at Philadelphia, Captain Gardner, from New York bound for Key West with 200 tons ballast. Wrecked off of North Beach, Mosquito Inlet, April 3, 1878, diagonally across the wreck of the Narragansett (see #56). Years later both were blown up with dynamite. Source: 14, 52, 97 (Strickland, Alice. "Ponce De Leon Inlet." Vol. XLIII No.3, January 1965, pp. 244-261).

94. *Sarah B.* — Schooner. Stranded on the St. Johns Bar, June 1878. A partial loss. Source: 14.

95. *Sarah L. Thomas* — Schooner, of Middletown, Conn., 196 tons, built in 1865, Captain Cole, from New York bound for Jacksonville with assorted cargo. Stranded during a storm, July 12, 1878, 1/2 mile south of the St. Johns Bar. Some cargo saved. Source: 14.

96. *Lucy M. Collins* — Schooner. Stranded on Jacksonville Bar, August 1878. A partial loss. Source: 14.

97. *Jessie B. Smith* — Schooner, of Middletown, Conn., 322 tons, built in 1866, Captain Williams, from Milk River, Jamaica, bound for New York with logwood. Stranded at Mayport Beach, Sept. 11, 1878, at 6 a.m. A total loss. Source: 14.

98. *Elim* (one source says *Dora Ellen*) — Norwegian bark, cargo of mahogany. Stranded three miles north of Mosquito Inlet, during the September 1878 hurricane. Some cargo saved. Source: 14, 97

(Strickland, Alice. "Ponce De Leon Inlet." Vol. XLIII No.3, January 1965, pp. 244-261).

99. *Pinta* — Central American schooner, carrying 125,000 coconuts. Wrecked during the September 1878 hurricane, four miles south of Mosquito Inlet. Cargo scattered for miles. Source: 14.

100. *Abbie S. Oakes* — Schooner. Stranded during the September 1878 hurricane, one mile north of St. Augustine Light. A total loss. Source: 14.

101. *Sally Brown* — Brig. Wrecked at New Smyrna during the September 1878 hurricane. Valued at $30,000. A total loss. Source: 14.

102. *Hattie Ross* — Schooner. Stranded north of Cape Canaveral during the September 1878 hurricane. One life lost. A total loss. Source: 14.

103. *Minerve* — French bark. Sprang a leak and stranded off the St. Johns Bar during the September 1878 hurricane. A partial loss. Source: 14.

104. *City of Houston* — Steamer (iron), 1,515 tons, built in 1871 at Chester, Pa., owned by C.W. Mallory & Co., rebuilt in 1875, 290' x 33' x 20', from New York bound for Galveston. Hit by a hurricane Oct. 20, 1878, off Fernandina. Started leaking on Oct. 22. Her fires went out on the 23rd and distress signals were fired. By 8 A.M. she drifted over Frying Pan Shoals off Fernandina with 10 feet of water in her hold (Note: I only know of a Frying Pan Shoals, Carolina). The steamer *Margaret* rescued passengers and crew. Source: 40 (Vol. 3, 1964).

105. *Lizzie L. Smith* — Schooner. Stranded three miles south of Mosquito Inlet, October 1878. A total loss. Source: 14.

106. *Salvador* — Spanish brig. Dismasted off the St. Johns Bar, October 1878. A partial loss. Source: 14.

107. *Mary A. Holt* — Schooner. Wrecked off Fernandina, November 1878. A total loss. Source: 14.

108. *Belle of Texas* — Steamer. Foundered off Mosquito Inlet, February 1879. A total loss. Source: 14.

109. *Destino A* — Austrian brig, 430 tons, built in 1872, Captain Manasteriotte, from St. Marys, Ga., bound for Marabelle, Spain, with yellow pine lumber. On March 10, 1879, she was being towed in New Channel at the entrance to the St. Marys River during a gale when she struck bottom. Her lines parted, and she stranded on the

north breakers on Pelican Shoals, between red buoy #2 and black bouy #3, approximately 300 yards from red buoy #2. A total loss. Source: 14.

110. *Annie Bell(?)* — Schooner, of Wilmington, 150 tons, built in 1872, Captain Betts, from Alexandria bound for Jacksonville with terra cotta pipe. Stranded on the North Breakers of the St. Johns Bar, Oct. 5, 1879, at 2 P.M. A total loss. Source: 14.

111. *Lizzie Baker* — Wrecked in the North Channel at the mouth of the St. Johns River, April 1880. Source: 20.

112. *Hattie* — Sidewheel steamer, of Jacksonville, 217 tons, built in 1863 at Jacksonville, rebuilt in 1868, 191' x 25.3' x 5.4', Captain Jones, from Jacksonville bound for Bings Ferry, Ga. Stranded ½ mile off Governors Cut, July 9, 1880. She could not be gotten off and the crew salvaged what they could. Source: 14, 40 (Vol. 5, 1967).

113. *City of Vera Cruz* — See Shipwreck Narratives.

114. *Caroline Eddy* — Brig, Captain George Warren, from Fernandina bound for New York with lumber. Went ashore at Mantanzas during the hurricane of Aug. 28, 1880. Crew saved after spending two days and one night in the rigging. Source: 99 (Sept. 4 and 5, 1880).

115. *City of Austin* — Steamer, of New York, 1,294 tons, built in 1871, Captain Stevens, from Nassau bound for New York, via Fernandina, with 65 passengers and a crew of 38, and a cargo of sugar, sponge, fruit and vegetables. Stranded at Fernandina, April 24, 1881, on the North Breakers, 1/2 mile from Buoy #9. Only 10% of her cargo saved. Source: 14.

116. *Albina* — Bark, of New York, 801 tons, built in 1870, Captain Madison, from Manassa Island, West Indies, bound for Baltimore with 1,100 tons of guano. Sprang a leak and wrecked at Fernandina, Oct. 6, 1881, at 2 P.M., on the South Breakers, 2-1/2 miles offshore east 3/4 mile north of Main Light. A total loss. Crew taken off by the pilot boat. Source: 14.

117. *Puntaluna* — Brig, of Santo Domingo, 260 tons, built in 1863, from New York bound for Fernandina. Stranded on the North Breakers on Pelican Shoals, October 1881, due to an incorrect 1875 chart of the harbor. Source: 14.

118. *Magnolia* — Vessel of Jacksonville, 22 tons, built in 1878, from Jacksonville bound for Smyrna. Stranded on the north point of Mos-

quito Inlet, March 9, 1882. A total loss. Source: 14.

119. *Mary F. Carson* — Schooner, of Philadelphia, 277 tons, built in 1873, Captain Williams, from New York bound for Jacksonville with coal. Stranded on the South Breakers of the St. Johns Bar, March 3, 1883, at 2:20 P.M. Cargo a total loss; 25% of vessel saved. Source: 14.

120. *Fred W. Hoyt* — Schooner, of Fernandina, 59 tons, built in 1881, burned at Amelia Beach, Dec. 18, 1883, at 2 A.M., at the mouth of Amelia River. Fire believed to have started from the cook's stove. Source: 14.

121. *R.W. Johnson* — Schooner, of Bridgeton, N.J., 252 tons, built in 1868, Captain Cobb, from Baltimore bound for Mosquito Inlet with a cargo of bricks for the Lighthouse. Stranded on the north beach of Mosquito Inlet, Jan. 15, 1886, at 6:50 A.M. A total loss. Two crew members of the seven on board lost. Source: 14.

122. *Athlete* — Vessel, type unknown, of Jacksonville, 178 tons, built in 1878, Captain Parsons, with general merchandise including a piano and an organ. Burned at New Smyrna Wharf, Feb. 2, 1886, at 4 P.M. A total loss. Source: 14.

123. *Theodore S. Parker* — Schooner, of New York, 33 tons, built in 1848, from New York bound for Mosquito Inlet with furniture, bricks, and salt. Stranded on Mosquito Inlet Bar, Feb. 9, 1886, at 9:30 A.M. Little cargo saved. Source: 14.

124. *Nathan Cobb* — Schooner, of Portland, Maine. Disabled during a storm, Dec. 5, 1886, and wrecked at Ormond Beach. One life lost. An inscribed boulder was sent from relatives in Maine to mark the resting place of the lost sailor. It is in the area of the wreck. Source: 14.

125. *Virginia Lee Hickman* — Schooner. Lost on the St. Augustine Bar, Jan. 26, 1888. Source: 9.

126. *Lady Banerman* — British schooner, of Nassau, 78 tons, 34 years old, Captain Thompson, from Jamaica bound for Jacksonville with fruit. Lost her foremast and wrecked 15 miles north of Cape Canaveral, Jan. 13, 1889. A total loss. Source: 14.

127. *Mattie Langdon* — Three-masted schooner, of Jacksonville, 303 tons, built in 1874, Captain Ross. Stranded on a shoal, Sept. 6, 1889, at 4 P.M., between the north and south jetty at the mouth of the St. Johns River, while being towed out to sea. Source: 14.

128. *David Clark* — Vessel, type unknown. Burned at Fernandina, Oct. 7, 1889. Source: 20.

129. *Svanen* — Bark. Lost on Fernandina Bar, March 23, 1890. Source: 9.

130. *Ethel* — Schooner, of Jacksonville, 32 tons, built in 1862, Captain Garrison, from Jacksonville bound for Nassau with lumber and miscellaneous cargo. Foundered 18 miles northeast of Cape Canaveral, April 5, 1890, at 10:30 P.M. Crew saved. Source: 14.

131. *Franconia* — Tramp steamer, of New York, 808 tons (another source says 445 tons and another 674 tons), built in 1864 at Kennebunkport, Maine, 179' x 30' x 18'5". She left New York bound for Fernandina, July 23, 1890, in ballast to pick up a cargo of phosphate. On July 28 the pilot boat *Agnes Bell* hailed her about three miles off Fernandina Bar. The *Fraconia*'s captain declined the pilot's help and she soon was blown off course. She grounded near the wreck of the *City of Austin,* on the bar on North Pelican Bank, Cumberland Sound, July 28, 1890, at 5 P.M. On Aug. 4, she caught fire and burned. Source: 14. 40 (Vol. 4, 1966), 52.

132. *Soli Deo Gloria* — Bark. Lost at Nassau Inlet, Oct. 19, 1891. Source: 9.

133. *T(?) Louise* — British schooner, 223 tons, from Fernandina bound for Barbados with phosphate. Stranded on the North Breakers of Fernandina Bar, Jan. 14, 1892, at 4 P.M. Source: 14.

134. *Mascott* — Vessel, type unknown. Wrecked on Cumberland Beach, March 29, 1893. Source: 20.

135. *Maggie Jones* — Schooner, of Fernandina. Driven ashore during a storm the night of Aug. 16, 1893, near the shingle mill at Fernandina. Source: 14.

136. *J.E. Stevens* — Vessel, type unknown. Burned at Mayport, July 26, 1894. Source: 20.

137. *Steam Tug* — Of Tabasco, Mexico, 75 tons, built in 1881, from Key West bound for Wilmington. Sank off the Mosquito Bank, May 25, 1896, at 11 A.M. A total loss. Source: 14.

138. *City of Brunswick* — Sidewheel steamer (formerly the *Thomas Collyer*), of Brunswick, Ga., 194 tons, built in 1850 at New York, 123.8' x 22.7' x 6.9'. Caught fire at her dock at Mayport after discharging all cargo and passengers, Sept. 11, 1897. Cut loose and sank

on the St. Johns Bluff at Sisters Creek, where she burned to the water's edge. Source: 20, 40 (Vol. 6, 1969), 52.

139. *Commodore* — Steamer, built in 1882 at Philadelphia, 123' x 19' x 11.5', Captain Murphy. Sank approximately 12 miles off Daytona Beach in 1897. Now lies in 70 feet of water. The author Stephen Crane was on board when she sank. He and three others took to one of the lifeboats and spent 30 hours before reaching shore at Daytona, where one of the four drowned when the boat capsized. The event inspired his writing of the short story "The Open Boat." On board were munitions bound for the Cubans fighting for independence from Spain. Don Serbouseck has an admiralty claim on this site. Source: 94 (Barada, Bill. "Commodore." May 1987, pp. 128-132), 94 (Boyd, Ellsworth. "Wreck Facts." May, 1988, p. 26).

140. *Lina* — German bark (steel), 1,199 tons, built in 1871. Abandoned at sea, and eventually grounded on the beach, April 6, 1898, at 9 A.M., 12 miles south of Fernandina. Unknown if salvaged. Source: 14.

141. *Amelia* — Steamer, 21 tons, built in 1898 at Fernandina, 42' x 10' x 4.6'. Foundered at Fernandina, Oct. 2, 1898. Source: 14.

142. *Ida E. Latham* — Schooner, of Connecticut, 462 tons, built in 1874 at Belfast, Maine, 136.6' x 33.4' x 15.4', from New York bound for Fernandina with salt. Stranded north of the channel at Fernandina, Jan. 14, 1899, at 3 A.M. A total loss. Source: 14.

143. *General Whitney* — Steamer (iron), of the Metropolitan S.S. Co., 1,848 tons, built in 1873 at Wilmington. On April 23, 1899, she was northbound with a heavy cargo of copper billets and molasses. Off St. Augustine she was hit by a severe storm and foundered. The crew barely made it to the boats. One of the boats capsized in the breakers, drowning the captain and 16 of the crew. A total loss. Source: 40 (Vol.1, 1953).

144. *John H. Tingue* — Schooner, 552 tons, built in 1884 at New Haven, 136.6' x 33.4' x 12.2,' Captain Taylor, from Philadelphia bound for Jacksonville with 699 tons of coal. Struck the beach at Cumberland Island (just north of Fernandina in Georgia) during a storm, Oct. 5, 1899. The residents of the island helped the crew. Source: 14.

145. *John R. Anidia(?)* — Schooner, 32 tons, built in 1857, Captain Millan (possibly the schooner *John R. Wilder,* of Fernandina, 34 tons, built in 1854 at Savannah, 62' x 16' x 7.8'). Sank in Fernandina Harbor, Oct. 6, 1899, during a strong gale. Source: 14.

1900

146. *Providenza R* — Italian bark, of Genoa, 895 tons, built in 1856, from Barbados bound for Fernandina, in ballast. Stranded on Amelia Beach, Dec. 4, 1901, approximately two miles south of Cumberland Sound Bar. Source: 14.

147. *Orithyia* — Schooner yacht, of New York, 38 tons, built in 1890 at Greenwood, N.Y., 54' x 16.5' x 8.3'. Stranded on the St. Johns Bar, Dec. 11, 1901. Source: 14.

148. *Mary F. Godfrey* — Schooner, of Somers Point, N.J., 446 tons, built in 1882 at Tuckahoe, N.J., 140.4' x 34.5' x 12.3'. Sprang a leak on May 10, 1903. An attempt was made to tow her into the St. Johns River, but she broke up within an hour. Note: One source says she broke up after entering the river. Source: 14.

149. *Oregon* — Steamer, of St. Augustine, 21 tons, built in 1899 at Daytona, 60' x 11' x 4'. Burned at Ormond, July 29, 1904. Source: 14.

150. *Peconic* — Steamer (iron), 1,855 tons, built in 1881. Foundered off Fernandina, Aug. 28, 1905. Twenty lives lost. Source: 14.

151. *Pasadena* (formerly *Erastus Wiman*) — Schooner, of New York, 596 tons, built in 1880 at Bath, 148.6' x 36.3' x 15.5', from New York bound for Crandell, Fla. Parted her chain and wrecked at the Fernandina Jetty, Nov. 22, 1905, at 11 P.M., during a storm. Source: 14.

152. *Ruby* — Norwegian ship, of Skien, 1,418 tons, built in 1878 in Nova Scotia, 208.8' x 39.6' x 23.8', stranded off Quarantine Station, Fernandina, Jan. 15, 1907, and was condemned. (See Figure 46). Source: 80, Florida State Archives.

153. *Marie Gilbert* — Four-masted schooner, of New London, 586 tons, built in 1906 at Mystic, 166.6' x 36.2' x 12.6'. Stranded on Nassau Bar near Mayport, April 20 or 22, 1907. Source: 14, 80.

154. *Glad Tidings* — Schooner (formerly a barkentine), of New London, 654 tons, built in 1884 at Belfast, Maine, 159.2' x 33.1' x 17', from Baltimore bound for Mayport with coal. Struck a shoal, passed over it and sank, Oct. 16, 1907, at 1 P.M., west-northwest of St. Andrews Lighthouse. A total loss. Source: 14, 80.

155. *Alma H.* — Gas vessel, 37 tons, built in 1908. Burned at St. Augustine, Dec. 9, 1908. Source: 14.

Figure 46: Norwegian ship *Ruby*, stranded off Quarantine Station, Fernandina, 1907. Note the tug *Wade Hampton* in the background. FLORIDA STATE ARCHIVES.

156. *Chatham* (formerly the *Vulcan*) — Sidewheel steamer (iron), of the Merchants and Miner Transportation Co. (M&M Line), 2,728 tons, built in 1884 at Philadelphia, 265.4' x 40' x 15.6'. Stranded on the north jetty of the St. Johns River during a dense fog while attempting to enter the river, Jan. 14, 1910. A total loss. (See Figure 47). Source: 14, 20, 80.

157. *Gracie D. Buchanan* — Four-masted schooner, 1,141 tons, built in 1888 at Bath, 194.6' x 40' x 18.1'. Stranded at Nassau Inlet, Feb. 10, 1910. Source: 14.

158. *Majik City* — Steamer, 315 tons, built in 1876. Was rammed and sunk by the *Parthian,* Feb. 16, 1910, off Pilot Town (Mayport). Source: 14, 20.

159. *William W. Converse* — Schooner, 745 tons, built in 1886 at New Haven, 168.8' x 37.8' x 18'. Stranded at Halifax River Beach, Oct. 18, 1910. Three lives lost. Source: 14.

160. *Jessie A. Bishop* — Four-masted schooner, of New Haven, 754 tons, built in 1908 at Rockland, Maine, 188.9' x 38' x 14.9'. Stranded at Nassau Inlet, Jan. 1, 1912. Source: 14, 80.

161. *Emily B* — Listed as a both a gas vessel and a schooner, 43 tons,

Figure 47: Steamer *Chatham,* wrecked in 1910. THE STEAMSHIP SOCIETY COLLECTION, UNIVERSITY OF BALTIMORE LIBRARY.

90' x 18' x 5', built in 1887 at Jacksonville as a schooner. Lost off Ponce Park, near Daytona, in 1912. Source: 14, 48.

162. *Alert* — Gas vessel (formerly a schooner yacht), 99 tons, built in 1888 at Boston, 92.5' x 23.1' x 11'. Stranded on Nassau Bar, Nov. 24, 1914. Source: 14.

163. *L. McNeill* — Sidewheel steamer, 145 tons, built in 1899 at Jacksonville, 93.3' x 22.2' x 5.7'. Stranded at Mosquito Inlet, June 8, 1916. Source: 14.

164. *Nanon* — Gas vessel (formerly a cutter yacht), 26 tons, built in 1889 at South Boston, 50.3' x 16.5' x 6.6'. Stranded at Anastasia Island, Sept. 3, 1916. Source: 14.

165. *Manatanzas* — Gas vessel, 43 tons, built in 1906. Stranded at Matanzas Inlet, Dec. 18, 1916. Source: 14.

166. *Fanny Sprague* — Steamer, 56 tons, built in 1872 at South Boston, 79.2' x 16.6' x 7.8'. Stranded at Fort George Inlet, April 30, 1917. Source: 14.

167. *Ethel* — Gas vessel, 718 tons, built in 1918. Foundered off St. Augustine, Oct. 23, 1918. Source: 14.

168. *Daisy Farlin* — Three-masted schooner, of Bath, 466 tons, built in 1891 at Bath, 151.6' x 34.2' x 11.3'. Sank on Nov. 18, 1919, at approximate Lat. 31-00-00, Long. 80-10-00. (See Figure 48). Source: 1, 14, 80.

Figure 48: Schooner *Daisy Farlin*, wrecked in 1919. MAINE MARITIME MUSEUM.

169. *Lejok* — Schooner, 371 tons, built in 1901 at Milbridge, Maine, 134.6' x 32' x 10.6'. Foundered, March 4, 1920, at Lat. 29-12-00, Long. 79-10-00. Source: 14.

170. *Northwestern* (formerly *Orizaba*) — Steam freighter, of Cleveland, 1,645 tons, built in 1881 at Cleveland, 247.6' x 36.3' x 20.2'. Stranded at Mantanzas Inlet, March 22, 1920. One life lost. Source: 14.

Figure 49: Schooner *Margaret Thomas*, stranded off Mosquito Lagoon, Feb. 29, 1924. PENOBSCOT MARINE MUSEUM.

185

171. *Minerva* — Schooner, 222 tons, built in 1863 at Black River, Ohio, 125.5' x 26.7' x 9.8'. Stranded at Anastasia Island, June 25, 1920. Source: 14.

172. *Swordfish* — Gas yacht, of New York, 151 tons, built in 1901 at Nyak, N.Y., 116.8' x 17.7' x 4.9'. Burned near Amelia, April 29, 1921. Source: 14.

173. *Victory* — Steam tug, of New York, 337 tons, built in 1918 at West New Brighton, N.Y., 115.4' x 30.8' x 14'. Burned off Mantanzas Inlet, May 11, 1921, at Lat. 29-27-14, Long. 80-52-50, in 81 feet of water. Source: 14.

174. *Hercules* — Steam freighter, of New York, 163 tons, built in 1905 at Tomkins Cove, N.Y., 93' x 24.8' x 9.6'. Foundered June 9, 1923, at Lat. 30-43-00, Long. 79-35-00. Source: 1, 14.

175. *Margaret Thomas* — Four-masted schooner, of Boston, 1,427 tons, built in 1904 at Thomaston, Maine, 201.1' x 47' x 19.6'. Stranded off Mosquito Lagoon, Feb. 29, 1924. (See Figure 49). Source: 14, 80.

176. *Hermitage* — Schooner barge (steel), of Pittsburgh, 2,111 tons, built in 1919 at Baltimore, 306.2' x 50.2' x 20.3'. Foundered Nov. 22, 1924, at Lat. 30-16-00, Long. 79-43-00. Source: 14.

177. *Comanche* — Steamer (steel), of New York, 3,856 tons, built in 1895 at Philadelphia, 300' x 46' x 18.9'. Left Jacksonville Oct. 17, 1925, with a cargo of resin. Three hours later she caught fire and had to be abandoned. Source: 14, 42, 80.

178. *Walborg Potter* — Steamer, 44 tons, built in 1906. Foundered at Cape Canaveral, Nov. 9, 1926. Source: 14.

179. *Piute* — Motor vessel, 79 tons, built in 1925. Stranded at Mosquito Inlet, Jan. 27, 1927. Source: 14.

180. *Santa Clause* — Freight vessel (gas), of St. Augustine, 78 tons, built in 1922 at Daytona, 58.6' x 18' x 5.4'. Burned at St. Augustine, March 30, 1927. Source: 14.

181. *Social* — Fishing vessel (gas), 21 tons, built in 1922 at Fernandina, 42.4' x 13.5' x 5.7'. Burned at Fernandina, July 29, 1928. Source: 14.

182. *Service* — Fishing vessel (oil), of Miami, 33 tons, built in 1917 at

Eden, Fla., 59.2' x 14.6' x 5.7'. Foundered at Flagler Beach, March 10, 1929. Source: 14.

183. *Ada Tower* — Four-masted schooner, of Petersboro, Nova Scotia, 573 tons, built in 1916 at Port Greville, Nova Scotia, 175.5' x 36.4' x 12.9'. Wrecked at Jacksonville, Oct. 10, 1929. Source: 80.

184. *Naya* — Gas vessel, 24 tons, built in 1911. Stranded at Cape Canaveral, April 27, 1930. Source: 14.

185. *Tamarco* — Four-masted schooner, of Tampa, 686 tons, built in 1902 at Bath, 172.8' x 36.6' x 14'. Foundered off Flagler Beach, Sept. 5, 1929 (another source says Sept. 24, 1932). One life lost. Source: 14, 80.

186. *Bill Nye* — Schooner, 80 tons, built in 1893 at Madison, Md., 82' x 24.3' x 6.6'. Stranded at Fernandina, Aug. 7, 1933. Source: 14.

187. *Ojus* — Oil vessel, 22 tons, built in 1929. Stranded on the beach, Dec. 21, 1936, approximately 500 yards north of the bar at Ponce de Leon Inlet. Source: 14.

188. *Fortuna II* — Oil vessel, 38 tons, built in 1907. Stranded 16 miles north of St. Augustine, Feb. 1, 1938. Source: 14.

189. *Caroline* — Motor vessel, 109 tons, built in 1918 at St. Marys, Ga., 107.2' x 19.1' x 6.6'. Foundered in Cumberland Sound, Aug. 11, 1939. Located in 1949 at Lat. 30-47-00, Long. 81-24-00. Source: 1, 14.

190. Unknown Wreck — Charted in 1944, though she sank before WWII, at Lat. 30-26-48, Long. 81-19-06, in 65 feet of water. Source: 1.

191. *Ruby Lee II* — Gas vessel, 79 tons, built in 1924. Wrecked at the mouth of the St. Johns, July 4, 1941. Source: 14.

See World War II section for Section 6 wrecks during that period.

192. *Dixie Crystal* — O/V, 123 tons, built in 1895. Stranded at Nun Buoy 152, opposite Vilano Beach, St. Augustine, Sept. 21, 1945. Source: 14.

193. *Mary Linda* — O/V, 35 tons, built in 1945. Collided with range light, Nov. 4, 1946, one mile northeast of jetty at Mayport. Source: 14.

194. *Hudson* — O/V (iron), 124 tons, built in 1893 at Camden, N.J., 93.2' x 20.5' x 9.9'. Foundered on jetties at entrance to St. Johns River, Dec. 19, 1946. Source: 14,

195. *Valkyrie* — G/V, 58 tons, built in 1915. Stranded at Medicis Creek ten miles north of St. Augustine, Nov. 3, 1947. Source: 14.

196. *Trawler* — Sank in November 1947, at Lat. 30-23-30, Long. 81-19-00. Source: 1.

197. *Sea Breeze* — O/V, 32 tons, built in 1944. Foundered off False Cape, north of Cape Canaveral, Jan. 17, 1948. Source: 14.

198. *Uncle Sam* — O/V, 26 tons, built in 1940. Stranded one mile south of Ponce de Leon Inlet, Feb. 27, 1948. Source: 14.

199. *Red Snapper* — O/V, 33 tons, built in 1938. Lost 11 miles south of New Smyrna Beach, Dec. 25, 1948. Source: 14.

200. *Little Stevie* — O/V, 27 tons, built in 1943. Foundered at approximate Lat. 29-02-00, Long. 80-25-00, Nov. 29, 1949. Source: 14.

201. *Marion* — O/V, 35 tons, built in 1946. Beached one mile south of the South Jetty, Fernandina Beach, June 15, 1950. Source: 14.

202. *Gypsy Girl* — O/V, 52 tons, built in 1945, burned 2-1/2 miles north of the North Jetty range line, July 17, 1950, at the Fernandina Harbor entrance. Source: 14.

203. *Trawler* — Sank in September 1950, in 40 feet of water, at Lat. 30-43-15, Long. 81-21-30. Source: 1.

204. *Seafarer* — M/V, 63 tons, built in 1952. Foundered Oct. 1, 1952, at Lat. 28-36-00, Long. 80-35-00. Source: 14.

205. *Wanderer* — O/V, 44 tons, built in 1948. Foundered off Crescent Beach, at Mantanzas Inlet, Dec. 6, 1954. Source: 14.

206. *American Eagle* — O/V, 38 tons, built in 1953. Stranded at Mantanzas Beach, Dec. 6, 1954. Source: 14.

207. *Donald Ray* — O/V, 34 tons, built in 1950. Lost off Mayport, March 8, 1957. Source: 14.

208. *Miss Ilse* — O/V, 31 tons, built in 1950. Stranded on Flagler Beach, Nov. 22, 1957. Source: 14.

209. Unknown wreck — Charted in 1957, in 126 feet of water, at Lat. 30-46-28, Long. 80-15-00. Source: 1.

210. *Elizabeth Perry* — O/V, 47 tons, built in 1949. Foundered 2,000 feet south of the jetties, St. Augustine, Dec. 14, 1958. Source: 14.

211. *Deepwater II* — O/V, 44 tons, built in 1954. Lost on Jan. 24, 1960, at approximate Lat. 30-31-00, Long. 80-28-00. Source: 14.

212. *Big Lady* — O/V, 48 tons, built in 1910. Foundered at entrance to Nassau Sound, at the south end of Amelia Island, May 11, 1960. Source: 14.

213. *Majo* — O/V, 30 tons, built in 1947. Stranded at Ponte Vedra Beach city limits, Aug. 31, 1960. Source: 14.

214. *Jackie B* — O/V, 44 tons, built in 1948. Foundered approximately 20 miles off Mayport, Nov. 8, 1960. Source: 14.

215. *D&D II* — O/V, 46 tons, built in 1945. Foundered southeast of St. Augustine, Nov. 30, 1960. Source: 14.

216. *Chichemo* — O/V, 39 tons, built in 1953. Burned approximately 14 miles south of Jacksonville Beach, April 28, 1962. Source: 14.

217. *Cape Charles* — F/V (oil), 33 tons, built in 1945 at Fernandina, 53.2' x 16.1' x 6'. Lost during a storm, Nov. 26, 1962, at Lat. 28-36-04, Long. 80-35-18. Source: 14.

218. *Miller Brothers* — F/V (oil), 63 tons, built in 1952 at St. Augustine, 58.7' x 18.5' x 8.2'. Foundered approximately two miles south of Turtle Mound, seven miles south of New Smyrna Beach, Nov. 22, 1963. Source: 14.

219. *John Wayne* — F/V (oil), 34 tons, built in 1944. Wrecked on the beach, Jan. 7, 1965, seven miles south of Ponte Vedra Beach. Source: 14.

220. *Rhea* — F/V (oil), 63 tons, built in 1953 at St. Augustine, 58.7' x 18.5' x 8.2'. Foundered at False Cape, five miles offshore, three miles north of Cape Canaveral, Jan. 3, 1966. Source: 14.

221. *Captain Ike Lewis* — O/V, 44 tons, built in 1950. Collided with the North Jetty in the St. Johns, at Mayport, April 5, 1967. Source: 14.

222. *Sea Eagle* — F/V (oil), 65 tons, built in 1953. Stranded 1/4 mile east of the North Jetty, St. Augustine, Nov. 11, 1968. Source: 14.

223. *Granada* — O/V, 45 tons, built in 1947. Lost during a storm, Nov. 25, 1969, in Fort George Inlet, 3/4 mile north of the Mayport

Jetties. Source: 14.

224. *Sea Boy* — O/V, 31 tons, built in 1949. Stranded 50 feet east by southeast of the North Jetty, Ponce de Leon Inlet, Dec. 9, 1969. Source: 14.

225. *Outcast* — O/V, 64 tons, built in 1958. Stranded off Fort George Inlet, Jan. 14, 1970. Source: 14.

226. *Lady M. Johnson* — F/V (oil), 46 tons, built in 1947. Foundered in the St. Johns, at the North Jetty between Buoy 8 and 10, March 18, 1970. Source: 14.

227. *Patricia M* — F/V (gas), 67 tons, built in 1964 at St. Augustine, 62.2' x 18.3' x 8.4'. Stranded north of Ponte Vedra, south of Jacksonville Beach, June 26, 1970. Source: 14.

228. *Joan & Ursala* — F/V (oil), 60 tons, built in 1937. Foundered ten miles south of St. Augustine, Aug. 5, 1972. Source: 14.

229. *Oriental Warrior* (formerly the *Hamburg*) — One of the first combi-vessels (passenger cargo ships), 8,269 tons, built in 1954 in Germany, 538' x 64', single screw. She carried 81 first-class passengers and could do 16.5 knots. She was from New York bound for Hong Kong. On May 25, 1972, approximately 40 miles northeast of Daytona Beach, an explosion in the engine room caused a fire, which then spread further in the ship. She arrived at Jacksonville two days later and sank. On Sept. 25, she was refloated and found to be unsalvageable. On Oct. 1, 1972, she was towed to Lat. 30-23-00, Long. 79-23-00, and sunk. Source: 82.

230. *Nina Fay* — F/V (oil), 47 tons, built in 1952. Lost during a storm off St. Augustine Beach, Dec. 16, 1972. Source: 14.

231. *Miss Libby* — F/V (oil), 30 tons, built in 1958. Stranded at Crescent Beach, Dec. 16, 1972. Source: 14.

232. *Miss Lula* — F/V (oil), 30 tons, built in 1954. Stranded off Ponte Vedra Beach, June 3, 1974, at Lat. 30-14-00, Long. 81-22-28. Source: 14.

233. *Pan Dallas* — F/V. Sank in 1980, at approximate Lat. 29-36-00, Long. 80-54-00. Source: 1.

234. *Free Spirit Enterprise* — 43'. Burned and sank in 1981, at Lat. 28-39-42, Long. 80-23-18. Source: 1.

235. *Ghost* — F/V, 68'. Sank in 1981, at Lat. 29-04-48, Long. 80-53-00. Source: 1.

Figure 49A: Copy of original woodcut from story of the *Alna*. THE TRAGEDY OF THE SEAS; OR, SORROW ON THE OCEAN, LAKE, AND RIVER, FROM SHIPWRECK, PLAGUE, FIRE AND FAMINE BY CHARLES ELLMS. (See narrative on pages 278–281).

Section 7: Inland Waters

1700

1. Spanish ship — Sometime before 1763 a ship was lost in a river near Warrington, Fla. All men lost. Source: 54.

2. *Britannia* — British sloop. Blown up by the Americans on the St. Mary's River, August 1776. The British schooner *Ponpey* was captured at the same time. Source: 59.

1800

3. *Sangamon* — Sidewheel steamer, 103 tons, built in 1832 at Portland, Ky. Stranded at Kent River, March 1, 1835. Source: 52.

4. *Ohion* — Sidewheel steamer, 104 tons, built in 1833 at Pittsburgh. Burned at Ocheesee (near present-day Blountstown) on the Apalachicola River, April 23, 1836. One life lost. Source: 52.

5. *Boatwright* — Sidewheel steamer, 184 tons, built in 1835 at New York. Stranded on Indian River, April 23, 1838. Source: 52.

6. *Tempest* — Sidewheel steamer, 105 tons, built in 1835 at Pittsburgh, snagged on the Chatahoochee River (probably confused it with Apalachicola River), at Ocheesee, Nov. 26, 1838. Source: 14, 52.

7. *Commerce* — Sidewheel steamer, 124 tons, built in 1836 at New Albany, Ind. (one source says 124 tons, built in 1834 at Pittsburg, 110' x 17' x 5'). Exploded on the Apalachicola River, March 5, 1839. Five lives lost. Source: 14, 52.

8. *Little Rock* — Sidewheel steamer, 156 tons, built in 1837 at Cincinnati. Stranded on the Boeuf River, April 3, 1840. Source: 52.

9. *LeRoy* — Sidewheel steamer, 83 tons, built in 1836 at Brownsville, Pa. Exploded at Iola, on the Apalachicola River, Oct. 25, 1840. Six lives lost. Source: 52.

10. *Chamois* — Sidewheel steamer, 125 tons, built in 1936 at Pittsburgh. Exploded at River Junction (Gadson County), Oct. 31, 1842. Source: 52.

11. *Robert Fulton* — Sidewheel steamer, 187 tons, built in 1839 at Madison, Ind. Snagged at Iola, July 9, 1843. Source: 52.

12. *Fanny Ellsler* — Steamer. Her boilers caught fire and she burned

to the waterline on the Apalachicola River in 1844. Source: 103

13. *Siren* — Sidewheel steamer, of Apalachicola, 110 tons, built in 1838 at Cincinnati, carried 200 bales of cotton. Exploded Feb. 8, 1845, a few miles below Chattahoochee, Fla. Nine or ten lives lost. Source: 103

14. *Lowell* — Sidewheel steamer, 159 tons, built in 1839 at Jeffersonville, Ind. Snagged below Fort Gaines, March 4, 1845. Source: 52.

Note: The steamers *Charleston* (146 tons, listed as wrecked at Gibsons Reach, Ala., in 1848), and the *Apalachicola* (149 tons, listed as wrecked at Kings Rocks, Ala., in 1848), are also listed from the District of Apalachicola as having wrecked on the Apalachicola River in May 1848. Source: 14, 52.

15. *Eagle* — Sidewheel steamer, 200 tons, built in 1852 at Shousetown, Pa., from Columbus bound for Apalachicola with 1,300 bales of cotton. Destroyed by fire, Jan. 29, 1854, below Columbus (one source says on the Apalachicola River). Four lives lost. Source: 52, 99 (Feb. 3, 1854).

16. *Franklin* — Sternwheel steamer, 181 tons, built in 1851 at Brownsville, Pa. Burned on the Apalachicola River, January 1854. One life lost. Source: 52.

17. *Seminole* — Sidewheel steamer, 319 tons, built in 1854 by D.P. Landershire of Savannah, 152'6" x 26' x 9'. Burned at the wharf at Jacksonville, Dec. 20, 1855, and drifted to the opposite shore. A total loss. Another source states that her hull was later raised. Source: 52, 60, 97 (Mueller, Edward. "East Coast Florida Steamboating, 1831-1861." Vol. XL, No.3, January 1962, pp. 241-260,).

18. *Cusseta* and the *Union* — The *Cusseta*, sidewheel steamer, 201 tons, built in 1851 at Cincinnati, and the *Union*, 209 tons, built in 1852 at Cincinnati. Collided with each other on the Apalachicola River, Feb. 5, 1856. Source: 52.

19. *Major William Barnett* — Sidewheel steamer, 116 tons, built in 1851 at Camden, N.J., and sailed on the St. Johns River. Her boilers exploded, Aug. 3, 1859, killing the captain and three passengers. Source: 20, 52.

See Civil War Section for Section 7 wrecks during that period.

20. *Widgeon* — Steamer, 56 tons, built in 1864 at Ogdensburg, N.Y.

Burned at Jacksonville, April 8, 1867. Source: 52.

21. *Sylph* — Sidewheel steamer, 290 tons, built in 1844 at New York. Burned March 31, 1868, at Julington Creek near Jacksonville. Source: 52.

22. *General U.S. Grant* — Steamer, 58 tons, built in 1863 at Philadelphia. Burned at Jacksonville, Aug. 2, 1869. Source: 52.

23. *J.D. Swain* — Sidewheel steamer, 228 tons, built in 1859 at Jeffersonville, Ind. Sank as a Confederate steamer but was raised in 1864. Stranded on the Escambia River in 1869. Source: 52.

24. *Fanny Fern* — Steamer, of Jacksonville, 17 tons, built in 1868 at Jacksonville. Exploded at Jacksonville, Jan. 21, 1873. Source: 52.

25. *Nick King* (formerly *St. Marys*; see Civil War Section) — Steamer (iron), 337 tons, built in 1857 at Wilmington. Struck an obstruction on the St. Johns in mid-1874 (one source says she wrecked Jan. 24, 1873, on the Altahama River, Ga.). A total loss. Source: 20, 52.

26. *Oyster Boy* — Steam tug, 84 tons, built in 1864 at New Brunswick, N.J., Captain Wilson, from Jacksonville bound for Trout Creek. Burned at Cold Hill on the St. Johns, May 24, 1876, and was scuttled. A total loss. Source: 14, 52.

27. *Ocklawaha* — Sternwheel steamer (recessed wheel), of Jacksonville, 60 tons, built in 1867 at Palatka, Captain Hart. Caught fire near Hart's Orange Grove, Aug. 31, 1877, while moored on the bank of the St. Johns. A total loss. Source: 14, 52.

28. *Lollie Boy* — Steamer, of Jacksonville, 86 tons, built in 1873, Captain Jones, from Silver Springs bound for Jacksonville with cotton, oranges, and hides. Sank while enroute, Nov. 11, 1877. Some cargo saved. Source: 14.

29. *Starlight* — Sidewheel steamer, of Jacksonville, 261 tons, built in 1866 at Portland, Maine, Captain Coxetter, from Jacksonville bound for Enterprise. Burned at the wharf at Sanford, May 11, 1878 (or 1879), at 2 A.M. Passengers and crew narrowly escaped. A total loss. Source: 14, 20, 52.

30. *Magnet* — Steamer. Burned at Jacksonville, May 1879. A partial loss. Source: 14.

31. *L.T. Knight* — Schooner, of St. Marys, 203 tons, built in 1853, from St. Marys bound for Rio with yellow pine lumber. Stranded at

the east point of Tiger Island, June 5, 1879, at the mouth of the Amelia and St. Marys rivers. A total loss. Source: 14.

32. *Abbie* — Steamer, of Jacksonville, 18 tons, built in 1877, from Clay Springs bound for Sanford. Stranded at Dyles Wharf, Melbourne, Aug. 29, 1880, at 8 p.m. Source: 14.

33. *Representative* — Schooner, of Pensacola, 13 tons, from Berry's Mill bound for Barrancas with lumber. Sank at Barrancas Wharf during a storm, Aug. 2, 1881, and broke up. Some cargo saved. Source: 14.

34. *Star* — Vessel, type unknown, 236 tons, built in 1861, burned at Crescent Lake, Nov. 2, 1881. Note: Seems to be the same vessel as *Seth Low*. Source: 20.

35. *Seth Low* — Sidewheel steam tug, of Jacksonville, 236 tons, built in 1861 at Keyport, N.J., 126' x 23' x 8'. Burned at the mouth of Trout Creek on the St. Johns, Nov. 2, 1888, next to the wreck of the *Oyster Boy* (1876). The *Seth Low* was famous in that she was the vessel that towed the *USS Monitor* from New York to Hampton Roads, March 1862. Source: 52, 80.

36. *City of Sanford* — Steamer, of Jacksonville, 145 tons, built in 1880, Captain Roberts, from Palatka bound for Jacksonville with vegetables and palmetto buds. Burned at Point La Vista, April 24, 1882. Nine lives lost. A total loss. Source: 14, 20.

37. *Jarlington* — Schooner, of Jacksonville, 17 tons, Captain Moore, from Jacksonville bound for Fruit Cove. Capsized off Fruit Cove on the St. Johns, Sept. 15, 1882. A total loss. Source: 14.

38. *Heather Barker* — Schooner, of Jacksonville, 74 tons, built in 1874, Captain Moore, from Jacksonville bound for Fruit Cove with lumber. Sank off Black Point on the St. Johns, Oct. 15, 1882. Cargo saved. Source: 14.

39. *Isis* — Sternwheel steamer (iron), 73 tons, built in 1870, Captain Summerville, from Volusia bound for Jacksonville with oranges, flour, and honey. Foundered in Lake George, Nov. 6, 1882, at 4 A.M., approximately 2-1/2 miles southeast and 1/4 mile south of Lake George Wharf House, east end of Drayton Island. Three lives lost. A total loss. Source: 14, 20.

40. *Volusia* — Steamer, of Jacksonville, 102 tons. Sank after a boiler explosion, Dec. 2, 1882, at 1:30 P.M., at the wharf at the foot of Newman St., Jacksonville. A total loss. Source: 14.

41. *Arrow* — Sidewheel steamer, 123 tons, built in 1855 at New Castle, Del., 142' x 21' x 4.4'. Came to Jacksonville in 1879 and ran on the St. Johns. Sank off St. Johns Bluff on the St. Johns, in 1883 or 1884. A total loss. Source: 52, 60.

42. *Dictator* — Sidewheel steamer, 735 tons, built in 1863 at Williamsburgh, N.Y., rebuilt in 1865, 205.8' x 30' x 8.6', bought by James McKay of Tampa in 1883. From Manatee bound for Tampa. She grounded at the mouth of the Hillsborough River on Dec. 24 or 26, 1884, and later that evening caught fire. A total loss amounting to $42,000. Source: 40 (Vol. 5, 1967), 60.

43. *Ida Stockton* — Sternwheel steamer, of Pensacola, 64 tons, built in 1864. Burned at the Hoodless Ship Yard, Milton, Aug. 3, 1885. A total loss. Source: 14.

44. *Schooner* — 16 tons. Lost off Fort George, Aug. 22, 1885. Source: 14.

45. *Fannie Duggan* — Sidewheel steamer, built in 1872, 165'. Stranded in Lake Monroe in 1885. Source: 20.

46. *W.D. Ellis* — Steamer, 146 tons, built in 1882, from Apalachicola bound for Columbus, Ga., with a general cargo. Ran ashore near Apalachicola River, Dec. 1, 1885, at 10 P.M. Source: 14.

47. *City of Georgetown* — Vessel of Jacksonville, 78 tons, from Jacksonville bound for Lake Jessup with general merchandise. Collided with the vessel *City Of Monticello*, Feb. 11, 1886, opposite Palatka, at 4 A.M. Source: 14.

48. *Bertha Lee* — Steamer, 121 tons, from Columbus bound for Apalachicola with general merchandise. Wrecked May 2, 1886, at head of a slough, 50 miles above Apalachicola on the Apalachicola River. Source: 14.

49. *Rosalie* — Sternwheel steamer, 41'. Sank near the Fort Thompson rapids, near the mouth of the Kissimmee River, in 1886. Source: 84.

50. *Lourah* — Schooner, of Pensacola, 36 tons, built in 1877, from Pensacola bound for Point Washington. Caught fire at Criglor & Sons Mill, July 18, 1887. A total loss. Source: 14.

51. *Port Royal* — Sidewheel steamer, of Jacksonville, 136 tons (also listed at 187 tons), built in 1861 at Staten Island, N.Y.. Burned at the wharf while under repair at Jacksonville, Oct. 31, 1887. A total loss. Source: 14, 52.

52. *Henry Nin(?)* — Vessel, type unknown, of Jacksonville, 98 tons, built in 1871, Captain Watts. Burned at Palatka Wharf, Dec. 14, 1887. A total loss. Source: 14.

53. *Ridgeman* — Schooner, of Jacksonville, 282 tons, built in 1864, Captain Grace. Burned on the St. Johns River, May 9, 1888, at the mill, with a cargo of lumber. Source: 14.

54. *Melzingah* (formerly *William Tittamer*) — Sidewheel steamer, of Pensacola, 134 tons (also listed at 184 tons), built in 1864 at Keyport, N.J., Captain Allen. Burned at the dock on Blackwater River, Sept. 6, 1888, at 10 P.M., 1/2 mile below Milton. A total loss. Source: 14, 52.

55. *North Star* — Paddlewheel steamer, of Jacksonville, 146 tons, built in 1868. Burned at Sand Fly Point, Nov. 2, 1888, on the St. Johns. Source: 14.

56. *Oyster Boy* — Paddlewheel steamer, of Jacksonville, 54 tons, built in 1878. Burned along with the *North Star*, Nov. 2, 1888, at Sand Fly Point. Source: 14.

57. *Chipola* — Steamer, 32 tons, built in 1886, Captain Stone, from Iola bound for Magnolia Bluff on the Chipola River. Sank at Magnolia Landing, Aug. 12, 1889, at the wharf on the Chipola River. Source: 14.

58. *Falcon* — Vessel, type unknown, of Pensacola, 90 tons, from Alabama bound for Carryville. Burned at Carryville, Dec. 25, 1889. Source: 14.

59. *Louise* — Sidewheel steamer, of Jacksonville, 44 tons, built in 1857, Captain Floyd, from Mayport bound for Jacksonville with fish. Hit a sunken lighter opposite the lumber mill at East Jacksonville and sank, Feb. 10, 1890. Vessel valued at $10,000 ($8,000 loss). Cargo a total loss. Source: 14.

60. *H. B. Plant* — Paddlewheel steamer (iron), of New Haven, 287 tons, built in 1882, Captain Hall, from Jacksonville bound for Sanford with miscellaneous cargo. Burned at Lake Beresford, April 29, 1890. Three lives lost. A total loss. Source: 14.

61. *Marion* — Flat-bottomed boat, of Jacksonville, 61 tons, built in 1871. Burned at Harts Point, opposite Palatka, Oct. 31, 1890, at 8 A.M. A total loss. Source: 14.

62. *Authur Hauch Jr.* — Tug, of Pensacola, 42 tons, built in 1884,

Captain Chaffin. Burned at Chaffins Mill Wharf, Milton, May 7, 1891. A total loss. Source: 14.

63. *Mechanic* — Sidewheel steamer (ferryboat), of Jacksonville, 215 tons, built in 1856 at Camden, N.J. Stranded at Jacksonville, Aug. 15, 1891. Taken out of service. Lies under the south Jacksonville waterfront. Source: 20, 52.

64. *Rosalie* — Steamer, of Tampa, 22 tons, built in 1884, Captain Grogran. Sprang a leak and sank on the south shore of Lake Okeechobee, April 7, 1892. Towed to shallow water to try to save her machinery. Source: 14.

65. *Camusi* — Vessel, type unknown. Burned at Palatka, Jan. 26, 1894. Source: 20.

66. *Ravenswood* — Sidewheel steamer (ferryboat), of Jacksonville, 430 tons, built in 1867 at New York. Burned at her slip at South Jacksonville, Jan. 13 or March 31, 1895. Source: 20, 52.

67. *Santa Rosa* — Sternwheel steamer, of Pensacola, 82 tons, built in 1879, Captain Wilson, from Pensalcola bound for the Escambia River. Foundered five miles above the mouth of the Escambia River, July 8, 1896, at 12 P.M. A total loss. Source: 14.

68. *California* — Schooner, of Tampa, 16 tons. Ran ashore on the Anclote River, September 1896. A total loss. Source: 14.

69. *David Kemps* — Vessel, type unknown. Burned on Black Creek, off the St. Johns, June 18, 1897. Source: 20.

70. *Walnatronica* — Steamer, of Pensacola, 30 tons, built in 1885, Captain Mason, from Pensacola bound for Milton. Accidentally burned at the wharf at Milton, Oct. 4, 1898. A total loss. Source: 14.

1900

71. *Commodore Barney* (formerly the *USS Commodore Barney; Ethan Allen*) — Sidewheel steamer (ferryboat), 538 tons (also listed at 513 tons), built in 1859 at Brooklyn, 143.6' x 33.9' x 12.2.' Stranded off Jacksonville, Sept. 22, 1901. Sank at the foot of the dock at Newman Street, Jacksonville, September 1901. After several months she was raised and towed to the railroad bridge, where her remains now lie. (See Figure 50). Source: 20, 40 (Vol. 4, 1966), 52.

72. *Lewis* — Sidewheel steamer, of Tampa, 127 tons, built in 1901. Burned at McKenzies Wharehouse, Oct. 11, 1902, at 8 P.M., on the Manatee River. A total loss. Source: 14.

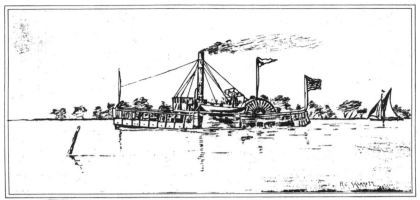

Figure 50: Drawing of the *USS Commodore Barney* by R.G. Skerrett, made during the Civil War. Became the *Commodore Barney*, sunk in 1901. FROM *OFFICIAL RECORDS OF THE UNION AND CONFEDERATE NAVIES ON THE WAR OF THE REBELLION* (See Bibliography).

73. *Trojan* — Steamer, 60 tons, built in 1900. Burned near Green Cove Springs, March 2, 1903. Source: 14, 20.

74. *Evangeline* — Steamer, of Pensacola, 21 tons, built in 1889 at Chicago, 59.6' x 12.5' x 4'. Burned in Horseshoe Lake, Feb. 15, 1904. Source: 14.

75. *Marquedora* — Gas vessel, 58 tons, built in 1902. Burned on the Carrabelle River, Aug. 23, 1905. Source: 14.

76. *Fearless* — Steamer, of Bath, 24 tons, built in 1897 at Palatka, 50' x 15.3' x 3.1'. Burned at Collee, April 29, 1907. Source: 14.

77. *Venice* — Gas vessel, of Tampa, 74 tons, built in 1902, Captain Fogarty. Abandoned on the Manatee River, Jan. 4, 1908, near Bradenton. Source: 14.

78. *Enterprise* — Steamer, of Pensacola, 40 tons, built in 1896 at Tottenville, N.Y., 67.2' x 16.5' x 5.2'. Burned at Milton, July 31, 1908. Source: 14.

79. *Alligator* — Sidewheel steamer, of Jacksonville, 69 tons, built in 1888 at Norwalk, Fla., 81.4' x 18.7' x 3.5'. Burned at Cross Cut Lake, Nov. 5, 1909. Source: 14.

80. *Martha Helen* — Steamer, 75 tons, built in 1878 at Berkley, Va., 82' x 16.7' x 7.4'. Burned at the foot of Ocean Street in Jacksonville, Feb. 6, 1910. One life lost. Source: 14, 20.

81. *Eulalia* — Sidewheel steamer, 231 tons, built in 1896 at Palatka, 94' x 27.6' x 4.8'. Burned at Beresford, April 25, 1910. Source: 14.

82. *Sultana* — Schooner, of Key West, 24 tons, built in 1891 at Bradentown, 53' x 18' x 3.8'. Stranded on Rogers River, Oct. 17, 1910. Source: 14.

83. *White Scud* — Schooner, 25 tons, built in 1890 at Key West, 53.3' x 18.5' x 2.7'. Foundered at Man River, Oct. 17, 1910. Source: 14.

84. *Levi H. Pelton* — Steamer, of Jacksonville, 46 tons, built in 1892 at Jacksonville, 70' x 18.4' x 11.' Foundered at Moser Channel, Oct. 17, 1910. Source: 14.

85. *Mistletoe* — Steamer, of Tampa, 43 tons, built in 1885 at Norwalk, Fla., 75.3' x 16.4' x 4.4', Captain Thompson. Sank at her dock on the Hillsborough River during a storm, Oct. 18, 1910. Some cargo saved. Source: 14.

86. *Mawagra II* — Gas vessel, 23 tons, built in 1906. Exploded on the St. Johns, Nov. 3, 1910. Source: 14.

87. *Terra Ceia* — Sternwheel steamer, of Tampa, 243 tons, built in 1882 at Jacksonville, 126' x 31.4' x 53.' Sank in the Hillsborough River, Jan. 15, 1911 (another source says Oct. 1, 1910). A total loss. Source: 14, 80.

88. *Bertha Ritter* — Steamer, 27 tons, built in 1899. Burned off Black Point on the St. Johns, Feb. 25, 1911. One life lost. Source: 14, 20.

89. *Columbia* — Sidewheel steamer, of Pensacola, 149 tons, built in 1900 at Pensacola, 104.5' x 19.8' x 5.8'. Burned at Milton, March 13, 1911. Source: 14.

90. *Hester* — Sternwheel dredge, of Tampa, owned by Hillsboro Dredging Co., 206 tons (also listed at 95 tons), built in 1889, Captain Hoob. From Sarasota bound for Clearwater. Burned at the narrows of Indian River, July 23, 1911. Source: 14.

91. *Madeleine* — Schooner, of Tampa, 79 tons, built in 1869 at Rye, N.Y., 92.5' x 24' x 7', Captain Scaurly, from Tarpon Springs bound for Tampa. Sank on Hillsborough River, Sept. 1, 1911. Source: 14.

92. *Cero* — Gas vessel, 28 tons, built in 1899. Burned on the Orange River, Sept. 30, 1912. Source: 14.

93. *W.W. Phipps* — Tug, of Tampa, 13 tons, built in 1906, Captain Fielding, from Tampa bound for Gulf City. Burned on the Alafia River, Oct. 11, 1912, at 5 A.M. Source: 14.

94. *Senrab* — Gas vessel, 23 tons, built in 1908. Burned at Phoenix Park on the St. Johns, Oct. 30, 1912. Source: 14.

95. *Biscayne* (formerly *J.W. Sweeney*) — Sidewheel steamer, 276 tons, built in 1888 at Abbeville, Ga., 118.9' x 27.7' x 4.4'. Stranded at Pine Island, North River, April 12, 1913. Source: 14.

96. *Kennedy* — Sidewheel steamer, 140 tons, built in 1901. Burned on the St. Johns, Feb. 24, 1914. Source: 14.

97. *Planter* — Steamer, 499 tons, built in 1876 at Charleston, 155' x 32.8' x 9.1'. Burned at Fort Myers, June 17, 1914. Source: 14.

98. *Melba* — Gas vessel, 27 tons, built in 1907. Burned on Trout Creek, off the St. Johns, Dec. 22, 1914. Source: 14.

99. *Homer Hand* — Gas vessel, 37 tons, built in 1913. Burned on the Imperial River, Nov. 21, 1915. Source: 14.

100. *City of Athens* — Sternwheel steamer, 65'. Sank at Fort Thompson, on the Kissimmee River, in 1915. Source: 84.

101. *Missinglink* — Steamer, 36 tons, built in 1916. Burned at Milton, May 23, 1919. Source: 14.

102. *Richmond* — Schooner, 1,719 tons, built in 1919. Stranded at Jacksonville, Jan. 5, 1920. Source: 14.

103. *Misery* — Gas vessel, 34 tons, built in 1919. Stranded on the St. Johns, March 16, 1920. Source: 14.

104. *City of Eufaula* — Sidewheel steamer, of Apalachicola, 216 tons, built in 1912 at Apalachicola, 161' x 34.7' x 4.9.' Burned near Neals Landing, Feb. 11, 1921. Source: 14.

105. *Bay Queen* (formerly *Clermont; Chamary*) — Sidewheel steamer, of Tampa, 289 tons, built in 1892 at Brooklyn, N.Y., 164.9' x 25.6' x 10.6'. Burned on the Hillsborough River at Tampa, July 21, 1921. (See Figure 51). Source: 14.

106. *Kona* — Gas yacht, of Miami, 43 tons, built in 1909 at Baltimore, 60' x 17.4' x 6.8'. Foundered at Jacksonville, October 1921.

Figure 51: Sidewheel steamer *Bay Queen* after she had burned on the Hillsborough River at Tampa, 1921. FLORIDA STATE ARCHIVES.

Two lives lost. Source: 14.

107. *John W. Callahan* — Sidewheel steamer, of Apalachicola, 202 tons, built in 1907 at Apalachicola, 153' x 34.6' x 5.6'. Stranded at White River, March 25, 1923. Source: 14.

108. *Broward* — Dredge, 165 tons, built in 1923. Burned at Hollywood, April 11, 1924. Source: 14.

109. *R.B. Trueman* — Gas vessel, 78 tons, built in 1918. Burned at Jacksonville, June 18, 1924. Source: 14.

110. *Bruce* — Steamer, 84 tons, built in 1922. Burned at White City, Sept. 8, 1925. Source: 14.

111. *Lavinia* — Gas vessel, 29 tons, built in 1897. Burned at Green Cove Springs, October 1925. Source: 14.

112. *Suwanee* — Thomas Edison enjoyed chartering this vessel. She wrecked at Moore Haven during the 1926 hurricane. Henry Ford salvaged her engines and built a replica. Note: Possibly the sidewheel steamer *Suwanee*, 82 tons, 70' x 16.5' x 4.4', built at Branford, Fla. in 1888. Source: 14, 39.

113. *Palatka* — Steamer, of Jacksonville, 73 tons, built in 1923 at Palatka, 63.5' x 22.1' x 6.8'. Foundered at Mandarin Point, Dec. 3, 1926. Four lives lost. Source: 14.

114. *Swan* — Oil vessel, 50 tons, built in 1908. Burned at Milton,

April 27, 1927. Source: 14.

115. *Globe* — Gas vessel, 23 tons, built in 1928. Foundered at Jacksonville, July 10, 1928. Source: 14.

116. *Magnolia* — Gas vessel, 47 tons, built in 1918. Burned at Jacksonville, Oct. 28, 1928. Source: 14.

117. *Bernice* — Freight boat, 64'11", four-cylinder 25-horsepower engine, built in Florida. Delivered goods along the Palm Beach Canal. Wrecked on the beach at Canal Point, on Lake Okeechobee, during a storm in 1928. Source: 84.

118. *Corona* — Steamer, old vessel which sailed on Florida's lakes and rivers, (possibly the 16-ton *Corona* of Key West, built 1908, 57'). Wrecked at Canal Point, on Lake Okeechobee, in 1928. Source: 14, 84.

119. *Oklahoma* — Gas vessel, 26 tons, built in 1916. Burned at Angel Fish Creek, April 27, 1930. Source: 14.

120. *Tot* — Gas vessel, 24 tons, built in 1924. Burned at Orange Park, April 9, 1930. Source: 14.

Figure 52: Abandoned steamboat *Hiawatha*, in a photo taken on the St. Johns River in 1963. FLORIDA STATE ARCHIVES.

121. *Nassauvian* (formerly three masted schooner *J.W. Somerville*) — Converted to motor power, 547 tons, built in 1919 in Maryland, 160.2' x 35.2' x 12.7'. Burned at Jacksonville, April 27, 1930. Source: 14, 80.

122. *Captain Fritz* — Steamer, 57 tons, built in 1892 at Mosspoint, Miss., 99.8' x 21.6' x 3.4'. Burned at Cedar Tree Landing, Sept. 19, 1930. One life lost. Source: 14.

123. *Robin Hood III* — Gas vessel, 23 tons, built in 1913. Burned at Switzerland, Fla., Dec. 27, 1930. Source: 14.

124. *Hiawatha* — Freight motor vessel, of Jacksonville, 88 tons, built in 1926 at Arlington, Fla., 63.7' x 22.6' x 4.8'. Burned at Eastport, Sept. 30, 1931. (See Figure 52). Source: 14.

125. *Utility* — Steamer, 77 tons, built in 1899 at Peaks Island, Maine, 73.1' x 19.6' x 6.2'. Burned on the St. Johns, Feb. 21, 1932. Source: 14.

126. *Libbie* — Motor vessel, 66 tons, built in 1929. Burned at Kings Ferry, April 26, 1932. Source: 14.

See World War II section for Section 7 wrecks during that period.

127. *Homestead* — Tanker. Hit by lightning while in Jacksonville Harbor, Aug. 5, 1946, and burned for eight days. Source: 42.

128. *Josephine H. II* — G/V, 36 tons, built in 1912. Burned on the Nassau River, near Nassauville, July 22, 1947. Source: 14.

129. *Norvell* — Sternwheel oil vessel, 45 tons, built in 1935. Foundered at the junction of the Chatahoochee and Apalachicola rivers, December 1949. Source: 14.

130. *Transfer No. 8* — Steamer (iron), believed to be a tug, 131 tons, built in 1891 at Elizabeth, N.J., 90.1' x 22.2' x 10.5.' Foundered on the St. Johns, at Jacksonville, Dec. 15, 1950. Source: 14.

131. *Paladin* — O/V, 74 tons, built in 1928. Burned one mile south of the intersection of the St. Johns and the Intracoastal, July 20, 1951. Source: 14.

132. *Miss Jo* — O/V, 44 tons, built in 1950. Burned on Lake Okeechobee, April 3, 1952, near Moore Haven. Source: 14.

133. *Big Lady* — O/V, 26 tons, built in 1954. Burned at the mouth of Pond Creek, Blackwater River, near Bagdad, May 4, 1959. Source: 14.

134. *Gulf King* — O/V, 66 tons, built in 1954. Burned approximately 1/4 mile from the mouth of the San Sebastian River, on the east bank, May 22, 1961. Source: 14.

135. *Grace* — O/V, 24 tons, built in 1929. Stranded on the San Sebastian River, St. Augustine, Jan. 1962. Source: 14.

136. *Flying Cloud* — O/V, 28 tons, built in 1911. Foundered in Lake Worth at Lake Worth, July 1969. Source: 14.

137. Unknown wreck — Charted in 1959 in shallow water, at Lat. 27-02-26, Long. 81-58-50. Verified in 1983. Source: 1.

138. *Little David* — O/V (steel), 58 tons, built in 1944. Foundered between Fort Myers and Port Sutton, Feb. 7, 1960. Source: 14.

139. *Helma* — G/V, 172 tons, built in 1925. Destroyed by a hurricane, Sept. 10, 1960, at 148 N.W. North River Dr., Miami River. Source: 14.

Figure 52A: Anchor chain from a nineteenth-century wreck. AUTHOR.

Section 8: Unknown Locations or Dates

1500

1. *San Antón* — Spanish nao, 100 tons, Captain Gonzalo Rodríquez, from Cuba bound for Spain. Lost on "the shallows" in 1521, after leaving Cuba. Possible Florida wreck. Source: 54.

2. Spanish caravel — Part of an expedition under Don Lucas Vasquez de Ayllon. Lost near Cape St. Helen (believed part of the panhandle) in 1525. Indians killed all 200 survivors. Source: 54.

3. Spanish ship — A ship carrying Don L'Escalante Fonteneda. Wrecked off Florida in 1545, possibly in the Keys. Until his rescue in 1565, he lived with the Tequesta Indians near Cape Canaveral. Source: 22.

4. Spanish ship — Lost in the Espíritu Santo River on the coast of Florida sometime before 1550. Possible Florida wreck since much of the American coast was considered Florida at this time. Source: 54.

5. *Vistacion* — Spanish nao, 200 tons, Captain Pedro de la Torre. Left Havana bound for Spain with $200,000 in treasure. Lost during a hurricane off the Keys in 1550. Source: 67.

6. Four Spanish ships — Four ships of a fleet under the command of Cosme Rodriguez Farfan. Lost on the coast of Florida in 1554, after being caught in a storm in the Bahama Channel. Source: 67.

7. Spanish vessels — Ships of the fleet under Angel de Villafone y Garcia de Escalante Alvarado. Lost off the coast of Florida in 1554. Source: 57.

8. *Santa Catalina* — Spanish nao, 120 tons, Captain Francisco Morales Camacho, from Santo Domingo bound for Spain. Was attacked and robbed of its treasure by a French ship and sunk in the Gulf of Florida in 1554. Possibly one of the above fleets. Source: 54.

9. *Santa María del Camino* — Spanish nao, 200 tons, Captain Alonso Martín Morejon, from South America bound for Spain by herself. Lost in the Bahama Channel in 1555. Possible Florida wreck. Source: 54.

10. Three Spanish naos — All under Captain Gonzalo de Carbajal, from Puerto Rico bound for Spain. Wrecked on the Florida coast in 1556. Two were 120 tons of the same name, *Sancta Salbador*, Captains Guillen de Lugo and Martín de Artaleco. The other is unknown. Source: 54.

11. Spanish vessel — A vessel, type unknown, from Campeche bound for New Spain with maize, chickens, and wool blankets. Went aground on the Florida coast during a storm in 1561. This may not be a Florida wreck, since much of the southeastern United States was considered Florida at this time. Source: 7.

12. Spanish urca — Of Tristan de Salvatierra. Lost in the Bahama Channel along with 35 lives. Possible Florida wreck. Source: 54.

13. *Santa Clara* — Spanish galleon, 300 tons, Captain Juan Díaz Bozino, of the Armada de Tierra Firme. Lost in the Bahama Channel in 1564 near Isla de Mine. Treasure and crew saved by the galleon *San Pelayo*. Another source says the *San Pelayo* wrecked at the same location. It might have also sunk or maybe was mistaken for the other ship. Possible Florida wreck. Source: 54.

14. Spanish nao — Of a fleet under Pero [sic] Menéndez de Avilés. Lost on the Florida coast in 1567. Source: 54.

15. Spanish ship — A ship was sent from St. Augustine bound for Havana in 1570, but wrecked on shoals soon after. Crew members made their way back to St. Augustine. Source: 7.

16. *San Ignacio* and the *Santa María de la Limpia Concepción* — Both galleons. the first was 300 tons, Captain Juan de Canavas, 22 iron cannon. The other was 340 tons. Together they carried 2,500,000 pesos in treasure. They were lost on the Florida coast during a storm in 1571. Only a few survivors made St. Augustine in two longboats. Nothing salvaged. Source: 54.

17. Spanish nao — Of the Armada de Tierra Firme, from Havana bound for Spain. Was separated in a storm and went to Puerto Escondido near Puerta de las Palmas (believed to be Tampa Bay) and sank in the port in 1576. All gold and silver was salvaged. Source: 54.

18. Spanish ships — A message dated Feb. 12, 1578, from Don Francisco Correño to the king tells of more than 20 ships having been lost off the Florida Keys. Source: 18.

19. Spanish frigate — From Havana bound for St. Augustine. Wrecked on Florida's east coast in 1579. All crew made it safely to St. Augustine by land. Source: 54.

20. *La Salvadora* — Spanish nao, 120 tons, Captain Melchor Rodríquez, from Puerto Rico which joined the Nueva España Flota at Havana. Sunk in the Bahama Channel in 1582. Many of the pearls she

207

carried were later salvaged, indicating she sank in shallow water. Possible Florida wreck. Source: 54.

21. *San Francisco* and *Nuestra Señora de la Concepción* — Two Spanish vessels, 120 tons each, Masters Alonso and Rixo, left Puerto Rico and joined the New Spain Fleet in Havana bound for Spain in 1586. Sixty-one ships left Havana and met a storm while in the Bahama Channel. These two, as well as six or seven others, were lost. Marx identifies one of the vessels that sank as the nao *San Juan*, 120 tons, Captain Martín de Irigoyen, from Mexico. Possible Florida wreck. Source: 10.

22. Spanish nao — Sank off the coast of Florida in 1587, but not before most of the treasure was transferred to the *Capitana* in a launch. Source: 54.

23. Spanish ships — Seventy-seven ships left Havana June 27, 1591. They encountered storms and 29 ships were lost, many on Florida's coast. They were not carrying any registered treasure. Source: 54.

1600

24. Spanish ship — Of 200 tons, Captain Diego Rodríquez Garrucho, from Mexico and Havana. Wrecked off Florida due to bad navigation in 1600. Carried much treasure including 245 chests of valuables from the Far East. Two years later the Spanish salvaged three bronze cannon, but no cargo since it was buried. Source: 54.

25. Spanish ship — Of a fleet under General Garibay. Wrecked on a key during a storm sometime before Sept. 25, 1602, before entering the Bahama Channel. Eight people made three boats from the wreckage and arrived at Havana. Possible Florida wreck. Source: 54.

26. Spanish patache — Wrecked in March 1618 at "la Boca de Matasissos" on Florida's coast. Some survivors made it to St. Augustine. Source:54.

27. Spanish ship — From Campeche with hides and indigo. Wrecked in the Keys, March 24, 1618. Crew made it to St. Augustine. Source: 54.

28. *Santa Ana María* — Spanish nao, 180 tons, Captain Goncolo [sic] de la Roche. From Santo Domingo and Havana bound for Spain. Lost during a storm off the Florida coast in1622. Source: 54.

29. Spanish ship — A vessel bringing uniforms, salaries, and supplies to the soldiers at Puerto Rico sank in the Bahama Channel in 1624. Possible Florida wreck. Source: 54.

30. Two Galleons — Under command of D. Antonio de Oteiza. Lost in the Bahama Channel in 1630 while carrying reinforcements to Florida. Crew saved. Source: 57.

31. Spanish fleet — When the treasure fleet of 1634 sailed into the Bahama Channel, a storm hit, wrecking some of the fleet on the Florida coast. The Vice Admiral's ship and a patache reached Cadiz in November, and the almiranta arrived at Cadiz six weeks later. However, Marx says that the almiranta and a patache were lost and that most of the fleet survived. Source: 7, 54.

32. Spanish Fleet — This fleet left Havana on Jan. 1, 1656. On board a galleon was the Marquis de Monte Alegre. On Jan. 5 a severe storm hit the fleet in the Bahama Channel. The almiranta was lost, while the other ships were scattered to New Spain and elsewhere. Source: 7.

33. *Santissima Concepción*, also called *El Grande* — Spanish galleon, 700 tons. Wrecked on the east coast of Florida during a storm in 1683. She was loaded with treasure. Only four of the 500 on board survived and reached St. Augustine. None of the treasure was salvaged. All her cannon were bronze. Source: 54.

34. Spanish nao — Lost in the Florida Keys in 1688. Source: 54.

1700

35. Two Spanish frigates — Of the Armada de Barlovento, under command of D. Francisco Cornejo. Wrecked in the Bahama Channel in 1720. All hands saved. Possible Florida wrecks. Source: 54, 57.

36. Spanish nao — Sailing alone to Spain. Lost on Florida's coast at "Rio Seco" in 1733. Source: 54.

37. Spanish ship — Owned or under Don Geronimo Baroso. Wrecked on Florida's coast at Rio Seco in 1734. Source: 54.

38. *Santo Cayetano* — Spanish frigate, 24 guns. Lost off the Florida coast in 1738. Two salvage vessels brought survivors and some cargo to Havana Jan. 3, 1740. Source: 54, 67.

39. *HMS Wolf* — British naval sloop, 244 tons, 14 guns, 87' x 25'. Wrecked on the coast of Florida, March 2, 1741. Source: 13 (Vol. III), 16.

40. *Naffaw* — British merchantman, Captain Bradshaw, from Jamaica bound for Bristol, England. Reported October 1741 as lost in the Florida Keys. Crew saved. Source: 54.

41. *Rose* — British merchantman, Captain Murdock, from Jamaica bound

for London. Reported May 1747 as lost in the Gulf of Florida. Source: 54.

42. *Prince Arthur* — British merchantman from Jamaica bound for London. Reported April 1748 as lost in the Gulf of Florida. Source: 54.

43. *Betsey* — British merchantman, Captain Slater, from Jamaica bound for Bristol. Reported May 1750 as lost in the Gulf of Florida. Crew saved. Source: 54.

44. *Great Britain* — British merchantman, Captain Hume, from Jamaica bound for London. Reported December 1751 as lost in the Gulf of Florida. Crew saved. Source: 54.

45. Note: The following seven vessels, plus an unknown Spanish man-of-war, a Spanish schooner, and three other ships, were all lost in a hurricane, Oct. 22, 1752, in the Gulf of Florida. Source: 54.

a. *Alexander* — British merchantman, Captain Mudis, from Jamaica bound for London.
b. *Lancaster* — British merchantman, Captain Lowery, from Jamaica bound for Lancaster. .
c. *Dolphin* — Captain Pedrick, from Jamaica bound for Liverpool.
d. *Queen Anne* — British merchantman, Captain Rymer, from Jamaica bound for Bristol.
e. *May* — British merchantman, Captain Crawford, from Jamaica bound for Glasgow.
f. *Rhode Island* — American merchantman, Captain Ball, from Jamaica bound for New York.
g. *Statea* — American merchantman, Captain Jones, from Honduras bound for Rhode Island.
h. *Phillis* — British merchantman, Captain Baker, from Jamaica bound for London. This was reported later than the above and is possibly one of the three unidentified vessels mentioned.

46. *Mary & Pricilla* and the *Kingston* — Both British merchantmen; the *Mary & Pricilla*, Captain Ham, from Jamaica bound for London; and the *Kingston*, Captain Littlejohn, from Jamaica bound for Philadelphia. Both lost in a hurricane, Nov. 2, 1752 (probably same storm as above), in Lat. 25 degrees in the Gulf of Floirda. Both crews saved. Source: 54.

47. *Pompey* — British merchantman, Captain England, from Jamaica bound for London. Lost in the Gulf of Florida in 1752. Source: 54.

48. *Two Brothers* — British merchantman, Captain Coats [sic] from Jamaica bound for London. Lost in the Gulf of Florida, April 26, 1753.

Crew saved. Source: 54.

49. *Myrtilla* — British ship, Captain March, from Jamaica bound for London. Reported November 1757 to have foundered in the Gulf of Florida. Crew saved. Source: 54.

50. *Elizabeth* — British merchantman, Captain Brewer, from Jamaica bound for London. Reported March 1760 as lost in the Gulf of Florida. crew saved. Source: 54.

51. Three British merchantmen — Reported July 1761 as lost in the Gulf of Florida. Source: 54.
a. *Mary* — Captain Rycraft, from Jamaica bound for London. Ninety puncheons of rum and four hogsheads of sugar saved.
b. *Bella* — From Jamaica bound for Liverpool.
c. *Jamaica Packet* — Captain Flyn [sic], from Jamaica bound for London.

52. *Albinia* — British merchantman, from Jamaica bound for London. Reported June 1763 as wrecked on Florida's coast. Crew saved. Source: 54.

53. *Santa Barbara* — Spanish frigate, Captain Josef Antonio de Urrismi, from Havana bound for Spain with 2,000 serons of indigo. Lost at entrance to the Bahama Channel, July 17, 1766. Total loss. Only seven survivors. Possible Florida wreck. Source: 54.

54. *General Conway* — British ship, Captain Bail, from Jamaica. Reported September 1766 as lost in the Florida Keys. Crew saved. Source: 54.

55. *Anna Theresa* — British paquetboat, Captain Dyer, from Pensacola bound for Falmouth. A ship saw her aground in the Keys and on fire, July 30, 1768. Crew saved. A Spanish ship and a brig from Boston were also wrecked in the same area. Source: 54.

56. *Jazo e Santa Anna*, alias *Nisma del Puerto* — Spanish ship, from Havana bound for Cadiz. Reported November 1768 as lost in the Florida Strait. (Possibly the same as # 7 in Section 6). Source: 54.

57. Unknown vessel — Captain Codington, from Montego Bay bound for Rhode Island with rum. Reported November 1768 to have caught fire by lightning in the Florida Gulf. Crew and vessel lost. Source: 54.

58. Spanish ship — Reported from Jamaica that a large Spanish ship wrecked in the Keys during a storm in 1769 or 1770.

A total loss. Source: 54.

59. *St. Mary* — British merchantman, Captain Carr, from Jamaica bound for London. Reported September 1770 as lost in the Gulf of Florida. Source: 54.

60. Unknown vessels — A number of vessels were reported wrecked in the Keys and the Florida east coast after July 1771. Source: 54.

61. *Fortune* — British ship, Captain Richardson, from Jamaica bound for London. Lost near the Florida coast, Nov. 18, 1772. Two men drowned. Source: 54.

62. *Dove* — British slave ship, from Africa bound for St. Augustine with slaves. Wrecked on the Florida coast, Oct. 18, 1773. The captain, two crew, and 80 of the 100 slaves were lost. Source: 54.

63. *Rhee Galley* — British ship, Captain Hunter, from Honduras bound for Bristol. Reported July 1774 as lost on the Florida Keys. Source: 54.

64. *Jamaica Planter* — British merchantman, from Jamaica bound for Bristol. Reported November 1775 as a total loss in the Gulf of Florida. Crew saved. Source: 54.

65. *Fly* — British merchantman, Captain North, from Jamaica bound for London. Reported May 1776 as lost in the Gulf of Florida. Source: 54.

66. *William* — Ship, from Honduras bound for Hull. Reported May 1776 as lost in the Gulf of Florida. Source: 54.

67. *Belieze* [sic] — British ship, Captain Gillis, from Honduras bound for London. Lost on Florida's coast, Oct. 12, 1776. Source: 54.

68. *Minerva* — Ship, Captain Callahan. Reported April 1777 as lost on the Florida coast. Source: 54.

69. *Salisbury* — English ship, Captain Williams, from Mobile bound for Cork. A Spanish ship rescued the crew of this vessel off Florida as she was sinking, May 16, 1777. Source: 54.

70. Spanish man-of-war — The *London Chronicle* of June 24-26, 1777, mentions news from the Bahamas of a recent hurricane. It states that a Spanish man-of-war foundered in the Gulf of Florida. All hands lost. Source: Naval Historical Center. "Naval Records of the Revolution." Vol. 9., 1986.

71. *Claudina* — British ship, Captain Valliant, from London bound for Pensacola. Reported December 1777 as lost on the Florida coast. Source: 54.

72. British merchantman — Three-decked, of a fleet from Jamaica. Reported September 1779 as lost on shore in the Gulf of Florida. Source: 54.

73. *HMS Felicity* — British naval brig. Left Pensacola bound for Jamaica, May 23, 1780, and was never heard from again. Possible Florida wreck. Source: 79.

74. Spanish ships — Of a fleet of Don Bernardo de Galvez, from Havana bound for Pensacola. A hurricane hit the fleet in 1781 and four capital ships and a number of others were totally lost. Over 2,000 lives lost. Possible Florida wrecks. Source: 54.

75. *Emanuel & Hercules* — British merchantman, Captain McDougal, of a fleet from Jamaica bound for London. Reported July 1782 as wrecked in the Gulf of Florida and as it could not be saved was burned. Another source mentioned an English ship wrecked in the Florida Keys the same year. Likely the same vessel. Source: 54.

76. Spanish frigate — Left Philadelphia bound for Havana, June 10, 1784. Ran aground in the Keys, June 29, 1784, at 3 A.M. All survivors reached Havana in lifeboats. Source: 75.

77. *Santa Anna* — Spanish frigate, Captain Miguel Ysnardy. Wrecked on a reef by Aroquito Key during a storm in 1784. Some made their way back to Havana in a boat. One was Thomas Hasset, the parish priest of St. Augustine. Source: 49.

78. Ship — A large ship was seen on Aug. 31, 1785 wrecked in the Florida Keys, with wreckers nearby. Source: 54.

79. *Caroline* — British merchantman, Captain Grant, from St. Mark's bound for Charleston and London. Reported May 1786 as lost in the Gulf of Florida. A total loss. Source:54.

80. *San Josef* — Spanish schooner. Lost in August 1787 after leaving St. Augustine bound for Havana. Three officers and 40 men of the Inmemorial del Rey Regiment were lost with her. Possible Florida wreck. Source: 75.

81. *Albion* and the *Alfred* — British merchantmen, Captains Whitehead and Stupart, from Jamaica bound for London. Reported

October 1787 as wrecked in the Gulf of Florida. Some cargo saved. Source: 54.

82. *Evenly* — British merchantman, Captain Hebden, from Honduras bound for London. Reported September 1788 as wrecked on the Florida Keys. Source: 54.

83. *Mary & Jane* — British merchantman, Captain Pennymont, from Jamaica bound for Liverpool. Reported November 1788 as lost on the Florida coast. Crew saved. Source: 54.

84. *Infanta* — Spanish brigantine, 18 cannon, commanded by Teniente de Navio Casamiro de Lamadrid. Lost in the Bahama Channel in 1788. Possible Florida wreck. Source: 54.

85. *Friendship* — British merchantman, Captain Lamb, from Jamaica bound for London. Reported October 1789 as lost in the Gulf of Florida. Some cargo saved. Source: 54.

86. *Fly* — British ship, Captain Walker, from Jamaica bound for Africa. Reported in December 1789 as lost on the Florida Keys. Source: 54.

87. *Thetis* and the *Abby* — British merchantmen, Captains Moore and Braithwaite, bound for London and Dublin. Reported October 1790 as lost in the Gulf of Florida. Source: 54.

88. *Hope* — British merchantman, Captain Chappel, from Jamaica bound for Charleston. Lost on the Florida coast in 1790. Source: 54.

89. *Lively* — British brig, Captain Morse, from Jamaica bound for Bristol. Reported in September 1791 as lost on the Florida Keys. Most cargo saved. Source: 54.

90. *Diana* — Spanish mail boat (frigate), Captain Manuel de Abona. Lost in the Bahama Channel in 1791. Crew saved. Source: 54.

91. *Ross* — British packetboat, Captain Best, from Honduras. Reported February 1792 as lost in the Gulf of Florida in 1791. Source: 54.

92. *Prince of Austurias* — Ship (probably Spanish), from New Orleans bound for Bordeaux. Reported February 1792 as lost in the Gulf of Florida in 1791. Source: 54.

93. Ship — A large ship was seen wrecking in the Florida Keys on June 5, 1792. A total loss. Source: 54.

94. *Sarah* — British merchantman, Captain Youd [sic], from Jamaica bound for Liverpool. Reported September 1792 as lost in the Gulf of Florida. Source: 54.

95. *Lovely Ann* — American merchantman, Captain Green, from Jamaica bound for New York. Reported in December 1792 as lost on the Florida Keys. Source: 54.

96. *Brothers* — British merchantman, Captain Withers, from Jamaica bound for Liverpool. Reported April 1793 as lost in the Gulf of Florida. A total loss. Source: 54.

97. *General Clark* — British merchantman, Captain Lilburn, from Jamaica bound for Savannah. Reported in July 1793 to have wrecked on a reef in the Florida Keys. Crew saved. Total loss. Source: 54.

98. *Echo* — American merchantman, Captain Nicol, from Jamaica bound for New York. Reported April 1794 as lost in the Gulf of Florida. Source: 54.

99. *Catherine Green* — British merchantman, Captain Rose, from Jamaica bound for London. Wrecked on a reef on the Florida Keys, Aug. 8, 1794. Most cargo saved. Source: 54.

100. *Vigilant* and an unknown ship — *Vigilant* was a British ship, from Honduras bound for London. Both were lost in a hurricane in the Gulf of Florida, Aug. 28, 1794, near the Cape (probably Cape Florida). Source: 54.

101. *Noah's Ark* — American merchantman, from New Orleans bound for Philadelphia. Reported in July 1795 as lost on the Florida Keys. Source: 54.

102. *Ranger* — British transport, Captain Dobsen, from Jamaica. Lost in the Gulf of Florida, August 1796. Source: 54.

103. *Jolly Tar* — Ship, from Jamaica bound for Norfolk. Reported in November 1796 as wrecked on the Florida coast. Source: 54.

104. *Flora* — British ship, Captain Scott, from Charleston bound for Havana. Reported April 1798 as lost on the Florida Keys. Source: 54.

1800

105. *Hector* — Ship, from Havana bound for Nassau. Reported October 1800 as lost on a reef in the Florida Keys. Source: 54.

106. *Eagle* — British ship, Captain Dennet, from Havana bound for Philadelphia. Wrecked on the Florida side of Maranzie Reef in the Florida Keys, Dec. 15, 1801. Crew and cargo saved. Source: 54.

107. *John* — Ship, from Jamaica bound for Liverpool. Reported June 1802 as wrecked on shore in the Gulf of Florida. Source: 54.

108. *Neptune* — British ship, Captain Cushley, from New Orleans bound for Nassau. Reported August 1802 as lost on the Florida coast. Crew and most cargo saved. Source: 54.

109. *Maria* — British merchantman, from Honduras bound for Charleston. Reported April 1803 as wrecked on the Florida coast. Crew and cargo saved. Source: 54.

110. *Britannia* — British merchantman, Captain Wright, from Jamaica bound for London. Reported October 1803 as lost on the Florida Keys. Some cargo saved. Source: 54.

111. *Mercury* — Ship, Captain Hume, from Africa bound for Havana. Reported May 1804 as lost in the Straits of Bahamas. Possible Florida wreck. Source: 54.

112. *Mary Ellen* — Ship, from Africa and Demerara bound for Havana. Reported June 1804 as lost in the Straits of the Bahamas. Crew and passengers saved. Possible Florida wreck. Source: 54.

113. *Calliope* — American merchantman, Captain Nash, from Jamaica bound for Virginia. Reported July 1804 as lost on a reef in the Florida Keys. Source: 54.

114. *Providence* — Ship, Captain Gibson, from New Orleans bound for Bordeaux. Wrecked in the Florida Keys, Sept. 17, 1805. Source: 54.

115. *Andromache* — Ship, Captain Hickles, from Jamaica bound for New York. Wrecked in the Florida Keys, Dec. 6, 1805. Most cargo saved. Source: 54.

116. *Trusty* — British merchantman, Captain Smith, from Jamaica bound for Halifax. Reported May 1806 as lost on shore in the Gulf of Florida. Some cargo saved. Source: 54.

117. *Zenobia* — British naval schooner, ten guns, 112 tons, built in 1806 in Bermuda, 68' x 20', Commander A. Hamilton. Listed as having wrecked off the Florida coast in both Gilly's and Colledge's

books, and Gosset has her wrecking 20 miles south of Cape Henry Light, Florida, Oct. 24, 1806. The only Cape Henry that I know of is in Virginia. Gosset states the *Zenobia* picked up a pilot at Lat 36-50, which puts her near Cape Henry, Va. Source: 16, 35, 36.

118. *Seaflower* — Ship, Captain Pitch, from Jamaica and Havana bound for New York. Reported March 1807 as lost on the Florida coast. Source: 54.

119. *Flora* — British merchantman, Captain Adams, from New Orleans bound for Liverpool. Reported May 1807 as wrecked on the Florida coast. Source: 54.

120. *Fame* — American merchantman, Captain Bennett, from New Orleans bound for Liverpool. Reported December 1810 as lost on the Florida coast. Crew saved. Source: 54.

121. *Cabinet* — British merchantman, Captain Montgomery, from New Orleans bound for Liverpool. Lost on a reef in the Florida Keys, Oct. 26, 1811. Crw and most cargo saved. Source: 54.

122. *Orion* — American merchantman, Captain Brown, from Aux Cayes bound for Philadelphia. Lost on a reef in the Florida Keys, Feb. 20, 1812. Source: 54.

123. *Gipsey* — American ship (possibly the 207 ton brig, *Gipsey*, built in 1809 in Maine, 89' x 24' x 11'), Captain Long, from Havana bound for Boston. Lost in the Gulf of Florida, April 20, 1812. Crew saved. Source: 54, 105.

124. *Three Brother*s — British merchantman, Captain Roach, from Jamaica bound for London. Lost in the Gulf of Florida, June 1812. Crew saved. Source: 54.

125. *Lord Wellington* — British merchantman, Captain Flynn, from Jamaica bound for Cork. Reported July 1812 as lost in the Gulf of Florida. Some cargo saved. Source: 54.

126. *Americano* — Spanish merchantman, Captain Abrew, from Havana bound for Lisbon. Wrecked on a reef in the Florida Keys, July 26, 1814. Source: 54.

127. *Watt* — Ship, Captain McGee, from Jamaica bound for New York. Reported October 1815 as lost on a reef in the Florida Keys. Source: 54.

128. *Jerusalem* — Spanish ship, from Havana bound for Africa. Lost on a reef in the Florida Keys, Nov. 13, 1815. Crew and cargo saved. Source: 54.

129. *Atlas*, *Cossack*, *General Pike*, and the *Zanga* — These wrecked in a storm between June 5th and 8th, 1816. The *Atlas*, of Glasgow, Captain Thompson, from Jamaica bound for Glasgow, wrecked on a reef in the Florida Keys. The *Cossack*, Captain Flint, from Havana bound for Hamburg, wrecked in the Florida Keys, crew and cargo saved. The *General Pike*, Captain Emery, from Charleston bound for Mantanzas, wrecked at Sound Point, some cargo saved. The *Zanga*, of Nassau, Captain Russell, wrecked at Sound Point, all cargo saved. Source: 54.

130. *Minerva* — Ship (possibly the ship *Minerva* of 224 tons, built in 1798 at Haverill, Mass., 84' x 24'10" x 12'5"), from New Orleans bound for Le Havre. Reported June 1816 as lost in the Bahama Channel. Possible Florida wreck. Source: 54, 105.

131. *Narraganet* — American ship, Captain Wolf, from Havana bound for Bristol, Rhode Island. Wrecked in the Gulf of Florida, June 8, 1816. Source: 54.

132. *Rebecca* and the *Catherine Osmond* — The *Rebecca*, from Cadiz and Havana bound for Savannah, and the *Catherine Osmond*, Captain Vicaiz [sic], from Havana bound for Salem. Reported December 1816 as wrecked "at Florida." Some cargo saved. Source: 54.

133. *Magdalen* — British merchantman, Captain Sawyer, from New Orleans bound for Liverpool. Reported December 1816 as wrecked on a reef in the Florida Keys. Cargo saved. Source: 54.

134. *Galga* — Spanish *goleta* (type of vessel). Ran aground and exploded in 1816, in the Bahama Channel. Possible Florida wreck. Source: 54.

135. *Anna Maria* — Ship, from New Orleans bound for Philadelphia. Wrecked on Bason Bank off east Florida, March 23, 1817. Crew saved. Source: 54.

136. *Marquis de Pombal* — Portuguese ship, from Pernambuco bound for Oporto. Captured by a privateer in March and ran aground on a reef in the Florida Keys, May 5, 1817. Cargo saved. Source: 54.

137. *Europa* — Ship, Captain Rich, from St. Jago de Cuba bound for America. Wrecked on a reef in the Florida Keys, May 1817. Source: 54.

138. *Merrimack* — American brig, from Havana bound for New York. Reported October 1817 as lost "on the Floridas." Crew saved. Cargo lost. Source: 54.

139. Ship — A ship which left Jamaica Nov. 16, 1817 bound for England, reported seeing a two-decked ship, believed to be Spanish, ashore in the Gulf of Florida. Source: 54.

140. *Venus* — Ship, Captain Pinder, from Jamaica bound for New York. Reported February 1818 as lost on the Florida coast. Crew and some cargo saved. Source: 54.

141. *Iris* — Ship, Captain Bailey, from Havana bound for the Cape Verde Islands. Wrecked April 7, 1818, "on the side of the Gulf Stream." Possible Florida wreck. Source: 54.

142. *Marianne* — Dutch ship, Captain Beckman, from Antwerp bound for Havana. Reported April 1818 as lost in the Bahama Channel. Possible Florida wreck. Source: 54.

143. *Betsy* — American merchantman, Captain Grafton, from Havana bound for Rhode Island. Reported in July 1818 on a reef in the Florida Keys. Some cargo saved. Source: 54.

144. *Quebec* — British merchantman, Captain Fiott, from Jamaica bound for London. Lost on a reef in the Florida Keys, Aug. 7, 1818. Crew saved. A total loss. Source: 54.

145. *Solway* — British merchantman, Captain Bennett, from Jamaica bound for Withsharon. Wrecked on a reef in the Florida Keys, Aug. 10, 1818. Eighteen wrecking vessels worked to save her cargo. Source: 54.

146. *Bonee Adelle* — Ship, from Havana. Wrecked on the Florida coast, Feb. 5, 1819. Crew saved. Source: 54.

147. *Anie of Scarbro* [sic] — Ship, Captain Stanley, bound for England. Lost on a reef in the Florida Keys, June 29, 1819. Some lives lost. Source: 54.

148. *Sandwich* — British merchantman, Captain Fraser, from Havana bound for Guernsey. Reported July 1819 as wrecked in the Florida Keys. Little cargo saved. Source: 54.

149. *Barilla* — American brig, Captain Jones, from New Orleans bound for Philadelphia. Reported November 1819 as wrecked on a

reef in the Florida Keys. Source: 54.

150. *Lively* — American schooner, Captain Avery, from New Orleans bound for Baltimore. Wrecked the same time as the *Barilla*. Source: 54.

151. *Royal Desire* — French ship, Captain Feuardant, from Havana bound for Le Havre. Lost on the Florida coast in early June, 1821. Crew saved. Source: 54.

152. *Cosmopolite* — Ship, Captain Selliman, from Charleston bound for New Orleans. Wrecked in a gale, Sept. 14, 1821, in the Florida Keys. Source: 54.

153. *General Jackson* — American sloop., Wrecked on the Florida coast sometime before October 1821. Crew saved. Source: 54.

154. *Almirante* — Spanish *bergantine-goleta (type of ship)*, 20 cannon, commanded by Teniente de Navio Ignacio Chacon. Wrecked in the Bahama Channel in 1821. Twenty-five men drowned. Possible Florida wreck. Source: 54.

155. *Frances & Lucy* — British merchantman, Captain Barnaby, from Jamaica bound for Halifax. Lost on a reef in the Florida Keys, Jan. 14, 1822. Source: 54.

156. *Ann of London* — British merchantman, Captain Campbell, from Havana bound for Buenos Aires. Lost on the East Florida Keys, late April 1822. Some cargo saved. Source: 54.

157. French brig — From Honduras with indigo, logwood, and mahogany. Lost same time and place as the *Ann of London*. Source: 54.

158. *Neptune* — British merchantman, Captain Duncan, from Jamaica bound for Dublin. Reported July 1822 as wrecked on the Florida shore where she quickly broke up. Source: 54.

159. *Waterloo* — British ship, Captain Kelcher, from Jamaica bound for Cork. Wrecked on the Florida coast, October 1822. Cargo saved. Source: 54.

160. Spanish ship — From Havana bound for Cadiz. Lost in the Gulf of Florida. crew rescued by another ship, Jan. 30, 1823. Source: 54.

161. *Leopard* — American sloop, from St. Augustine bound for Havana. Reported July 1823 lost in the Florida Keys. Crew saved. Source: 54.

162. *Parker & Sons* — British merchantman, Captain Hodgson, from New Orleans bound for Clyde. Reported October 1823 to have struck on Honda Rock in the Gulf of Florida. Was gotten off and run ashore to prevent her sinking. Source: 54.

163. *Andromache* — Ship, from Jamaica bound for New York. Wrecked on a reef in the Florida Keys, Nov. 18, 1823. Source: 54.

164. *Franklin* — American merchantman, Captain Taper, from Philadelphia bound for Pensacola. Reported December 1823 as wrecked in the Florida Keys. Crew and most cargo saved. Source: 54.

165. Brig — A large brig was seen Aug. 29, 1824, wrecked at Palmerstone inlet on the Florida coast. Several small vessels were alongside. Source: 54.

166. *Majica* — Spanish bergantine-goleta , 7 guns, Comandante Joaquin Santolalla. Lost in the Bahama Channel in 1824. Possible Florida wreck. Source: 54.

167. *Hercules* — Vessel, type unknown. Wrecked in the Keys in 1824. Cargo salvaged and sold at Key West. Source: 11.

168. Unknown ship — Was seen flying a distress flag, Feb. 26, 1825, near East Key in the Gulf of Florida. A small schooner went to assist. Unknown if salvaged. Source: 54.

169. *Johan Carl* or *John Carl* — From Havana bound for the Mediterranean with 100 boxes of sugar. Reported April 1825 as lost in the Florida Keys. Seventy-four boxes of sugar saved. Source: 54.

170. *Maria* — Ship. Wrecked in the Keys in 1831. Source: 11.

171. *Byron* — Ship. Wrecked off the Florida coast in 1839. Source: 38.

172. *Cora Nelly* — Vessel, type unknown, from Havana bound for Marseilles with coffee and sugar. Lost June 16, 1840. Key West wreckers were awarded $15,606. Possible Florida wreck. Source: 37.

173. *St. George* — Ship, left London bound for New Orleans on April 29, 1841. Lost on the Florida coast. Only three survivors. Ship and cargo valued at 12,000 pounds sterling. Source: 54.

174. *John Parker* — Vessel, type unknown, of Boston, from Mantanzas bound for Hamburg with sugar. Wrecked in the Keys, April 1846. Valued at $105,000. Though the cargo was saved in a

damaged state, the vessel was a total loss. Source: 14.

175. *Mandarin* — Scottish vessel, of Glasgow, from Jamaica bound for Liverpool with sugar. Wrecked in the Keys, April 1846. Valued at $60,000. Vessel a total loss. Damaged cargo saved by wreckers. Source: 14.

176. *Nelson* — British vessel, of London, from Jamaica bound for London with coffee. Went ashore in the Keys, June 1846. Enlisted aid of wreckers. Unknown if salvaged. Source: 14.

177. *Telamon* — Ship. Reported from Key West to have wrecked, Feb. 15, 1852. $23,695 worth of dry goods saved. Likely same vessel as # 72 in Section 3. Source: 99 (Feb. 24, 1852).

178. *Cairo* — British bark, of London. Found sinking on Sept. 13, 1853, on the south edge of the Gulf Stream by the schooner *Waldron*, which took off her crew. Possible Florida wreck. Source: 99 (Nov. 2, 1853).

179. *Walter J. Dodge* — Schooner, of Beaufort. Foundered at sea, Jan. 18, 1854. Crew taken to Key West by the bark *Edward*. Possible Florida wreck. Source: 99 (Jan. 28, 1854).

180. *Zephyr* — Vessel, type unknown, 650 tons, built in 1853 in Maine, from Pensacola bound for Buenos Aires with timber. Abandoned at sea in 1857. All hands taken to Charleston by the ship *Florida*. Possible Florida wreck. Source: 99 (Sept. 22, 1857).

181. *Noticioso* — Spanish brig, from Havana bound for Hamburg. Caught in a gale three days out of Havana. The crew manned the pumps for four days. On Oct. 28, 1857, a bark took off her crew, and she was abandoned with seven feet of water in her hold. Possible Florida wreck. Source: 99 (Nov. 9, 1857).

182. *Belle* — British brig. Reported from Key West to have run ashore. A total loss. Source: 99 (Nov. 2, 1857).

183. *Owenee* — Brig, of Baltimore, 286 tons, built in May, 1857, from Mobile bound for Cuba. Lost at sea, November 1857. Possible Florida wreck. Source: 99 (Nov. 26, 1857).

184. *Sarah Bartlett* — Schooner. Reported from New Orleans to have been left to drift in the Gulf of Mexico, with $40,000 in coins secured on board. A ship was sent to search for her, but to no avail. Possible Florida wreck. Source: 99 (May 3, 1858).

185. *Kinderhook* — Ship. Reported as a total loss by the steamer *Atlantic*, traveling from Key West to New Orleans. Possible Florida wreck. Source: 99 (July 28, 1858).

186. *R. Bingham* — Brig, of Key West, 133 tons, built in 1852 on the Mississippi River, Captain Southack, from New York bound for Key West. Reported by a schooner to have wrecked on the Florida coast, June 21, 1859. Wreckers saved some cargo. Source: 99 (June 29, 1859).

187. *Fé* — Spanish brig. Left New Orleans on June 14, 1859. Caught fire and burned while at sea. Crew escaped and landed on the Florida coast. Possible Florida wreck. Source: 99 (July 20, 1859).

188. *King Bird* — Brig. Sprang a leak and was abandoned before she sank, Oct. 24, 1859. Crew was picked up and arrived at Key West on Nov. 6. Possible Florida wreck. Source: 99 (Nov. 17, 1859).

189. *Silas Holmes* — Ship, 645 tons, from New York. Reported ashore in the Keys, Dec. 3, 1859. She was freed, but wrecked again on Dec. 9, and was reported in a dangerous condition. In Cutler's book she is listed as having foundered on Dec. 18, 1859, with the loss of Captain Charles Berry and 32 passengers and crew. Likely was gotten off and foundered soon after. Source: 19, 99 (Dec. 14, 1859).

190. *Elizabeth Allen* — Ship, from New Orleans. Reported from Key West to have gone ashore and bilged, December 1859. Note: this ship was likely the *Elizabeth Ellen*, # 49 in Section 5. Source: 99 (Ibid).

191. *W.C. Young* — Steamer, from Pensacola bound for Ship Island (off Mississippi). Struck by a gale in August 1860. Seven lives lost. A total loss. Possible Florida wreck. Source: 99 (Aug. 17, 1860).

See Civil War section for Section 8 wrecks during that period.

192. *D.H. Mount* — Steamer, 321 tons, built in 1863 at Bound Brook, N.J. Foundered on a voyage from Cape Hatteras bound for Jacksonville, Oct. 23, 1865. Twenty-four lives lost. Possible Florida wreck. Source: 52.

193. *Monga* — Brig. Believed to have wrecked in the Keys, Oct. 24, 1865, with cargo of flour, sardines, and other goods. Vessel lost. Wreckers awarded $4,088. Source: 37.

194. *Indian River* (formerly the *Neptune*, a British steamer captured in 1863; *USS Neptune*; *USS Clyde*) — Sidewheel steamer, of New York, 250 tons, built in 1861 at Glasgow. Lost off Florida's east coast,

December 1865. (See Figure 53). Source: 52.

195. *R.N. Browne* — Schooner, 133 tons, Captain Dupress, from Mobile bound for Havana. Found waterlogged and abandoned, with her mainmast overboard, Oct. 12, 1866. Crew picked up. Possible Florida wreck. Source: 99 (Oct. 28, 1866).

Figure 53: Sidewheel steamer *Indian River*, lost off Florida's east coast in 1865. Photo shows her when she was the *USS Clyde*. U.S. NAVAL HISTORICAL CENTER.

196. *Alexander Galatia* — Steamer, from Port au Prince bound for Boston. Sank on Sept. 15, 1870. Crew picked up and taken to Key West by the schooner *Tampico*. Possible Florida wreck. Source: 99 (Sept. 21, 1870).

197. *Mariposa* — Sternwheel steamer, 1,089 tons, built in 1864 at Greenpoint, Long Island, N.Y. Foundered off the Florida Coast, Oct. 9, 1870. Thirty-six lives lost. Source: 52.

198. *Mary A.R.* — Schooner. Wrecked off the coast of Florida, October 1870, while on a voyage from Cedar Keys to Jacksonville. A total loss. Source: 14.

199. *Washington* — Schooner. Became a partial loss in the Gulf Stream off Florida, October 1876. Source: 14.

200. *Franklin* — Schooner. Wrecked off the coast of Florida, October 1876, while on a passage from Galveston to New York. A partial loss. Source: 14.

201. *Conservative* — Schooner, of Galveston, 293 tons, built in 1862, Captain Terry, from Galveston bound for New York. Wrecked in the Keys, June 11, 1877, at 11 P.M. Cargo saved and vessel condemned. Source: 14.

202. *Lizzie Dakens* — British schooner, of St. John, New Brunswick, 121 tons, built in 1871, Captain Buckman, from Havana bound for New York with sugar. Foundered in the Gulf Stream, Oct. 19, 1878. Possible Florida wreck. Source: 14.

203. *Sally* — Barkentine, of Key West, 226 tons, Captain Alvarez, from Pensacola bound for Havana with yellow pine lumber. Lost in the Gulf of Mexico, April or May, 1879. Loss of six of the eight on board. Possible Florida wreck. Source: 14.

204. *James Buenaventura* — Spanish brig, of Bilboa, 1,331 tons, built in 1871, Captain Larrimaga, from New Orleans bound for Liverpool. Wrecked on the south coast of Florida, April 4, 1882, at 5 a.m. Source: 14.

205. *Lepantr(?)* — Bark, of Boston, 272 tons, Captain Hansen, from Pensacola bound for Cienfuegos, Cuba, with lumber. Stranded in the Gulf of Mexico, March 11, 1883. Vessel valued at $7,500 ($6,000 loss). Half the cargo saved. Possible Florida wreck. Source: 14.

206. *Arietis* — Schooner, of Key West, 88 tons, built in 1858, from

Key West bound for Apalachicola. Left Key West April 21, 1886, and was never heard from again. Source: 14.

207. *Nellie Parker* — Schooner, 183 tons, Captain Barkhouse, from Havana bound for Fernandina, wrecked two miles south of Smith Creek Station, March 29, 1893. Source: 14.

208. *Mary C. Mariner* — Brig, of Key West, 273 tons, built in 1861, Captain Griffin, from Key West bound for Pascagoula. Lost Oct. 2, 1893. Source: 14.

1900

209. *Fannie L. Child* — Schooner, 425 tons, built in 1881 at Waldoboro, Mass., 140' x 32.1' x 11.8'. Sailed from Jacksonville Oct. 28, 1902, for Fall River, Mass., with pine lumber and a crew of seven. Never heard from again. Source: 14.

210. *Celeste* — Schooner, 403 tons, built in 1902. Stranded at Green Run Inlet, Fla., Jan. 10, 1903. Source: 14.

211. *E.H. Weaver* — Schooner, 686 tons, built in 1882 at Bath, 153.6' x 35.4' x 15.5'. Sprang a leak during a gale and was abandoned off the Florida coast, March 31, 1903. Source: 14.

212. *Sophie Behrmann* — Schooner, 49 tons, built in 1874 at Brick Township, N.J., 61.5' x 19' x 5.6'. Stranded at Sunbass Pass, Fla., May 12, 1903. Source: 14.

213. *A. Hayford* — Schooner barge, 153 tons, built in 1872 at Belfast, Maine, 102' x 27.5' x 7.5'. Stranded at Lozee Head, Fla., Jan. 8, 1905. Source: 14.

214. *Ruth* — Sternwheel steamer, of Pensacola, 42 tons, built in 1897 at Caryville, Fla., 89' x 19.3' x 3.4', foundered at Durham Point, Fla., Jan. 27, 1905. Source: 14.

215. *Asa T. Stowell* — Schooner, 419 tons, built in 1891 at East Providence, R.I., 133.7' x 36' x 11.6'. Left Pensacola Sept. 22, 1906, bound for Havana, with a crew of seven. Never heard from again. Source: 14.

216. *Rita* — Gas vessel, 29 tons, built in 1902. Sailed from Miami bound for New York, March 30, 1907, with a crew of eight. Never heard from again. Source: 14.

217. *Northern Eagle* — Schooner, 36 tons, built in 1857 at Gloucester, 61' x 20' x 6'. Sailed from Key West Jan. 3, 1908, bound for Tampico, Mexico, with a crew of nine. Never heard

from again. Source: 14.

218. *Stillman F. Kelly* — Schooner, of Thomaston, Maine, 685 tons, built in 1905 at Thomaston, 173.5' x 37.5' x 14'. Stranded on Salt Key Bank, Sept. 14, 1909. Source: 14.

219. *Martha S. Bement* — Three-masted schooner, 479 tons, built in 1881 at Bath, 146.2' x 35' x 12.4'. Left Jacksonville, Dec. 12, 1909, with a crew of seven. Never heard from again. Source: 14.

220. *Maggie S. Hart* — Schooner, 679 tons, built in 1885 at Waldoboro, Maine, 174' x 35' x 18.3'. Left Jacksonville, Dec. 18, 1909, with a crew of eight. Never heard from again. Source: 14.

221. *Auburn* — Four-masted schooner, 633 tons, built in 1906 at Phippsburg, Maine, 171.4' x 36.3' x 13.5'. Left Jacksonville, Dec. 23, 1909, bound for Philadelphia, with a crew of nine. Never heard from again. Source: 14.

222. *Anna R. Bishop* — Schooner, 448 tons, built in 1880 at Wilmington, 146' x 34.2' x 12'. Left Jacksonville, Dec. 25, 1909, bound for Elizabethport, N.J., with a crew of seven. Never heard from again. Source: 14.

223. *Geo. A. Lawry* — Schooner, 108 tons, built in 1886 at Jonesboro, Maine, 85.7' x 23.8' x 7.6'. Left Jacksonville, Dec. 17, 1913, bound for New York, with a crew of six. Never heard from again. Source: 14.

224. *Fitz J. Babson* — Schooner, 69 tons, built in 1871 at Essex, Mass., 74.9' x 21.1' x 7.6'. Left Jacksonville, Feb. 27, 1914, with a crew of seven. Never heard from again. Source: 14.

225. *Maude B. Krum* (formerly *Grace Bailey*) — Schooner, 687 tons, built in 1883 at Bath, 159.1' x 35.5' x 16.7'. Sailed from St. Andrews, April 20, 1915, bound for Buenos Aires, with a crew of seven. Never heard from again. Source: 14.

226. *Loando* (formerly *Promise*) — Steam yacht, 42 tons, built in 1877 at Greenpoint, N.Y., 88.4' x 16.9' x 5.2'. Foundered off the coast of Florida, May 20, 1915. Source: 14.

227. *Clara P. Sewall* — Schooner, 52 tons, built in 1894 at Gloucester, 75.8' x 19.6' x 8'. Left Pensacola to go fishing, Dec. 18, 1915, with a crew of seven. Never heard from again. Source: 14.

228. *Limit* — Schooner, 38 tons, built in 1900. Sailed from the Keys,

Oct. 31, 1916, with a crew of four. Never heard from again. Source: 14.

229. *Lizzie E. Dennison* — Schooner, 528 tons, built in 1890 at East Deering, Maine, 141.5' x 33' x 14.9'. Stranded at Hetzel Shoal, Fla., March 10, 1918. Source: 14.

230. *Corydon* — Steam freighter (steel), of Detroit, 2,351 tons, built in 1918 at Ecorse, Mich., 253.4' x 43.7' x 25.1'. Foundered off the Florida coast during a hurricane, Sept. 9, 1919. Twenty-seven lives lost. Source: 14.

231. *Larimer* — Steam tanker (steel), of Port Arthur, Texas (owned by The Gulf Refining Co.), 3,737 tons, built in 1903 at Camden, N.J., 352.5' x 46.4' x 26.2'. Left Baltimore for Port Arthur, Texas, and Tampico, Mexico, where she picked up a cargo of oil, then headed back to Baltimore. She was last heard from Sept. 8, 1919, by wireless from Sand Key, eight miles south of Key West, in direct line of a hurricane. Never heard from again. All 36 of crew lost. Source: 14, 89 (Oct. 3, 1919).

232. *Lake Conway* — Steam freighter (steel), of Detroit, 1,948 tons, built in 1918 at Wyandotte, Mich., 251' x 43.8' x 18.5.' Left Philadelphia with a crew of 32, Sept. 3, 1919, bound for Havana. Not heard from since. Most likely sank in the September 1919 hurricane. Possible Florida wreck. Source: 14.

233. *Munisla* — Steam freighter (steel), of New York, 1,697 tons, built in 1916 at Ecorse, Mich., 243.3' x 43.1' x 17'. Sailed from Mobile with a crew of 28, Sept. 9, 1919, bound for Havana. Not heard from since. Most likely sank in the September 1919 hurricane. Possible Florida wreck. Source: 14.

234. *Bagdad* — Schooner, of Pensacola, 790 tons, built in 1918 at Milton, Fla., 176.3' x 37.8' x 16.7'. Sailed from Key West, Oct. 27, 1921, bound for Arecibo, Puerto Rico, with a crew of eight. Never heard from again. Source: 14.

235. *Uncle Sam* — Schooner, 21 tons, built in 1918. Sailed from Tampa, Oct. 3, 1924, bound for the Gulf, with a crew of six. Never heard from again. Source: 14.

236. *Genessee* — Steamer (steel), 212 tons, built in 1900 at Elizabeth, N.J., 119' x 27.7' x 13.7'. Stranded at Zero, Fla., October 1925. Source: 14.

237. *William Russell* — Schooner, 63 tons, built in 1907 at
Pocomoke City, Md., 81.4' x 23.4' x 6.6'. Foundered off Olympia,
Fla., Nov. 29, 1925. Source: 14.

238. *Maurice R. Thurlow* — Schooner, of Boston, 1,270 tons, built in
1920 at Stockton Springs, Maine, 202.6' x 40.1' x 22.2'. Stranded on
Diamond Shoal, Fla., Oct. 14, 1927. Source: 14.

239. *Albert Meyer* — Schooner, 459 tons, built in 1896 at Fairhaven,
Calif., 156' x 36' x 11.9'. Stranded in the Keys, Dec. 31, 1927.
Source: 14.

240. *Ruby Lee* — Motor vessel, 131 tons, built in 1903. Foundered at
Olympia, Fla., April 27, 1930. Source: 14.

241. The following St. Johns riverboats are listed in Frederick Davis's
book *History of Jacksonville & Vicinity 1513-1924* as having
wrecked. The dates they wrecked are not listed and I could find no
further information, but they likely all wrecked during the late 1800s
to the early 1900s. Source: 4.
  Armsmear — Burned at Palatka while running as a ferryboat.
  Arrow — Sank at south Jacksonville.
  Cadillac — Sank at Palatka.
  Catherine G — Sank above Palatka.
  Comet — Sank at Crescent City.
  Escort — Burned near Palatka.
  Euphemia — Stranded on shore at Dunns Lake.
  Everglade — Burned at Jacksonville.
  Georgea — Burned on the St. Johns.
  Harry Lee — Sank near Palatka.
  Howland — Sank at south Jacksonville.
  Mermaid — Burned at Jacksonville.
  Pastime — Sank at Tampa.
  Pelton — Lost during a storm while working on the overseas
    railroad at Key West.

See World War II section for Section 8 wrecks during that period.

242. *Marine Sulfur Queen* — A converted T-2 tanker, of Wilmington,
7,240 tons, built in 1944 at Chester, Pa., 504' x 68.2' x 39.4'. Her con-
version was widely publicized as a breakthrough in transportation of
liquid sulphur at high temperature. She left Beaumont, Texas, Feb. 2,
1963, with a crew of 39, bound for Norfolk, Va., with a full load of
molten sulphur. On Feb. 4, she sent a routine radio call while approximately 270 miles from Key West. She was never heard from again.
On Feb. 20, a Navy vessel retrieved some identifiable floating wreckage from the *Marine Sulphur Queen*, about 12 miles southwest of

Key West, though no trace of the ship was ever found. What happened to her remains a mystery. The American Hull Insurance Co. paid $1,080,000 for her loss, and an investigation into the incident lasted for some years. Source: 46, 58.

243. *Demerara* — O/V, 74 tons, built in 1962. Foundered off the Florida coast, Oct. 17, 1977. Source: 14.

Figure 53A: Don Kree with a bronze railing brace from an unidentified wreck. AUTHOR.

Section 9: Unidentified Wreck Sites

There are many wreck sites where the ship has not been identified. I've listed a few sites that have produced coins and other valuable artifacts.

1. Hillsboro Inlet-Pompano Beach — The area south of the Hillsboro Inlet to the Pompano Beach Pier has yielded artifacts over the years. Cob coins and a 17th-century Spanish cannon have been found here. There are many stories of gold and silver coins having been found here in the 1950s. The coins may have come from one of the 1715 Fleet vessels, or possibly from a vessel that had salvaged the fleet and was returning to Havana. A beach restoration project has buried the shallow reef just offshore and, most likely, any trace of a wreck, although recently the dredge at the inlet has dredged up coins from the 1715 period.

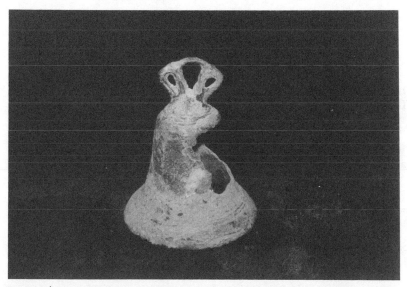

Figure 54: Bronze bell recovered at 1,500 feet on a wreck off the Tortugas, believed to be one of the 1622 Fleet wrecks. ERNIE RICHARDS.

2. Lantana — Beachcombers have found coins along the beach here for years. An 18th-century cannon was found here a few years ago. I have also seen one- and two-real coins dated 1694 and 1695 from this area.

3. Jupiter — For years, a wreck was known to be near here, but it wasn't until 1987 that a lifeguard saw a ship's remains off the public

231

beach just south of Jupiter Inlet. A silver bar dated 1652 and more than 2,500 gold and silver coins have been found using no mechanical devices. In 1991, two five-pound gold bars were found buried under six feet of sand in 11 feet of water. Dominic Addario and Peter Leo hold the lease on this site. Litigation with the State of Florida has been resolved, and they are actively working the site with a salvage vessel. The wreck could be the Spanish vessel *San Francisco y San Antonio*, which wrecked in 1659. The salvors believe it might be the *San Miguel el Archangel*, a Spanish dispatch boat that wrecked here in 1660.

4. Naples — Gold and silver coins have been found on the beach after a storm. Don Johnson and Terry Fulmer have a state lease to work a wreck site eight miles off Vanderbilt Beach.

5. Cedar Key — Coins, mostly silver, reportedly have been found on the western shore of this island.

6. Bradenton Beach — Coins reportedly have been found here and on Longboat and Siesta keys.

7. Kings Ferry — During the late 1960s, divers found large amounts of gold coins in the St. Marys River at Kings Ferry. In 1972, they found hundreds of Spanish silver coins dated 1773-1794. Many other artifacts have been found in this area. Though most of the coins were salvaged, some might remain. Source: *Skin Diver*, January 1983.

8. Cape Canaveral — Randy Lathrop has received permission to work an 18th-century wreck site off the cape. The site has yielded coins.

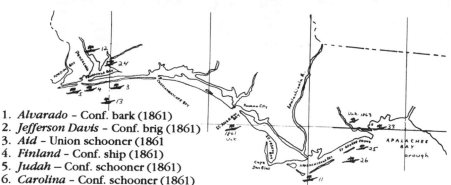

1. *Alvarado* – Conf. bark (1861)
2. *Jefferson Davis* – Conf. brig (1861)
3. *Aid* – Union schooner (1861
4. *Finland* – Conf. ship (1861)
5. *Judah* — Conf. schooner (1861)
6. *Carolina* – Conf. schooner (1861)
7. *Stag* – Conf. schooner (1861
8. *Anna Smith* – Conf. schooner (1862)
9. *Caroline* — Conf. sloop (1862)
10. *Spitfire* – Conf. schooner (1862)
11. *Rose* – Conf. schooner (1862)
12. *Fulton* – Conf. sidewheel steamer (1862)
13. *Helen* – Conf. steamer (1862)
14. *Havana* – Conf. steamer (1862)
15. *Menemon Sanford* – sidewheel steamer (1862)
16. *Patriot* – schooner (1862)
17. *Ann* – Conf. sloop (1862)
18. *Elizabeth* – British sloop (1862)
19. *Florence Nightingale* – Conf. schooner (1863)
20. *Ida* – Conf. schooner (1863)
21. *Helen* – Conf. sloop (1863)
22. *Berosa* – Conf. steamer (1863)
23. *Inez* – British schooner (1863)
24. *Preble* – Union sloop-of-war (1863)
25. *G.L. Brokenborough* – Union 4th rate sloop (1863)
26. *Amanda* – Union bark (1863)
27. *Mary Jane* – British schooner (1863)
28. *Director* – British schooner (1863)
29. *Madison* – Conf. steamer (1863)
30. *Kate Dale* – Conf. sloop (1863)
31. *Scottish Chief* – Conf. steamer (1863)
32. *Powerful* – Conf. steamer (1863)
33. *Caroline Gertrude* – Conf. schooner (1863)
34. *Young Racer* – British sloop (1864)
35. *Mary* – Conf. sloop 1864)
36. *Nan Nan* – Conf. steamer (1864)
37. *Etta* – Conf. schooner (1864)
38. *Maple Leaf* – Union transport steamer (1864)
39. *General Hunter* – Union transport steamer (1864)
40. *Good Hope* – Conf. schooner (1864)
41. *Harriet A. Wood* – Union steamer (1864)
42. *Columbine* – Union steamer (1864)
43. *General Finegan* – Conf. sloop (1864)
44. *Alice C. Price* – Union steamer (1864)
45. *Restless* – Union schooner (1864)
46. *Anna* – Union 4th rate schooner (1864)
47. *Sort* – Conf. schooner (1865)
48. *Rob Roy* – Conf. blockade runner (1865)
49. *George C. Collins* – steamer (1865)
50. *Harriet Deford* – steamer (1865)
51. *Annie* and the *Florida* – Conf. sloops (1865)

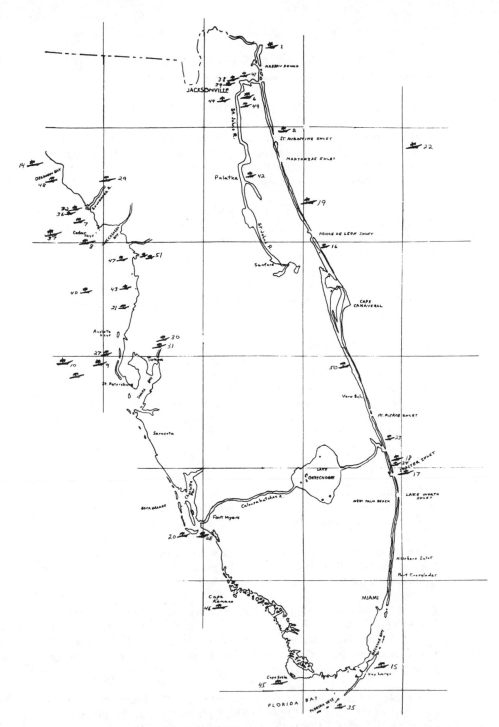

Figure 55: Map of Civil War wrecks.

235

Section 10: Civil War

The Civil War began on April 12, 1861, when Fort Sumter was fired upon, and ended on April 19, 1865, when Robert E. Lee signed the South's surrender at Appomatox. The vessels listed in this section all wrecked or were destroyed during the war. Most were wrecked or destroyed due to circumstances related to the war, though some wrecked due to other mishaps.

Florida Panhandle

1. *Aid* — Captured Confederate schooner, of Mobile, 100 tons. Sunk by Union forces to block the pass at the east end of Santa Rosa Island, Aug. 23, 1861. Source: 28, 71.

2. *Finland* — Confederate ship. Engaged by the Union vessel *R.R. Cuyler*, Captain Ellison, in Apalachicola Bay, Aug. 26, 1861. Burned. Source: 62.

3. *Judah* — Confederate schooner, 250 tons, four 42-pounders, and one long pivot gun amidships. Four boats from the Union vessel *Colorado*, under command of Lieutenant John Russel, attacked the *Judah* while she lay under the guns of the Pensacola Navy Yard, Sept. 14, 1861, at 3:30 A.M. She was set on fire and burned to the water's edge. While burning, she was set free, and drifted down opposite Fort Barrancas, where she sank. Three Union men were killed and 15 wounded. (See Figure 56). Source: 62, 63 (Series 1, Vol. 16), 71, 99 (Sept. 28, 1861).

4. Unknown Schooner — Driven ashore by the Union vessel *Bienville* at St. Andrews, Dec. 15, 1861, and was burned. She had a cargo of coffee, cigars, blankets, and shoes. Source: 62, 71.

5. Two Confederate gunboats — Both were burned to prevent capture at the head of Pensacola Bay, March 11, 1862. Both were under construction. Source: 71.

6. Three Confederate vessels (*Rose, Cygnet, Mary Olive*) — The Union vessels *Mercedita* and the *Sagamore* engaged six Confederate vessels off Apalachicola, April 2, 1862, capturing three and burning the *Rose* (schooner), *Cygnet* (pilot boat), and the *Mary Olive* (pilot boat). Source: 62.

7. *Fulton* and an ironclad — The *Fulton* was a Confederate sidewheel steamer, 698 tons, four 32-pounders, built in 1837 at the Brooklyn Navy Yard, 180' x 34'8" x 13'. She was formerly a Union vessel but

was captured by the Confederates when they took the Pensacola Navy Yard, Jan. 12, 1861. On May 10, 1862, she was destroyed, along with an ironclad, on the Escambia River at the Pensacola Yard, to prevent capture during the Federal reoccupation. (See Figure 57). Source: 28, 71.

8. *Helen* — Confederate steamer. Burned at Pensacola to prevent capture, May 1862. Note: This might be confused with the steamer *Helen* in Section 2, #6. Source: 71.

9. *Ewing* — Confederate vessel, owned by E. Simpson of Pensacola. Burned at the end of the wharf at Pensacola in 16 feet of water, to prevent capture, in 1862. She had one gun on the bow. Source: 14.

10. *Preble* — Union sloop-of-War, 566 tons, four eight-inch 32-cwt, twelve 32-pounders, two 20-pounder parrot rifles, one 12-pounder, built in 1839 at Portsmouth Naval Yard, 117' x 32' x 15'. Burned by accident, April 27, 1863, off "Little Bayou," approximately 1-1/4 miles below Pensacola, in Pensacola Bay. Later, a Mr. Tucker contracted to remove her. He blew up the wreck after removing most of the guns. Her copper was not salvaged, nor were two or three brass pieces. There was also considerable copper in boxes left on the wreck, worth $3,000 to $5,000 in 1870. (See Figure 58). Source: 28, 62, 63 (Series II, Vol. 1).

11. *G.L Brockenboro* (also spelled *Brockenborough*) — Union 4th-rate sloop, one howitzer, originally a blockade runner. Scuttled in the Apalachicola River in 1862 and later raised. Ran aground during a severe gale in St. George's Sound, May 27, 1863. Source: 28, 71.

12. *Andrew Manderson* — Bark, carried coal. Wrecked on Sand Island during the storm of May 27, 1863. Source: 103.

13. *Amanda* — Union bark, 368 tons, six 32-pounder smooth bore, one 20-pounder parrot, one 12-pounder howitzer, built in 1858 in New York, 117'6" x 27'9" x 12'6". Blown aground during a gale at the East Pass of St. George Sound. On May 29, 1863, she was burned by her crew. Source: 28, 71.

14. *Caroline Gertrude* — Confederate schooner, Captain Meeker. Captured and destroyed by the Union steamer *Stars And Stripes*, Master Willcomb, Dec. 28, 1863, while aground on the bar at the mouth of the Ochlockonee River. Source: 62, 71.

Florida's West Coast

1. Nine Confederate vessels — On Jan. 16, 1862, the Union vessel

Hatteras, under Captain Emmons, engaged and destroyed nine vessels at Cedar Keys Harbor, along with the Florida Railroad Wharf. Only the vessel *Fanny* escaped. The vessels carried turpentine, rosin, cotton, lumber, and other cargo. Source: 28, 62, 63 (Series 1, Vol. 17).

The vessels were:
Anna Smith — Schooner, 198 tons, Captain Edwards.
Ancilla — Schooner, 81 tons, Captain Burrows.
Dudly (or *Pinckney*) — Sloop, 57 tons, Captain Artiga.
Rattler — Sloop, 66 tons.
Stag — Schooner, 200 tons, Captain Burns.
Wyfe (or *Nye*) — Schooner.
William H. Middleton — Sloop, 69 tons, Captain Roberts.
Unknown saiboat.
Unknown ferryboat.

Figure 56: Union Navy boats burn the Confederate schooner *Judah* in Pensacola Harbor in 1861. U.S. NAVAL HISTORICAL CENTER.

2. *Caroline* — Confederate sloop. Sunk by the Union vessel *Ethan Allen*, Captain Eaton, in Clearwater Harbor, Feb. 18, 1862. Source: 62.

3. *Spitfire* — Confederate schooner. Sunk the same time as the *Caroline*. Source: 62.

4. *Mary Nevis* — Cutter. Was being towed by the Union bark *Ethan*

Figure 57: *USS Fulton*, destroyed on the Escambia River at Pensacola in 1862. U.S. NAVAL HISTORICAL CENTER.

Allen when she grounded and then bilged, Feb. 19, 1862, at Bayes Pass, Cedar Keys. Everything that could be saved was, and then she was burned. Source: 63 (Series 1, Vol. 17).

5. *Ida* — Confederate schooner. Captured by Union vessel *Chambers*, run aground on the beach and destroyed, March 4, 1863, on Sanibel Island. Source: 71.

Figure 58: U.S. Naval Ship *Preble*, burned in 1863. U.S. NAVAL ACADEMY MUSEUM.

6. *Helen* and a schooner — Seven boats from the Union vessels *St. Lawrence, Sagamore*, and *Ft. Henry*, while on expedition under Acting Lieutenant McCauley. Captured the Confederate sloop (one source says a small steamer) *Helen*, with a cargo of corn, April 2 or 3, 1863, at Bayport and then burned her. On April 4, the expedition burned another schooner at Bayport. Two other sloops and two schooners were also run aground during the expedition in Bayport Harbor. Source: 28, 62, 71.

7. *Havana* — Confederate steamer. Surprised by the *USS Isilda*, June 5, 1863 (one source says 1862), while in Deadman's Bay. Her crew burned and deserted her. Source: 63 (Series II, Vol. 1).

8. *Mary Jane* — British schooner. Chased ashore and destroyed by the Union steamer *Tahoma*, Lieutenant A.A. Semmes, June 18, 1863, at Clearwater, at Lat. 28-00, Long. 82-53. Source: 62, 71.

9. Steamer — The Union prize steamer *James Battle*, under Lieutenant Commander A.A. Semmes, encountered an iron steamer (camouflaged with branches), one mast and one funnel, apparently more than 200 feet long, English-built, though reported to sail under a French flag, inside the harbor at Bayport, Fla., Sept. 15, 1863. Rebels set the steamer and a wharehouse full of cotton on fire after they were seen. Semmes watched for three hours to make sure the steamer was destroyed before sailing to Cedar Keys. Source: 63 (Series 1, Vol. 17).

10. *Director* — British schooner, Captain Johnson, cargo of rum and salt. Destroyed by the Union bark *Gem Of The Sea*, Lieutenant Baxter, Sept. 30, 1863, at Punta Rassa. Source: 62.

11. *Powerful* — Confederate steamer. Captured and destroyed by the Union schooner *Fox*, Captain Ashbury, Dec. 20, 1863, at the mouth of the Suwanee River. Source: 62, 71.

12. *Etta* and a schooner — The *Etta* was originally the *Uncle Ben*, a Lake Erie tug, and was later fitted out as a privateer schooner. She was captured and destroyed by the Union vessel *Sagamore*, March 31, 1864, near Cedar Key. The schooner was burned by her crew to prevent capture. Source: 28, 71.

13. *General Finegan* — Confederate sloop, with a cargo of turpentine and cotton. Captured by the Union vessel *Ariel*, May 28, 1864. After the cargo was discharged, she was destroyed just north of Chassahowitzka Bay. Source: 71.

14. *Anna* (also called *Annie*) — Union 4th-rate schooner (originally

the *La Criolla*). Captured Feb. 26, 1863, on the Suwanee River, 27 tons, built in 1857, 46'2" x 14'9" x 5', one 12-pounder smooth bore pivot gun. Left Key West Dec. 30, 1864, and was discovered two weeks later off Cape Roman, a total wreck, apparently the victim of an explosion. Another Union vessel found her remains in February 1865 off Cape Roman, sunk in six fathoms, bearing northeast by north approximately ten miles, with her mast protruding above the water. A few items, including an octant, were salvaged. Source: 28, 63 (Series 1, Vol. 17).

15. *Sort* — Confederate schooner. Forced aground by the Union vessel *Honeysuckle,* Feb. 28, 1865, on a reef at the mouth of the Crystal River. Eventually destroyed. Source: 71.

16. *Rob Roy* — Famous blockade runner, 60 tons, 78' x 22' x 6'6". Chased ashore and run aground by the Union vessel *Fox,* Master Burgess, March 2, 1865, at Deadman's Bay, with assorted cargo. Her crew set her on fire. Wreckers awarded $528. Source: 37, 62, 71.

Lower Florida Keys

1. *Malvina Cezard* — Ship, from Manzanillo bound for Bordeaux with palm leaves, mahogany, fustic, and other cargo. Wrecked on Pine Key Bar, Aug. 15, 1861. Vessel lost. Wreckers awarded $1,150. Source: 37.

2. *Sebra Crooker* — Bark, from Mantanzas bound for Portland with molasses. Wrecked on Looe Key, July 8, 1864. Vessel lost. Wreckers awarded $3,405. Source: 37.

3. *Atlantic* — Brig, from Philadelphia bound for New Orleans with coal and the materials of the ship *Conqueror.* Wrecked on East Key, Tortugas, April 6, 1865. Vessel lost. Wreckers awarded $850. Source: 37.

Upper Florida Keys

1. *Franklin* — Brig, from Mantanzas bound for New York with sugar. Wrecked on Conch Reef, May 19, 1861. Vessel lost. Wreckers awarded $2,043. Source: 37.

2. *Sir Walter Raleigh* — Bark, from Jamaica bound for New Orleans with assorted cargo. Wrecked on Pacific Reef, Aug. 18, 1861. Vessel lost. Wreckers awarded $163. Source: 37.

3. *Ben Cushing* — Brig, from Havana bound for Portland with molasses and cigars. Wrecked on French Reef, Feb. 22, 1862. Vessel lost. Wreckers awarded $380. Source: 37.

4. *Director* — Bark, from Jamaica bound for London with sugar, ginger, honey, and beeswax. Wrecked on Carysfort Reef, March 21, 1862. Vessel lost. Wreckers awarded $3,128. Source: 37.

5. *Lady Franklin* — Bark, from Jamaica bound for Liverpool with sugar, honey, rum, and logwood. Wrecked on French Reef, May 25, 1862. Vessel lost. Wreckers awarded $3,735. Source: 37.

6. *Menemon Sanford* — Sidewheel steamer, chartered by U.S. government, 904 tons, built in 1854 at New York (also listed as built at Greenpoint, Long Island, N.Y.), 237' x 34' x 12'. Stranded on Carysfort Reef, Dec. 9, 1862, 1-1/2 miles south of the light. Soon reduced to wreckage. Her engine was later salvaged. The pilot on board was believed to be a Southern sympathizer who deliberately grounded her. Wreckers awarded $1,753. Source: 37, 40 (Vol. 1, 1953), 52.

7. *Sparkling Sea* — Ship, from Fort Monroe, with troops and supplies. Wrecked on Ajax Reef, Jan. 8, 1863. Vessel lost. Wreckers awarded $3,026. Source: 37.

8. *Adelayda* — Schooner, from New York bound for Mantanzas with dry goods. Wrecked on Elbow Reef, March 26, 1863. Vessel lost. Wreckers awarded $7,713. Source: 37.

9. *Joseph Meigs* — Ship, from Boston bound for New Orleans with government stores. Wrecked on what was believed to be Fowey Rocks, July 14, 1863. Vessel lost. Wreckers awarded $1,725. Source: 37.

10. *Restless* — Schooner, of Boothbay, Maine, 59 tons. Sunk by the Confederate vessel *Tallahassee*, Aug. 15, 1864, off Cape Sable. Source: 69.

11. *N.M. Terry* — Brig, from Philadelphia bound for New Orleans with coal. Wrecked on French Reef, Nov. 7, 1864. Vessel lost. Wreckers awarded $1,864. Source: 37.

12. *Margaret Kerr* — Ship, from Mantanzas bound for Greencock with sugar. Wrecked on Crockers Reef, Feb. 22, 1865. Vessel lost. Wreckers awarded $13,898. Source: 37.

13. *Annie Baldwin* — Bark, from Florida Keys bound for Liverpool with guano. Wrecked on Conch Reef, April 16, 1865. Vessel lost. Wreckers awarded $734. Source: 37.

Florida's Lower East Coast

1. Two unknown schooners — One was burned and the other sunk

by the Union vessel *Sagamore*, Captain English, Dec. 5, 1862, off Jupiter Inlet. Source: 62.

2. *Ann* — Confederate sloop, with a cargo of salt and coffee. Destroyed by Union bark *Gem Of The Sea*, Captain Baxter, Dec. 30, 1862, off Jupiter Inlet. Source: 62.

3. *Elizabeth* — British sloop, Captain Sweeting. Destroyed by the Union vessel *Sagamore*, Captain English, Jan. 28, 1863, at the mouth of Jupiter Inlet. Source: 62, 71.

4. *Inez* — British schooner, Captain Edgett. Destroyed by the Union bark *Gem Of The Sea*, Lieutenant Baxter, April 18, 1863, at the Indian River Inlet, with a cargo of salt. Source: 62, 71.

5. *Young Racer* — British sloop, with a cargo of salt. Chased ashore and destroyed by the Union bark *Roebuck*, Captain Sherrill, Jan. 14, 1864, north of Jupiter Inlet. Source: 62, 71.

Florida's Upper East Coast

1. *Alvarado* — Bark, of Boston, Captain G.C. Whiting. Left Cape Town, Africa, June 3, 1861, with wool, sheep- and goatskins, buckskins, hides, old copper, and 70 tons of iron. Captured by the Confederate brig *Jefferson Davis* at Lat. 25-04-00, Long. 50-00-00.. Later she was chased ashore and destroyed, Aug. 5, 1861, on a bar off Fernandina, by the *USS Jamestown,* Captain Green. (See Figure 59). Only a few items belonging to Captain Whiting, including the log, were saved. Source: 62, 63 (Series 1, Vol. 6).

2. *Jefferson Davis* — Confederate full-rigged brig, formerly the slaver *Echo*, 187 tons, built in 1845 at Baltimore (originally the *Putnam*), 10'6" draft, two 32-pounders, two 24-pounders, one long 18-pounder pivot (all guns were 60-year-old British guns), Captain Coxetter. Grounded on the bar at the entrance to St. Augustine Harbor during a gale, Aug. 18, 1861. The crew threw the heavy guns overboard, but to no avail. The crew and small arms were saved. Source: 28, 63 (Series II, Vol.1), 71, 99 (Sept. 4, 1861).

3. *Patriot* — Centerboard schooner. Found beached and stripped by the *USS Carolina*, Aug. 27, 1862, 12 to 15 miles south of Mosquito Inlet. Source: 71.

4. *Florence Nightingale* — Confederate schooner. Destroyed by the Union vessel *Sagamore*, Feb. 23, 1863, off New Smyrna. Source: 62.

5. *Petee* — Confederate sloop. Captured and destroyed by the Union

Figure 59: *USS Jamestown* drives ashore and burns the Confederate bark *Alvarado* near Fernandina in 1861. U.S. NAVAL HISTORICAL CENTER.

bark *Gem Of The Sea*, March 10, 1863, while trying to enter the Indian River Inlet with a cargo of salt. Source: 71.

6. *Berosa* — Confederate steamer. Sailed from the St. Mary's River. Sprang a leak and was abandoned in the Gulf Stream, April 8, 1863, at Lat. 29-50-00, Long. 79-50-00. Source: 28.

7. Confederate vessels — A number of vessels were destroyed at New Smyrna by the Confederates, to prevent capture by the Union vessels *Beauregard, Orleander, Sagamore,* and *Para*, July 28, 1863. Some were loaded with cotton and ready to sail. Source: 28, 71.

8. *Delaware* — Union sidewheel steamer, 616 tons, built in 1851 (or 1852) at New York, 225' x 29' x 10.6'. Left Hilton Head, May 24, 1864 bound for Florida and was lost after stranding inside the St. John's Bar, May 1864. Most furniture and equipment was salvaged. Source: 40 (Vol. 1, 1953), 52.

Florida's Inland Waters

1. *Carolina* — Confederate schooner. Driven ashore on the St. Johns River, Dec. 11, 1861, by the Union vessel *Bienville*. Source: 62.

2. Confederate schooner — During a Union expedition up the Ochlockonee River, March 2-4, 1863, a Confederate schooner was burned, despite severe fire from shore. Source: 28.

3. *Onward* (believed to be renamed *Emma*) — Confederate schooner. Destroyed while loading cotton on the Ochlockonee River, by

boats of the Union bark *Amanda* under Master R.J. Hoffner, between March 20 and 23, 1863. At least one Union sailor was killed and five wounded. Note: Possibly same vessel as #2. Source: 63 (Series 1, Vol. 17).

4. *Madison* — Sidewheel steamer, of Cedar Keys, 99 tons, built in 1855 at New Albany, Ind., Captain James Tucker, ran supplies up the Suwanee River. At the beginning of the Civil War, the Captain raised a company of Cofederate soldiers and, with the *Madison,* captured a Union gunboat one night. In September 1863, Tucker left his vessel with some civilians for them to make one more trip up the river. Afterwards she was to be sunk at Old Troy Spring, with the intention of raising her after the war. Her boilers and funnels were salvaged during the war, and used for salt and sugar production. Her remains are visible today. Source: 52, 88 (Vol. 6, No. 1, January 1989).

5. *Kate Dale* — Sloop. Destroyed by the Union steamers *Tahoma* and *Adelia*, Oct. 16, 1863, on the Hillsborough River, with a cargo of cotton. Source: 62.

6. *Scottish Chief* — Steamer. Destroyed along with the *Kate Dale*. She also had a cargo of cotton. Source: 62.

7. *Schooner* — This vessel was destroyed by Union forces at Bear Creek on Dec. 10, 1863, with 100 bales of cotton on board. Source: 71.

8. *St. Marys* — Confederate sidewheel steamer (iron), built in 1857 at Wilmington. Sunk by Confederates in 1862 to avoid capture. Raised by Confederates and renamed *Nick King*. She was later trapped and sunk in McGirts Creek, off the St. Johns River, on either Feb. 7 or 9, 1864, by the Union steamer *Norwich*. She was later raised and rebuilt and reportedly became the *USS Genesee*, later renamed again the *Nick King,* which wrecked on the St. Johns in 1874. Source: 52, 60, 62, 71.

9. *Nan Nan* — Confederate steamer, with a cargo of cotton. Chased ashore by the Union vessel *Nita*, Feb. 24, 1864, at the east pass of the Suwanee River. Burned by her crew. Source: 71.

10. *Maple Leaf* — U.S. Army transport steamer, 508 tons, built in 1861 at Kingston, Ontario, 173'2 x 24.7' x 18.6,' from Palatka bound for Jacksonville. Sunk by a torpedo (floating mine), April 1, 1864, on the St. Johns River, off Mandarin Point., approximately 12 or 15 miles above Jacksonville. Sank within 12 minutes, taking four men with her. This wreck was found in the 1980s, and is being excavated. (See Figure 60). Source: 21, 40 (Vol. 5, 1967), 71.

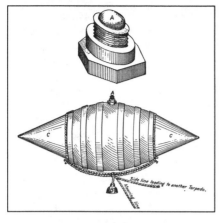

Figure 60: Sketch of a torpedo similar to the one that sank the *Maple Leaf*, found in the St. Johns River. Explanation – **A**, thin sheet-lead cover to exploding apparatus; **B**, balance-ball to keep exploding apparatus uppermost; **C**, cones of pine wood serving as buoys. *OFFICIAL RECORDS OF THE UNION AND CONFEDERATE NAVIES ON THE WAR OF THE REBELLION* (SEE BIBLIOGRAPHY).

11. *General Hunter* — Union troop transport steamer. Sunk by a torpedo, April 16, 1864, on the St. Johns River, near Mandarin Point not far from the wreck of the *Maple Leaf*. Sank immediately with valuable quartermaster's stores. One man drowned. Source: 21, 71.

12. *Good Hope* — Confederate schooner, 150 tons, with a cargo of salt and dry goods. Captured and burned by the Union schooner *Fox*, Captain Chase, April 18, 1864, at the mouth of the Homosassa River, Lat.28-34-00, Long.83-10-00. Source: 62, 71.

13. *Harriet A. Weed* — Union transport sidewheel steamer, 210 tons, built in 1863 at Newburgh, N.Y. Sunk by a Confederate torpedo, May 9 or 10, 1864, on the St. Johns River. Six men went down with her. Source: 21, 52, 71.

14. *Columbine* — Union sidewheel steamer, tug rig, 133 tons, 117' x 36' x 6'2", two 20-pounder parrot rifles. On the evening of May 23, 1864, she was engaged by Confederate soldiers under Captain Dickinson and Lieutenant Bates at Horse Landing, Palatka. She was disabled by artillery fire and grounded after 45 minutes of battle. Unable to fight and having lost 20 to 25 men, she struck her colors. She was burned to prevent recapture after Confederates confiscated 42 rifles, 28 cartridge boxes, 2,000 rounds ammunition, 35 bayonets, five swords, eight pistols, four cutlasses, two nautical compasses, two chest bomb fuses, two spyglasses, three stand of colors, and two boats. Both Dickinson and Bates each received one of the swords for their success. Source: 28, 63 (Series 1, Vol. 15), 71.

15. *Alice C. Price* — Union sidewheel steamer, 283 tons, built in 1853 at New York, lengthened in 1861, 320 tons, 169' x 26.6' x 7.6'. Struck a torpedo and quickly sank, June 19, 1864, on the St. Johns River, approximately eight miles above Jacksonville. Was returning

from the Nassau River for Jacksonville with machinery that had been captured. The machinery and most of the fixtures were salvaged. Source: 12, 40 (Vol. 4, 1966), 52.

16. *George C. Collins* — Steamer, 234 tons, built in 1862 at East Haddam, Conn. Stranded on the St. Johns River, March 27, 1865. Source: 52.

Note: The monitor *Milwaukee* has been incorrectly listed by some sources as having sunk in Florida in March 1865. She sank in the Blakely River off Mobile Bay in March 1865 and later was salvaged.

17. *Annie* and the *Florida* — Both Confederate sloops. Destroyed by the Union schooner *Sea Bird*, Master Robbins, April 1, 1865, on the Crystal River. Their cargoes of cotton were taken to Key West. Source: 62.

18. *Harriet Deford* — Steamer, 149 tons, built in 1864 at Baltimore. Burned on the Indian River, April 7, 1865, with a loss of three lives. Source: 52.

19. *Spray* — Confederate steam gunboat, tug-rigged, two guns. Sunk by the Confederates in the St. Mary's River. Probably salvaged, since one source says she surrendered in May 1865. Source: 28, 63 (Series II, Vol.1).

Unknown Locations

1. *Glen* — Bark, of Freeport, Maine, 287 tons, bound for Fort Jefferson, Tortugas, with coal. Captured and burned by the Confederate vessel *Dixie*, off Florida, July 23, 1861. Source: 69.

2. *Santa Clara* — Brig, of Eastport, Maine, 198 tons. Captured and burned off the Florida coast, Aug. 6, 1861, by the Confederate brig *Jefferson Davis*. Source: 69.

3. *John Carver* — Ship, of Bath, 1,250 tons (also listed at 976 tons), built in 1860 at Bath, 182'9 x 33'9, Captain Edge. Captured and burned off the Florida coast, Aug. 11, 1861, by the Confederate brig *Jefferson Davis*. Source: 6, 14, 69.

4. *Estelle* — Bark, of Millbridge, Maine. Captured and burned by Confederate vessel *Florida*, Jan. 1, 1862, north of Cuba. Possible Florida wreck. Source: 69.

5. *Swan* — Confederate steamer (May 24, 1862), of Key West, 487 tons. Captured May 24, 1862. Foundered on a voyage from Key West to New Orleans, Feb. 19, 1863. Possible Florida wreck. Source: 52.

6. *Anglo Saxon* — Bark, of Rockland, Maine, built in 1852. Captured by the Confederate vessel *Florida* and burned, Aug. 20, 1863, off the Florida coast. Source: 69.

7. *Mary* — Confederate sloop, with a cargo of cotton. Captured by the *Roebuck*, Captain Sherill, Jan. 19, 1864. On Jan. 22, 1864, she ran aground and wrecked in the Keys. Source: 71.

8. *Wild Pigeon* — Confederate schooner, 37 tons. Sunk by the Union sidewheel steamer *Hendrick Hudson*, Captain McDougal, March 21, 1864, off the coast of Florida. Source: 62.

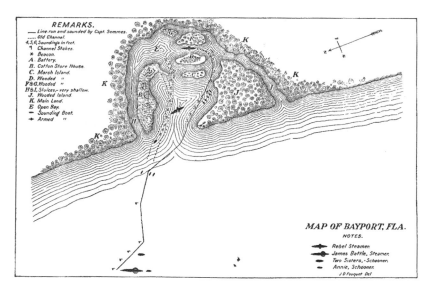

Figure 60A: Map depicting the location of the steamer in #9 on page 240.
U.S. GOVERNMENT PRINTING OFFICE.

Section 11: World War II

Though the war on land was far away, the war on the sea was brought right to our doorstep. During the early part of the war, German U-boats wreaked havoc on Allied shipping along the eastern coasts of both North and South America, including the Caribbean and the Gulf of Mexico. After the implementation of sonar, upgraded patrols, and improved air power, the U-boats were nearly eliminated from our coast during the later part of the war.

Shipping off the Florida coast was some of the hardest hit by U-boats in 1942 and 1943. Many older residents still remember seeing allied ships burning off this coast from U-boat attacks. On June 17, 1942, U 584 landed four German spies along with clothing, IDs, money, and explosives on the beach just south of Ponte Vedra Beach. They made their way to Jacksonville, where they spent the night. Two were later captured in New York, and the other two in Chicago. There was even a humorous incident in which the sewer outfall pipe off Miami was depth-charged because someone believed it to be a U-boat. A Navy blimp, the K-74, spotted a U-boat near Miami and prepared to attack, but the sub surfaced and shot the blimp down with deck guns. Divers have found and are still finding many shells, bombs, and torpedoes from the war off Florida's coast. Much of Florida's coast was used for military exercises during the war.

Since I started diving in Florida, I have heard numerous rumors of sunken U-boats off our coast. The July 1967 issue of *Skin Diver* magazine showed a photo of the supposed conning tower of a sunken U-boat in 90 feet of water off Broward County, supposedly on the outside of the third reef. The photo was taken by a Fort Lauderdale diver. Local fishermen referred to an area off Pompano in 500 feet of water as "the sub." When investigated with a TV camera, it proved to be only a reef. One resident told me he saw a U-boat attacked off Deerfield Beach, though there was no evidence that it sank.

Diver Bill Parks told me of a sub he dove on during the 1950s off Palm Beach in 90 to 100 feet of water. The bow would cover and uncover in the sand facing west, with the stern always covered. There seemed to be no damage and he believed she was scuttled. We looked for her recently, but couldn't find her. She probably remains buried under the sand.

I've heard rumors of a U-boat off Martin County, and another off the Fort Myers area. Another rumor involves U 166, which sank off New Orleans, Aug. 1, 1942. It reportedly has been seen drifting along the bottom from Mobile to Tampa, though this seems highly unlikely.

The U 157 is the only U-boat I know of that was sunk off our coast during the war. Another U-boat was captured, served in our Navy, and was sunk after the war off the Keys.

All in all, the German U-boats were one of the most feared weapons

1. *Ontario*
2. *Empire Mica*
3. *Norlindo*
4. *Munger T. Ball*
5. *Joseph M. Cudahy*
6. *Torny*
7. *Baja California*
8. *USS Sturtevant*
9. *Faja de Oro*
10. *Hermis*
11. *U-157*
12. *Managua*
13. *Bosiljka*
14. *Edward S. Luckenbach*
15. *Nicholas Cuneo*
16. *Andrew Jackson*
17. *Gertrude*
18. *Port Antonio*
19. *Santiago de Cuba*
20. *Manzanillo*
21. *Gulfstate*
22. *R-12* (accident)
23. *Benwood*
24. *Potrero del Llano*
25. *Nicarao*
26. *Umtata*
27. *Pan Massachusetts*
28. *Republic*
29. *W.D. Anderson*
30. *Cities Service Empire*
31. *Korsholm*
32. *Laertes*
33. *Sama*
34. *Ocean Venus*
35. *Amazone*
36. *Halsey*
37. *Ohioan*
38. *Lubrafol*
39. *Esparta*
40. *Gulf America*
41. *Leslie*
42. *Esso Gettysburg*
43. *Gulfland* (collision)
44. *Gunvor* (accident)
45. *San Pablo* (accident)
46. *Elizabeth Massey* (accident)
47. *Vamar* (accident)

О All were sunk by torpedo, gunfire, or mine unless otherwise noted.

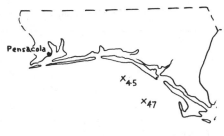

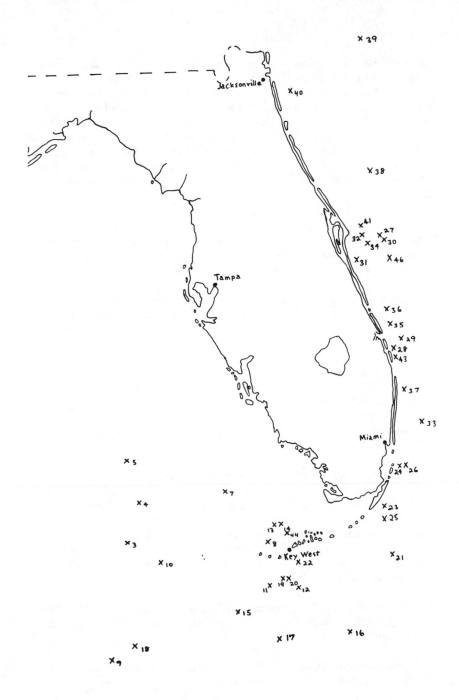

Figure 61: Map of World War II wrecks.

251

used by the Axis. From September 1939 to May 1945, these U-boats sent 23,351,000 tons of Allied shipping to the bottom of the ocean.

The following is a list of vessels sunk during WWII by enemy and allied action, or other mishap. Many have become popular diving and fishing areas, but many others were destroyed by the Navy and Coast Guard, both for navigational reasons and to prevent U-boats from using them as sonar camouflage. Note: Many of the vessels listed give the Latitude and Longitude where they were torpedoed or shelled. Some of these remained afloat for a time and drifted to another location where they sank.

Florida Panhandle

1. *Vamar* (fifth name she sailed under) — Freighter, of Wilmington, 598 tons, built in 1919 at Middlesboro, 170' x 30' x 15.7', cargo of lumber. Capsized after stranding, March 21, 1942, at Lat. 29-54-00, Long. 85-27-54, in 25 feet of water. Now a popular dive site. Source: 1, 14, 80.

2. *Ontario* — Honduran freighter (another source says she was from Baltimore and owned by the M & N Line), 3,099 tons, built in 1904 at Camden, N.J., 292.2' x 42.2' x 15.9'. Torpedoed by *U 507*, May 8, 1942, at Lat. 28-11-00, Long. 87-32-00. Source: 1, 68, 80.

3. *Empire Mica* — British tanker, 8,032 tons. Torpedoed by *U 67*, June 29, 1942, at Lat. 29-25-00, Long. 85-17-00. Sank at Lat. 29-56-54, Long. 85-21-05, approximately 52 miles from Panama City. The wreck was demolished to 50 feet, and lies in 110 feet of water. She is a popular dive site today, with her bow intact and upper deck at 60 feet. Source: 1, 68.

4. *San Pablo* — Panamanian steam freighter, of the United Fruit Co., 3,305 tons, built in 1915, 315.2' x 44.2' x 28.8'. Torpedoed and sunk by *U 161*, July 3, 1942, at her pier in Port Limon, Costa Rica. She was refloated and was being towed to Mobile for repairs when she sank nine miles off Pensacola Beach, Sept. 25, 1943, in 75 feet of water, at Lat. 30-11-20, Long. 87-13-03. She is now a popular dive site. It has mistakenly been referred to as a Russian freighter which sank in 1957. Source: 1, 80.

5. *A.G.T.N. No. 34* — Barge (steel), 265 tons, built in 1937 at Mobile, 128' x 32' x 7.5'. Foundered in the pass into Pensacola Bay, Nov. 22, 1942. Source: 14.

6. Barge — Sank in 1942 in 16 fathoms, at Lat. 30-00-00, Long. 87-21-00. Now a popular dive site. Source: 1.

7. *Viking* — Oil vessel, 52 tons, built in 1925. Burned seven miles east of Graton Beach, Dec. 23, 1943. Source: 14.

8. *Gelmer* — Dredge. Sank in 1943, at Lat. 29-19-00, Long. 84-55-00, in 88 feet of water. Source: 1.

9. *Anona* — Vessel, type unknown, 150 tons. Sank June 11, 1944, at approximate Lat. 29-10-00, Long. 87-49-00. Source: 1.

10. *Lapwing* — Oil vessel, 34 tons, built in 1901. Wrecked on the beach, Dec. 5, 1944, 500 feet south of the jetty at Fort Macrae, Pensacola Bay. Source: 14.

11. Unknown wreck — Reported in 1944 to be in 80 feet of water, with her stack and two masts protruding above the water, at Lat. 30-12-00, Long. 87-13-00. Source: 1.

Florida's West Coast

1. *Norlindo* — Steam freighter, of Baltimore (owned by the M & N Line), 2,686 tons, built in 1920 at Superior, Wis., 255.4' x 43.8' x 26.9'. Torpedoed and sunk by *U 507*, May 4, 1942, at Lat. 24-57-00, Long. 84-00-00. Source: 1, 14, 68, 80.

2. *Munger T. Ball* — Steam tanker, of Baltimore (owned by Sabine Transportation Co.), 5,104 tons, built in 1920 at Savannah, 391.9' x 51.2' x 30'. Torpedoed and sunk by *U 507*, May 4, 1942, at Lat. 25-24-00, Long. 83-46-00. Source: 14, 68.

3. *Joseph M. Cudahy* — Steam tanker, of Sinclair Refining Co., 6,949 tons, built in 1921 at Chester, Pa., 430' x 59.2' x 33.4'. Torpedoed and sunk by *U 507*, May 5, 1942, at Lat. 25-57-00, Long. 83-57-00, in 50 fathoms. Source: 1, 14, 68.

4. *Torny* — Norwegian freighter, of Bergen, 2,424 tons, built in 1919. Torpedoed by *U 507*, May 8, 1942, at Lat. 26-40-00, Long. 86-40-00. Source: 68.

5. *Baja California* — Honduran freighter, 1,648 tons, built in 1914 in Norway, 265.6' x 38.6' x 18', from New Orleans bound for Guatemala with a miscellaneous cargo. Torpedoed by *U 84*, July 19, 1942, at Lat. 25-14-00, Long. 82-27-00, and soon after sank in 114 feet at Lat. 25-25-51, Long. 82-31-50. She lies approximately 80 miles south-southwest of Mantanzas Pass. Local dive charter boats offer trips to the site. Source: 68, 80, 93 (Sanders, Dale. "Wreck of the Baja California." Vol. 1 No. 2, pp. 17-21).

6. *Gulfport* — Dredge (steel), 682 tons, built in 1930 at Nashville, 164.2' x 40' x 7.7'. Foundered 18 miles off Clearwater, either Feb. 13 or 14, 1943, at Lat. 28-00-00, Long. 82-50-00. Still visible

in 1983. Source: 1, 14.

7. *Dolores* — Freighter, 82 tons. Sank Sept. 26, 1943, at Lat. 27-01-00, Long. 82-19-00. Source: 1.

8. *Antonio Ensen* — Freighter, 200 tons. Sank Oct. 31, 1943, at Lat. 27-05-12, Long. 82-41-00, in 36 feet of water. Still visible in 1983. Source: 1.

9. Unknown wreck — Sank in 1943, at Lat. 27-35-30, Long. 83-59-30. Still visible in 1983. Source: 1.

10. Dredge — Sank in 1943, at Lat. 27-56-48, Long. 83-07-42. Source: 1.

11. Dredge — Sank in 1943, at Lat. 27-58-00, Long. 83-07-00. Source: 1.

12. Unknown wreck — Reported in 1944, at Lat. 27-05-12, Long. 82-41-00, in 35 feet of water. Source: 1.

Lower Florida Keys

1. *USS Sturtevant* — Navy destroyer, 1,190 tons, commissioned July 29, 1920, 314'4" x 30'9" x 9'3". Sank after striking a mine, April 26, 1942, at Lat. 24-45-00, Long. 82-01-00. Fifteen lives lost. She now lies in 68 feet of water. Some Key West dive charter boats make the trip to this site, less than 12 miles from Key West. (See Figure 62). Source: 44, 45.

2. *Faja de Oro* — Mexican government steam tanker, 6,067 tons, built in 1914 at Newcastle, England, 433.5' x 54.6' x 32.4'. Torpedoed by *U 106*, May 21, 1942, at Lat. 23-30-00, Long. 84-24-00. Source: 68, 80.

3. *Hermis* — Panamanian freighter, 5,234 tons. Torpedoed by *U 158*, June 7, 1942, at Lat. 23-08-00, Long. 83-30-00. NOAA says she sank at approximate Lat. 24-36-00, Long. 83-32-00 (accurate between one and three miles). Source: 1, 68.

4. *U 157* — German submarine, 740 tons, built in the early part of WWII, 244'6" x 20'4" x 13'6", Captain Henne. Sunk by U.S. Coast Guard vessel *Thetis*, off Key West, June 13, 1942, at Lat. 24-13-00, Long. 82-03-00. Source: 1, 44.

5. *Gunvor* — Norwegian freighter, of Trondheim, 1,942 tons, built in 1935, 277.7' x 43.2' x 18.1'. Sank on June 14, 1942, at Lat. 24-56-54, Long. 81-46-36, and was later demolished. Source: 1, 80, Norsk Sjofartsmuseum.

Figure 62: Destroyer *USS Sturtevant*, sunk in 1942. NATIONAL ARCHIVES.

6. *Managua* — Nicaraguan freighter, of Bluefield, 2,220 tons, built in 1919 at Portland, Ore. Torpedoed by *U 67*, June 16, 1942, at Lat. 24-05-00, Long. 81-40-00. Source: 1, 68, 80.

7. *Bosiljka* — Yugoslavian freighter, of Orebic, 3,009 tons, built in 1896 at Glasgow, 322' x 42.3' x 16.9'. Sunk by a Navy mine, June 19, 1942, at Lat. 24-57-00, Long. 81-57-30 (accurate within one mile). Source: 1, 80.

8. *Edward S. Luckenbach* — Freighter, of New York, 7,934 tons, built in 1916 at Quincy, Mass., 436.5' x 57.2' x 37.6'. Sank on July 2, 1942 (possibly from a mine), 30 miles north of Key West, at Lat. 24-57-06, Long. 81-54-00, in 65 feet of water. On board was $1,500,000 million in ore (reportedly 1/6 the world's supply of tungsten), which was later salvaged. Source: 1, 70, 80.

9. *Nicholas Cuneo* — Honduran freighter, 1,051 tons. Sunk by gunfire from *U 571*, July 9, 1942, at Lat. 23-54-00, Long. 82-33-00. Source: 68.

10. *Andrew Jackson* — Steam freighter, of the Waterman S.S. Co., Mobile, 5,990 tons, built in 1920 at Harriman, Pa., 400.7' x 54.2' x 30.4'. Torpedoed by *U 84*, July 13, 1942, at Lat. 23-32-00, Long. 81-02-00. Source: 14, 68.

11. *Gertrude* — Trawler, 16 tons. Sunk by gunfire from *U 166*, July 16, 1942, at Lat. 23-32-00, Long. 82-00-00. Source: 68.

12. *Port Antonio* — Norwegian steam freighter, of Oslo, 1,266 tons, built in 1913. Torpedoed by *U 129*, July 19, 1942, at Lat. 23-39-00, Long. 84-00-00. Source: 68, Norsk Sjofartmuseum.

13. *Santiago de Cuba* — Cuban freighter, of Havana, 1,685 tons, built in 1908 at Bostock, 261.4' x 40'. Torpedoed and sunk by *U 508*, Aug. 12, 1942, at Lat. 24-20-00, Long. 81-50-00, in ten fathoms. Source: 1, 68.

14. *Manzanillo* — Cuban freighter, of Havana, 1,025 tons, built in 1915, 216.5' x 34.1' x 14.8'. Sunk by *U 508* at the same time as the *Santiago De Cuba*. Source: 68, 80.

15. *YC 898* and *899* — Open lighters. Sank off Key West, Sept. 29, 1942. Source: 44.

16. *Coot* — Freighter, 154 tons. Sank Dec. 17, 1942, at approximate Lat. 24-37-00, Long. 82-35-00. Source: 1.

17. *Norman H. Davis* — Dredge (steel), 664 tons, built in 1911 in Maryland, 150' x 40' x 11'. Burned at Key West in 1942. Source: 14.

18. *Majestic* — Motor vessel in 1939 (formerly a bugeye a ketch-rigged sailing vessel), of Reedville, Md., 26 tons, built in 1901 at Fairmont, Md., 67.3' x 19.6' x 5.5'. Stranded at Key West, Jan. 7, 1943. Source: 80.

19. *Gulfstate* — Steam tanker, owned by Gulf Oil, 6,882 tons, built in 1920 at Alameda, Calif., 435' x 56' x 33.8'. Torpedoed by U 155, April 3, 1943, at Lat. 24-26-00, Long. 80-18-00. Loss of 31 of 49 crew on board. Source: 14, 68.

20. *YC 891* — Open lighter. Sank off Key West, April 18, 1943. Source: 44.

21. *R-12* — U.S. Navy submarine, 530 tons, 186'1" x 17'6" x 13'8", built in 1918, Lieutenant Commander E.E. Shelby. Sank June 12, 1943, at Lat. 24-24-30, Long. 81-38-30, in 600 feet of water. Forty-two lives lost including four U.S. Navy officers, two Brazilian Navy officers and 36 U.S. Navy enlisted men. Only the personnel on the bridge survived: two officers, including the commanding officer, and three enlisted men.

The book *United States Submarines Losses World War II* states: "At the time of the accident R-12 was engaged in normal operations off Key West, Florida, being underway to take up position for a torpedo practice approach. She was rigged for diving (except main induction was open and batteries were ventilating into the engine room) and riding the vents. The Commanding Officer was on the bridge in the act of turning the Officer of the Deck watch over to another officer when the collision alarm was sounded from below and the report that the forward battery compartment was flooding was passed to the bridge. Although the Commanding Officer gave immediate orders to blow main ballast and close the hatches, the ship sank in an estimated 15 seconds from the time the alarm was sounded until the bridge was completely under water."

The Court of Inquiry assumed that rapid flooding through a forward torpedo tube was the cause of the sinking. (See Figure 63). Source: 44, 81.

Figure 63: Submarine *R - 12,* lost off Key West in 1943. NATIONAL ARCHIVES.

22. *YCK 8* — Open cargo lighter. Sank off Key West, Dec. 12, 1943. Source: 44.

23. Unknown wreck — Charted in 1943, 6.8 miles, 62 degrees from American Shoal Light, at Lat. 24-34-40, Long. 81-24-32. Destroyed March 24, 1944. Source: 1.

24. Unknown wreck — Listed in 1943, at Lat. 24-35-16.20, Long. 81-48-04.80. Source: 1.

25. Unknown wreck — Located in 1943, at Lat. 24-42-03, Long. 80-52-00. Source: 1.

26. *YP 331* — Patrol vessel, 24 tons. Sank March 23, 1944, at Lat. 24-56-07, Long. 81-53-00. (See Figure 64). Source: 1, 44.

27. *Vitric* — Freighter, 765 tons. Sank March 29, 1944, at approximate Lat. 24-58-00, Long. 80-19-00. Source: 1.

Figure 64: U.S. Navy patrol vessel *YP -331*, lost in 1944. Photo taken at Key West in 1942. NATIONAL ARCHIVES.

28. Unknown wreck — Located March 31, 1944, at Lat. 24-42-00, Long. 80-52-00, in 16 fathoms. Source: 1.

29. *H.H. Conway* — Trawler, 78 tons. Sank April 24, 1944, at approximate Lat. 24-40-00, Long. 81-04-00. Source: 1.

30. *Maria* — Sank April 29, 1944, at approximate Lat. 24-41-00, Long. 81-05-00. Source: 1.

31. *Spindrift* — Freighter, 134 tons. Sank Nov. 16, 1944, at approximate Lat. 24-40-00, Long. 81-48-00. Source: 1.

32. *S -16* — U.S. Navy submarine, 790 tons, 231'6" x 21'6" x 12'6", built in 1919 in Connecticut, decommisioned Oct. 4, 1944, after serving in both the Pacific and Caribbean. After being stripped, she was sunk as a target, April 3, 1945, off Key West, at Lat. 24-25-13, Long. 82-02-24, approximately 14 miles west-southwest of Key West, in 250 feet of water. (See Figure 65). Source: 1, 28, 44, Naval Historical Center.

Upper Florida Keys

1. *Benwood* — Norwegian freighter, of Xiansand, 3,931 tons, built in 1910 in England, 344.9' x 51.3' x 25.3'. The *Benwood* had been rammed in her stern by the vessel *Robert C. Tuttle*. Leaking and with pumps working, she headed for port. On the night of April 9, 1942, five shells hit her and she sank at Lat. 25-03-06, Long. 80-20-00, in present-day John Pennekamp State Park. She is now one of the most

Figure 65: Submarine *S - 16*, sunk off Key West in 1945. U.S. NAVAL HISTORICAL CENTER.

popular dive sites in the park. Source: 1, 56, 80.

2. *Potrero del Llano* — Mexican tanker, of Tampico, 4,000 tons, built 1912 at Newcastle, England, 564' x 47.5' x 26.6', was torpedoed by U 564, May 14, 1942, at Lat. 25-35-00, Long. 80-06-00, eight miles south-southeast of Fowey Rocks, with 35,000 barrels of diesel oil. This attack on the neutral tanker hastened Mexico's declaration of war against Germany. Source: 34, 68, 80.

3. *Nicarao* — Steam freighter, of the New York Central Rail Road, 1,445 tons, built in 1912 at Newburgh, N.Y., 183.7' x 40' x 16'. Torpedoed by U 751, May 16, 1942, at Lat. 25-20-00, Long. 74-19-00 (Bahamas), though the U.S. Archives say she sank off the Florida Keys (quite possibly she did not sink immediately). Source: 14, 68.

4. *Umtata* — British freighter, 8,141 tons. Torpedoed and sunk by U 571, July 7, 1942, at Lat. 25-35-00, Long. 80-02-03. The crew blamed the lights of Miami for making her an easy target. This was the second time the *Umtata* had been torpedoed. In March of 1942, she was hit by U 161 in the harbor at Port Castries, Santa Lucia, but was salvaged and repaired. Source: 1, 34, 68.

5. *J.A. Moffet Jr.* — Tanker, of Wilmington, 9,788 tons, built in 1921 at Kearny, N.J., 499.2' x 68.1' x 30.5'. Took two torpedoes and 20 hits from the 88-mm gun of U 571, July 8, 1942, off Islamorada. Towed to harbor and declared a total loss. Source: 68, 80.

6. *Montgomery* — Barge, of Miami, 294 tons, built in 1920 on Long Island, N.Y., 146.3' x 20.3' x 10.9'. Foundered Jan. 27, 1943, at Lat. 25-27-00, Long. 80-45-00. Source: 14.

7. *Athene* — Trawler, 82 tons. Sank May 31, 1943, at Lat. 25-35-00,

Long. 80-05-00. Source: 1.

8. *Rugged* — Gas vessel, 52 tons, built in 1905. Burned July 15, 1943, 50 miles southeast of Miami. Source: 14.

9. *Francis V. Silvia* — Gas vessel, 93 tons, built in 1904. Foundered 25 miles south of Miami, Nov. 16, 1943, at Lat. 25-22-00, Long. 80-08-00. Source: 1, 14.

10. *Mimiva* — Freighter, 355 tons. Sank Feb. 24, 1944, at approximate Lat. 25-23-00, Long. 80-03-00. Source: 1.

11. *Charles G. Joyce* — Schooner, 122 tons, built in 1882 at Baltimore, 97.9' x 26.9' x 7.6'. Foundered at McArthur Causeway Dock, Miami, May 13, 1944. Source: 14.

Florida's Lower East Coast

1. *Nancy Moran* — Oil vessel (steel), 212 tons, built in 1941. Collided with S.S. PC 451, Dec. 20, 1941, approximately 18 miles east of Port Everglades. Source: 14.

2. *Key West* — Oil vessel, 347 tons, built in 1928. Burned at Cocoa Beach, Jan. 10, 1942. Source: 14.

3. *Pan Massachusetts* — Steam tanker, owned by National Bulk Carriers, Del., 8,201 tons, built in 1918 at Alameda, Calif., 456.1' x 56' x 35.4'. Torpedoed by *U 128,* Feb. 19, 1942, at 7:45 p.m., at Lat. 28-27-00, Long. 80-08-00. Only 18 of a crew of 38 survived. Source: 14, 68.

4. *Elizabeth Massey* — British freighter, 2,598 tons. Sank in 40 fathoms, Feb. 19, 1942, at Lat. 28-09-10, Long. 80-00-40. I've heard she had a cargo of copper, which was partially salvaged recently. Source: 1.

5. *Republic* (formerly *Liberty Minguas*) — Tanker, of Wilmington, 5,287 tons, built in 1920 at Philadelphia, 390.8' x 51.3' x 28.8'. Torpedoed by *U 504,* Feb. 22, 1942, at Lat. 27-00-36, Long. 80-02-42. Eventually beached in 20 feet of water. Five of 34 crewmen lost their lives. The wreck was demolished in June 1944. Source: 14, 29, 68.

6. *W.D. Anderson* (formerly *Tamiahua*) — Tanker, 10,227 tons, built in 1921 at Oakland, Calif., 500' x 71.2' x 31.2'. Torpedoed and sunk by *U 504*, Feb. 22, 1942, at Lat. 27-09-00, Long. 79-57-00, approximately 14 miles east of Stuart, in 40 fathoms. There was only one survivor of the 36 men on board (one source says there were 34 on board). Frank Terry and another sailor had just finished dinner and left most of the crew in the mess room to have coffee on the fantail.

Frank then noticed a torpedo heading straight for the ship and jumped overboard, swimming underwater as long as he could. When he surfaced, burning fuel was all around him so he took a breath and went underwater again, swimming as far as he could. This time he came up in clear water. After many hours, he was rescued by the Coast Guard. Source: 14, 29, 41, 68, 80.

7. *Cities Service Empire* (formerly *Ampetco*) — Steam tanker, of New York, 8,103 tons, built in 1918 at Sparroes Point, Md., 464.7' x 60.2' x 26.3'. Torpedoed and sunk by *U 128*, Feb. 22, 1942, at Lat. 28-25-00, Long. 80-02-00, 25 miles north of Bethel Shoals Gas Buoy. Twelve of 36 lives lost. Demolished in 1944. Source: 1, 14, 68, 80.

8. *Korsholm* — See Shipwreck Narratives.

9. *Laertes* — Dutch freighter, of Amsterdam, 5,825 tons, built in 1919 at Hong Kong, 423.9' x 52.3' x 28.9.' Torpedoed by *U 109,* May 3, 1942, at Lat. 28-21-00, Long.80-23-00. NOAA lists her as sunk at Lat. 28-29-42, Long. 80-22-00, where she was demolished to a depth of 38 feet. Source: 1, 68, 80.

10. *Sama* — Nicaraguan freighter, 567 tons. Torpedoed and sunk by *U 506*, May 3, 1942, at Lat. 26-04-00, Long. 79-45-00. Source: 23.

11. *Ocean Venus* — British freighter, 7,174 tons. Torpedoed and sunk by *U 564*, May 3, 1942, at Lat. 28-23-16, Long. 80-17-40. Later demolished to a depth of 40 feet, Aug. 13, 1944. Source: 1, 68.

12. *Amazone* — Dutch freighter, of Amsterdam, 1,294 tons, built in 1922 at Zalt Bommel, 255.1' x 36.8' x 13.3', cargo of coffee, sisal, orange peel, and oil burners. Torpedoed and sunk by *U 333*, May 6, 1942, at Lat. 27-23-39, Long. 80-03-08, in 13 fathoms. Demolished by the Coast Guard in 1944. Source: 29, 68, 80.

13. *Halsey* — Steam tanker, 7,088 tons, built in 1920 at Alameda, Calif., 435' x 56' x 32', cargo of 80,000 barrels of fuel oil, gasoline, and naptha. Torpedoed and sunk by *U 333*, May 6, 1942, in eight fathoms, at Lat. 27-33-00, Long. 80-08-00. Two of her masts protruded above the water after she sank. Source: 14, 29, 68.

14. *Ohioan* — Steam freighter, of American Hawaiian Steamship Co., 6,078 tons, built in 1920 at Vancouver, Wash., 401.4' x 53.2' x 31.9', cargo of manganese ore, licorice root, and wool. Torpedoed and sunk by *U 564*, May 8, 1942, in 92 fathoms, at Lat. 26-31-00, Long. 79-59-00. Source: 29, 68.

15. *Lubrafol* — Panamanian tanker, 7,138 tons. Torpedoed by U 564, May 9, 1942, at Lat. 26-26-00, Long. 80-00-00. NOAA says she sank at Lat. 29-14-00, Long. 80-10-00. (See Figure 66). Source: 1, 68.

Figure 66: Panamanian tanker *Lubrafol* after being torpedoed off the Florida coast on May 9, 1942. NATIONAL ARCHIVES.

16. *Maurice R. Shaw Jr.* (formerly the four-masted schooner *Charles M. Struven*) — Converted to a barge, 598 tons, built in 1917 at Pocomoke City, Md., 171.1' x 37' x 13.1'. Foundered on Nov. 4, 1942, four miles from Point Jupiter Light. Source: 14, 80.

17. Unknown Wreck — Located April 19, 1943, at Lat. 27-04-10, Long. 80-03-41, in ten fathoms. Source: 1.

18. *Gulfland* — Tanker, 5,277 tons, built in 1918 at Camden, N.J., 391.1' x 51.2' x 30.2'. Traveling north under blackout on Oct. 20, 1943, she collided with her sister-ship, the *Gulf Bell*, at 10:50 p.m. She immediately blew up, and both ships caught fire. The *Gulf Bell*, which was empty, was towed away. The *Gulfland* was left and remained burning for 53 days. She drifted northward and grounded off Hobe Sound, near the wreck of the *Republic*. Holes were punched in her bottom, and she sank in approximately 15 feet of water. Salvage was attempted in 1944 and she was raised, but she broke in two and the bow settled back on the ocean floor. The stern was towed away, and the bow still remains off Hobe Sound in 28 feet of water, at Lat. 26-56-00, Long. 80-01-00 Loran 7980-Z-62026.2 and W-14351.8, and is a popular dive site today. Source: 14, 29.

19. *Franklin Baker 2nd* — Trawler, 100 tons, built in 1925. Sank Nov. 13, 1943, at Lat. 26-09-00, Long. 79-52-00. Source: 23.

20. *Conmar* — Freighter, 231 tons. Sank in September 1944, at approximate Lat. 26-00-00, Long. 80-00-00. Source: 23.

21. *Elvira Gaspar* — Trawler, 185 tons, built in 1929 at Essex, Mass., 87.9' x 21.6' x 10.8'. Sank Nov. 24, 1944, at approximate Lat. 28-27-00, Long. 80-32-00. Source: 1, 14.

22. *Paz* — British ship. Sank off Cape Canaveral during WWII. Two thousand cases of Scotch whiskey washed ashore. Source: 26.

Florida's Upper East Coast

1. *Esparta* — Steam freighter (refigeration ship), of New York (owned by United Fruit Co.), built in 1904 at Belfast, 330.6' x 44.5' x 28.9', cargo of food. Torpedoed by *U 123*, April 9, 1942, at Lat. 30-50-45, Long. 81-09-58. One life lost. Found in 1944, lying on her side in 56 feet of water. Source: 1, 34, 68, 80.

2. *Gulf America* — Tanker, 8,081 tons, built in 1942, Captain Anderson. On her maiden voyage from Port Arthur, Texas, bound for New York with 90,000 barrels of fuel oil. Sunk by *U 123*, April 11, 1942 at 10:20 PM, by both torpedo and gunfire, at Lat. 30-16-40, Long. 81-13-40, 7-1/2 miles southeast of the St. Johns Lightship. Thirty lives lost. The silhouette of *U 123* could be seen in front of the burning wall of flames as hundreds of people along the shore watched in disbelief. She protruded two feet above the water until cleared by the Navy to 50 feet. Source: 1, 14, 34, 68.

3. *Leslie* — Freighter, 2,609 tons, built in 1919 at Duluth, Minn., 251' x 43.7' x 25.8', Captain Ericksson, from Antilla, Cuba, via Havana to New York with 3,300 tons of sugar. Torpedoed and sunk by *U 123*, April 13, 1942, at Lat. 28-35-00, Long. 80-19-00, in 15 fathoms, three miles southeast of Hetzel Shoals Gas Buoy. Four lives lost. Source: 14, 34, 68, 80.

4. Unknown Wreck — Reported in 1942, at Lat. 30-45-00, Long. 80-11-00. Source: 1.

5. *Esso Gettysburg* — Tanker, of Wilmington, 10,173 tons, built in 1942 at Chester, Pa., 503' x 68' x 39.3'. Torpedoed by *U 66*, June 10, 1943, at Lat. 31-02-00, Long. 79-17-00, more than 100 miles offshore just north of Florida. Source: 14, 68, 80.

6. Unknown wreck — Located in 1943 in 11 fathoms, at Lat. 30-06-00, Long. 81-00-00. Source: 1.

7. *Brunswick* — Located in 1944 in 36 feet of water, lying on her side, off Cumberland Island, Ga., just north of Fernandina, at Lat. 30-50-45, Long. 81-09-58.20. Source: 1.

8. Unknown wreck — Reported in 1944, at Lat. 30-33-00, Long. 81-09-15, in 60 feet of water. Source: 1.

Florida's Inland Waters

1. *Standard* — Dredge, of Jacksonville, 175 tons, built in 1926 at Jacksonville, 71' x 29.4' x 6'. Burned at Arlington (Duval County), March 14, 1944. Source: 14.

Unknown Locations

1. *YP 492* — District patrol vessel. Sank after a collision off Florida's east coast, Jan. 8, 1943. Source: 44.

2. *Norwalk* — Steam freighter, owned by East Steamship Lines Inc., 2,157 tons, built in 1920 at Wilmington, 250.8' x 42.6' x 25.6'. Sank north of Cuba after a collision, Jan. 10, 1943. Possible Florida wreck. Source: 1, 14.

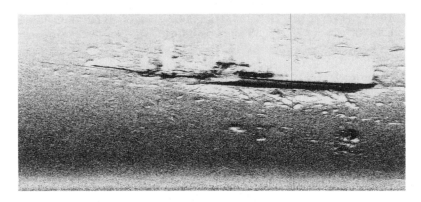

Figure 66A: Side-scan image of WWII sub 0-9 found off New Hampshire in 1997. GARY KOZAK, KLEIN ASSOCIATES.

SHIPWRECK NARRATIVES

The Athenaise

The "Wreck of the *Athenaise*" is reprinted from "El Escribano" Vol. 4, No.1, pp.5–15, with permission from the St. Augustine Historical Society. It is a first-person account by Lieutenant G. J. Honey, originally printed in the *London Mercury*. Honey had arrived at Port Royal, Jamaica, on July 22, 1804, to serve on a ship, but he became ill with fever and was put on the *Athenaise* to be returned to Europe.

⊙　　⊙　　⊙

The ship in which I was to take my passage was named *L'Athenaise* and 182 French prisoners and two women were put on board on September 30th. I went on board on October 1st, and we sailed the next morning. As it may be amusing to see how things are too often conducted, I shall give the general fit-out of the ship. She was of 350 tons, built in Normandy, and copperbottomed; at the capitulation of Cape Francois she had fallen into our hands, and had lain at Port Royal for over fourteen months exposed to the sea, and now became a cartell to Morlaix. As it was necessary to man her from the ships of war, an order was given to send all invalids to her. I believe that it had been intended to have included some able men, but when we got to sea we found that only five, out of thirty-four seamen, were capable of going aloft. Luckily there were some active young French sailors in the ship, who volunteered to do duty, and we gave these men full rations, instead of the two-thirds usually given to prisoners.

A boat had been fitted for us at the dockyard, and as far as paint went was very fine, but on hoisting her in the night before our departure, she actually broke in two, being too rotten to bear her own weight. This was to have been the only boat for a ship containing 212 lives, namely 184 French and 38 English, including invalid officers and the wife of an old quartermaster. As we were to sail at daybreak, an officer went to the dockyard to ask for another boat, but the only thing they would give us was a canoe about 14 feet long, which had been taken from a negro caught stealing something from the dockyard. This would contain two people with difficulty, but it was better than nothing, for it afterwards answered very well to bathe the fever patients....The fever had increased greatly since we left Jamaica, and we had now buried one Englishman and one Frenchman. The treatment given was cold bathing in the canoe, with doses of calomel and salts, or cupping as appeared best in our judgment. In a few days another Englishman and another Frenchman died, and the prisoners observed that at this rate they would soon have the ship to themselves.

The wind continued to blow a fresh breeze from the East, and as there was no one in the ship at all acquainted with the currents, we continued to beat about, first on the Cuba side, where we nearly lost the ship on the Coloradoes without making any ground, and then on the Florida side, where we made no more progress. Finally, a westerly breeze sprang up and carried us as far as the Matanzas, to the East of Havana. When off the latter port, another Frenchman died, but there was then every hope that the disease would soon leave us.

On October 30th we made the Salt Keys, and as we were fairly in the Gulf Stream, we hoped to be soon clear of that navigation. On the following evening we took the bearings of the Little Isaacs at sunset, E.N.E., the ship was wore and put under snug sail. On referring to the chart, we decided to stand on until a quarter before four the next morning, and as the master had the middle watch (i.e., from 12 to 4 A.M.), he agreed to wear her at that hour. The wind increased to a fresh gale in which the foresail was split, and as we had not sufficient men to go aloft and bend another, it was cut from the yard. As the main topsail was now the only one set, the ship naturally made a considerable drift, for being light, the wind forced her to leeward in spite of the current.

The Master who had been sent in command of this ship had been a mate in a merchantman belonging to the agent victualler at Kingston, and, being found unfit for his station, was given charge of this unfortunate vessel in order to get rid of him. We found it necessary to keep him from liquor by every means in our power, but he escaped all our vigilance, and after cutting away the foresail took the desperate resolution of getting drunk.

Consequently the ship was not wore, and, standing on, soon gained the eddy current, which runs to the southward along the coast of Florida. If common attention is paid, the change of colour in the water along this coast gives the seamen full time to avoid danger; however, in our case, the first thing seen was breakers about a mile away on the lee beam. The seaman who made the discovery instantly told the Master, whom he found quite drunk and half asleep on the poop, and after an altercation was knocked down. A sufficient noise was soon made on deck to alarm everyone, but the loss of the ship was inevitable. Directly I went on deck the anchor was cut away; but before she brought up, the ship struck on a coral reef with a tremendous crash. The scene that followed is indescribable; there were upwards of two hundred men crouching on the deck, naked, and mostly praying and confessing their sins, whilst the sea broke over her mast heads, and to heighten the confusion, the mizzen mast fell across the deck, breaking one man's ankle and maiming several others.

The sea soon threw the ship over the reef into deep water, and fortunately she remained afloat until she reached the beach. She was gradually sinking, and on striking the beach a few seas soon filled her. It was then about half-past four, and still so dark that we could see nothing but breakers all around us, there was no sign of land, and little prospect that the ship would hold together much longer. We were kept in this state of suspense for nearly an hour, but when day dawned at last we saw a low, sandy beach, about six ship's lengths off, or perhaps a little more, and a most barren-looking country.

Our attention was now turned to saving what provisions we could, but as the ship had sunk low in the sand and was full of water, it was impossible to get any from below. The only food on deck was half a cask of pork which had been put in the harness tub the evening before, and the four turtles which we were carrying home as presents.

The next question was how to reach the shore. To swim through so high a surf with any chance of reaching the land seemed a forlorn hope, but after many proposals, some volunteered to take the end of a line ashore by which we could send a hawser. As soon as the line was found, five men undertook the hazardous enterprise, and to our great joy succeeded, though with the loss of two Frenchmen. A hawser was sent after making one end fast to the bowsprit end and the other was held by the men on the beach. The fore and main masts, being in a tottering state, were now cut away to prevent the ship falling over more on her larboard side. We hoped to use these as a raft, but the current soon carried them away with three or four of our fellow sufferers who were never heard of again. When everything was adjusted, we began to descend by the hawser and haul ourselves through the surf, whilst those who landed first helped the others. By the evening we had all landed with the exception of a few persons who, disregarding every sense of decorum, had got drunk; the master was among the number, and he could not be persuaded to leave the wreck that night, though it was unlikely that she could remain together long. As we could not get the women on shore by the same method as the men, another line was taken to the beach, the three women tied together, launched off the lee bow, and drawn safely through the surf to the beach.

As the wind had lulled considerably and the sea gone down during the night, the ship was left within twice her length of the shore, and at first there seemed a chance of obtaining some provisions. We found however, that she was too full of water, and the sand had got in and formed a bed over the casks, with five feet of water over that. After many efforts the attempt was given over and the little saved, which did not amount to one pound each, was equally distributed. The Master now landed with the rest of his drunken companions, and was met by the remainder of the crew as the wretch who had brought on their misfortunes. The Frenchmen nearly all wanted to hang him, the tree was pointed out and everything was ready when the English obtained pardon for him. Had he met his fate here it would have been no more than he deserved, but he was always treated with great abuse, to which he was prudent enough not to reply.

We had formed ourselves into Messes to receive equal portions of the turtles, which were made into broth, but although four small turtles did not make very good soup for two hundred men, it was all we could afford ourselves. Fortunately there was a good supply of water and plenty of firewood, and for the first two nights we kept up good fires in the woods about half a mile from the wreck.

As soon as the ship was lost I had been careful to keep the part of the chart on which I knew the wreck had occurred. On taking an observation, we found that our Latitude was 26°10' N. (near Cape Florida), whereas we had supposed ourselves at least eighty miles more to the Northward and consequently nearer to an inhabited country. A consultation was now called by the French Sergeant-Major, who had been nominated to regulate the marches, etc. The only thing to do appeared to be to make our way towards St. Augustine, which was at least 270 miles from us, but several decided to remain by the wreck rather than perish by the way.

We agreed to commence the march on the following afternoon, and we all hoped that we might be assisted by the Indians of the country. We did not know then that we had been driven on an Islet, of which the sea shore of East Florida is composed, formed by the Gulf of Florida on the East, the Indian River on the West, and intersected by inlets from the sea, viz., Hillsborough, Indian River, Musquito or New Smyrna, Matanzas, and lastly by that which forms the entrance into St. Augustine harbour.

When everything was arranged as to the time our march should commence, the English were taken into custody in case we should go by ourselves. We commenced our march soon after noon on November 4th, leaving by the wreck two old English quartermasters, the wife of one, the Frenchman with the broken ankle, and two others with yellow fever. Mr. Brierly, a midshipman, and like myself, an invalid passenger, told me afterwards in England that one of these men had been taken off. Before we left, this man had said, "I have been wrecked twice before on this coast and Johnston took me off; he may come again." This Johnston has been a wrecker all his life and has made a good living by it. These wreckers make what they can out of stranded vessels, and have their own laws regulating how they shall work if two or more come upon the same prey.

After two hours' march from the wreck we passed over what had evidently once been an inlet of the sea but was now dry, and here the Indian River came very near the beach, whence we were glad to replenish our water bottles. Shortly afterwards a Frenchman killed a small rattlesnake, about the size of a man's arm and between five and six feet long, by running a nail which he had at the end of his stick into its head. At sunset, we all halted and made several fires. The snake was skinned and made into soup, of which I made a very tolerable meal, though there was not enough to make a hearty one. We considered that we had marched about twelve miles, and I was so fatigued that, having collected some palm leaves for a bed near a fire, I was soon sound asleep in spite of the noise of the bullfrogs. As the day broke the Sergeant-Major, whom we had always called La Major, gave orders to prepare for the march, and in a few minutes we set off. My stock of clothes consisted of one hat, two shirts, and a pair of trousers, but I had no shoes or stockings, as some villain had stolen them when I first landed.

November the 5th was, until the breeze set in, intolerably hot, and our feet and legs suffered considerably on the white sandy beach. At noon we halted, and on taking the sun's altitude we found that we had only advanced about twenty miles due North, instead of the twenty-six we had counted on. From the nature of the country, we were obliged to keep to the beach and go around the different bays, often two or three miles out of our direct line.

Nothing special happened during this day, and at sunset we again went into the woods and made fires near fresh water. Some oatmeal was made into Burgoo, and two parrots, which had been carried by one of the Frenchwomen, were killed to improve the mess. The night was excessively cold, and as rain fell during the greater part of it, and we had no shelter, we did not get much rest. When the Sergeant gave his orders at daybreak, he was not attended to for some time, but he encouraged them and at length succeeded in getting all to move off together.

We commenced this day (November 6th) in a pretty hungry state, as the little saved from the wreck was totally exhausted. The effect of the bad night was obvious, there was nothing but dejection, and the only voice heard was that of the Sergeant's exhorting them to hold up and not give way. After two hours' walk we rested for a few minutes, and again about noon, but too late for an observation, which was disappointing. On proceeding, five of the unfortunate invalids and three Frenchmen, who could walk no longer, gave in with a determination to remain by each other. Their feet were in a dreadfully ulcerated state, but my spirits were too far gone to dwell on their miseries and I went on, leaving them to their fate. As we were now fifty miles from the wreck, their case was desperate, for they had neither provisions nor means to kindle a fire, nor even enough strength to get water from the lagoon two miles across the island.

During the afternoon our loss was increased by two more falling down totally exhausted, and they were left to their fate without anyone appearing the least concerned.

About three in the afternoon, a schooner was seen working through the Gulf with the wind in the N.N.E,., and as she stood towards us a long time, coming nearer the shore than vessels would usually do, we all hoped that we had been seen, and that (in spite of her American flag) our distress would be relieved. Great was the disappointment when she tacked and stood from us, and I am certain that we must have been seen, as a body of a hundred and sixty men on a white sandy beach would be bound to attract the attention of a vessel as near as she was. We displayed the Union Jack on first seeing her to show that we were not Indians, and a flag was flying at her main peak, which must have been for us as she was near neither fort, ship, nor even inhabited land.

The party now became very much dejected, and there were stragglers many miles behind, picking up what they could from the sea shore or woods. On this coast there is a small land crab, about three inches in length, which leaves its hole to crawl into the sea about sunset. When one of these little creatures left its hole, there was a scramble between those who happened to be near, but I was too far gone for that, and contented myself by watching for them where there was no likelihood of contest, and even so was seldom able to catch one. This was the cause of many being left behind, and this evening Mr. Brierly and myself were perfectly knocked up from our efforts to procure them.

We sat down on the stump of a tree to rest for a few minutes, and after a short lamentation we fell asleep and did not wake until the tide had come in and broke a gentle sea over us. There was no sign of the party, but after two hours' walking we joined their fires at midnight. However, our rest was short as the party was assembled at daybreak, and we went on ten fewer than on the preceding day.

November 7th. After two hours' walk we all rested and searched the woods for water, and here we found some berries not unlike the hips on the hedges of this country, but they were far from plentiful. There was also a dwarf plant with a fruit like a small potato apple which, though not at all agreeable, helped to fill the stomach. During the forenoon's march, I picked up the head of a dolphin which must have been sun-dried for some weeks; there was little on it, but it was too valuable to be thrown away, and I added it to the scanty stock in my knapsack.

Near noon, we halted at a very fine spring of fresh water which was very refreshing, but many drank to such an excess as to produce convulsions. During this forenoon five men had been lost, being left singly as they fell. The sun had not proved so troublesome as on the day before and there was a cool breeze, but want of provisions had become general, and failure of strength became more frequent from that cause.

We had most of us washed by this refreshing spring, and after replenishing our bottles walked on, but two of our companions were left in the agonies of death, and others moved on in almost as wretched condition. During the next hour, two more fell and the party straggled very much. I had become one of the last, and my feet were swelled to double their usual size and much ulcerated.

About 3 o'clock, I sat down to rest without a hope of being saved, and reflected that it was the day of my birth [his twentieth birthday] and probably the last I should ever spend on earth. The party was at least three miles from me and out of sight, and as it was impossible for me to go on for some time, I lay down hoping to get some rest and be enabled to go on again in the evening. I had fallen into a sound sleep when the French Sergeant awoke me with the joyful tidings of a town having been seen across the first inlet which they had now reached, and that a boat had come to their assistance. This worthy man (which I hope it will not be treason to say he was, although a Frenchman) came back the instant he missed me and assisted me to join the party. It was a most noble action of a man who knew it was not in my power to repay him.

The boat proved to belong to an American sloop which had been wrecked within half an hour of ourselves, and her cargo of flour, apples, potatoes and onions had been partly saved and was in a tent near her. As soon as we reached this joyful spot a distribution was made, and all were eagerly employed preparing messes of such things as first came to hand, and we had a feast which I shall ever remember. In spite of previous examples, many ate and drank to such excess that convulsions and delirium were brought on. Although the water here was very bad (coming from a swamp) and there was a great scarcity of firewood, we were in a paradise compared with the sufferings of the last five days.

The American sloop was going from New York to St. Augustine, and in an unaccountable way was driven at least 170 miles to leeward of her port. She had been off St. Augustine bar the day before, and the only way to account for the loss of either her or the *Athenaise* is that the current must have changed its usual course. This coast is very little known and most erroneously laid down on the English charts.

We remained by the American wreck until the morning of the 9th, when it was agreed to push on for St. Augustine, as the journey had to be undertaken and delay could do no good. Flour, onions, and a small quantity of salt pork was served out by the American, who wisely gave it with good grace, for if he had not done so, we should certainly have helped ourselves. However, he shamefully misled us by stating that St. Augustine was only 39 leagues off, and we attributed our supposed distance to the damaged state of our quadrant, and for some reason, no observation was taken during the day we were by the wreck. The cause of this I do not know, for after washing and drying my only shirt (having thrown away my spare one on the third day's march) I collected a few pimento leaves and slept the whole day through, in spite of the mosquitos and sandflies, which were almost insufferable.

The morning after our arrival by the wreck, a boat was sent to the inlet to see if any of the stragglers had reached it, and soon returned with three of the most wretched objects to be conceived. They had been there some hours, and were in such a helpless state that they had to be lifted in and out of the boat, and it was quite obvious that they would soon fall if they continued the march.

With the idea that St. Augustine was at so short a distance, we calculated on reaching it in four or five days, and knowing that we had provisions for that time we agreed that we should proceed in a collected body and aid each other. Unfortunately, having been misled, we did not practice sufficient economy in the use of our provisions. On the night of the 9th, we made our fires amongst pimento trees on the highest ground we had yet passed over.

On the morning of the 10th, we entered on the march with some hopes, thinking that we had covered one-fourth of the distance. Shortly after noon we saw an opening in the pimento forest, and entering it we found a person just beginning a settlement, in which he proposed trying the coffee plant. He had six negro men and women with him, and had just commenced the undertaking. His name was Atkinson, and as we afterwards learned at St. Augustine, he was a most cruel brute. He had lived at Savannah, Georgia, where he made a purchase of eight negroes, gave his creditors the slip with what he could collect, went to East Florida, and put himself under the protection of the Spanish laws. A grant of some hundred acres was soon made him, and he began clearing away the wood. One of his negro boys ran away and after a long search was found and brought back. A fire was made in the form of a ring, the culprit being placed in the middle, and the other slaves being employed adding fresh fuel to the flames, until the wretched master (fearing he would lose his slave) made room for him to crawl out. Death followed in two days, but the only punishment given to the brute for this deed was to inflict a small fine.

As Indian River inlet was at hand, Atkinson offered to take us across in his boat, and we thankfully accepted. We were all anxious to know the distance to St. Augustine, and he soon undeceived us by saying it was at least 150 miles off. The curses of the party now poured down upon the American, and many thought of returning to the wreck, but as we had proceeded at least 40 miles, and as Atkinson assured us that we should find beds of oysters further on, we all were determined to go on. By four o'clock that afternoon we were all across the inlet with the exception of three or four who had been left behind under circumstances little less desperate than those before our relief. The number of sharks and alligators that followed the boat across was rather alarming, but fortunately no accident occurred, no doubt to the disappointment of those monsters, as they were so little afraid that they kept opening their tremendous jaws within two or three feet of us.

When we were all across, we marched on until sunset and made our fires in the woods near fresh water. The country about Indian River inlet is the highest part of the coast, and covered with cabbage palm and stately pitch pine, the former providing a very pleasant eatable not unlike the stalk of a cabbage, and as it alleviated thirst it was found a great luxury.

So wretched were we all now getting that delirium was very common, and produced by the most trifling circumstances. I had always carried a pebble in my mouth, and the relief from thirst which this gives is almost incredible; that was a great object as we frequently had much difficulty in procuring water. We used to dig pits on the beach, but I believe that the water so obtained did more harm than good, as it was always brackish. We were in such a state at this time that none of us kept an exact record of our sufferings, and I was content to make a note of the principal occurrences later on when still fresh in my memory.

The marches were regulated by the Sergeant-Major as before, but our stores were again reduced and we had no resource but the snakes, such things as were driven on the beach, and the berries in the woods. Many experiments were tried by boiling roots, but without success, as they proved too bitter. On the second day after crossing the inlet we found a dead alligator on the beach, and although the back was perfectly sun-dried, the belly was in a sadly putrid state. This was a prize indeed, it afforded a sumptuous repast to all, and allowed many to fill their knapsacks with its flesh, which was either broiled or made into soup, and though coarse was far from disagreeable. We lost five men during this day owing to their excess in eating.

On the following day we reached the banks of the New Smyrna inlet, and having kindled large fires were soon observed by a settler named Ladd, who came to our assistance with a boat. He carefully avoided taking us near his farm, but he gave us some Indian meal, and told us that we were in the neighborhood of oyster beds. The distance to St. Augustine was yet 70 miles, but we concluded that there was no fear of suffering much more from hunger. Our numbers were now reduced to 140, and evidently many of these could not hold out much longer, although our prospects were so much brightened.

Having found the oyster beds, fires were made, by which we stayed all night, and our only complaint was that the water was very brackish. In the morning we again proceeded, and as I now had eight ulcers on my feet, I provided myself with a crutch and a stick, but in spite of their aid, I was left miles behind the main body. I came up with them in time to share the last of an alligator which they had killed on a sandbank five or six hundred yards from the water. Some twenty of the party had attacked it with sticks and stones, which they threw into its mouth when it opened it to charge them, and being quite unwieldy in such a situation, after a long contest it had become their prey. It was at least eighteen feet in length, and was relished much better than the sun-dried one we had before. Our numbers had again decreased, and I found that the Master of the *Athenaise* (James Cox) had been taken by Ladd to his farm — he had always said that he would not go back to England.

We had proceeded about eighteen miles from Smyrna inlet when we rested for the night, and went on again at daybreak. After going five or six miles there was not a breath of wind, and as my feet became so painful from the sun I decided to stay by myself during the day. I lay down in the woods and went to sleep, waking up about eight o'clock in the evening much refreshed, and went on in the hopes of overtaking the party. By resting at intervals I made good progress and realised how much better it was walking by night than by day. At about four o'clock, I crawled in amongst the prickly pear plants and slept soundly until seven o'clock, when I resumed my toils. I had not proceeded far when I fancied that I saw a house among the trees, and keeping my eyes fixed on it, I soon saw smoke issuing from it. So delighted was I that I neglected the cut path (which appeared circuitous) and went straight through the bushes to it, having many falls on the way.

About eight o'clock I entered the cottage and was very kindly received by the old Irish woman who kept it; her husband had gone to ferry the party across the inlet and did not return for some time. I proposed that he should take me to St. Augustine by water, a distance of about 23 miles, but as he did not appear to come into my plan I offered to give him one dollar for my passage and showed him my stock of money, which consisted of a guinea, a two dollar piece, and a half-dollar. This had the desired effect, and it was settled that we should go by the night flood tide. The old woman now began to improve, and instead of kind words, gave me something to eat. Seville orange-leaf tea and Johny cake were provided, and after a good breakfast I bathed my feet in warm water and went to sleep in a blanket, under the first covering for fourteen days and nights. About one o'clock I was called to a dinner of salt pork, hominy, and rice, and felt more refreshed that I could have imagined possible. The old Irishman took his aquadente pretty freely after dinner, and then attacked the English for not emancipating the Catholics, finally becoming so bitter that I was glad to get out of his way and saw no more of him until nine o'clock at night when we embarked in a small canoe for St. Augustine.

I never exactly made out the history of these people, but I believe the man deserted from the British Army during the war with America. He obtained a livelihood by burning oyster shells to lime, and by selling the juice of Seville oranges for between five and six pounds per ton.

At the time of my departure I asked the old woman what I owed her; "As you have not much money," said she, "we'll only have the half-dollar, but you must leave your spoon." This I did with great reluctance as it had been given to me by one of the Frenchmen the day after the wreck and had been made by him out of the lead which covered the capstan head of the unfortunate ship.

It blew pretty fresh against us all the way, but the tide ran strong and carried us to our destination about one in the morning. Great secrecy was observed in landing to avoid the patrol, but I was soon safely lodged in a boarding house kept by one Long. He was very kind and seemed as happy to do everything he could, as if I had been an old and intimate friend. A bed was soon got ready, and I slept in perfect ease, it being the fifteenth night since my clothes were off. Next morning breakfast assured me of good fare, for tea, coffee, venison steaks, fish, rice, hominy, and Johnny cake, composed this sumptuous meal. When it was all over I went to Long, candidly told him my situation, and asked his advice as to obtaining money. He said that the person able to assist us was the Governor, an Irishman born, but brought up in the King of Spain's Hibernian Regiment.

Having purchased a pair of shoes and stockings, I proceeded to the Governor's house and showed him my commission to command the *Snapper* schooner. He read it and then said, "This, Sir, is a sad thing bringing so many men to this place, what am I to do with them? We have hardly provisions for the garrison." I replied, "I hope, Sir, you will be able to assist us, as we have lost everything." He was not long in giving me fully to understand that I had nothing to expect; "For," said he, "the troops are unpaid for want of money, and I have advanced everything I had for that purpose." On returning to my lodgings Long told me that the Governor had the reputation of detesting the English, and had more than once behaved ill to persons of this nation wrecked on Florida.

I now went to a doctor to get something for my feet, which were in a dreadful state, and it was only by cutting away almost all the upper leather of the shoes that I could bear them on. As I was little inclined to walk for some days, I amused myself by taking down some account of our march, and by mending my clothes.

When the main party was seen opposite the town, canoes went and brought them over, and on counting numbers we found that there were 131 all told, 81 less than embarked at Jamaica. We now all went in a body to the Governor, who showed his partiality for the French by listening attentively to all they had to say and promising them food and quarters. He was as good as his word, for he gave them a Spanish barrack room and plenty of fuel, whereas the English seamen had a miserable dungeon without even straw to lie on, until an American merchant sent

Figure 67: British Admiralty anchor believed to come from the *Athenaise*. AUTHOR.

them an old carpet and some wood. All the sick, to the number of about 50, were received into the hospital. It was proposed to Governor White that a small schooner should be sent down the coast to try and save some of those left behind, or alternatively that some provisions should be sent along the beach on horses, but he would do neither. If these steps had been taken 20 lives would probably have been saved, but as we remained at St. Augustine until December 2nd and during sixteen days no more arrived, the absentees must have mostly perished.

After much trouble I obtained 40 dollars for a bill on the Consul at Charleston, and was thus enabled to pay for my board at a dollar a day, the passage to Charleston, and a few necessaries for the voyage. Our passages were taken in a small American schooner laden with oranges in bulk, and skins of bear and deer. Lieutenant Moore, since lost in the *Blenheim*, Mr. Brierly, midshipman, with myself and five seamen, were the English survivors embarked in her, and on December 5th we anchored at Charleston.

❂   ❂   ❂

It's possible that this is the wreck that lies just off the beach, just south of the Barefoot Mailman Hotel at Hillsboro Beach, Fla. It was salvaged in the 1960s, and was referred to locally as the "Barefoot Mailman Wreck." Figure 67 shows an anchor believed to have come from the *Athenaise*.

Figure 67A: Author's salvage boat *Chelsea*. AUTHOR.

The Alna

The following story is taken from the book *The Tragedy Of The Seas; Or, Sorrow On The Ocean, Lake, And River, from Shipwreck, Plague, Fire And Famine*, by Charles Ellms, published in Philadelpha by W.A. Leary and in Boston by W.J. Reynolds & Co., 1848.

○　　○　　○

On the 19th of August, 1838, the brig *Alna*, of Portland, Maine, Captain Thomas, sailed from St. Jago de Cuba, bound to Boston. Owing to light and baffling winds, it was some time before the vessel got round the island, when she took her departure from Matanzas, and left the coast with a light breeze. But on the 5th of September, it came on to blow very hard; the sail on her was reduced, but the wind still increased, so that on the 7th it blew a violent gale from the northeast. The brig was about fifteen miles off the Florida coast, and drifting rapidly on a lee shore. A heavy press of canvas was now carried, to endeavor, if possible, to claw off. But the head of the bowsprit was carried away; and the sea making a clear breach over her, sweeping the decks fore and aft, the brig was again hove to, but drifted rapidly to leeward. As it was found impossible to keep the vessel off the land, the captain determined to run her on shore in the daytime, so as to have a better chance of saving the lives of those on board. Accordingly, the mainsail was lowered, and the helm put hard up. The vessel soon struck the bottom, about twenty miles north of Cape Florida, and was shortly after lifted so high on the beach by the heavy breakers that the crew could easily jump from her to the shore. As the tide ebbed, great exertions were made to land the stores and clothing; and a sufficient quantity of provisions and water were secured on the beach to last a month. Here the unfortunate captain and his crew remained until Sunday, the 9th of September. "On that fatal day, about noon," says Mr. Wyer, "the first Indians which appeared nigh our tent were four in number. They were armed with rifles. The mate was packing his clothes in his chest, which he had been drying that day; and the first notice we had of the Indians was the smart crack of a rifle; and at the same instant the mate exclaimed, 'O dear!' having received the ball in his hand, passing into the abdomen, as we supposed. The same Indian, being behind a tree, reloaded, and marked me for his next object, (myself, Cammett, and Captain Thomas, crouching down) which gave me the ball through the hand, passing up laterally through the thigh, coming out just below the hip joint, making a journey through the flesh of eight or nine inches. We took to the beach (it being warm, we were barefooted) and they pursued us. Captain Thomas, having taken a long walk with Cammett, was tired, and gave out. We halted, being thirty yards ahead of him, to see what his fate might be. I saw him shot, the ball whizzing by me; and he fell on his face, and seemed to die instantly. After this, we expected no quarter, if taken. I felt approaching weakness from loss of blood, and feared I must soon give up. We very soon entered the bushes, Cammett going ahead. I soon lost him, and made my way along till night, among the palmettos, which cut my feet cruelly; added to this, were mosquitos, which were a formidable foe. At dark, on Sunday night I came out on the beach, and traveled till nearly daylight. Finding my wounds bleeding profusely, I tore off the bottom of my flannel shirt, and bound them up, which continued to bleed all the next day. I lay down, and sometimes fell down, often thinking I should not be able to rise again. My fears were increased from the trail of blood which I left behind, knowing this to be a good mark for them. Monday I continued to travel the beach — went to the river, running parallel with the sea, for water — ate nothing that day — came to New River, waded in to my neck, and swam off, finding the current setting from both shores to the center, making it very doubtful to me, from the long time I was there, whether I could ever reach the opposite shore. Here I was about to despair. I finally got foothold and gained the shore, but found myself very much exhausted. I should think the river was a quarter of a mile wide. It was about night. I kept on — occasionally would lie down during the night, gathering the seaweed to cover me, while asleep — when I awoke, would go on again till weary, and then take a nap.

"Tuesday morning, fair weather — saw a house ahead, which proved to be the Patterson House, as I was told by the wreckers. It is a one-story frame house, and has a long time been vacated. I hoped here to find something to satisfy my hunger, but I was disappointed. Here was another river to swim. For the first time, I saw two large alligators; and the river was full of sharks of the largest kind. I was divested of fear, and in I plunged, and landed safe on the other side, feeling no enemy to be worse than the Indians. I traveled on, my feet being very sore — oftentimes would climb a tree to see if any danger was at hand, and hoping to see marks of civilization, to encourage me in my lonely journey — ate nothing this day — swam and forded several small streams and creeks, which was very painful in my wounded situation.

"Wednesday morning came with fair weather — continued my journey as the day previous — clambered a tree, and found a huge snake had ascended before me: he lay out on one of the limbs, coiled up, as if asleep. I was well armed with a club, but took good care not to arouse him. His size round was as large as my ankle. I had been without food three days and nights, and was very hungry. I hoped to find something to eat among the wrecked matter that had washed up to the shore, but found nothing but dead fish; and it was a hard scramble to know whether I or the pelicans and other birds should be served first, as they exist in acres, and are so numerous that fish are all taken up before they get old. A dead fish was a great luxury; and when I had satiated my appetite, I would put them on my hat to dry, while journeying on.

"An hour or two before sunset, I saw two sail, that did not appear to notice me; soon after, I saw two more, who were in pursuit of a Dutch brig. I now hoisted my shirt on a pole, and waved it with all my strength. They discovered me; and happy was I to be rescued from the many perils that I had encountered. Indians, sharks, the moccasin snake, arabs, and various other reptiles, were foes in my way; but, thank God, I have been spared to return to my friends, and tell my perilous tale."

Mr. Cammett, who escaped at the same time with Wyer, when the captain was massacred, says, "My story, in regard to the shipwreck of the *Alna*, and being surprised by the Indians on the coast of Florida, cannot be otherwise than the same as Wyer's, until we entered the bushes, where we unfortunately got separated. I remained quiet, in concealment, until the dusk of the evening; then I thought it prudent to start. I walked across the beach to the bushes, to see if their trail continued — took care to use the same tracks back, so as to deceive them — got along the beach five or six miles, and encountered a party of Indians. They saw me, and raised a horrid yell, and pursued me. I ran into a swamp, where the mud and water were about waist high. Two Indians remained where I entered, while the rest seemed to be surrounding me. They avoided the water on account of the snakes, the wreckers told me.

"I was about an hour there — concluded it would not do to stop till morning, for they would get me — got out, and took to the shore — was careful to go so close to the shore that every ripple of the water should wash out my tracks — came across a well of water that was covered, and a village of low huts, said to have been some old barracks. I took them to be Indian huts; as I saw no tracks beyond them, I was puzzled to know how to pass them. The palmettos were like sharks' teeth, and made a noise in getting through. I was then on the border of the river — finally thought I would wade up to my neck, that no trace of me could be seen — got by in safety, lost their tracks and began to feel as if I was delivered.

"Monday, still on the river, with trees and bushes growing to the edge. I was obliged to travel, and occasionally swim round — came to a place which I took to be two rivers that intersected this. I swam over, and found it to be an island covered with water, and the roots of the trees starting out two or three feet above ground, making a sort of bridge to walk on — tasted the water, and found it fresh — stopped and rested — a severe current on both sides. Seeing a number of sharks, I made a raft of drift-wood; but it was water-logged, and would not support me — abandoned it — took a lot of driftwood, but could hardly keep it under me, the force of the current being so severe — reached the shore in safety; there I found the seashore, and kept on till 12 o'clock on Monday night. My feet were deeply cut with shells and palmettos, and ankles so swollen, I could not bend them — my toes raw up between, and cruelly sore.

"Tuesday and Wednesday, swam several streams. I suffered with the intense heat — had no hat, and was obliged to wet my head to keep it cool — found a tar bucket to carry water in — slept on board a wreck, with nothing but a quarter-deck left — my neck so swollen with mosquito bites that I could scarcely move my head — ate six dead fish on Tuesday, and eight on Wednesday. Wednesday afternoon, crawled into a large log. The hole being too short to admit my whole length, I took a barrel up from the shore to make out the length. Had a good nap — waking, I felt something under my chin — gave it a brush off — was stung that instant by a centipede — got up, looked out, and saw four sloops making up the shore — wind light — I anxiously kept along with them, but they did not see me — no sleep that night.

"At daylight, saw them standing in for the shore. I seized my tar bucket to a long pole, with my knife lanyard, and hoisted it as a signal of distress; they saw it, and to my unutterable joy I was taken on board the wrecking sloop *Mount Vernon,* where I found my lost friend, Wyer, who, to my astonishment, called my name from over the side of the vessel. Thus ended my cruel adventure; and not till then was I fully sensible of my soreness. Under the blessing of God, I have been saved to return to my friends in perfect health."

Those who were murdered by the Indians were Captain Charles Thomas, Andrew J. Plummer, mate, and John Sheafe, seaman, all of Portland, and William Reed, of Salem, cook. The only survivors were Wyer and Cammett, who published the following grateful tribute:

"It is our humane and highly pleasing duty to say of Captain George Alden and his crew, of the wrecking sloop *Mount Vernon*, that our treatment was in the highest degree kind, hospitable, over-generous — dressing our wounds, nursing us with parental kindness, giving us clothing, regretting, when we left, that they had no money to give us, and all of us feeling as if attached with the strongest ties of friendship. On board the *Index* they were equally hospitable; and on board the revenue cutter *Madison*, Captain Howard (our old friend and acquaintance) gave us a feeling reception, and the most cordial welcome.

"To correct wrong impressions and wicked prejudices that exist against the wreckers on the coast of Florida, we feel bound by every thing sacred to state that instead of being 'plunderers and pirates,' as they are often represented, it is the height of their ambition to save lives and property."

The Enterprise

The following story is taken from the *New York Times*, July 14, 1859, copyright 1859, by The New York Times Company. Reprinted with permission. It tells the tale of murder, robbery, and shipwreck.

○   ○   ○

From the Key of the Gulf, July 2

On the 26th of June, the U.S. revenue cutter *John Appleton*, Lieut. Comdr. William B. Randolph, returned to this port from a cruise along the reef, bringing four of the crew of the schooner *Enterprise*, fallen in with at Cape Florida, and who were suspicioned with having murdered their captain.

The four men being arrested and brought before U.S. Commissioner J. B. Browne, for examination, it was ascertained that the schooner *Enterprise*, Capt. B. A. Morantes, sailed from Havana about the 4th or 5th of June, bound to Carthagena, New Granada, for cattle. On the third or fourth day after leaving Havana, a dispute arose between some of the crew and Capt. Morantes with regard to the provisions. On that occasion one of the crew was heard to say, "Never mind, it will all be right soon." A day or two after this, the vessel was run ashore near Hillsborough, as it is believed intentionally, and the master most horribly murdered. It was stated that the vessel first struck the reef about 2 o'clock in the morning, (about the 8th of June), and by daylight had drifted broadside onto the beach, so near that it was not difficult to get ashore without a boat. About 7 o'clock two of the men — the cook and a Spaniard named Jose Maria — asked permission of Capt. Morantes to go along the beach to see if a settlement could be found, to which he consented, and they left. Soon after, three others of the crew — called Charlie, Frank and Joe — went to the captain and asked permission to take the foresail out of the schooner and go on shore and put up a tent, to which he also assented. After the tent had been erected, the same three men returned to the schooner and asked permission to carry the provisions ashore. Capt. Morantes objected, saying that a vessel might come along at any moment and they could all go on board. This they seemed not to like, and after going forward, cursing among themselves, again returned to the Captain, when Charlie struck him with his fist. The Captain clinched him, and while in that position, Frank stepped up behind the Captain and stabbed him in the temple. He and Charlie then threw him overboard. The Captain, being only wounded, endeavored, by keeping close under the vessel, to get out of sight of his pursuers, but whenever his head would appear, they would throw iron pots or anything they could find at him. He then went out into deep water, but did not remain there long, before he approached the beach, with his hands crossed on his breast, begging them to spare him. Frank

282

went out in the water to meet him, giving him to understand at the same time that he would not further molest him, but as soon as he got to him he again stabbed him in the head: the Captain again went back into deep water. Charlie, Frank, and Joe then went on board the vessel and lowered the stern boat, and proceeded for the Captain, but the sea being rough, they capsized. Charlie and Frank jumped out, but Joe was caught under the boat and drowned. Captain Morantes, with his hands crossed as before, came towards Charlie and Frank, begging them to spare him, but as soon as he got up to them, Frank stabbed him with a knife, and Charlie beat him over the head with an iron pump-break until he was dead. They then dragged him ashore and buried him, leveled the sand over the grave, and covered it with grass. They then got Joe's body, which was still under the boat, and buried it also.

After this, they broke open the Captain's trunk and took out his money, in all about $1,600.00, and divided it among the crew, Charlie and Frank retaining the largest portion for themselves. After this, they all took to the boat, and proceeded up the coast until they fell in with the U.S. lighthouse schooner *Delaware*. They went on board, and after being there a few days Captain Owen had good reason to believe that all was not right, and he arrested and sent them to Key West by the U. S. revenue cutter *John Appleton*. Previous to the arrest, Charlie and the cook made their escape in the boat. Captain Owen (Deputy Marshal for the occasion) is in pursuit of them with the *Delaware*, and it is to be hoped they will be caught and brought to punishment for this cold-blooded, horrible murder. They will all be committed for trial at the next term of the Court.

Captain Morantes, the murdered Captain, was well known in this city, and was a French Creole, a native of Louisiana, and was evidently bound for the coast of Africa.

The City of Vera Cruz

One of the worst marine disasters in recent history was that of the *City Of Vera Cruz.* She was a wooden screw steamship of 1,874 tons, brigantine-rigged, with auxiliary engines. She was built at Greenpoint, Long Island, N.Y., in 1874 at John English's shipyard, for Alexandre & Sons, to be used on their New York-to-Havana-and-Mexico run. She was 296' x 37' x 26' and had three decks. She had two compressed cylinder engines and a reinforced hull. She had cabins and staterooms for 100 passengers.

The cargo consisted of a wide variety of merchandise. The largest of the stores were 1,000 barrels of potatoes, 500 drums of fish, 800 tierces (42-gallon barrels) of lard, and 500 bushels of corn. There was one streetcar on board for the Mexican Central Railway, and several other cars in pieces. Other items on board were candles, glassware, firecrackers, wine, beer, pistols, carbines, clocks, a billiard table, corsettes, machinery, and horses.

She sailed from Pier No. 3 North River, New York, on Wednesday afternoon, Aug. 15, 1880, with 28 passengers and a crew of 49. The Captain was Edward Van Sice, who had over 20 years' experience in the Gulf trade. The first mate was Frank Harris, who was captain of the famous Confederate blockade runner *Kingfisher.* One passenger was General A.T.A. Torbert, the famous Union Calvary officer and ex-consul-general to Paris.

The *Vera Cruz* sank during a hurricane at 6 A.M., Aug. 28, 1880. The following is a partial reprint of the story printed in the *New York Times,* Sept. 4 and 5, 1880. Copyright 1880, by The New York Times Company. Reprinted with permission.

○ ○ ○

The *Vera Cruz* was about 30 miles offshore when the cyclone burst upon Saturday evening. The heavy seas which she shipped made their way into the engine-room. The fires were extinguished. It became impossible to keep her under control, and preparations were made to abandon her. Several of the boats were launched, filled with passengers and members of the crew, and were dashed to pieces before they reached the water. While the remaining passengers and crew clung to the ship, paralyzed with fear, the vessel suddenly broke in two and went down, carrying them with her. How the seven men escaped to tell the story is almost a miracle. The account given by Mason Talbot, one of the seven, and a seaman, is intensely interesting.

"We were," he said, "about 30 miles from the coast when the great seas began to pile up over the ship and to fill the hold. We were put to work at the pumps, but as fast as we made a little headway another sea caught us, and the water gradually gained so fast that pumping became useless. The water poured into the engine-room, and, work as hard as they could, the firemen could not keep up the fires. These burned so low that it was impossible to make steam, and then the danger really began. The vessel's head could not be kept into the wind, and finally a heavy drag was rigged forward and thrown over the side. This helped matters a little, and, although we were tossing like an eggshell, now on top of a mountain wave, the next instant far down in the trough of the sea, with the mountain breaking over us, we had hopes of weathering the gale. The passengers and many of the crew seemed to be panic-stricken, and, having provided themselves with life-preservers, were only waiting for the first favorable moment to abandon the vessel. The lifeboats were cut loose and swung out upon their davits ready for instant service. Life-preservers were distributed to such as were un-proved, and everybody prayed for the morning light. When day broke the condition of affairs was no better. It brought more coolness, however, to the officers and crew. It was determined to abandon the ship, as the water had gained so rapidly in the hold during the night that it was evident she could not long remain afloat. One of the boats was swung over the side and manned with a crew. The passengers tumbled into her as best they could. When she was filled, the signal to let go was given. The boat went down with a run, but before she had gone 10 feet, the side of the ship coming up with a roll struck it, and those who were not crushed to death outright were dropped, half stunned, into the sea, where they were drowned before our eyes. It was a pitiful sight to see them struggling almost within our grasp, and then disappear one after another beneath the waters. Another boat was got ready, and was left off in the same manner. It, too, was ground to splinters against the ship's side, and its occupants met with the same fate as those in the first boat. Meantime, the steamer was found to be slowly settling. Every sea shook her from end to end, and if she had not been as stiff and strong as she was, she must have been wrenched to pieces during the night. Those who now remained aboard were so completely unnerved by the horrible sights which they had seen, and the shrieks of the drowning, that they refused to enter one of the boats. The Captain and some of the officers were in one of the boats. It was about 5:30 o'clock when they went over the side. Such a scene I never before witnessed as that now presented. Men and women were in the cabin praying and shrieking, and screaming. All of a sudden there was a snapping sound as of many timbers giving way, and a shock that was felt all over the vessel. She had broken completely in two. She gave one or two plunges, the water rushed in through the wide-open seams and cracks, and the next minute the *Vera Cruz* went down, carrying all on board.

"I was clinging to the deck and was sucked down with the vessel. I came to the surface, breathless and choking with the salt water I had swallowed. Then one person and another came to the top, grasping wildly for something to support them. The water was dotted with their heads and was filled with heavy pieces of wreck. Some of them were struck by this stuff, and so much stunned that they went down again never to come up. I saw one or two women drowned in this way. I got hold of a piece of wreck, but the sea tore it away from me, and then tossed it back again, as if to tantalize me. When I first came on the surface, the water around me was thick with human beings. Some of them caught me, and I had to dive to get rid of their grip. I did this in several cases. I had to do the same thing to avoid pieces of wreck that had bolts sticking out of them. Whoever was struck by one of these bolts was sure to be so maimed as to become helpless. I was tossed up and down all that day until late in the afternoon. Occasionally, as I rose to the crest of some wave, I could see a human being on the crest of another one. Then I was down in the hollow again dodging the timbers. Many times I was driven down two or three fathoms under the water, and if I was lucky enough to grasp a timber when I came to it, it was almost sure to be snatched away from me the next moment. I saw a mother and her daughter tightly clasped together. They rode past me on a wave and disappeared. Their bodies came ashore, still bound in the same embrace. All that Sunday night I was tossed about, and finally, at 7:30 o'clock Monday morning, after having been in the water 26 hours, I was hurled up on the beach. I lay there exhausted for a long time. The other six came ashore on the same beach, although at long distances apart.

"The last I saw of General Torbert alive, he was on the after part of the vessel with Mr. Owen. He was breathing, I was told, when he was cast ashore. A boy dragged him up as far as he could on the beach and then ran for help. When he came back with assistance, General Torbert was dead. His dead body was removed to the little village of Port Orange, which is at the entrance to the Mosquito Inlet. There I saw it. His head was covered with bruises, showing that he must have been struck several times by the pieces of wreck. His body was buried at Daytona."

Talbot added that all his companions were more or less bruised by the drifting debris of the wreck. One of them, stripped of his clothing and in a naked state, swam until he was cast up on the beach. He had no life-preserver and was the first one to come ashore. At Mantanzas, 17 miles south of St. Augustine, the body of a young man, wearing nothing but shirt and drawers, was found. A few miles further south, the bodies of a man between 50 and 60 years of age, an elderly lady, a girl, and a child were washed ashore.

Daytona, where the body of General Torbert was buried, is 50 miles south of St. Augustine, on the west bank of the Halifax River. Port Orange is about 15 miles to the southeast of Daytona, on the east bank of the Halifax River. Halifax River is nothing more than a channel between the mainland and a long strip of beach which was been thrown up by the sea. Mosquito Inlet is the channel connecting the river with the sea. From this city to Cape Canaveral, the shore is covered with wreckage. Within a coastline of 50 miles, the wrecks of eight vessels are visible. The brig *Caroline Eddy* is ashore at Mantanzas, and about a mile and a half from land can be seen a vessel bottom-side up, whose anchors fasten her to the spot. Captain George Warren and his crew, of the *Caroline Eddy,* were saved. This vessel was from Fernandina to New York and was loaded with lumber. The only piece of wreck belonging to the *Vera Cruz* that has yet come ashore is a red plush sofa, with iron castings, on which are stamped the words: "M. and H. Shrenkheiser, N.Y. Pat. May 23, 1876."

This coast swarms with wreckers who have no hesitation in robbing the dead bodies that may fall into their hands, and stories are told that some of them are fiendish enough to hasten the death of wrecked sailors and passengers in order to steal their property. There are no life-saving stations along the coast, and no organized crews to prevent this piratical work, or to render assistance to survivors. In many instances if the proper aid were at hand, the lives of those who are in critical condition might be saved. The rings and jewelry on the bodies that came ashore near Mantanzas have been secured and await identification. A number of private letters were also found.

Later information from the south is to the effect that several trunks have just been found, and their contents rescued from the hands of the pirates, into which they had fallen. The three men referred to in the first portion of this dispatch are expected to reach St. Augustine either tonight or tomorrow morning. The telegraph lines were all blown down in this region, and it is extremely difficult to obtain satisfactory information regarding the discoveries along the coast to the south.

Only 11 people survived of the 77 on board. According to a Mrs. Peaters, who was the wife of "Portguese John," a seaman for five years on the *Vera Curz*, he had told her that she was one of the worst ships he had been on in a heavy sea. He said she never rose buoyantly upon the waves and her stern struck right through them. The bow and the woodwork forward had been broken and splintered by the heavy seas several times. His wife asked why he didn't ship on another ship and he replied "No, I've shipped for five years on her, and I'll fight it out or die on her." His wife was to be a stewardess on this voyage, but her husband said to wait till winter for fear of yellow fever.

An officer of the Atlantic Mutual Marine Insurance Co. stated in the *Times* that the Captain should have avoided the storm and must have seen the barometer drop. "He had plenty of warning. He was undoubtedly a brave man, but like all sea Captains, especially on the Gulf routes, he could not bear the idea of being detained and getting in a day or two late, and perhaps getting censured by the owners. That is what sent many a fine steamer to the bottom, and will send many another yet, until companies and Captains learn that safety is preferable to any number of fast passages." He also criticized the crew in that they delayed throwing the deck load, the cars, etc., overboard until after the ship was partially swamped.

○   ○   ○

The deputy collector of customs at the Port of New Smyrna at this time was Charles H. Coe, who wrote an article called "Memorable Florida Wrecks" for the *St. Augustine News*, Jan. 8, 1898, which mentioned the *City Of Vera Cruz*. Here is a quote from this article.

"One of the first mails after the storm brought me instructions from Capt. House, the collector at St. Augustine, to "warn all persons having wrecked property in their possession to turn the same over to the Customs officer." As boat after boat came in loaded with barrels and tins of lard, and other goods, I notified their owners as instructed.

For thus doing my duty I was laughed at and even threatened. But I could not blame the salvors for refusing to part with the goods they had labored so hard to save. My instructions were explicit, however, and I carried them out to the best of my ability under the circumstances. I learned afterward from the collector, that he himself had been threatened, and by no less a person then the worthy mayor of St. Augustine, who had turned wrecker himself, for the time being."

○   ○   ○

This wreck was located by fishermen in 1980, and is currently under an admiralty salvage lease held by Shipwrecks Inc. She lies in 78 feet of water, and her Loran position is 60910.45 and 44071.65. Her steam engines rise 30 feet off the ocean bottom. Source: 14, 94 (Nielsen, Robert R. "Florida Jewelry Wreck, Wreck of the City Of Vera Cruz." Vol. 1, No. 1, pp. 27-31).

Figure 67B: Author's sketch of the *City of Vera Cruz*.

The Valbanera

Undoubtedly the worst disaster off the Florida coast in this last century — in terms of lives lost from a single ship — was the sinking of the *Valbanera*.

The *Valbanera* was built in 1905 at Glasgow, Scotland, by C. Connell & Co., for the Pinillos, Izquierdo & Co., of Cadiz, Spain. Tonnage: 5,099. Dimensions: 399' x 48.' Single screw, capable of 12 knots. Triple expansion engines. Two masts and one funnel. She could carry 1,000 passengers in three classes.

The *Valbanera* left Spain for New Orleans via Havana. On board were 400 passengers and 88 crew members. Almost all the passengers were either Spaniards or Cubans, and most were to disembark at Havana. The ship carried a general cargo, which included wines and liquors. The trip was uneventful until she approached Cuba. She arrived off Morro Castle at Havana Harbor on Sept. 9, 1919, but a hurricane was sweeping across the island at this time. Rather than risk trying to enter the harbor, Captain Morton decided to ride the storm out at sea.

Figure 68: Spanish steamer *Valbanera*, sunk in 1919. THE STEAMSHIP HISTORICAL SOCIETY COLLECTION, UNIVERSITY OF BALTIMORE LIBRARY.

At 1:15 p.m. on Sept. 12, the *Valbanera* radioed Key West and asked if there were any messages for her. Ten minutes later the Key West station radioed back, but there was no response from her. The hurricane was raging with considerable violence at the time, and it is most probable that the *Valbanera* sank within minutes after her call to Key West.

On Sept. 19 the United States Sub-Chaser 203 and the Coast Guard vessel *Tuscarora* found the *Valbanera* sunk in 40 feet of water near the Rebecca Shoal Lighthouse, Dry Tortugas. Ensign L.B. Roberts, commander of the U. S. Sub-Chaser 203, stated that he had seen the nameplate of the *Valbanera* on the sunken vessel. The *Valbanera* lay in water which covered a bed of quicksand. No bodies or wreckage were seen in the vicinity of the wreck when first discovered. Ensign Roberts' statement was corroborated by divers who, on order of the Cuban consul at Key West, investigated the sunken vessel.

A search was made for survivors, but to no avail. Examination of the wreck was made by divers under direction of Cuban Consul Domingo Milord. Rear Admiral Decker, commander of the Seventh Naval District, headquartered in Key West, reported that divers investigating the steamer's davits found that no effort was made to lower the port lifeboats, indicating that most passengers went down with the ship. Divers also found no structural damage.

It was reported that for a few days after the *Valbanera* sank, faint calls by wireless were being picked up from survivors of the *Valbanera,* asking for help. This was never verified, since no survivors or bodies were ever found, even though an extensive search was made. Most on board were believed to have been trapped inside the ship when she went down.

The *Valbanera* must have sunk quite suddenly and without warning. Since there were no survivors, one can only speculate what actually happened. Had she entered Havana Harbor, she might have survived. Instead, 488 people lost their lives in one of Florida's worst maritime disasters.

Source: 73, 82, 98 (Sept. 20-22, 1919), 99 (Sept. 20-22, 1919).

Figure 68A: Large eighteenth-century anchor lost off Palm Beach County. AUTHOR.

The Korsholm

World War II came right to our doorstep, as the crew of the *Korsholm* could attest to. The *Korsholm* was a Swedish freighter of Gothenburg, built in 1925 by the Aktieb shipyard of Gothenburg, for the Swedish American Mexican Line. She was 2,647 tons, 336.2' x 45.6' x 19.9.'

After loading 4,593 tons of phosphate at Tampa, she left on April 11, 1942, bound for Liverpool, England, via Halifax, Nova Scotia.

The German U 123, under the command of Lieutenant Reinhard Hardegen, was continuing an extremely successful second mission off the U.S. coast, having sunk or crippled a number of vessels. Lieut. Hardegen was one of the most successful U-boat commanders during WWII, and probably the most successful in the use of artillery fire.

The U 123's first success on this trip was on March 22, 1942, when she attacked the tanker *Muskogee* by torpedo, at Lat. 28 N, Long. 58 W. The tanker sank soon after. On March 24, the U 123 attacked the tanker *Empire Steel* by both torpedo and gunfire, at Lat. 37.45 N, Long. 63.17 W, and the *Empire* was also sunk. On the 27th, the U 123 attacked the Q-ship (a heavily armed ship disguised as a merchant vessel) *Atik*, by both torpedo and gunfire, at Lat. 36 N, Long.70 W. The *Atik* was also sunk with all hands, though she did manage to inflict some damage on the U 123.

Figure 69: Sketch of the freighter *Korsholm*, torpedoed in World War II. AUTHOR.

On April 2, the U 123 attacked the tanker *Liebre*, by both torpedo and gunfire, at Lat. 34.11 N, Long. 76.08 W, but succeeded only in damaging her. On April 8, the U 123 hit the tanker *Oklahoma* with one torpedo and five gunshots at 0752 hours, at Lat. 31.18 N, Long. 80.59 W. The *Oklahoma* was beached and later salvaged. At 0844 hours on the same day, the U 123 torpedoed the tanker *Esso Baton Rouge* at Lat.

31.02 N, Long. 80.53 W. Though the tanker was also beached in a damaged state, she was salvaged.

The next day, the U 123 attacked the steamer *Esparta* by torpedo, at Lat. 30.46 N, Long. 81.11 W, and sank it in shallow water. On the night of the 11th, she attacked the tanker *Gulfamerica* off Jacksonville, by both torpedo and gunfire, at Lat. 30.10 N, Long. 81.15 W in full view of the residents of Jacksonville Beach. The tanker sank soon after. Not long after her attack of the *Gulfamerica*, the U 123 was attacked by depth charges from a destroyer, and was almost ordered to be scuttled, when the barrage suddenly stopped, and she later slipped away. On April 13, the U 123 attacked the steamer *Leslie* by torpedo, at Lat. 28.35 N, Long. 80.19 W, and the steamer soon sank in 15 fathoms. A short time later on the same day, the U 123 spotted and attacked the *Korsholm*, at Lat. 28.21 N, Long. 80.22 W.

On April 13, 1942, the *Korsholm* was headed north under blackout off Cape Canaveral, unaware that the U 123 was stalking her, waiting for the proper moment to commence an attack. The U 123 had used her store of torpedoes, having expended the last on her attack on the *Leslie* a short time earlier, and would now have to attack with artillery fire only. At 2 A.M., without notice, the U 123 attacked the *Korsholm* with both artillery shells and machine guns. The first shell hit the bridge, causing grave damage, and also destroyed the radio. The starboard lifeboat was broken by another shell, and several of the men were killed or severely wounded. Some of the crew abandoned ship shortly after.

The firing was intense, and after some time the *Korsholm* caught fire. At 0400, a plane from the Banana River Naval Air Station arrived at the scene and dropped life rafts and flares. The *Korsholm* was still afloat early in the morning, and two of the crewmen were rescued from her at this time by the Dutch steamer *Bacchus,* which had been directed to her by the naval aircraft which had spotted her previously. The other surviving crewmen had taken to the lifeboat soon after the attack. One other survivor was rescued from the water by the *SS Esso Bayone.* Of the 26 crewmen on board, nine lost their lives. One washed up on the beach, and eight others, including the captain, were reported missing.

The *Korsholm* sank soon after at Lat. 28-12-10, Long. 80-29-16. Sometime during 1944 she was demolished to a depth of 60 feet. Her remains are a reminder of how close the war came to the Florida coast.

After attacking the *Korsholm*, the U 123 was still not finished with her mission of destruction. Even though she had no more torpedoes, she had enough shells and bullets for one more attack. On April 17, she attacked the steamer *Alcoa Guide*, at Lat. 35.34 N, Long. 70.08 W, by gunfire, and the steamer sank the same day. Hardegen received the Knight's Cross with oak leaves for his service.

Source: Statens Sjohistoriska Museum, Stockholm, 34, 68.

APPENDICES

Appendix A: Research

Unless you are lucky enough to stumble upon a shipwreck of interest, the key to finding a particular wreck is through research. It's hard to believe that investors still sink large amounts of money into salvage projects where little or no research has been done.

Though a wreck might have no historical or monetary value, it is still satisfying to identify one you have found, or one that is a favorite dive location. The stories behind some of these wrecks can be fascinating.

Shipwrecks in the Americas in the 15th and 16th centuries were predominantly Spanish or Portuguese. Unfortunately, most of the documents concerning Portuguese ships in the New World were deposited in the Casa da India in Lisbon, which was destroyed during an earthquake in 1763. Most Portuguese vessels sailed to Brazil and the surrounding area, which was under their control. According to the Treaty of Tordesillas in 1494, a line of demarcation assigned the east coast of Brazil to Portugal, and the rest of the hemisphere to Spain. The Spanish had control of the Caribbean, Florida, and the west coasts of South and Central America. Fortunately, most Spanish documents concerning early New World shipping have survived and are in the Archives of the Indies in Seville, and in the Simancas Archives near Valladolid.

When Sir Henry Morgan took Panama City in 1670, he destroyed all the records of shipping, land grants, and other Spanish transactions stored there. Many archives in Cartegena, Bogota, and Vera Cruz have been lost due to humidity and war. Fortunately, many of Cuba's archives have survived and remain in Cuba and in the Archives of the Indies in Seville. Also, the Spanish always kept more than one set of records, in both the New World and in Spain. With enough digging, there is a good chance of finding records pertaining to a Spanish shipwreck of interest.

Though these records do exist, finding what you are looking for can be a monumental task — one best undertaken by a competent professional trained in the art of finding and deciphering these early Spanish documents. Documents concerning the New World are stored in bundles called *legajos*, and many have still never been read. Though the language is basically the same as today, the style of writing is a script called *procesal*. Even for someone fluent in Spanish, it is difficult to translate without proper training. For example, there were many variations of the same Spanish letters during the last few centuries.

If you want to do your own research in the archives of Spain, it would be helpful to take a course in Spanish paleography, the study of deciphering ancient writings. One is offered at the University of Florida. You should also become familiar with early Spanish place names and their modern counterparts.

The cost of hiring a professional to research Spanish documents is minuscule compared to the cost of searching for a wreck that does not exist, one that already has been salvaged, or one that wrecked far from where you thought it had. Good research saves both time and money. Moreover, a shipwreck project that has good research behind it is more likely to get the financial backing needed to continue.

It is important to remember that in the 16th century, Spain referred to much of the United States as the continent of "Florida," so many ships listed as wrecked on the coast of Florida could be elsewhere. For example, an early Spanish narrative mentioned the 1553 Fleet as having wrecked on the coast of Florida, but it wrecked in an area that is now off Texas.

To find someone to research a wreck for you, contact the appropriate museum, archive, or records office. That institution can usually refer you to a professional researcher.

England has a variety of sources available for shipwreck information. The following are major sources:

• National Maritime Museum, Park Row, Greenwich, London SE10 9NF.

• Public Records Office, Kew, Richmond, Surrey TW9 4DU. Has the operational records of the Royal Navy, from 1660 to 1914.

• Department of Transport, Marine Library, Room G7, Sunley House, 90-93 High Holborn, London WC1V 6LP. Has wreck reports from 1876 on, although it also has done some earlier research.

• Keeper of the Lloyd's Marine Collection, Guildhall Library, Aldermanbury, London EC2P 2EJ. Has information on marine casualties going back to 1740.

• Many regional libraries and museums in England also can help with research. Some of the above sources will refer you to them.

Here are some sources for information on marine casualties in other countries of Europe.

• Belgium: National Scheepvaartmuseum, Steenplein, 1, Antwerp.

• Denmark: 1) Danish Admiralty Collection, Naval Museum, Royal Dockyard, Copenhagen. 2) Danish National Museum, Vikingeskibs-hallen, Roskilde.

• Finland: Bureau of Maritime Archaeology, National Museum, Helsinki.

• France: 1) Underwater Archaeology Commission, CMAS Secretariat, Paris. 2) Musée de la Marine, Paris. 3) Archives Nationales, 60 rue de Francs, Bourgeois, Paris III.

• Germany: Deutsches Schiffahrts Museum, Bremerhaven, Germany.

• Ireland: National Maritime Museum, Haigh Terrace, Dun Laoghaire Dublin, Ireland.

• Netherlands: Maritime Museum Prins Hendrick, Rotterdam.

• Norway: Norsk Sjofartsmuseum, Bygdoynesvn. 37, 0286 Oslo 2.

• Portugal: 1) Museo da Marinha, Praca do Imperia, Belem, 1400 Lisbon. 2) Arquivo Nacional, Largo S. Bento, Lisbon 2.

• Sweden: Statens Sjohistoriska Museum, 115 27 Stockholm.

These are but a few of the European sources available. Many will refer you to another source if they do not have the information requested.

For shipwreck information in Caribbean and South American countries, and also Mexico, contact local museums, universities, or libraries for information on local history and newspaper and shipping records. Here are a few sources:

• Antigua: The Nelson Museum, Nelson's Dockyard, Antigua.

• Bahamas: Bahamas Historical Society Museum, P.O. Box N1715/Elizabeth Avenue, Nassau.

• Brazil: Museu Naval, Rua Dom Manuel 15, Rio de Janeiro, Guanabara.

• Columbia: Museo Geologico Nacional, Carrera 30 No. 51-59, Apdo. Aero 4865, Bogota.

• Dominican Republic: Comision de Rescate Arqueologica Submarino, Museo de Las Casas Reales, Calle Las Dames Esq. Mercedes, Santo Domingo.

• Jamaica: West India Reference Library, 14-16 East St., Kingston.

• Martinique: Musée Departemental, Place de la Savane, 97200, Fort-de-France.

• Mexico: Archivos Generales de la Nacion, Calle Soledad, Mexico D.F.

For records of Canadian vessels, here are a few sources:

• Public Archives of Canada, Trade and Communications Records Center, 395 Wellington Street, Ottawa, K1A ON3

• Toronto Marine Historical Society, Marine Museum of Upper Canada, Exposition Park, Toronto 138, Ontario.

• Wheelhouse Maritime Museum, 222 Cumberland St., Ottawa 2, Ontario K1N 7H5.

• Maritime Museum, The Foot of Cypress Street, Vancouver 9, British Columbia.

• Maritime Museum of British Columbia, 28 Bastion Square, Victoria, British Columbia.

There are many records of U.S. shipping available. Unfortunately, many records of vessels before 1814 were lost when the British burned Washington that year, and most of the duplicate registers, enrollments, and licenses filed were destroyed.

Some custom-house records also have been destroyed by fire or other mishap from time to time. The main custom-house records were kept in New York, Boston, Baltimore, and Philadelphia. Any of these records that survived are probably kept now in the National Archives.

Some of the best sources of information on shipwrecks in the United States are newspaper records. Shipping news was reported daily in the newspapers of New England, Boston, New York, New Orleans, Charleston, Savannah, Key West, and other port cities. Many of these newspapers were saved and are available on microfilm in local museums and libraries. Some date back to the 18th century. Insurance companies that dealt in marine insurance also might have records of particular shipwrecks.

Some U.S. government sources are:

• National Archives and Record Service, 8th and Pennsylvania avenues, N.W., Washington, D.C. 20408.

• U.S. Dept. of Commerce, NOAA, National Ocean Service, Hydrographic Surveys Branch, 6001 Executive Boulevard, Rockville, Maryland 20852. (This department can provide files from the Automated Wreck and Obstruction Information System, or AWOIS).

• U.S. Govt. Printing Office, Washington D.C. 20402. (This office has printed a pamphlet on treasure maps and charts available in the Library of Congress.)

• Naval Historical Center, Washington Navy Yard, Washington, D.C. 20374.

• U.S. Naval Academy, The Museum, Annapolis, Maryland 21402.

• Smithsonian Institution, Museum of American History, Washington, D.C. 20560.

The following is a list of some maritime museums in the United States:

• Mariners Museum, Newport News, Virginia 23606.

• Mystic Seaport Museum, Mystic, Connecticut 06355.

• Maine Maritime Museum, 963 Washington St., Bath, Maine 04530.

• National Maritime Museum, J. Porter Shaw Library, Foot of Polk St., San Francisco, California 04109.

• Peabody Museum, East India Square, Salem, Massachusetts 01970.

• Penobscot Marine Museum, Searsport, Maine 14974.

• Steamship Historical Society of America, University of Baltimore Library, 1420 Maryland Ave., Baltimore, Maryland 21201.

Figure 69A: Jack Pennell with a bronze rudder gudgeon and a small cannon found off Boca Raton. AUTHOR.

Appendix B: Search & Salvage

SEARCH

Once the research has been done, you begin the search for your shipwreck. Searching for a wreck has become much easier with the use of equipment such as magnetometers, side-scan sonar, sub-bottom sonar, and underwater metal detectors.

Some companies specialize in this field, using computers and precise navigational instruments to pinpoint areas of interest. Their services are expensive, but they might save you money in the long run by pinpointing a wreck site in a very short time.

Still, you can do the search successfully by yourself. Magnetometers come in a wide range of prices and options, and there are good, inexpensive models on the market. The same holds true for side-scan units, underwater metal detectors, and sub-bottom sonar.

Magnetometer

A magnetometer is an electronic instrument that measures variations in the earth's magnetic field. It should be noted that the strength of the earth's magnetic field also varies depending on the geographic area. A magmetometer will only detect ferrous metals underwater, which distort the earth's magnetic field: The larger the object, the greater the distortion.

The "proton" magnetometer is the type most widely used in searching for shipwrecks. A coil is encased in a probe (referred to as a towfish) filled with a hydrocarbon fluid, usually kerosene. This coil is alternately connected to either a polarizing circuit or a high gain amplifier. The probe is towed behind a boat where the free spinning protons in the kerosene align themselves with the earth's magnetic field.

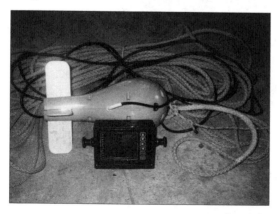

Figure 70: The MX500
Magnetometer System.
AUTHOR.

When the coil is connected to the polarizing circuit, a much stronger magnetic field is induced within the kerosene which causes the protons to realign with this new magnetic field. The longer the polarize time, the more protons aligned with this magnetic field, and the greater the signal strength. Polarize times can be adjusted on some of the new magnetometer units; two seconds is usually sufficient for good signal strength. When choosing a polarize time, you must consider several things, such as the size of the objects you are searching for, the depth at which they are buried, and tow speed. Searching for small objects—cannonballs, for instance—might require a one half–second or one-second polarize time. For larger objects, a two- or even three-second polarize time may be used.

When the polarizing circuit is switched off, the detection phase begins. The protons act like little gyroscopes, which now try to realign to the prevailing direction of the earth's magnetic field. While doing this, they induce a small signal voltage which is then amplified by the high gain amplifier, which in turn is displayed on the computer screen or chart recorder as an anomaly. Some units even have an audible alarm, which I recommend. Staring at a screen for hours is no fun.

Another consideration is voltage. Some units can run on either twelve or twenty-four volts. The higher the voltage, the greater the signal strength. In areas with a weak magnetic field, you should use twenty-four volts or more.

Units such as the MX500 magnetometer system are inexpensive and are just as sensitive as those costing much more. This unit has memory capability and can interface with most Geographical Positioning System (GPS) and Differential Geographical Positioning System (DGPS) units on the market. With an onboard computer, you can download information all day. This and most other units are available with software that allows you to store information in memory and to download to a personal computer. If you are interfacing with a DGPS and have accounted for your towfish cable length, you can pinpoint potential wrecksites to within a few feet.

For those who don't have software or interface capabilities, bouys are just as efficient. Once you get a good hit, do a north-south run. On each run, throw a buoy when your hit is recorded. Then do an east-west run through the middle of the two buoys already thrown, dropping two more buoys. In the middle of the four bouys you've thrown should lie the ferrous object or wreck you detected.

Side-Scan Sonar

A side-scan sonar produces an image using the reflected vibrations of acoustic signals. The side-scan sonar sends out these sonar signals at an angle, which helps to cover much larger areas than if the signals were sent straight down, hence the name "side-scan."(See Figures 74 and 75.)

As with a magnetometer, a "fish" is towed behind a boat. The sonar signals are transmitted and received through it, then transmitted to the console, which produces a sonar image of any object on the ocean floor. Some of the larger "fish" used in deep-water searches require a large vessel with miles of cable for towing the unit.(Figure 76).

Figures 77 and 78 show sonar images of a submarine and a biplane found off the coast of California in 1,400 feet of water. The image was done by Oceaneering International, Inc. (Search Division), of Fort Lauderdale.

Side-scan sonar will detect objects only above the sea floor. It is most commonly used to search for deep-water wrecks such as the *Central America* and the *Titanic* (though it was a remote underwater video camera which actually found the latter).

You might consider a side-scan unit to search for nonferrous materials, since a magnetometer cannot detect these. The cost, usually in thousands of dollars, will depend on the application.

Sub-Bottom Sonar

If a wreck is buried under sand, silt, or mud, a sub-bottom sonar unit might be more effective than a magnetometer (Figure 79). The sub-bottom sonar unit transmits acoustic signals straight to the ocean floor, penetrating shallow sediment to the bedrock. These sound pulses reflect off the bottom, revealing sonar images of objects under the sediment, along with a profile of the ocean floor. A good unit can be very expensive.

Underwater Metal Detectors

Hand-held underwater metal detectors will detect both ferrous and nonferrous metals. There are many good units on the market. A decent unit will cost a few hundred dollars. (See Figure 80.)

Once a wreck site has been found, these detectors become invaluable for finding small artifacts and coins. How deep a unit will detect depends on the unit and on what is being found. A detector might find a cannon under six feet of sand, but a coin under only six inches of sand.

You can learn to operate the new detectors in a few hours. They are self-tuning and work just as well on land.

Underwater Video Systems and ROVs

A remotely operated vehicle (ROV) might also be considered for certain applications. The cost of these units can vary from a few thousand dollars into the millions. Though they are used for search purposes, as

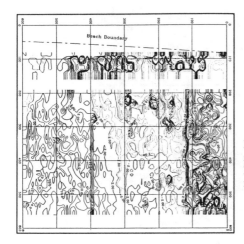

Figure 71: Magnetometer survey map of a 19th-century wreck site off Hillsboro Beach. MARINE ARCHAEOLOGICAL COUNCIL INC.

Figures 72 (above, right) and 73 (below): A surveyor stays in contact with the magnetometer operator offshore in a boat. Traffic cones on the beach help the boat with the magnetometer to run its course. These photos show steps in the process that produced the magnetometer map shown in Figure 71. AUTHOR.

301

Figure 74: Rick Horgan of Oceaneering International Search Division holds a side-scan sonar fish next to the cable apparatus needed to tow the fish. AUTHOR.

Figure 75: Rick Horgan next to the U.S. Navy's "Orion" side-scan sonar fish used for deep-ocean search. Notice the difference in size from the fish in Figure 74. AUTHOR

Figure 76: Rick Horgan next to the cable apparatus needed to tow the larger fish. AUTHOR.

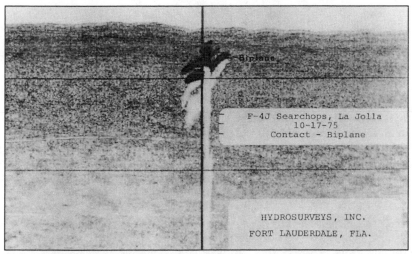

Figures 77 and 78: A side-scan image of a submarine and a biplane in more than 1,400 feet of water off California. OCEANEERING INTERNATIONAL INC., SEARCH DIVISION, FT. LAUDERDALE.

Figure 79: A sub-bottom sonar (Chirp sonar) fish, weighing over 200 pounds, developed by two professors at Florida Atlantic University. AUTHOR.

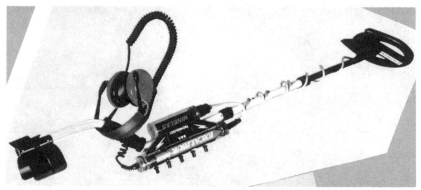

Figure 80: Minelab's Excalibur underwater metal detector incorporates the newest technologies. MINELAB.

in the case of the *Titanic*, they can do the actual salvage when combined with mechanical arms, as in the salvage of the *Central America* in over 8,000 feet of water.

There are also towable video units and ones that are simply lowered from your boat. These are usually less expensive than remotely operated units. (See Figures 81 and 82.)

What to Look For

The easiest and least expensive way to search for a wreck site, assuming it is in shallow water with good visibility, is simply a visual search. If the wreck is exposed, this can be just as effective as using expensive search equipment.

You can find a wreck site using a sled, or simply a rope to tow a diver, though you need to know what to look for. Most divers could swim right over an old wreck site and not even realize it.

If you are searching an area with very good visibility, you might consider a search by air. This can sometimes be the easiest and fastest way to locate a wreck, since a large area can be covered in a short time.

Figure 81: An underwater TV camera being lowered into the ocean. AUTHOR.

Figure 82: An underwater TV camera equipped with sonar. AUTHOR.

A modern steel or iron wreck is usually quite obvious to a diver, but an earlier wooden vessel has usually deteriorated, destroyed by the teredo worm or by nature. All that usually remains visible is the ballast pile or large metal objects such as cannon, anchors, or windlass. In Florida, these objects usually become coral-encrusted, making them even harder to identify. You need to look for any straight line shapes, (Figures 83–86) since this could indicate a cannon or anchor. Straight lines are not natural to the ocean floor. Ballast piles can also indicate a wreck site, though ballast found near a port area may have been discharged to make room for cargo. Ballast comes in all shapes and sizes (Figure 87).

Figure 83: An obvious cannon. AUTHOR.

Figure 84: Two not-so-obvious coral-encrusted cannons. Can you find them? Look for the straight lines. AUTHOR.

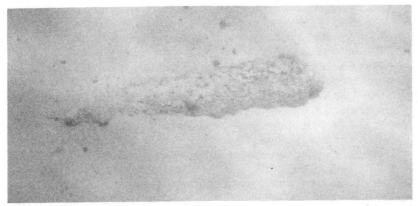

Figures 85 (above) and 86 (below): An unidentified object sticking out of the sand (notice the straight lines). Most divers would swim right over this. With a little hand fanning a cannon is uncovered. AUTHOR.

Figure 87: The ballast pile of the *El Lerri* (1733), which wrecked in the Keys. AUTHOR.

Many vessels, if they were taking on water, jettisoned heavy objects such as cannon, cannon balls, and cargo to lighten the ship. If this was the case, you need to follow this trail to the actual wreck, if indeed it did wreck.

If a vessel grounded on a reef or sandbar, heavy objects would have been jettisoned, in hopes of getting the vessel off.

Vessels wrecked during severe storms, such as the *Atocha* and the ships of the 1715 Fleet, were scattered over large areas, sometimes miles, so the trail of wreckage could take months and even years to follow until the actual cargo is found.

Since most ships in danger of wrecking on a reef or shore would let their anchors out in hopes of holding the vessel in place, anchors are often found with no wreckage nearby. Follow the direction of the anchor shank. If it wasn't simply a lost anchor, it might lead you to the wreck site. Most sailing vessels carried a few anchors, and more often than not anchors found on the bottom were simply lost.

Unfortunately, Florida's coastline has not been kind to wreck sites. Most wrecks lie in shallow water, and with constant storms, wave action, and currents, are deteriorating a little more each year. Wrecks on inland waterways are more protected. They may remain preserved for years, covered by mud or silt in inland lakes and rivers — as long as pollutants or dredging projects don't destroy them.

SALVAGE

Once you have found the wreck you were searching for, you can begin excavation (uncovering) of the site as long as you have legally obtained permission. A modern wreck site may not need any excavation work done, but that doesn't mean the salvage will be easy. There is still danger in entering old ships or in working at depths which require commercial deep-sea divers and a diving bell.

Most salvage in Florida is done on older wrecks carrying gold and silver from the mines of Mexico and South America. These were constructed of wood and sank long ago, with the majority of the wrecks buried under sand, silt, or mud. Excavation removes these overlying materials.

There are three basic ways to remove sand from a wreck site. The most popular with treasure salvors is the prop wash, also called a blower or blaster (Figure 88). This device, when lowered over the propeller, directs the force from the prop to the ocean floor, blowing the sand away and uncovering the wreck site. Since many treasure wrecks are scattered over acres and even miles, this is the fastest and most efficient way to salvage these wrecks.

The force from the blower is controlled by raising or lowering the RPMs (revolutions per minute) of the engine. Running the engine at low RPMs, after the initial hole is blown, will keep sand from falling back into the hole and also will direct clean surface water below for better visibility. The force from some of the larger blowers can be quite strong.

Figure 88: Blowers on the salvage vessel Virgalona, one of the most successful treasure salvage boats in Florida. AUTHOR.

Another way of removing sand is to use a dredge, an apparatus that sucks up material from the ocean floor like a vacuum. If your wreck site is intact, you might consider using a dredge since this will give you greater control over smaller areas than a blower, though a blower could be used to remove the initial top layer of sand. Some wrecks can be buried under 10 or more feet of sand.

A small dredge can be built at home (Figures 89 and 90). All you

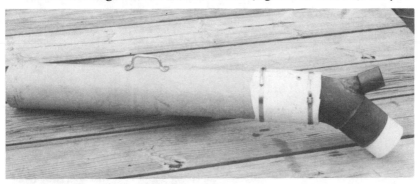

Figure 89: Homemade suction dredge. AUTHOR.

need is a gas-driven pump (a hydraulic pump also can be used), a rigid hose that won't collapse for the intake, a long flexible hose for the discharge from the dredge, and some PVC or metal pipe. The size of your dredge depends on how big a pump you use. Angle the suction end downward so it can be easily used. The length to the discharge end can vary depending on the circumstances. You might consider an extension pipe.

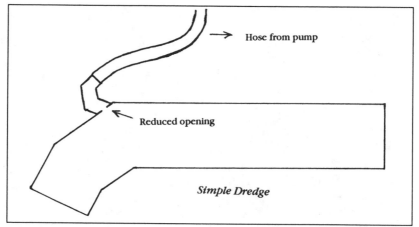

Figure 90: Sketch of a suction dredge. AUTHOR.

Attaching the discharge hose from the pump just above the suction end of your dredge, at an angle towards the discharge end of the dredge, will force the water into your dredge, creating suction, which will remove sand quite efficiently. The connection for the pump discharge hose and the dredge must be tapered to create a pressure differential (venturi effect). If your discharge hose is two inches in diameter, the hole at the connection on the dredge should be approximately one-half inch in diameter to create suction in the dredge.

A third way to remove sand is with an air lift, a device with an air

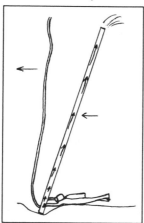

Figure 91: Sketch of an air lift. A hose (at left) from the air compressor supplies air that, as it rises in the pipe on the right, expands and creates suction. AUTHOR.

compressor that creates suction to lift sand from the ocean floor (Figure 91). It will work only in water at least 20 to 25 feet deep since anything shallower leaves no room for air to rise and create suction. Air lifts have been used with great success in the Mediterranean, where ancient wrecks all lie in deep water.

Figure 92 : Don Kree taking a sextant reading from a boat on the *Nieves* (1715) site. AUTHOR.

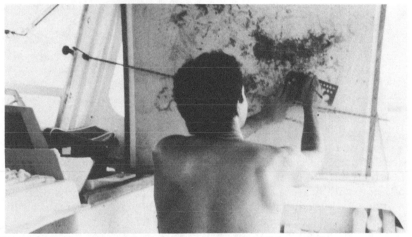

Figure 93: Author plotting the sextant readings on a real "treasure" map. AUTHOR.

They are highly efficient and easily made from an air compressor, hose, and PVC pipe. The compressor forces air through the hose, which is attached to the PVC pipe just above the intake end. The length and width of the PVC pipe will depend on your depth and compressor size. As the air rises up through the PVC pipe, it expands, creating suction and lifting with it the sand from the bottom — hence the name air lift. The force of the suction can be very strong, so be careful not to get your hand caught in the intake end.

You can extend the discharge end out of the water and direct all discharge through a screen rigged to float on the surface, catching any objects missed on the ocean floor.

Mapping the wreck site is most important, whether it is an archaeological or treasure salvage project (Figures 92 and 93). An intact wreck is usually mapped using a PVC grid fixed over top of the site. This puts the site in perspective and allows you to pinpoint the location of all artifacts. Figure 94 shows a hand-drawn site plan of a wreck off Hillsboro Beach. There are a few good underwater archaeology books, which explain how to map and survey an underwater site. They are listed in the Bibliography.

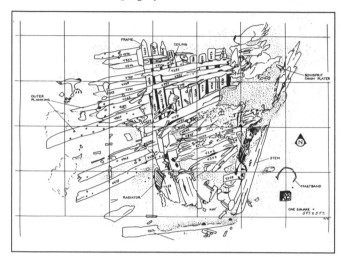

Figure 94: A hand-drawn site plan of one of two wrecks in the magnetometer survey (Figure 71). MARINE AR-CHAEOLOGICAL COUNCIL INC.

Wrecks strewn over large areas also can be mapped accurately. The *Nieves* site of 1715 off Fort Pierce is a good example. The area I've worked on under Bob Weller encompasses approximately 50 acres of ocean floor. The state of Florida erected three range markers on the beach off this site. With a sextant, we could pinpoint the salvage boat's position within a couple of feet. This eliminates the possibility of working the same area again, and helps in finding a particular area again. All artifacts and treasure are recorded and plotted on a map. As the area is worked, we can look at the map, plot how the ship broke up and follow the scatter pattern.

Where no land is visible, electronic positioning can be used to plot a map. This can be done on board a ship with Loran or with satellite navigation systems.

All the search and salvage equipment mentioned is readily available. A trade magazine such as *Sea Technology* or *Waves* will list many of the companies that sell this equipment or that specialize in search and salvage work. *Sea Technology* is available through Compass Publications, Suite 1000, 1117 No. 19th St., Arlington, VA 22209. *Waves* is published by Windate Enterprises, Inc., P.O. Box 368, Spring Valley, CO 91976.

Appendix C: Wreck Identification

While it is possible to find a ship's bell that shows her name and the date she was built, or another object that would instantly identify the wreck, this is rarely the case.

Usually it is like piecing together a puzzle. Many artifacts found on a wreck site can be dated. After you gather all this information together, you can get a fairly good idea of the type, age, and nationality of the wreck. The following are some of the artifacts to look for.

Cannon

Cannon are an excellent dating material. Some of the many good books on cannon and other armament are listed in the "Suggested Reading"

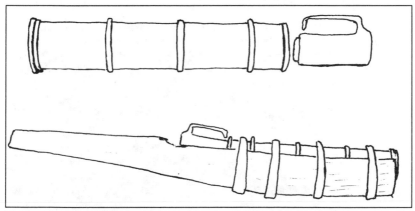

Figure 95: Upper: Early wrought-iron lombard and breech block from a European wreck dating 1490. Lower: Same cannon mounted in wood stock. AUTHOR.

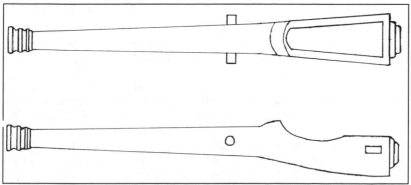

Figure 96: Early bronze verso (8.5 feet long), late 15th through 16th century. Upper: top view. Lower: side view. AUTHOR.

Figures 97 (above) and 98 (below): A bronze cannon from the wreck of the *San Martin* (1618), found south of Sebastion Inlet. A close-up shows the dolphin handles. DON KREE.

section at the end of this book.

Early ships visiting the New World used a breech-loading, wrought-iron cannon called a lombard or a *bombardeta* (Figure 95). It was made by laying iron bars on a round barrel mold, then heat welding rings around these bars to form a cannon. The *pasavolante* was another early iron cannon. It was narrower than the lombard and was muzzle-loading. Bronze and iron breech-loaders, called *versos*, were also common (Figure 96).

Bronze muzzle-loading cannon were predominant in the 1500s and early 1600s (Figures 97 and 98). Iron muzzle-loading cannon took over in the later 1600s. Cast-iron cannon, less expensive than bronze, began to be produced around 1550. Muzzle-loading cannon replaced most breech-loaders until the late 19th century, when improved breech-loading cannon again were used, resulting in today's modern weaponry.

Figures 99 (above, left), 100 (above, right) and 101 (below): Carl Ward with a rare Dutch bronze *steenstruck* he recovered from the *El Populo* (1733) wreck. The Spanish referred to this cannon as a *pedrera*. A close-up shows the maker's mark, identifying it as having been made in Amsterdam. ERNIE RICHARDS.

Small breech-loading swivel guns continued to be used into the 18th century, however. They were found on the 1715 Fleet and 1733 Fleet wrecks. Figures 99, 100 and 101 show a rare bronze Dutch cannon called a steenstruk (the Spanish called it a pedrero), found on the 1733 wreck *El Populo.*

Stone shot was used until around 1500, when iron shot came into use (though small amounts of stone shot were carried on English warships until 1625). The English also used lead in the 16th century.

Many cannon have marks that identify their maker and nationality. During the Tudor reign, the English stamped the Tudor "rose" on cannon of the Royal Navy. When that reign ended in 1603, they began stamping a broad arrow on all naval armament (Figures 102 and 103).

Figures 102 (above) and 103 (left): Early 18th-century British Admiralty cannons, recovered in 1962 off Hallandale Beach. Note the Royal Crest with "G.R." (George Rex), and the English "broad arrow" below the crest, marks used on all crown property. JIM WARD (PHOTOS ON FILE AT BROWARD COUNTY HISTORICAL COMMISSION).

Measuring cannon found on a wreck can help you date the wreck, because cannon were different sizes during different periods.

Knowing the age and nationality of cannon can help you determine the general date of a wreck, but you should not use cannon alone for this purpose. Some ships carried as ballast some old, outdated cannon, usually with the trunnions (projecting pivots) knocked off. The French Navy used the old iron breech-loaders for a time in the later 1600s. Some countries captured cannon of other countries: One wreck was found with cannon from five different countries.

When comparing what you find with the shipping records, remember that the British Navy rated its swivel gun as half a gun. The HMS *Wolf*, which wrecked off Florida in 1741, is listed as having 14 guns, but she actually had 20. She carried eight guns and 12 swivels, which counted as six guns.

Anchors

Anchors can also help date a wreck. Early anchors were hand-forged; later ones were cast in one piece. Wooden stock anchors were used until the late 1800s (Figure 104), when iron stock became the norm. Iron stock anchors appeared as early as the late 1700s on smaller anchors and are still being used (Figure 105). A British naval frigate built in 1794 had an iron stock on its smaller kedge anchor and a wooden stock on its larger anchors.

The earlier the anchor, the longer the shank in relation to the flukes (the part that catches in the ground). Flukes were more triangle-shaped (Figure 106) until the early to mid-1700s, and later became more round or spade-shaped (Figure 107). Earlier anchors had straight arms and later anchors had curved arms.

Rope anchor line was used until around 1820, when iron chain became popular. Yet there are exceptions to this rule. For instance, the *San Jose*, which wrecked in the Florida Keys in 1733, was excavated and found to have an anchor with chain. It's possible that this anchor was from another vessel. Yet the *HMS Mermaid*, which wrecked in 1760, was excavated recently and also had chain at the wreck site. It is difficult to determine when anchor chain was first used. The log of an English ship in 1686 mentions being held fast by her "chaine." It is possible that "chaine" meant rope in that instance.

Stud-link chain, in which the links were separated in the middle to prevent kinking, was patented in 1819 and was predominant by the late 1800s.

Anchors that used rope line will have a large ring at the top.

I've heard from reputable sources that bronze anchors have been found off the coast of Central America. Some of the Manila galleons may have used these anchors, which were made in the Far East.

Rigging

Rigging is the ropes, chains, and other gear used to support, position, and control the masts and sails of a vessel. Rope rigging was used exclusively up until the 1830s and 1840s, when iron rigging began to appear on some vessels. Steel rigging was produced after 1860. Nineteenth-century iron and steel rigging was usually wrapped around a rope core.

Despite advances in rigging, many vessels continued using rope rigging up to the present.

Figure 104: A large 19th-century wooden stock anchor. AUTHOR.

Figure 105: A typical mid-19th- to mid-20th-century iron stock anchor. AUTHOR.

Figure 106: A 17th-century anchor on the Jupiter Inlet treasure wreck site. Notice the triangle-shaped flukes. DON KREE.

Figure 107: A late 18th- or early 19th-century anchor found off Lauderdale-by-the-Sea. Notice the more rounded flukes. AUTHOR.

Figure 108: Some wood and iron deadeyes and other tackle from the wrecks of the vessels *Protector* (1877), *Oh Kim Soon* (1897), and a ship believed to be the *Georgie* (1894), all lost off Florida. AUTHOR.

Wood

In Florida, it is not unusual to find some of the ship's timbers still intact if they are buried under the ballast pile or surrounding sand. If buried, the keel, lower ribs (framing), and planking can survive the ravages of the wood-eating teredo worm and the elements, while exposed wood is destroyed within a few years. Vessels sunk in fresh water, such as the St. Johns River, can become covered with silt or mud and remain intact for many years.

The wood can help date a wreck and help determine where she was built. Laboratories such as the Forest Products Lab, in Madison, Wisconsin, will analyze wood samples for a fee. Using wood alone to answer questions about a wreck can be misleading, however, because timber from all parts of the world was shipped regularly to other countries.

Most Spanish ships built before 1565 had oak or pine frames and pine planking. After 1565, Spanish law required that vessels over 120 tons be built of all oak because it was the longest-lasting material.

Some Portuguese who sailed to Brazil in 1565 used ships built in India, so expect to find native wood like teak on such a wreck. However, this is not a definite determiner, because the Dutch and English also built ships in India in the 1600s. The *Margarita*, which sank in 1622, was built in Europe of all oak, while the *Atocha*, which sank at the same time, was built in Havana, Cuba, and had oak frames and planking of mahogany, which is native to Cuba.

American ships of the 17th century experimented with many of the new woods found on this continent, and by 1700 were familiar with the types that held up the longest. American ships before 1830 were built mainly of oak, with live oak the wood of choice. Live oak lasted 40 to 50 years, whereas white oak decayed within a few years and red oak in even less time. Other woods were nearly as good as live oak. Early Maine vessels with larch frames and white cedar planks, and Chesapeake Bay vessels with mulberry or laurel frames and juniper planks, could easily last 30 or more years.

A U.S. Navy frigate built in 1794 was made of the following materials: The frames were of live oak and red cedar (which also had a long life span). The stern post, all the stern frames, the upper piece of stem, nearly all the frame, the first, second, and third futtocks (rib pieces), three-fourths of the top-timber, stanchions, counter-timbers, bow-timbers, hawse-pieces, knight-heads, breast-hooks, partners for masts and knees, and floor timbers were all of live oak. One-fourth of the top timbers, the half top timbers, and half counter-timbers were of red cedar. The keel, keelson, beams, ledges, carlings, plank for the side, bottom, ceiling, deck-plank under the guns, dead-woods, lower piece stem and wales were of white oak. The decks were of Carolina pitch pine, and the trunnels (pegs) were of locust.

In John Edye's book of English naval vessel construction (*Calculations Relating to the Equipment, Displacement, etc. of Ships and Vessels of War*, published in 1832) he lists the timber used in constructing these vessels: English oak, Dantzic oak, African teak, Indian teak (Malabar teak was the heaviest, and Rangoon teak the lightest), Indian mast peon, cedar, larch, Riga fir, New England fir, elm, beech, and ash.

After 1830, oak became scarce in the United States, and other woods were substituted. Birch, maple, and red oak were substituted in framing, and yellow pine in planking.

Elm planking on oak frames most likely indicates a European-built ship, since elm was scarce in the United States. Some British warships had an elm keel and strake (a single line of planking extending along the hull of a ship from stem to stern) and oak trunnels. British or other European vessels usually will have oak trunnels, and American vessels will have locust trunnels.

During the Napoleonic wars, Britain tried various soft woods in ship construction due to the scarcity of oak, but those ships lasted only a few years.

Sheathing

Sheathing was put on vessels to ward off the damaging teredo worm. Since the worm thrived in warm, tropical waters, sheathing was needed more on vessels in those waters than on vessels in cold northern waters.

Before metal sheathing became popular, a thin sacrificial planking was sometimes used on top of the original planking. The teredo worm attacked the top layer, leaving alone the planking underneath. There was usually a bed of cloth, or tar and hair, placed between the two layers of planking. Felt or pitch found between the planks most likely indicates an American or British ship, and horsehair and pitch a Spanish or Portuguese vessel.

Lead sheathing was used on some Spanish Navy vessels as early as

Figure 109: This patent stamp "Muntz's Patent #22" was found on a piece of composite sheathing on a wreck off Hillsboro Beach, dating it post-1832. AUTHOR.

1514, and on some English merchant ships after 1553. The first British naval vessel sheathed in lead was the *Phoenix*, in 1670. The British Navy soon stopped using lead, however, because of the galvanic reaction between the lead and the iron fastenings, such as the rudder pintles. The British Navy tried a composition of metals on the vessel *Sheerness* in 1696, but it was unsuccessful. The Spanish stopped using lead for a time in the late 16th century. Some Portuguese vessels started using lead sheathing after 1580.

Copper sheathing was first used by the British Navy in 1758 (another source says 1761) on the 32-gun frigate *Alarm*, and again in 1764 on the 24-gun *Dolphin*. There was still a problem with galvanic reaction between the copper and the ironwork. The Navy tried applying a canvas or a felt with hot pine tar before the sheathing was put on, and this helped reduce the reaction.

The problem was finally resolved by using copper instead of iron fastenings in the underwater portion of the ship. This became standard practice after 1783. Between 1776 and 1785, nearly all British naval vessels were coppered. The *HMS Mermaid*, which sank off the Bahamas on January 6, 1760, was recently excavated, and was found to have copper sheathing. She was built in 1749, so it would be interesting to know if she was coppered before the *Alarm* in 1758.

By 1781, the French Navy was partially copper sheathing its vessels. The Spanish continued using lead sheathing until around 1810. Copper eventually was used by all naval vessels sailing in Caribbean waters since it not only helped impede the teredo worm, but also improved speed and performance and reduced growth on the hull. Lead and other metals discouraged the worm, but not to the extent copper and composites did.

It wasn't until the late 1700s that merchant vessels were being coppered, and usually only the large vessels, since it was an expensive addition. The better American schooners probably weren't coppered until the mid-1790s. Composite metal sheathing was introduced in the late 1820s, and was being used after 1830 as the Industrial Revolution progressed.

A wreck with no sheathing does not necessarily mean the ship wrecked before sheathing was used, since some vessels were not sheathed for lack of money, scarcity of material, or any number of other factors. Also, until around 1822, many ships in America continued using the familiar lime-and-tallow coating applied to the hull of the boat in place of sheathing.

Fastenings

Check the nails, spikes, fastenings, and trunnels. Are they handmade or machine-made? Are they of iron, copper, bronze, alloy, or wood? These can help date a wreck.

The iron forelock bolt has been found on the 15th- and 16th-century Spanish vessels. This was an iron bolt that had a flat piece of iron heated

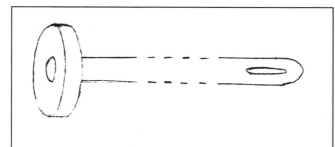

Figure 110: Iron "forelock" bolt, early Spanish (1400s – 1500s). Elongated hole at bottom is for locking wedge. AUTHOR.

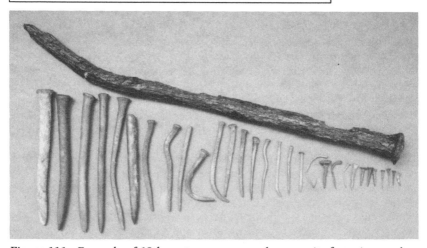

Figure 111: Example of 19th-century copper and composite fastenings and sheathing nails found off local wrecks, along with a preserved iron spike from a local wreck. AUTHOR.

and wrapped around the bolt to make a head (Figure 110). If a wreck has many of these, there's a good chance she is an early Spanish vessel. Only a few were found on the *Atocha* (1622), so they were probably being replaced by this time by other types of fastenings.

Until the later 1700s, iron and wood fastenings were the rule, though small amounts of copper or bronze fastenings were sometimes used. Copper fastenings were becoming popular in the later 1700s, and were the only type of fastening the British Navy used in the underwater portion of its ships after 1783. Copper-alloy fastenings were popular starting in the early 1800s, especially after the late 1820s (Figure 111). Lathe-turned trunnels came into use after 1830.

Construction

If part of the wooden structure of a wreck has survived, this structure can help determine the time period during which the vessel was built, and even her nationality.

Some good references on ship construction are listed in the "Suggested Reading" section. Anyone searching for a particular shipwreck should become familiar with that ship's type of construction. I'll briefly describe the types of construction likely to be found on a wreck off Florida.

Figure 112 shows the three types of framing that can be found on most vessels: scarfed frame, chock frame, or butted frame. Most ships that wrecked in Florida before 1715 will have a scarfed frame. Such a frame required large timbers, which were becoming scarce after 1715. Chock frame construction, in use after 1713, didn't require as large a

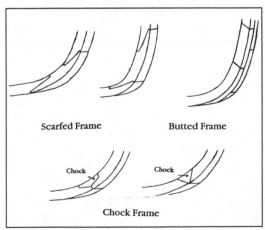

Figure 112: Examples of frames. AUTHOR.

timber as scarfed frame construction did. Chock frames were not as strong as scarfed frames, though, and scarfed framing continued when the materials were available. The method of butting the frames was first used in the late 1700s, and it became popular after 1811. Builders could use much smaller timbers than in scarf framing, yet build a stronger

323

frame than in chock framing.

Measuring the frame spacing can give a clue about a ship's nationality. Different countries used different units of measure. Are they in inches or feet, or in another unit of measure?

Checking the saw marks on the wood may provide another clue. Wood cut with a pit saw will have saw marks cut at an angle. In the early 1700s, sawmills began using the vertical band saw, which made straight, vertical saw marks. Circular saw marks show up after 1840. Figure 113 shows cross sections of these three wood cuts.

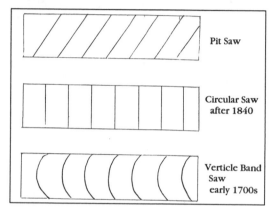

Figure 113: Cross section of three wood cuts.
AUTHOR.

Very large timbers were cut with an adze. Trunnels (also called treenails) were used as fasteners. A hole was drilled into the wood to be fastened and the trunnel was driven into the hole, fastening one piece of wood to another. Before 1830, trunnels were octagon-shaped and hatchet-roughed; after 1830, most were round and lathe-turned, though the rough octagon ones did continue in use after that date.

England was using iron in knees (braces) and straps on ships in the late 1700s. Between 1820 and 1860, almost all vessels constructed with iron were built in England. The British Navy tried iron knees, but went back to using wood knees on her wooden vessels in the early 1800s because they absorbed the shock from a cannon ball much better than iron did. The 1,051-ton ship *Columbia*, built in 1846, was the first American ship with iron knees and straps.

In the later 1800s, many sailing ships were being built with an iron frame and wood planking (composite construction). Teak was favored for much of the planking on these composite ships.

Iron ships disappeared after 1900, when steel replaced iron. The insurer Lloyds of London didn't approve steel for ship construction until after 1877. Until then, steel was too brittle for construction use. Underwater archaeologists and divers have found that a wreck built of iron seems to last much longer underwater than a wreck built of steel.

Riveted ships were popular until World War II, when the welded seam replaced the rivet. Welded ships were being built as early as the period between the two world wars.

Glass and China

Bottles are one of the best dating materials on a wreck site (Figure 114). Some good books on bottles and how to date them are listed in the "Suggested Reading" section.

English and Dutch wrecks seem to have carried many bottles (Figures 115, 116 and 117), whereas Spanish vessels seem to have carried very little glassware, using clay olive jars instead (Figures 118, 119 and 120).

The Manila galleons started to arrive in the New World after 1565. Part of their cargo usually consisted of porcelain china from the Far East. A wreck found off Florida with this china on board would have to have wrecked after 1565 and most likely would be a Spanish ship.

Pottery

As with glass, this is also an excellent dating material. Some good reference books on pottery are listed in the "Suggested Reading" section.

A wreck containing Indian pottery might indicate an early Spanish wreck site. Many Indian settlements were wiped out by the Spanish not long after their initial conquest of the New World, and Indian pottery became scarce.

Ballast

Most sailing ships had stone ballast. English naval ships from the late 1600s to the 1800s used iron ballast in bars, because they were easily shifted. Most of the Spanish wrecks of the 1715 and 1733 Fleets seem to have the same type of round granite river rock.

If a wreck contains a type of ballast particular to a certain part of the world, this might help identify the wreck's nationality. But ballast alone is not a reliable dating material, since it was loaded and unloaded in different ports.

Coins

Coins are always a great find since they are easily datable. Some excellent references on coins are listed in the "Suggested Reading" section.

The first Spanish mint in the New World was established in Mexico City and began producing coins in 1536. The short-lived mint in Santo Domingo, in what is now now the Dominican Republic, appeared at this time also. The Spaniards established other mints soon after, though some of these were also short-lived. The majority of Spanish shipwreck coins found off Florida to date are from the mints of Mexico, Lima, Potosi, and Bogota.

Most of these early minted coins are called *cobs*, possibly derived from the old English word cob, meaning a "small mass of something." Silver cobs were first coined in Mexico around 1556 and were produced until 1733. Gold cobs were first coined at the Bogota mint in 1621 or

Figure 114: Alex Okinczyc with a small portion of his vast collection of olive jars, bottles, and shipwreck artifacts, all recovered from the bottom of Key West Harbor. AUTHOR.

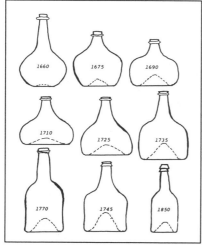

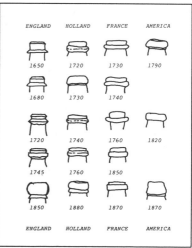

Figure 115: Evolution of English wine bottles (after Hume, 1963). From the globular shape of the mid-1600s, through the squats and mallets of the late 1600s and the early 1700s, to the cylinders of the mid- to late-1700s and the 3-piece cylinder of the mid-1800s. *PLUS ULTRA* NEWSLETTER, VOL. 7, NO. 3, 1989. DRAWINGS BY ERNIE RICHARDS.

Figure 116: Progression of lips and string-rings on wine bottles (after Dumbrell, 1983). The style of lipping and the type of laid-on ring is useful in determining the age and nationality of bottles and bottle fragments. Shipwrecks dating from 1650 yield lips for study. *PLUS ULTRA* NEWSLETTER, VOL. 7, NO. 3, 1989. DRAWINGS BY ERNIE RICHARDS.

Figure 117: Some 19th-century "Case Gin" bottles, an 18th-century Dutch "onion" bottle, and a 19th-century Schnapps bottle. AUTHOR.

1622. The cobs were cut from the end of a silver or gold bar, and clipped, chiseled, or filed until the correct weight was established. These blanks, or *planchets*, were then reheated and hand stamped between two dies using a hammer. A lower die was placed in a hole in an anvil, and the planchet placed on top of this die. Another die was then placed on top of the planchet and struck with a hammer. The process often resulted in only a partial imprint on the cob. Sometimes a die would break, and a die of another demomination would be substituted. I have seen 4-real pieces that had been struck with an 8-real die, and vice versa. No two cobs are the same shape.

Silver cobs, or *reals*, came in denominations of 8, 4, 2, 1, and 1/2 reals. Though 1/4-real coins were minted, they are very rare. The Mexico mint between 1536 and 1572 also produced some 3-reals, though they are also very rare. The 8-real coin was referred to as a "piece of eight."

Gold cobs, or *escudos*, came in denominations of 8, 4, 2, and 1 (Figures 121 and 122). The 8-escudo coin was called a doubloon. The "pillar" type of silver coin began being minted in 1732, and "bust" type of silver coin in 1772. Spanish coinage dominated much of the world trade for a time, and was the principal coinage used in this hemisphere up to the early 19th century. It was still accepted as supplemental currency in the United States until the mid-19th century.

Other Dating Material

There are many other items that could help date a wreck. A few are: navigational instruments such as a quadrant, octant, sextant (Figure 123) or astrolabe, and dividers (Figures 125); religious medals (Figure 126); clay

Figure 118: Olive jar shapes, by period (after Goggin). *PLUS ULTRA* NEWSLETTER, VOL. 7, NO. 3, 1989. DRAWINGS BY ERNIE RICHARDS.

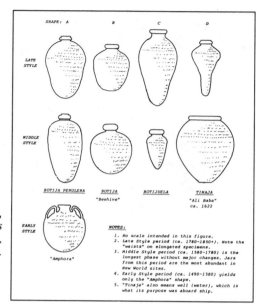

Figure 119: Olive jar lip/mouth details (after Goggin). *PLUS ULTRA* NEWSLETTER, VOL. 7, NO. 3, 1989. DRAWINGS BY ERNIE RICHARDS.

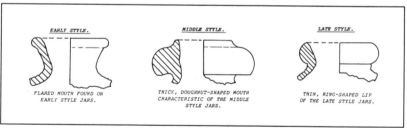

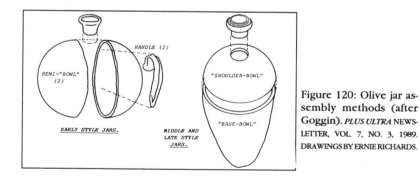

Figure 120: Olive jar assembly methods (after Goggin). *PLUS ULTRA* NEWSLETTER, VOL. 7, NO. 3, 1989. DRAWINGS BY ERNIE RICHARDS.

Figure 121 (top) and 122: Gold escudo set (Mexican Mint) — Photos show both sides of 8-, 4-, 2-, and 1-escudo pieces. Recovered from the *San Roman* (1715) *Fleet.* ERNIE RICHARDS.

pipes (Figure 127); military buttons; and armament such as pistols (Figure 128), swords, crossbows and guns (Figure 129). The navigational instruments are sometimes dated or have a maker's mark or name inscribed on them. They can be used for dating because they were used during certain periods. For instance, Hadley's octant was invented in 1731, and the sextant was an improvement on the octant some years later.

An early Spanish wreck might have carried gold Indian sculpture or statues. After the Spanish established their mints for producing coins in the New World, all Indian artifacts made of precious metals were melted down for use in coinage.

Figure 123: A 19th-century brass sextant inscribed W. Hogg, London. Found off Fort Lauderdale by John Noyes. AUTHOR.

Figure 124: Portuguese cast brass mariner's astrolabe recovered in 1985 from the pilot's chest in the wreck of the *Atocha*. One of the finest examples recovered. Note the date 1605 on the bottom. CHRISTIE'S, NEW YORK.

Figure 125: 18th-century brass dividers found by Jack Pennel off Palm Beach County. Note that the steel points have long since disintegrated. AUTHOR.

Figure 126: A religious pendant recovered from the wreck of the *Nuestra Señora de la Regla.* ERNIE RICHARDS.

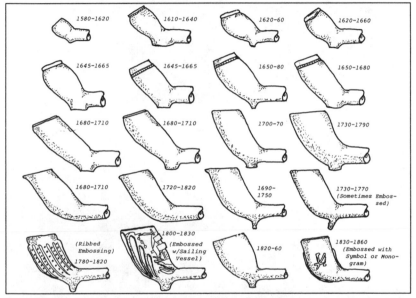

Figure 127: Evolution of English clay tobacco pipe bowl shapes. *PLUS ULTRA* NEWSLETTER, VOL. 8, NO. 1, 1990. DRAWINGS BY ERNIE RICHARDS.

Studying a wreck's construction and the various items found with it can give you a pretty good idea of its age and nationality. Here is how experts in one case used such clues to deduce information about a wreck. The Marine Archaeological Council, Inc., under the guidance of marine archaeologist Peter Throckmorton, excavated a wreck off Hillsboro Beach, Florida, in 1985. The wreck lay in the surf zone, and only about two days of work could be done. I worked with the group to piece together what was found:

• Glass: Though there were only a few fragments, two appeared free-blown and of a shape dating around 1830.

Figure 128: Author with coral-encrusted pistol from the wreck of the *Nieves* (1715). AUTHOR.

Figure 129: Author's daughter with the wooden stock of a Spanish arquebus or harquebus recovered in 1975 from the *Atocha*. AUTHOR.

• Pottery: There were only a few fragments, one of an olive jar dating post-1780.

• Fastenings: Iron fastenings seemed to be to inch/feet specifications. There were handmade copper fastenings dating to the early 1800s, as well as many copper sheathing nails of different types. The fact that no machine-made fastenings were found helped date the wreck as an early 19th-century vessel.

• Sheathing: Though the sheathing had deteriorated, traces of copper were found.

• Wood: Oak frames and planks with locust trunnels were used.

• Construction: The hull was approximately 80 feet long. Frame spacing was 18 inches. The number of sheathing nail holes and their spacing were counted on one of the planks, enabling us to conclude that the ship was refastened (received new sheathing) six times. Since most vessels were refastened every four years, this vessel would be approximately 25 years old. Trunnels were hand-finished.

From all this information, Throckmorton concluded that the vessel was most likely a 170-ton, 25-year-old New England-built merchant ship which sank around 1830.

Figure 129A: The late Peter Throckmorton, known as the father of marine archaeology, shown in Broward County teaching an archaeology class. AUTHOR.

Appendix D: Artifact Conservation (Metal)

Before I explain the process, I would like to make it clear that if you do not intend to preserve an object, especially iron, don't take it from the water. If it's not treated, it will only deteriorate. Though it does deteriorate in salt water, once it is removed from the water, the effects of deterioration increase rapidly.

Once you have removed a metal or wood object from the ocean, keep it wet until you start the treatment process. Do not chip off any encrustation until you are ready for treatment, since it helps keep the artifact from deteriorating.

The chemicals mentioned in this chapter can be obtained from a local chemical supply store.

Metals

Keep iron objects covered in a 5 percent solution of sodium carbonate until they can be preserved. Other metals can be kept in saltwater or fresh water, though fresh water is preferable.

Metal objects from the sea, with the exception of gold and lead, need treatment to remain intact (Figures 130 and 131). Electrolysis, which produces an oxygen-reduction reaction, is the most common and easiest way to stabilize them. You can treat only one type of metal at a time.

You will need an anode, a tank to hold the artifact and anode, a power source, and an electrolyte solution. The tank should be large enough for the solution to cover the artifact completely. For large objects such as anchors, you may be able to obtain a used storage tank from a local chemical company.

The anode can be of any metal, but stainless steel is the least

Figure 130: Cannon awaiting preservation. AUTHOR.

Figure 131: A cannon from the 1715 fleet on display by a municipality. An example of what happens to an iron cannon from the sea if left untreated. AUTHOR.

expensive and lasts longer than most metals. The most common electrolytes are sodium hydroxide (lye) and sodium carbonate. Use caution when handling sodium hydroxide, as it is poisonous and can cause burns. It is found at the grocery store in the form of crystal drain opener. It is not compatible with fiberglass (as sodium carbonate is), so if you have a fiberglass tank, coat it heavily with coal tar epoxy. Coat a metal tank, too, because it tends to become an anode itself and may leak.

Set the tank near a power source in a place where it will not be disturbed. Put the artifact in the tank. A heavy object such as a cannon should be set on pieces of wood which are cut to hold it in place(Figures

Figure 132: Cannon being set up in a preservation tank. AUTHOR.

132 and 133). A cannon also should be placed so the muzzle is elevated, to prevent any gasses from accumulating inside (Figure 134). The anodes should surround the artifact, but not touch it, as this would short-circuit the system (Figure 135). The muzzle of a cannon should

Figure 133: Two huge Civil War-era cannon being set up for preservation. STATE OF FLORIDA, DIVISION OF HISTORICAL RESOURCES.

be cleaned out (Figure 136), and an anode placed inside. A stainless steel speargun shaft is a good anode for the inside of a cannon. To prevent the shaft from touching the inside of the muzzle, wrap it in insulated wire or put it inside a PVC pipe that has holes drilled through it.

Connect the positive leads from your DC power source to your anodes, and the negative to your artifact, but do not turn the power on yet. If the artifact is encrusted, carefully chip away a portion to attach the wire to the metal. Electronic supply stores stock many sizes of clips you can use for this connection. With larger artifacts, however, you might have to improvise. For instance, cannon balls can be put on a board that has bolts to hold the balls in place (Figure 137). The negative lead is connected to the bolts, which are in contact with the cannon balls.

Once the power connections are established, fill your tank with fresh water until the artifact is covered. Deionized water is best. Add the electrolyte until you reach the ideal pH of 11, which can be checked with litmus paper or a pH meter. Then turn on the power. You don't need much power: 3 or 4 amps will stabilize a 7-foot cannon. If you run at a high amperage, the anodes will deteriorate much faster.

If you see bubbles coming to the surface, the system is working. If not, check for a short. Clean the tank and rotate the artifact 90 degrees in the middle of the treatment process.

The encrustation will begin to come off within a few hours or a few weeks, depending on the size of the artifact. When this happens,

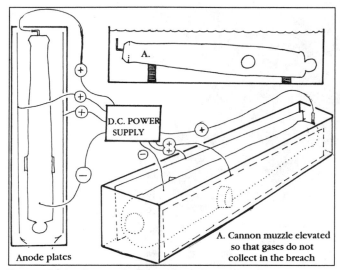

Figure 134: An illustration of how to set up a cannon for preservation. STATE OF FLORIDA, DIVISION OF HISTORICAL RESOURCES.

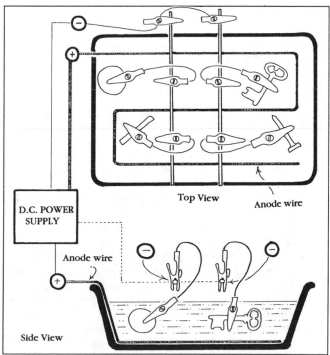

Figure 135: An illustration of how to set up small artifacts for preservation. STATE OF FLORIDA, DIVISION OF HISTORICAL RESOURCES.

Figure 136: A cannon being pre-pared for preservation. AUTHOR.

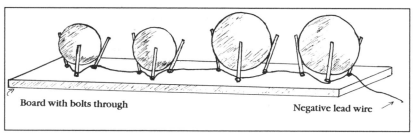

Board with bolts through   Negative lead wire

Figure 137: An illustration of how to set up cannon balls for preservation. AUTHOR.

turn off the power, remove the artifact from the solution, and take off as much of the remaining encrustation as you can without damaging the artifact. Return it to the tank and continue the electrolysis.

You should constantly monitor your treatment tank since a loss of power or an electrical short could turn your artifact into an anode itself. If the tank is running properly, a slight bubbling should be seen on the surface. If the bubbling is intense, you have too much current running into the system and the anodes will deteriorate much too fast.

The larger an artifact is, the longer the time needed to stabilize it. Iron objects will need a much longer treatment time than metals such as copper, bronze, or silver. There is no set rule for how long treatment will take. Silver coins usually take one to several days. Cannon balls, depending on size, could take two to 12 months. A small iron cannon might take six months to a year, and large iron cannon and anchors might take one to two years before becoming stabilized. Two iron objects of the same size might require different treatment times if one

Figure 138 (left): Author with ship's tackle before preservation. AUTHOR.

Figure 139 (above): Same ship's tackle after preservation. AUTHOR.

of them is of a different iron compound than the other. (If you have finished the process and, soon after, the object begins to rust again, you need to provide additional treatment.

When the artifact is done being treated (stabilized), the electrolyte will have penetrated the metal itself and will have to be removed from the artifact. Turn off the power. Drain the tank, making sure you dispose of the electrolyte properly, and clean it. Set up the artifact and anodes as before, and add fresh water only. Turn up the power, if possible, until you see some slight bubbling. Without the electrolyte, more voltage is required. This process will take several hours to several days depending on the size of the object.

After the treatment process, clean the artifact with a stiff nylon brush, being careful not to scratch it. If it is iron, don't let it dry, or rust will form. If the artifact is wrought iron, remove any soft spots in the metal with a pick.

While the artifact is damp, brush on a tannic acid solution in the following proportions: 850 milliliters water, 150 milliliters isopropyl alcohol, and 200 grams powdered tannic acid. Add the acid slowly while mixing to prevent it from clumping. After coating, let it dry. It will turn a blue-black color. Give it several coats until you achieve a universal blue-black color over the entire surface. Pre-mixed tannin-based solutions such as Zintex, used in the auto restoration field, are available from H.C. Fastener Co., Alvarado, Texas.

If the artifact will be kept inside, no more treatment is needed. If it will be outside, however, it will need extra protection from rain, snow, and humidity. Brush on several coats of primer, followed by several coats of outside epoxy or acrylic.

Appendix E: Rights To Wrecks

There has been much controversy surrounding the issue of who owns shipwrecks. More often than not it is because of "treasure," not historical importance, that this controversy has come about. Historically, on one side of the controversy have been the archaeologists and government, and on the other side have been treasure salvors and wreck divers. Both sides have their valid points, and both can be blamed for mistakes in the past. There is no reason why archaeologists and treasure salvors can't work together. Both could learn from each other, and the public would become the benefactor of their combined efforts.

Anyone interested in shipwrecks should be aware of the several laws that govern underwater archaeological sites. This section will acquaint you with the laws governing sites and your responsibilities should you discover a shipwreck.

The Federal Abandoned Shipwreck Act

In 1988 the Abandoned Shipwreck Act (43 U.S.C. 2101) was signed into law. The purpose of the Act was to vest title to certain abandoned shipwrecks that are located in state waters to the respective states, and to clarify that the states have management authority over those abandoned shipwrecks. Shipwrecks that fall under the Abandoned Shipwreck Act are those that are embedded in the submerged lands of a state, or embedded in coralline formations protected by a state; or those on submerged lands of a state and which are included in or determined eligible for inclusion in the National Register of Historic Places. A shipwreck can be eligible for the National Register if it is associated with events or persons significant to our history; or if it represents distinctive characteristics of a type, period, or method of construction; or if it has yielded, or is likely to yield, information important in prehistory or history.

The Florida Historical Resources Act

Florida's antiquities law (Chapter 267, Florida Statutes), and administrative rules (Chapters 1A-31 and 1A-32) govern the use of archaeological and historical resources located on state-owned lands. These include historical monuments, Indian sites, abandoned settlements, sunken or abandoned ships, engineering works, treasure troves, artifacts, and other objects relating to the history and culture of the state. Submerged lands that are state-owned include the bottoms of navigable streams and rivers, lakes, bays, and the adjacent bottoms of the Gulf of Mexico and the Atlantic Ocean. Florida's waters extend from the shoreline three marine leagues (nine geographical miles) in the Gulf of Mexico and three geographical miles in the Atlantic Ocean. Passed in 1967, the antiquities law is administered by the Division of Historical

Resources, Bureau of Archaeological Research, which has its office in Tallahassee. Excavation of archaeological or historical remains on submerged state lands requires a permit or contract from the Division and may require dredge and fill permits from the Florida Department of Environmental Regulation and the U.S. Army Corps of Engineers, as well as a form of consent from the Florida Department of Natural Resources.

Archaeological Research Permits

A permit to conduct survey and excavation in state waters may be obtained from the Division of Historical Resources under Rule 1A-32 of the Florida Statutes. Permits normally are issued to scientific and educational institutions such as museums, universities, and colleges, or to reputable organizations such as historical or archaeological societies. The permit requires that the permitee have the necessary professional archaeological expertise to perform proper field research, analysis, interpretation, conservation, and reporting. All materials collected under a research permit remain public property to be administered by the state, but may be placed on temporary or permanent loan to the permitted organization or institution for the purpose of further study, curation, or display.

Exploration and Salvage Contracts

Under Section 1A-31 of the Florida Administrative Code, the Division of Historical Resources is authorized to enter into contracts for the exploration and salvage of abandoned materials on state-owned submerged lands. These are not leases of state lands, but contracts to perform certain activities under the supervision of the state.

An Exploration Contract may be granted for a period of one year for the purpose of conducting a marine remote sensing survey to explore for historical period shipwrecks in an area up to a maximum of 18 square miles of submerged bottom. The fee for an exploration contract is $600. No salvage of material from wrecks located during the course of exploration under this type of contract is permitted without explicit permission from the Division and appropriate permits and/or consents from the Departments of Environmental Regulation and Natural Resources.

It is intended that the explorer, with no disturbance to the seabed, attempt to electronically locate magnetic or acoustical anomalies that may delineate the presence of historic shipwrecks, which can then be evaluated. Archaeological guidelines governing exploration activities include procedures for positioning and deploying survey instruments, recording of data, and reporting of such data to the Division. The entire contract area is to be explored during the term of the contract, and all wrecks or other archaeological remains are to be recorded in a log and on a chart so that this data may be incorporated into the Division's site files. Exploration contracts may be renewed after one year pending the contractor's performance.

A Salvage Contract may occasionally be granted to recover materials from a shipwreck either discovered in the course of an Exploration Contract or from a previously known or accidentally discovered site. Salvage contracts are only entered into by the State with commercial firms licensed to do business in Florida and who have demonstrated the experience and capability to conduct careful and conscientious work on an underwater site. A determination by state archaeologists must be made as to whether the site in question warrants commercial salvage as opposed to archaeological research or simple non-disturbance. This decision depends on whether the site is threatened by development or natural forces, or whether the site is likely to contain materials that make commercial recovery economically feasible. In any case, a contract applicant must conduct a detailed survey, which may include remote sensing of the site in question and an on-site inspection will be made by state personnel prior to determination of a site's eligibility for salvage.

A salvage contract usually is executed for one year with a fee of $1,200 and an option for renewal pending compliance with contract guidelines. These guidelines include rigourous archaeological controls and require that the salvor furnish funding for the employment by the State of a qualified marine archaeologist to actively participate in and to supervise the recovery of materials under the contract. The archaeologist also is responsible for insuring that proper recording and reporting procedures culminate in a professional quality report of the results of the contract work.

Artifacts and other materials recovered during the course of a salvage contract are to be given professional conservation treatment in approved laboratory facilitites, either at the expense of the salvor or in conjuction with the State Research and Conservation Laboratory in Tallahassee. At the conclusion of analysis and conservation treatment, 75 to 80 percent of these materials may be awarded to the salvor in compensation for his efforts and performance. The State generally retains the remainder of salvaged materials for research collections, museum specimens, or for public display.

Archaeological Reserve Areas

The State of Florida has set aside four Reserve Areas for the purpose of preserving a cross-sectional and representative sample of underwater cultural resources. Reserve areas are reserved exclusively for scientific investigations and may not be used for the commerical salvage of historical and archaeological resources. These areas, which occupy approximately 8.4% of state-owned coastal waters are described as follows:

1. On the Florida East Coast from 30 degrees North Latitude as a northern boundary to Latitude 29 degrees 40 minutes North as the southern boundary and extending seaward to the territorial limits of the State (St. Augustine to Matanzas Inlet area).

2. On the Florida East Coast from Latitude 27 degrees 10 minutes North as a northern boundary to Latitude 26 degrees 46.5 minutes North as a southern boundary extending seaward to the territorial limits of the State (between St. Lucie Inlet and North Lake Worth Inlet).

3. Entire area of the present John Pennekamp Coral Reef State Park.

4. On the Florida Gulf Coast from Longitude 84 degrees 10 minutes West as the eastern boundary to Longitude 85 degrees 30 minutes West as the western boundary to the territorial limits of the State (from St. Marks Lighthouse to just west of Cape San Blas).

For Further State Information

If you wish to search for a wreck or have found a wreck site, contact the state at this address:

Division of Historical Resources
(Bureau of Archaeological Research)
R.A. Gray Building
500 S. Bronough Street
Tallahassee, Fl 32399-0250

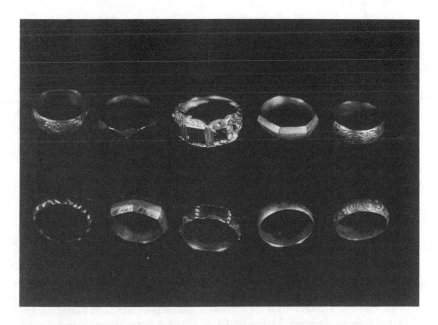

Figure 140: Gold rings found on the *Nieves* site (1715). ERNIE RICHARDS.

Bibliography

After each wreck in the listing section I have listed the source or sources by number, which will correspond with the following sources. * Denotes late-corrected sources which are out of alphabetical order.

1. *Automated Wreck and Obstruction Information System.* U.S. Department of Commerce, National Oceanic and Atmospheric Administration (NOAA). Rockville, Md.: July 1986.
2. Alden, Caroll S. *Lawrence Kearny, Sailor Diplomat.* Princeton, N.J.: Princeton University Press, 1936.
3. Allen, Gardner W. *Our Navy & The West Indian Pirates.* Essex Institute, 1929.
4. Anon. *A Geographical Description of the Coasts, Harbors, and Sea Ports of the West Indies.* Publisher unknown, 1739.
5. Arnade, Charles. *The Siege of St. Augustine in 1702.* Gainesville: University of Florida Monographs, No. 3. Summer of 1959.
6. Baker, William Avery. *A Maritime History of Bath, Maine, and the Kennebec River Region*, Vol. I and II. Bath: Marine Research Society of Bath, 1973.
7. Barcia Carballido y Zúñiga, Andres Gonzales de. *Barcia's chronological history of the continent of Florida ...from the year 1512, in which Ponce de León discovered Florida, until the year 1722*, trans. Anthony Kerrigan. Gainesville: University of Florida Press, 1951.
8. Beare, Nikki. *Pirates, Pineapples & People.* Miami: Atlantic Publishing Co., 1966.
9. Berman, Bruce D. *Encyclopedia of American Shipwrecks.* Boston: The Mariners Press Inc., 1973.
10. Bonet, Walter A. Cordona. *Shipwrecks in Puerto Rico's History*, Vol. 1 (1502-1650). San Juan, Puerto Rico: Self-published, 1989.
11. Browne, Jefferson B. *Key West — The Old & New.* Originally published in 1912 by The Record Company, St. Augustine. Gainesville: University of Florida Presses, 1973.
12. Cabell, James and Alfred Hanna. *The St. Johns.* New York: Rinehart Publishing, 1943.
13. Clowes, William Laird. *The Royal Navy, A History From the Earliest Times to the Present*, Vol. 1-4. London: 1898. Reprinted by AMS Press Inc., New York, 1966.
14. Congressional Information Service (CIS). *United States Serial Set Index*, Part 1-11, and *Records of the National Archives.* Washington, D.C.
From the National Archives are selected records of the U.S. Coast Guard (Record Group 26); the U.S. Customs Service (RG 36); the Bureau of Marine Inspection and Navigation (RG 41); and reports of the Steamboat Inspection Service. Particular records used include Collector of Cus-

toms Reports of Casualty 1873-1914; Life-Saving Stations Reports of Assistance Rendered, Eighth District 1881-1914; Light Stations Reports of Shipwrecks, Alligator Reef, 1874-1914; Report of the Apalachicola Collector of Customs, June 30, 1848 (Lighthouse Letters, Series P, Vol. 1849, p.119); Maritime Disasters off the Florida Coast, from Jan. 1, 1869, to June 30, 1879, (Life-Saving Letters Sent, Miscellaneous, Vol. 3, pp. 404-415); Table of casualties to vessels, Dec. 30, 1910–Nov. 22, 1918, at Gilbert's Bar House of Refuge; Letters received by the Secretary of the Treasury in 1870 from Collectors of Customs at particular ports reporting on wrecks of U.S. and Confederate vessels (RG 56, Records of the Cotton and Abandoned Property Division, File 1626); Abstracts of Shipwrecks near light stations in the 7th and 8th Lighthouse Districts, (1872-1873); Accidents and casualties to vessels 8th Coast Guard District (Florida House of Refuge), July 1, 1906-June 30, 1916; Annual Reports of the U.S. Life-Saving Service, 1876-1914; Merchant Vessels of the United States (annual volumes which, beginning in 1906, listed all casualties to American vessels).

The U.S. Serial Set Index also has records of the Merchant Vessels of the United States. Also used were selected "Reports of the Commissioner of Navigation" (annual reports which, beginning in 1903, listed all casualties to American vessels); selected records from the American State Papers, including a letter from the Secretary of Commerce and Labor on Losses of American Merchant Vessels at Sea, etc., Jan. 15, 1904; a report by Mr. Hubbard, April 17, 1840, in the U.S. Senate, about the steamer *John McLean*; a statement of vessels wrecked in the district of Key West and from other districts, from June 30, 1847, to June 30, 1848; Construction of Frigates Under Act of March 27, 1794; Compilation of Documented Merchant Vessels, March 15, 1904; Vessels in distress at Key West, from Jan. 1 to Dec. 31, 1846; Steamboat Accidents, Loss of Life, etc., a letter dated Dec. 21, 1840; Vessels in distress at Key West, from Jan. 1 to Dec. 31, 1846; Steamboat Accidents, Loss of Life, etc., from a report of the Secretary of the Treasury, Dec. 21, 1840; Report to the Committee of Naval Affairs for Captain Lewis Warrington and Others, March 28, 1850; Report to the Senate on the Capture of the *Epervier*, Oct. 3, 1814.

15. Coker, William and H. Coker. *The Siege of Pensacola, 1781, In Maps*. Pensacola: The Perdido Bay Press, 1981.
16. Colledge, J.J. *Ships of the Royal Navy*. Annapolis: Naval Institute Press, 1987.
17. Connor, Jeanette T. *Jean Ribaut*. Tallahassee: Florida State Historical Society, 1927.
*18. Escobeda, Alonso Gregorio de. *Pirates, Indians and Spaniards: Father Escobeda's La Florida*, Ed. James W. Covington, trans. A.F. Falcones. Saint Petersburg: Great Outdoors Publishing Co., 1963.
19. Cutler, Carl C. *Queens of the Western Ocean*. Annapolis: United

States Naval Institute, 1967.

20. Davis, T. Frederick. *History of Jacksonville & Vicinity 1513-1924.* Gainesville: University of Florida Press, 1964.

21. Davis, William W. *The Civil War & Reconstruction in Florida.* Originally published 1913. Gainesville: Reprinted by University of Florida Press, 1964.

*22. Escalante Fontaneda, Hernando d'. *Memoir of Do. d'Escalante respecting Florida.* Written in Spain approximately 1575, trans. Buckingham Smith, Washington, D.C., 1854, Ed. David O. True. Coral Gables: Glade House, 1945.

23. Dean, James and Steven Singer. *Shipwrecks of Broward County.* Florida: Self-published, 1984.

24. Dean, Love. *Reef Lights.* Key West: The Historic Key West Preservation Board, 1982.

25. Deloach, Ned. *Ocean Realm Diving Guide to Underwater Florida.* Miami: Ocean Realm Publishing Co., 1983.

26. De Wire, Elinore. *Guide to Florida Lighthouses.* Sarasota: Pineapple Press, 1987.

27. Dickinson, Jonathan. *Jonathan Dickinson's Journal*, Ed. Charles and Evangeline Andrews. New Haven: Yale University Press, 1945.

28. *Dictionary of American Naval Fighting Ships*, Vol.1-8. Washington: Navy Department, Office of the Chief of Naval Operations, Naval History Division, 1963 and 1977.

29. DuBois, Bessie W. *Shipwrecks in the Vicinity of Jupiter Inlet.* Florida: Self-published, 1975.

30. Edye, John. *Calculations Relating to the Equipment, Displacement, etc. of Ships and Vessels of War.* London: 1832.

31. Ellms, Charles. *The Tragedy of the Seas.* Philadelphia: W.A. Leary, 1848.

*32. Ellicot, Andrew. *The Journal of Andrew Ellicot, 1803.* Reprinted by Quadrangle Books, 1962.

33. Forbes, Allen. *Whale Ships and Whaling Scenes as portrayed by Benjamin Russell.* Boston: Second Bank–State Street Trust Co., 1955.

34. Gannon, Michael. *Operation Drumbeat.* New York: Harper & Row, Publishers, 1990.

35. Gilly, William O.S. *Narratives of Shipwrecks of the Royal Navy between 1793-1849.* London: 1850.

36. Gosset, W.P. *The Lost Ships of the Royal Navy, 1793-1900.* London: Mansell Publishing Ltd., 1986.

37. Hambright, Thomas L. *Selected Records in the Monroe County Public Library, Key West,* compiled by Mr. Hambright and others.

38. Hanna, Alfred and Kathryn Hanna. *Florida's Golden Sands.* Indianapolis: Bobbs-Merrill Co., 1950.

39. Hanna, Alfred and Kathryn Hanna. *Lake Okeechobee.* Indianapolis: Bobbs-Merrill Co., 1948.

40. Heyl, Erik. *Early American Steamers*, Vol. 1-5. Buffalo, N.Y.: 1953 to 1967.
41. Hoyt, Edwin P. *U-Boats Offshore*. New York: Stein and Day Publishers, 1978.
42. Hudson, K. and L. Nickolls, *Tragedy on the High Seas*. New York: A & W Publishers, 1979.
43. Jahoda, Gloria. *Florida, A Bicentennial History*. New York: W.W. Norton & Co., Inc., 1976.
44. Kafka, Roger and Roy L. Pepperburg. *Warships of the World*. New York: Cornell Maritime Press, 1946.
45. Kaplan, H.R. and Adrian L. Lonsdale. *A Guide to Sunken Ships in American Waters*. Arlington, Va.: Compass Publications, Inc., 1964.
46. Kusche, Lawrence D. *The Bermuda Triangle Mystery-Solved*. New York: Harper & Row, Publishers, 1975.
47. Lauther, Olive C. *The Lonesome Road*. Miami: Center Printing Co., 1963.
48. Linehan, Mary C. *Early Lantana, Her Neighbors & More*. St. Petersburg.: Byron Kennedy & Co., 1971.
49. Lockey, Joseph B. *East Florida 1783-1785*.Berkeley: University of California Press, 1949.
50. Lowery, Woodbury. *The Spanish Settlements—Florida 1562-1574*. Russel & Russel Inc., 1959.
51. Lubbock, Basil. *The Down Easters*. Glasgow: Brown, Son & Ferguson, Ltd., 1929 (reprinted 1930, 1953).
52. Lytle, William M. and Forrest R. Holdcamper. *Merchant Steam Vessels of the United States 1790-1868, "The Lytle-Holdcamper List."* New York: The Steamship Historical Society of America, Inc., 1952 and 1975.
*53. *The History of Castillo de San Marcos & Fort Mantanzas,* Ed. Albert C. Manucy. Washington, D.C.: National Park Service, 1955.
54. Marx, Robert F. *Spanish Treasure in Florida Waters, A Billion Dollar Graveyard*. Boston: The Mariners Press, 1979. (Updated as *Shipwrecks in Florida Waters*. Chuluota, Florida: The Mickler House, 1985.)
55. Mathewson, R. Duncan III. *Treasure of the Atocha*. New York: Pisces Books, 1987.
56. Meylach, Martin. *Diving to a Flash of Gold*. Port Salerno: Florida Classics Library, 1986.
57. Millás, José Carlos. *Hurricanes of the Caribbean & Adjacent Regions, 1492-1800*. Miami: Academy of the Arts & Sciences, 1968.
58. Mitchell, C. Bradford. *Touching the Adventures & Perils*. New York: American Hull Insurance Syndicate, 1970.
59. Mowat, Charles Loch. *East Florida as a British Province 1763-1784*. Gainesville: University of Florida Press, 1964.
60. Mueller, Edward A. *Steamboating on the St. Johns*. Melbourne, Fla.: Kellersberger Fund of the South Brevard Historical Society, 1980.
61. Munroe, Ralph M. and V. Gilpen. *The Commodore's Story*. Ives

Washburn Publisher, 1930. Reprinted by the Historical Association of Southern Florida, 1966.

62. Neeser, Robert W. *Statistical and Chronological History of the United States Navy 1775-1907*, Vol. II. New York: The Macmillan Co., 1909.

63. *Official Records of the Union & Confederate Navies on the War of the Rebellion*, Series 1, Vol. 1-17. Washington, D.C.: U.S. Government Printing Office, 1894. Also Series II, Vol.1, 1921.

64. Peters, Thelma. *Biscayne Country 1870-1926*. Miami: Banyan Books, 1981.

65. Peterson, Mendel. *History Under the Sea*. Washington, D.C.: Smithsonian Institute, 1965.

66. Peterson, William N. *"Mystic Built" Ships & Shipyards of the Mystic River, Connecticut, 1784-1919*. Mystic, Conn.: Mystic Seaport Museum, 1989.

67. Potter, John S. *The Treasure Diver's Guide*. New York: Doubleday & Co., 1972.

68. Rohwer, Jurgen. *Axis Submarine Successes 1939-1945*. Annapolis: Naval Institute Press, 1983.

69. Rowe, William. *The Maritime History of Maine*. W.W. Norton & Co., 1948. Reprinted by The Bond Wheelwright Co., Freeport, Maine.

70. Shepard, Birse. *Lore of the Wreckers*. Boston: Beacon Press, 1961.

71. Shomette, Donald G. *Shipwrecks of the Civil War*. Washington, D.C.: Donic Ltd., 1973.

72. Siebert, Wilbur H. *Loyalists in East Florida 1774 to 1785*. Vol. 1-2. Tallahassee: Florida State Historical Society, 1929.

73. Smith, Eugene W. *Passenger Ships of the World, Past and Present*. Boston: George H. Dean Co., 1963.

74. Snow, Edward R. *Sea Disasters & Inland Catastrophies*. New York: Dodd, Mead & Co., 1980.

75. Tanner, Helen H. *Zespedes in East Florida 1784-1790*. Coral Gables: University of Miami Press, August 1963.

76. Tebeau, Charlton. *Florida's Last Frontier: The History of Collier County*. Coral Gables: University of Miami Press, 1957.

77. Thurston, William N. *A Study of Maritime Activity in Florida in the Nineteenth Century*. Ann Arbor: University Microfilms International, 1983.Ph.D. dissertation, Florida State University, 1972.

78. Trupp, Phillip. *Tracking Treasure*. Washington, D.C.: Acropolis Books Ltd., 1986.

*79. *The Log of the H.M.S. Mentor 1780-1781*, Ed. James A. Servies. Pensacola: University Presses of Florida, 1982.

*80. *The Mariners Museum, Catalog of Marine Photographs*. Vol: 1-5. Boston: G.K. Hall & Co., 1964.

81. *United States Submarine Losses, World War II*. Washington, D.C.: Naval History Division, Office of Chief of Naval Operations, 1963.

82. Watson, Milton. *Disasters at Sea*. Wellingborough, Northamptonshire, England: Patrick Stephens Ltd., 1987.

83. Weller, Robert. *Sunken Treasure on Florida Reefs, The 1715 Spanish Plate Fleet.* West Palm Beach: Self-published, 1986.
84. Will, Lawrence. *Okeechobee Boats & Skippers.* St. Petersburg: Great Outdoors Publishing Co., 1965.
85. Wright, J. Leitch. *Florida in the American Revolution.* Gainesville: The University Presses of Florida, 1975.

Selected periodicals and newspapers. The selected issues are listed by date and author after each wreck.
86. *Broward Legacy.*
87. *El Escribano.*
88. *Florida Scuba News.*
89. *Fort Lauderdale News/Sun Sentinel.*
90. *Miami Daily Metropolis/The Daily Metropolis.*
91. *Plus Ultra.*
92. *Seafarers Journal of Maritime Heritage.* Vol. 1, 1987.
93. *ShipWrecks "The Magazine."*
94. *Skin Diver Magazine.*
95. *Tequesta.*
96. *The Charleston Courier.*
97. *The Florida Historical Quarterly.*
98. *The Miami Herald.*
99. *The New York Daily Times/The New York Times.*
100. *Treasure Magazine.*
101. *Underwater USA.*
102. *Waterfront News.*

Additional sources:
103. Rogers, William W. *Outposts on the Gulf.* Pensacola: University Presses of Florida, 1987.
104. Owens, Harry P. *Apalachicola Before 1861.* Ann Arbor: University Microfilms Inc., 1983. Ph.D. dissertation, Florida State University, 1966.
105. Cutler, Carl C. *Greyhounds of the Sea.* Annapolis: U.S. Naval Institute, 1967.

Suggested Reading

The following are additional sources on Florida shipwrecks, underwater archaeology, ships, and artifact identification.

1715 Spanish Plate Fleet

1. Burgess, F., and C. Clausen. *Florida's Golden Galleons*. Port Salerno: Florida Classics Library, 1982.
2. Wagner, Kip. *Pieces of Eight*. New York: E.P. Dutton & Co., Inc., 1966.

1622 Spanish Fleet

1. Daley, Robert. *Treasure*. New York: Random House, 1977.
2. Lyon, Eugene. *The Search for the Atocha*. Port Salerno: Florida Classics Library, 1982.

Other Shipwrecks

1. Earle, Peter. *The Treasure of the Concepcion*. New York: The Viking Press, 1980.
2. Horner, Dave. *The Treasure Galleons*. Port Salerno: Florida Classics Library, 1990.
3. Marx, Robert F. *Shipwrecks in the Americas*. New York: Bonanza Books, 1983.
4. Nesmith, Robert I. *Dig for Pirate Treasure*. New York: Bonanza Books, 1958.
5. Weller, Robert. *Famous Shipwrecks of the Florida Keys*. Birmingham, Ala.: EBSCO Media, 1990.

Nautical Archaeology and Ship History

1. Bass, George F. *Ships and Shipwrecks of the Americas*. London: Thames & Hudson, 1988.
2. Casson, Lionel. *Illustrated History of Ships & Boats*. New York: Doubleday & Co., 1964.
3. Chapelle, Howard I. *The Search For Speed Under Sail 1700-1855*. New York: Bonanza Books, 1967.
4. Greenhill, Basil. *The Evolution of the Wooden Ship*. New York: Facts on File, Inc., 1988.
5. MacGregor, David. *Merchant Sailing Ships*, Vols. 1 – 3 (covering the years 1775 to 1875). Annapolis: Naval Institute Press., 1981 to 1985.
6. Marx, Robert F. *The Underwater Dig*. New York: H.Z. Walck, 1975.
7. McKee, Alexander. *History Under the Sea*. London: Hutchinson & Co. Ltd., 1968.
8. Palacio, Diego Garcia de. *Nautical Instruction: A.D. 1587*. Printed in Mexico in 1587, translated by J. Bankston. Bisbee, Arizona: Terrenate Research, 1988.

9. Taylor, Joan du Plat. *Marine Archaeology*. New York: Thomas Y. Crowell Co., 1966.
10. Throckmorton, Peter. *Shipwrecks and Archaeology*. Boston: Little Brown & Co., 1970.
11. Throckmorton, Peter. *The Sea Remembers*. New York: Weidenfeld & Nicholson, 1987.
12. White, David. *The Frigate Diana*. Annapolis: Naval Institute Press, 1987. This is but one of "The Anatomy of the Ship Series" published by the Naval Institute Press. I recommend reading the others also.
13. Wilkes, Bill St. John. *The Handbook of Underwater Exploration*. New York: Stein & Day, 1971-1975.
14. *The Lore of Ships*. New York: Gallery Books, 1990.

Coins

1. Craig, Alan K. *Florida Archaeology, Gold Coins of the 1715 Spanish Plate Fleet*. Tallahassee: Florida Department of State, 1988.
2. Grove, Frank W. *Coins of Mexico*. Lawrence, Mass.: Quarterman Publishing, Inc., 1981.
3. Raymond, Wayte. *The Silver Dollars of North and South America*. Racine, Wisc.: The Whitman Publishing Co., 1964.
4. Sedwick, Frank. *The Practical Book of Cobs*. Maitland, Fla.: Self-published, 1987 (second edition, 1990).
Note: I also recommend some of the auction catalogues of shipwreck coins and artifacts. These are available from Christies' and other large auction houses, which auction treasure and artifacts excavated from sunken ships.

Ceramics, Pottery, and Glass

1. Deagan, Kathleen. *Artifacts of the Spanish Colonies of Florida and the Caribbean, 1500-1800*. Washington, D.C.: Smithsonian Institution Press, 1987.
2. Hume, Ivor Noel. *A Guide to Artifacts of Colonial America*. New York: Alfred A. Knopf, 1980.
3. Goggin, John M. *The Spanish Olive Jar, An Introductory Study*. New Haven: Yale University Publication in Anthropology, No. 62, 1960.

Armament

1. Blair, C. and L. Tarassuk. *The Complete Encyclopedia of Arms & Weapons*. London: B.T. Batsford Ltd., 1982.
2. Blair, C. *European and American Arms*. New York: Bonanza Books, 1962.
3. Blackmore, H.L. *The Armories of the Tower of London, The Ordinance*, Vol. 1. London: 1976

Other

1. *Plus Ultra*. Quarterly newsletter available from Florida Treasure Brokers, P.O. Box 1697, West Palm Beach, Fla. 33402.
2. *National Geographic*. Selected issues.
3. *The Seafarers Collection*, Time Life Books.
4. *International Journal of Nautical Archaeology and Underwater Exploration*.

Figure 141: Silver 1's, 2's, and 4's and an eight real compared to a modern quarter. AUTHOR.

SECOND EDITION
NEW INFORMATION

ADDITIONAL INFORMATION ON PREVIOUSLY LISTED WRECKS

Section 1

2. Spanish Ships — It's believed one of these ships has been found. Named the "Emanuel Point Ship," it lies in 12 feet of water in Pensacola Bay. It was excavated by Florida's Bureau of Archaeological Research, and the site can be viewed online at http://www.dos.state.fl.us/dhr.

74. *Mintie* — 48.4 tons. Source: 14.

76. *Jessie Rhynas* (correct spelling) — Source: 14.

83. *City of Manatee* — Steamer, 88.9 tons, built 1881 at Milville, Florida. Source: 14.

84. *C. Ervlin* — Paddle steam tug, of Apalachicola, Florida, 128.9 gross tons, built 1882 at Apalachicola. Source: 14.

86. *California* — Of Apalachicola, Florida, 16.67 gross tons. Source: 14.

87. *A.C. Monroe* — Built 1868 at Freeport, Florida, 27.48 tons. Source: 14.

88. *Samuel MacManemy* — Built 1870 at Marcus Hook, Pennsylvania, 310.21 tons, of Philadelphia. Source: 14.

91. *H.S. Rowe* — Built 1859 at Essex, Massachusetts, 59.47 tons. Source: 14.

92. *Sarah F. Bird* — Built 1873 at Rockland, Maine. Source: 14.

93. *Four Brothers* — Built 1867 at Biloxi, Mississippi, 44.58 tons. Source: 14.

100. *Carl D. Lathrop* — Built 1873 at Lubec, Maine, listed at 292.81 tons in 1884. Source: 14.

Figure 142: Diver carefully excavating an encrusted iron breastplate (circa 1510) from the Emanuel Point Ship.
FLORIDA BUREAU OF ARCHAEOLOGICAL RESEARCH.

Figure 143: Badly corroded copper coin from the Emanuel Point Ship identified as a blanca of Henry IV of Castille and Leon, minted in Spain between 1471 and 1474.
FLORIDA BUREAU OF ARCHAEOLOGICAL RESEARCH.

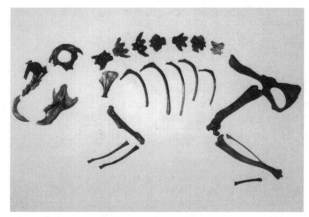

Figure 144: Bones of stowaways, such as rats and mice, were found in the bilge of the Emanuel Point Ship. FLORIDA BUREAU OF ARCHAEOLOGICAL RESEARCH.

Figure 145: Piece of an olive jar from the Emanuel Point Ship (note the early style neck). FLORIDA BUREAU OF ARCHAEOLOGICAL RESEARCH.

Figure 146: Ceramic fragments, identified as Aztec ceremonial pottery from the central valley of Mexico, found on the Emanuel Point Ship. FLORIDA BUREAU OF ARCHAEOLOGICAL RESEARCH.

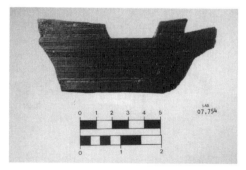

Figure 147: Tiny carving of a ship found on the Emanuel Point Ship. FLORIDA BUREAU OF ARCHAEOLOGICAL RESEARCH.

102. *John Pew* — Built 1852 at Essex, Massachusetts. Source: 14.

104. *James W. Wherren* — Built 1852 at Provincetown, Massachusetts. Source: 14.

105. *Hattie G. McFarland* — Built 1872 at Thomaston, Maine. Source: 14.

110. *Dexter Clark* — Built 1873 at Ellworth, Maine, listed at 141.75 gross tons in 1884. Source: 14.

111. *J.P. Allen* — Built 1872 at Dartmouth, Massachusetts. Source: 14.

114. *J.A. Bishop* — Of Apalachicola, built 1883 at Milton, Florida, 22.85 tons. Source: 14.

115. *Kanawha* — Built 1881 at Bath, Maine, 536 gross tons. Source: 14.

116. *Octavia A. Dow* — Built 1867 at Georgetown, Maine. Source: 14.

118. *George Jurgens* — Built 1878 at New Orleans. Source: 14.

119. *David Mitchell* — Built 1846 at Baltimore, 35.59 gross tons. Source: 14.

120. *Sea Foam* — Built 1860 at Booth Bay, Maine. Source: 14.

121/122. *Mary Potter* — Built 1868 at Noank, Connecticut., 53.5' x 19.2' x 4.3' Source: 14.

131. *Charles A. Swift* — Built 1885 at Bonsecour, Alabama, 25.72 gross tons, 54.3' x 19.2' x 4.3'. Source: 14.

Section 2

33. *Martha M. Heath* — Of Providence, Rhode Island, built 1870 at St. James, New York. Source: 14.

34. *Dictator* — 623.7 gross tons. Source: 14.

35. *Millie Wales* — Built 1875 at Booth Bay, Maine. Source: 14.

36. *Freddie L. Porter* — Built 1865 at Portsmouth, New Hampshire, 349.66 gross tons. Source: 14.

37. *Mary Ellen* — Believed built in 1867 at Islip, New York. Source: 14.

Section 3

11. The captured vessel was named the *Snow*, an English vessel crewed by Spanish interests. The *Snow* wrecked a cable's length west of the HMS *Looe*. Ed Link recovered the *Snow*'s anchor in the early 1950s. Source: 109.

22. *Concord* — Was saved later. A fishing vessel found her adrift and towed her to Key West. Source: 106 (April 20, 1831; October 13, 1831).

24. *Dumfries* — From Lisbon bound for New Orleans with a cargo of wine and salt, Captain Harvey, wrecked on Loggerhead Key, April 1, 1831. Some cargo saved. Source: 106 (April 20, 1831).

26. *Splendid* — Was saved. Source: 106 (April 27, 1831).

28. *Othello* — Was saved. Source: 106 (March 14, 1832).

32. *United States* — From Charleston bound for Key West, driven on shore a few miles north of Cape Florida (See Section 5), July 1835. Vessel a total loss, some cargo saved. Source: 106 (August 22, 1835).

36. *Eleanor* — British bark, was saved. Source: 106 (June, 1836).

52. *Conservative* — British brig, Captain Carrey. This source says lost at Key Largo. Source: 14(a).

53. *Zotoff* — Captain Murphy. Source: 14(a).

54. *Oconee* — New Orleans packet, built 1835 at New York, by Fickett & Thomas, 460 tons, 119'4" x 29'4" x 18'6". Possibly wrecked on Stirrup Key, Bahamas. Source: 108.

182. *Marcia Reynolds* — Of Somers Point, New Jersey, built 1871 at Lubec, Maine, 310.2 gross tons. Source: 14.

188. *Vidette* — Built 1881 at Essex, Massachusetts, 819.43 gross tons (429 net). Source: 14.

189. *Joshua H. Marvell* — Built 1864 at Laurel, Delaware, 104.69 gross tons. Source: 14.

190. *Arthur* — Likely a 201-ton barge of New York. Source: 14.

199. *Belle Hooper* — Believed to be a schooner, built 1874 at Boston, 475 gross tons (451 net) Source: 14.

200. *Joseph Baker* — Built 1873 at Brewer, Maine, 399.17 gross tons (379 net). Source: 14.

204. *Shannon* — Built 1867 at Millbridge, Maine, 393.34 gross tons (374 net). Source: 14.

212. *R. Bowers* — Built 1879 at Camden, Maine, 435 gross tons (413 net). Source: 14.

214. *Harry B. Ritter* — Built 1878 at Mauricetown, New Jersey, 643 gross tons (611 net). Source: 14.

255. *Brazos* — This source says she stranded November 13, 1917. Source: 113.

Figure 148: Diver preparing *Copenhagen* (1900) anchor for lifting. It was then returned to the wrecksite. AUTHOR.

Section 4

65. *Correrro* — From Havana bound for Cadiz, wrecked on Carysfort on April 2, 1832. Crew and some cargo saved including specie. Source: 106 (April 11, 1832).

66. *Marcella* — Had 984 bales of cotton, wrecked 4 miles from Cape Florida Light, 3/4 mile from Bear Cut. Source: 106 (March 21, 1831).

68. *Waverly* — Wrecked March 13, 1831. Source: Ibid.

70. *Lavinia* — Bound for New York, cargo—including $70,000 in specie—saved. Source: 106 (March 14, 1832).

71. *Kentucky* — Built 1827 by S&F Fickett of New York, 415 tons, of New Orleans, 118'8" x 27'10" x 13'11". Wrecked 50 miles north of Cape Florida (See Section 5), November 20, 1832. Source: 108.

101. *Newark* — Of the Savannah Line, built 1834 at New York, 306 tons, 104'10" x 25'6" x 12'9", wrecked on Carysfort Reef, 1845. Source: 108.

198. *Adelaide* — Believed built 1879 at Key West. Source: 14.

202. *Clyde* — Listed at 56 tons, built 1862 at Philadelphia. Source:14.

Section 5

91. *America* — Built 1863 at Portland, Connecticut, 781.8 gross tons. Source:14.

93. *Ilo* — Built 1863 at Port Jefferson, New York, 34.9 gross tons. Source: 14.

98. *Orrie V. Drisco* — Built 1873 at Columbia Falls, Maine, 321.34 gross tons. Source: 14.

100. *Breaconshire* — Schooner-rigged, iron-hulled steamer, built in 1883 at Sunderland, England, 299.7' x 37.2'. Was in ballast when wrecked. Source: 111.

101. *Georgie* — Of Windsor, Nova Scotia, built by W. S. Vaughn at Walton, Nova Scotia, in 1881, 239 gross tons, 107' X 29' X 11.5'. Listed as wrecked September 1894. Source: Lloyd's Register, courtesy Barbara Jones (Lloyd's).

103. *Nathan Cleaves* — Built 1871 at Essex, Massachusetts. Source: 14.

104. *Phoenix* — Built 1893 at Jacksonville, Florida, 60' x 40.5' x 18.2'. Source: 14.

108. *Copenhagen* — Wreck lies between the 5th and 6th mooring buoys, at latitude 26 12.349'N, longitude 80 05.108'W.

143. *Shuttle* — 227.4' x 40.5' x 18.2'. Source: 14.

170. *Richmond* — Built in 1908 at Sharptown, Maryland, 135.3' x 26.5' x 9'. Source 113.

Section 6

42. *Empecinada* — Spanish goleta, from Havana bound for Spain, wrecked at latitude 30.36 N, 81.26 W, January 3, 1815. Cargo, including gold and silver, saved. Source: 112.

114. *Caroline Eddy* — Of Bangor, Maine, 337.55 tons. Source: 1-4.

122. *Athlete* — Paddle steamer, built 1878 at St. Marys, Georgia, 178.85 gross tons. Source: 14.

123. *Theodore S. Parker* — Built 1873 at Brown's Point, New Jersey, 35.5 gross tons. Source: 14.

125. *Virginia Lee Hickman* — Built 1872 at Chester, Pennsylvania, 338.14 gross tons. Source: 14.

131. *Franconia* — Built 1873, 674 tons. Source: 14.

Section 7

43. *Ida Stockton* — Built 1874 at Orange City, Missouri. Source: 14.

45. *Fannie Duggan* — Of Jacksonville, Florida, built 1872 at Portsmouth, New Hampshire, 260.48 gross tons. Source: 14.

47. *City of Georgetown* — Paddle steamer, built 1879 at Portsmouth, Ohio. Source: 14.

51. *Port Royal* — 189.12 gross tons. Source: 14.

56. *Oyster Boy* — Built 1861 at New Brunswick, New Jersey. Source: 14.

60. *H.B. Plant* — Built 1880 at Wilmington, Delaware. Source: 14.

61. *Marion* — Believed to be a paddle steamer, built 1871 at Palatka, Florida, 67.43 gross tons. Source: 14.

67. *Santa Rosa* — Built 1878 at Pensacola, Florida, 122 gross tons, 107' x 31.2' x 4'. Source: 14.

69. *David Kemps* — Steamer, of Jacksonville, Florida, 57.82 gross tons, built 1891 at New Berlin, Florida, 87.5' x 20.9' x 6.6'. Source: 14.

70. *Walnatronica* — Built 1885 at Tallahassee, 70' x 13.4' x 4'. Also listed as *Walanatomica*. Source: 14.

121. *Nassauvian* — The *J.W. Sommerville* was listed as having foundered off Tampa, October 27, 1921. Must have been raised and renamed *Nassauvian*. Built 1919 at Pocomoke City, Maryland. Source 113.

Figure 149: Piece of Kang Hsi porcelain from the Cabin site (1715). AUTHOR.

Section 8

170. *Maria* — Captain M'Mullin, from Philadelphia bound for New Orleans, with a general cargo and 230 laborers for the canal, wrecked on Carysfort Reef (See Section 4), November 25, 1831. Crew and cargo saved. Source: 106 (November 30, 1831).

206. *Arietis* — Built 1857 at Key West. Source: 14.

208. *Mary C. Mariner* — Built 1861 at Cape Elizabeth, Maine. Source: 14.

236. *Genessee* — Stranded off Sand Point near Vero Beach, November 3, 1925, 120 feet long. Source: 111.

Section 11: Florida's Lower East Coast

9. *Laertes* — Had a cargo of war materials including 3 airplanes, 20 trucks, and 17 tanks. She lies about 9 1/2 miles due east of the Cape Canaveral Light. Source: 111.

11. *Ocean Venus* — 425' x 57', cargo included lead which was salvaged. Source: 111.

Figure 150: Assorted lead musket balls from the 1715 and other sites. Author.

SHIPWRECKS NOT
PREVIOUSLY LISTED

Surprisingly, ships are still being lost at an alarming rate. Even with improved weather forecasts and new, sophisticated electronic radar and positioning systems, ships still manage to collide, founder, or become wrecked. Some of the worst loss of life from shipwrecks has occurred in just the last five years.

A number of large vessels have run aground in the Florida Keys in the last few years, including a 170' research ship hired by the National Oceanographic Atmospheric Administration (NOAA) which, ironically, is supposed to protect the reefs. Most of these vessels have been salvaged, such as the 325' Panamanian freighter *Hind*, which went aground off Fort Lauderdale during a storm on March 18, 1998 and was towed offshore four days later. Others, however, have not fared as well. The 180' steel freighter, *Roatan Express*, foundered off Florida's west coast during a storm since the first edition of this book, and while writing this update, I read about the 430' freighter, *Merchant Patriot*, which foundered off the Bahamas the last week of 1997 during a storm. Both of these vessels sank.

Figure 151: The Panamanian freighter *Hind*, grounded off Fort Lauderdale, March 1998. AUTHOR.

Many factors—including weather, human error, and malfunctioning equipment—still contribute to the loss of ships, especially with older vessels registered where inspections are non-existent. As long as ships continue to sail the seas, the ocean will continue to claim her stake.

Section 1

1. *Matteawan* — British steamer, left Pensacola with a cargo of 11,000 bales of cotton. Caught fire January 14, 1904, and returned to Pensacola where she continued to burn. Source: 90 (January 15, 1904).

Section 2

1. *William & Frederick* — Schooner, from Apalachicola bound for Key West, Captain Fish, was lost on Sanibel Key, April 2, 1832. Source: 106 (April 11, 1832).

2. *Mary Anne* — Sloop, lost at Charlotte Harbor during the September 1835 storm. Source: 106 (September 26, 1835).

3. *Exchange* — Schooner, of Frankfort, Maine, no cargo, went ashore at Tampa Bay during a storm, January 31, 1836. Source: 106 (February 13, 1836).

4. *Kardyn Kage* — Schooner, went aground on Anna Marie Key, near Tampa, January 18, 1909. Crew saved; vessel a total wreck. Source: 107 (January 24, 1909).

5. *Cecil Anne* — Former U.S. Army cargo vessel, 62' long, foundered January 28, 1967, 50 miles southeast, 146 degrees from Carrabelle. Crew rescued by Coast Guard. Source: 110.

6. *Roatan Express* — Honduran freighter, 180' long, from Tampa bound for Roatan, foundered during a storm, 80 miles west of Fort Myers in 120' of water. Two lives lost. Source: 89 (date unknown; early 1990s).

Section 3

1. *Henry Bennett* — Brig, of Boston, was found abandoned near the Tortugas, August, 1832. Some cargo of lumber saved. Source: 106 (August 22, 1832).

Figure 152: Frame timbers from an unidentified wreck off Boca Raton.
AUTHOR.

2. *Glasgow* — British bark, from New Orleans bound for Europe, cargo of cotton, went ashore on Coffins Patch off Duck Key, June 24, 1832. Condemned and sold. Source: 106 (June 27, 1832).

3. *Collector* — Schooner, of Newport, Rhode Island, Captain Jacob Chapel, with cargo of lumber, dragged anchor during a gale for three miles and wrecked at entrance to Northwest Channel, 12 miles from Key West, December 31, 1834. Cargo saved. Source: 106 (January 3, 1835).

4. *Galaxy* — Schooner, of New York, Captain Warren, from Havana bound for Apalachicola with coffee, cigars and fruit. Sprung a leak and ran aground on the Tortugas, May 25, 1835. Some cargo saved. Possibly the 100-ton schooner built by J. Southwick at Vassalboro, Maine, in 1826, 65'6 x 20'6 x 8'8. Source: 6, 106 (June 6, 1835).

5. *Mary* — Brig, of Boston, Captain Nebemiah Hill, from New York bound for Mobile, wrecked on reef off Key Vacas, September 5, 1835. Most cargo saved. Source: 106 (September 12, 1835).

6. *Majestic* — Ship, of Boston, Captain Smith, from New Orleans bound for Liverpool with 1,060 bales of cotton and 100 hogsheads (casks) of tobacco. Driven ashore in a storm a few miles north of the Key West lightship, late September 1835. Some cargo saved. Likely the 390-ton ship built by Geo. F. Patten of Bath, Maine, in 1829, 114'3 x 27'6 x 13'9. Source: 6, 106 (September 26, 1835).

7. *Blakely* — Brig, from Portland bound for Havana with lumber and cod fish. Wrecked 2 or 3 miles north of the Key West lightship during the September 1835 storm. Some cargo saved. Source: Ibid.

8. *Jas. Dennison* — British bark, Captain Young, from Liverpool bound for Mobile, was a total loss on Cape Antonio, March 1844. Ship and cargo valued at $5,000. Source: 14 (a).

9. *Wellington* — British ship, Captain McIntyre, from New Orleans bound for Liverpool, was lost at the Tortugas, April, 1844. Ship and cargo valued at $56,000. Source: 14 (a).

10. *Alwida* — Brig, Captain Tallman, from Honduras bound for New York, was lost on Carysfort Reef, July, 1844. Ship and cargo valued at $9,000. Source: 14 (a).

11. *Louis XIV* — French ship, Captain Juge, from New Orleans bound for Havre, was lost on Long Key, July, 1844. Ship and cargo valued at $104,000. Source: 14 (a).

12. *Select* — Schooner, Captain Lewis, from New Orleans bound for Barbados, was lost on the Tortugas, August, 1844. Ship and cargo valued at $4,000. Source: 14 (a).

13. *Rothchild* — British ship, Captain Fell, from Apalachicola bound for Liverpool, was believed lost on Tortugas, August, 1844. Ship and cargo valued at $70,000. Source: 14 (a).

14. *Aitalia* — Bark, Captain Hammond, from Havana bound for Baltimore, was lost on Carysfort Reef, November, 1844. Ship and cargo valued at $12,000. Source: 14 (a).

15. *Statira* — Brig, 166 tons, built 1835 for the Center Line, New York, Captain Calvin Babbidge, from St. Marks bound for New York, was wrecked in Key West harbor during the October gale, 1844. Ship and cargo valued at $10,000. Source: 14 (a), 19.

16. *Lime Rock* — Brig, 174 tons, built 1840, transferred to the Commercial Line, New Orleans, in 1843, Captain Edward Auld, from Key West bound for New Orleans, sprung a leak at sea and was run ashore at the Tortugas, November, 1844. Source: 14 (a), 19.

17. *Tevonia* — British bark, Captain Davis, of London, from Jamaica bound for Liverpool, wrecked on Carysfort Reef, June, 1845. Ship and cargo valued at $40,000. Some cargo salvaged. Source: 14 (a).

18. *Nor'Wester* — Ship, built 1854 by S. Lapham of Medford, Massachusetts, 1267 tons, 186.6' x 38.6' x 23', Captain Frank C. Eldridge, owned by J. T. Coolidge & Company, Boston. Burned at Key West in 1873. Source: 105.

19. *Emily B* — Schooner, of Lake Worth, Captain Charles Earnest, lost within 4 miles of Key West in a storm, October 1894. Four lives lost. Source: 107 (October 4, 1894).

Section 4

1. *Veteran* — Flat bottom schooner, 14 tons, wrecked in Barnes Sound in the mangroves, October 18, 1831. Source: 106 (March 21, 1831).

2. *Amiable Gertrude* — Spanish brig, Captain Juan Ballabi, from Havana bound for Corona, with cocoa, wrecked near Caesar's Creek and bilged, November 12, 1834. Source: 106 (November 22, 1834).

3. *Maria* — Schooner, Captain Keatrag, from Thomaston bound for Pensacola with lime, caught fire and ran aground near lighthouse at Key West, November 26, 1834. Total loss. Source: 106 (November 29, 1834).

4. *Lion* or *Lyon* — Brig, of Bath, Captain Fullington, from Mantanzas bound for Savannah with molasses, wrecked on Pickles Reef, May 4, 1835. Most cargo saved. Likely the 190-ton *Lion*, built by John Henry at Bowdoinham, Maine, in 1822, 87'9 x 24'10 x 10'. Source: 6, 106 (June 6, 1835).

5. *Isabella* — Brig, of Baltimore, from Norfolk bound for New Orleans with pinewood, wrecked on Alligator Reef and bilged within 1/2 hour, May 9, 1835. Very little saved. Source: Ibid.

6. *John Britton* — British brig, of Halifax, Captain C. P. Morell, from Kingston, Jamaica, in ballast, wrecked on a reef off Tavernier Key, August 9, 1835. Total loss, crew saved. Source: 106 (August 15, 1835).

7. *Sea Drift* — Brig, of New York, Captain Hoyt, from New York bound for Mobile, went on Carysfort Reef and then beached high and dry at Key Largo during the September 1835 storm. Cargo saved. Source: 106 (September 26, 1835).

8. *Pizarro* — Wrecking schooner, lost during the September 1835 storm while salvaging the *Sea Drift*. Source: Ibid.

9. *Miami* — Sloop, found sunk near Cape Florida after the September 1835 storm. Source: Ibid.

10. *Natchez* — Brig, 228 tons, Captain A. Tyler, of the Center Line, from New York bound for Mobile, with assorted cargo, went ashore on Conch or Carysfort Reef, June 19, 1836. Vessel total loss, cargo saved. Source: 19, 106 (June 25, 1836).

11. *Franklin* — Brig, reported ashore on Pickles Reef, September 1836. Some cargo, including cotton, saved. Source: 106 (September 10, 1836).

12. *Dorothy Foster* — Ship, from Old Harbor, Jamaica bound for London, reported ashore between Pickles and Conch Reefs, September 1836. Vessel and most cargo lost. Source: 106 (September 10, 1836).

13. *Drot* — Norwegian bark, originally the *Almira Robinson*, built 1874 by Lemont & Robinson of Bath, Maine, 1,198 gross tons, 185.1' x 37.2' x 24', from Pascagoula bound for Buenos Aires with lumber, wrecked off Key Largo, August 11, 1899. Fourteen lives lost. Some survived through cannibalism. Source: 6, 110.

14. *Ada Bailey* — Three-masted schooner, 522 tons, 161' x 23.2' x 12.3', built 1884 by A. Sewall & Company of Bath, Maine, Captain Benett, from Tampa bound for Baltimore with a cargo of phosphate, sank 50 miles southeast of Cape Florida, November 15, 1894. Source: 6, 114.

Section 5

1. *Noble* — Brig, from Laguna bound for New York, with logwood, went ashore near Cape Canaveral during the September 1835 storm. Likely the 208-ton brig built at Brunswick, Maine, in 1833. Source: 6, 106 (September 26, 1835).

2. *LaFayette* — Schooner, Captain Snow, from Tabasco bound for New York, with logwood, went ashore near the *Noble*, September 1835. Possibly the 139-ton *LaFayette*, built 1832 at Pittston, Maine, 84' x 23'7 x 8'. Source: Ibid.

3. *Bessie B* — Schooner, of Hypoluxo, Captain Benson Lyman, wrecked on a reef south of Lake Worth Inlet during a storm, February 23, 1892. Vessel and most of the cargo lost. Source: 107 (February 25, 1892).

4. *Gladys* — Steam yacht, 20 tons, 67', of New York, en route to Nuevitus, Cuba, Captain M. Slavich, beached high and dry near Lake Worth Inlet, April 30, 1892. Source: 107 (May 5, 1892).

5. *Julia* — Brig, 200 tons, from Wilmington, Delaware, no cargo, wrecked high on beach on bar near Hillsboro Inlet, late September, 1894. Total loss. Source: 107 (October 4, 1894).

6. *Hattie* — Schooner, ashore near Lake Worth, November, 1894. Cargo of lumber saved. Source: 107 (December 6, 1894).

7. *Ethel* — Steamer, Captain John Dunn, swamped while coming in Lake Worth, April 27, 1895. Source: 114.

8. *Lofthus* — Norwegian bark, Captain O. Anderson, from Pensacola bound for Buenos Aires, with lumber. Wrecked just off where the *Oh Kim Soon* wrecked one year earlier at Hypoluxo, about 250' to 300' offshore, February 4, 1898. Source: 107 (February 10, 1898), 114.

9. *Doris* — Four-masted bark, of Baltimore, 944 gross tons, 189.1' x 36.8' x 17.1', built 1894 at Belfast, Maine, from Tampa bound for Baltimore with a cargo of phosphate, went aground on a reef just southeast of the Hotel Boynton, January 10, 1902. Mistook lights on shore for those of a passing vessel. Source: 14, 107 (January 10, 1904), 114.

10. *Pere Marquette* (also known as Steam Boat # 3) — Steamer, steel, 2,443 gross tons, 337.1' x 56' x 17', built at West Bay City, Michigan, beached during a gale at Palm Beach, January, 1902. Source: 14, 114.

11. *Melrose* — British steamer, wrecked at Hobe Sound, October 17. 1904. Nine lives lost. Source: 114.

12. Four-masted schooner — Reported ashore at Manalapan the same time as the *Melrose*. Unknown if saved. Source: 114.

Figure 153: Photo of the Norwegian bark *Coquimbo* shown wrecked off Boynton Beach. BOYNTON BEACH HISTORICAL SOCIETY.

13. *Massa e Gnecco* — Italian bark, of Genoa, Captain Pedro Musante, from Pensacola bound for Buenos Aires, with 785,116 feet of lumber, wrecked and bilged on the second reef about seven miles south of Palm Beach, January 15, 1905. Much of the cargo salvaged and auctioned. Also listed as wrecked about five miles south of Breakers Pier, Palm Beach. Crew made it to shore and took refuge in the wreck of the *James Judge*. Source: 107 (January 18, 1905), 114.

14. British brig— Wrecked at Jupiter, March 4, 1908. Source: 114.

15. *Coquimbo* — Norwegian bark, went aground in early 1909 off Boynton Beach, south of the Inlet. Her cargo of lumber was salvaged and her bell resides in the First Methodist Church. Some believe she was intentionally grounded for insurance purposes. Source: Boynton Beach Historical Society.

16. *Coylett* — British steam tanker, caught fire and was abandoned off St. Augustine, February 5, 1922. Sunk by the Coast Guard, 110 miles southeast of St. Augustine in 400' of water. Source: 114.

17. *Bahama Sun* — Steel freighter, 100', owned by the Bahama Transport Company, grounded off Palm Beach just off the beach between Jungle Road and Via da Selva, January 13, 1969. Could not be gotten off and was cut up. Source: 114.

18. *Abaco Sands* — Bahamian freighter, from West Palm Beach bound for Green Turtle Cay, with lumber, cement, and furniture, capsized off Palm Beach, November 3, 1983. Source: 114.

19. *Mariner* — Aluminum hull America's Cup–class sailboat, of Miami. Beached on South Palm Beach, October, 1996. Before she could be gotten off, a northeaster blew in and pounded her hull on the rocks.

20. *Venice* — Haitian freighter (wood), 65', caught fire December 19, 1997 off Port Everglades, and went ashore near the 1700 block of South Ocean Lane where she continued to burn and eventually broke up. Source: 89 (December 21, 1997).

21. *Hind* — Panamanian freighter, 325', went aground off Fort Lauderdale during a storm, towed offshore four days later (March 18, 1998).

Section 7

1. *Santa Rosario* — Converted steel shrimp trawler, 70.5' x 20' x 11.4', built 1973 at Larose, Louisiana. Turned over and sunk in 146' of water, July 23, 1984, 30 miles east of New Smyrna Beach. One life lost. Source: 110.

Section 8

1. *B.W. Morse* — Three-masted schooner, 589 tons, 156.6' x 35' x 13.6', built 1879 by B. W. & H. F. Morse of Bath, Maine. Left Jacksonville January 21, 1900, bound for San Juan, Puerto Rico. Two days out was hit by a storm and was abandoned. Possible Florida wreck. Source: 6.

2. *Alice Archer* — Schooner, Captain Arthur Gibbs, with cargo of railroad iron. Was abandoned off Florida's east coast, January, 1902. Likely the 447-ton, three-masted schooner built 1882 at Bath, Maine, 149.3' x 34.1' x 12.7'. Source: 6, 107 (January 24, 1902).

3. *Walker Armington* — Four-masted schooner, 771 tons, 178' x 38.3' x 16.7', built 1883 at Bath, Maine. Originally a steam schooner until she wrecked in 1897, when she was salvaged and her engine was removed. Reported lost a few years later on the coast of Florida. Source: 6 .

ADDITIONAL APPENDICES, BIBLIOGRAPHY, AND SUGGESTED READING

Appendix B: Search & Salvage

Side-Scan Sonar

Though several improvements have been made in side-scan sonar since this book's first printing, the most noticeable is digital imaging. The images produced by some of the newer, digitally enhanced side-scan units are quite extraordinary.

Underwater Metal Detectors

The ability to discriminate among different types of metal is the newest feature on some underwater detectors. They are still reasonably priced, and I recommend that you try a few before you buy one to see which one best fits your budget and purpose.

GPS and DGPS

Though navigation systems such as Loran C are still used, Geographical Positioning System (GPS) navigators are now the system of choice. These receive satellite signals and plot your position in latitude and longitude. Differential Geographical Positioning System (DGPS) navigators are also more common now. Both GPSs and DGPSs receive satellite and land-based signals, are extremely accurate, and can interface with most of the new electronic search equipment. Once cost-prohibitive, both are now quite affordable.

Figure 154: Side-scan image of a nineteenth-century schooner in Chesapeake Bay. GARY KOZAK, KLEIN ASSOCIATES.

Appendix C: Wreck Identification

Cannonballs

Though I briefly referred to cannonballs in the first edition, I failed to mention that bronze cannonballs were also used. An early seventeenth-century Spanish wreck with bronze cannonballs was recently found off Panama.

Stone cannonballs were recently found on the Emanuel Point Ship (1559) in Pensacola Bay.

Sheathing

Zinc sheathing was also used. The English-built *Admiral Collingwood* was sheathed in zinc in 1855.

Figure 155: Stone cannonballs fashioned by hand from limestone. Found in the stern of the Emanuel Point Ship. FLORIDA BUREAU OF ARCHAEOLOGICAL RESEARCH.

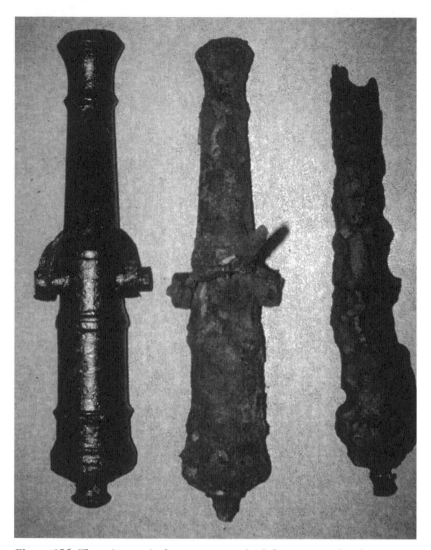

**Figure 156: Three iron swivel guns: gun on the left was immediately con-
served; gun in the middle has deteriorated and needs conservation; and
gun on the right was never conserved and has completely deteriorated.**
FLORIDA BUREAU OF ARCHAEOLOGICAL RESEARCH.

Metals

I now use soda ash for my electrolyte solution. It's much less dangerous to use than sodium hydroxide (lye) and is readily available at most pool supply stores.

I've also been using an automotive rust-preventive paint called POR 15 to coat my iron artifacts after conservation. It's best applied to the surface after a light rust forms. It seals out moisture and is very durable. Carefully read all directions before using.

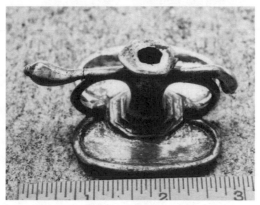

Figures 157 and 158: Before and after conservation photos of silver sword handle from 1715 wrecks. AUTHOR.

Underwater Archaeological Preserve Program

Six sites have already been designated under the State of Florida's new Underwater Archaeological Preserve Program: *Urca de Lima* (1715), *San Pedro* (1733), SS *Copenhagen* (1900), USS *Massachusetts* (1921), SS *Tarpon* (1937), and *City of Hawkinsville* (abandoned). Visit the preserves online at http://www.dos.state.fl.us/dostate/dhr/bar/.

If you know of a site—it should be in state waters, have easy accessibility, and have interesting features to explore and photograph—you may wish to nominate it as a future preserve site. Contact the state at the following address:

> Division of Historical Resources
> Bureau of Archaeological Research
> R. A. Gray Building
> 500 S. Bronough Street
> Tallahassee, FL 32399-0250

Bibliography

Note: Much of the additional material in this second edition came from "Lists of Merchant Vessels of the U.S." (source 14) and "List of Vessels Wrecked on the Florida Coast & Reef, Brought into Key West, from January 1, 1844 to January 1, 1845" [source 14 (a)].

Newspapers
1. *Key West Gazette/Key West Enquirer/Key West Inquirer*, Key West, Florida.

2. *The Tropical Sun*, West Palm Beach, Florida.

Books/Records

3. Albion, Robert G. *Square Riggers on Schedule*. Princeton: Princeton University Press, 1938.
4. Crile, Jane, and Barney Crile. *Treasure-Diving Holidays*. New York: The Viking Press, 1954.
5. The Historical Society of Palm Beach County (records on file).
6. McCarthy, Kevin M. *Thirty Florida Shipwrecks*. Sarasota, FL: Pineapple Press, Inc., 1992.
7. Mondano, Mark R. *Divers Guide to Shipwrecks-Cape Canaveral to Jupiter Light*. Roseland, FL: Sandman Productions, 1991.
8. Pickford, Nigel. *The Atlas of Shipwrecks and Treasure*. New York: Dorling Kindersley, 1994.
9. Snediker, Quentin, and Ann Jensen. *Chesapeake Bay Schooners*. Centreville, MD: Tidewater Publishers.

Figure 159: State of Florida archaeologist doing a video survey of the *Copenhagen* site (1900). AUTHOR.

Suggested Reading

Shipwrecks (Florida Area)

1. Breeden, Robert L., et. al., eds. *Undersea Treasures*. Washington, DC: The National Geographic Society, 1974.
2. Link, Marion Clayton. *Sea Diver*. New York: Rinehart & Company, Inc., 1959.
3. Weller, Robert. *The Dreamweaver*. Charleston: Fletcher Publishing Company, 1997.
4. Weller, Robert. *Galleon Hunt*. Self-published, 1992.

Nautical Archaeology and Ship History

1. Blot, Jean-Yves. *Underwater Archaeology*. New York: Harry N. Abrams, Inc., 1996.
2. Chaunu, Huguette et Pierre. *Seville et L'Atlantique (1504–1650)*. Paris: S.E.V.P.E.N., 1955.
3. Davis, Charles C. *American Sailing Ships*. New York: Dover Publications, Inc., 1984. (Originally published as *Ships of the Past* in 1929.)
4. MacGregor, David R. *Fast Sailing Ships*. Newfoundland: Haessner Publishing, Inc., 1973.
5. Magoun, F. Alexander. *The Frigate Constitution and Other Historic Ships*. New York: Dover Publications, Inc., 1987.
6. Smith, Roger C. *Vanguard of Empire*. New York: Oxford University Press, 1993.
7. Throckmorton, Peter. *Diving for Treasure*. New York: The Viking Press, 1977.
8. Walton, Timothy R. *The Spanish Treasure Fleets*. Sarasota: Pineapple Press, Inc., 1994.

Coins

1. Calico, Ferran, Xavier Calico, and Joaquin Trigo. *Monedas Espanolas Desde Felipe II A Isabel II*. Barcelona: Graficas Reclam, 1982.

Ceramics, Pottery, and Glass

1. Marken, Mitchell W. *Pottery from Spanish Shipwrecks, 1500–1800*. Gainesville: University Press of Florida, 1994.

Armament

1. Norman, A. V. B., and G. M. Wilson. *Treasures from the Tower of London*. London: Lund Humphries Publishers Ltd., 1982.

Silver/Gold Plate

1. Wyler, Seymour B. *The Book of Old Silver*. New York: Crown Publishers, Inc., 1969.

Index

381

Index to Second Edition New Information

If you enjoyed reading this book, here are some other Pineapple Press titles you might enjoy as well. To request our complete catalog or to place an order, write to Pineapple Press, P.O. Box 3889, Sarasota, Florida 34230, or call 1-800-PINEAPL (746-3275). Or visit our website at www.pineapplepress.com.

At the Edge of Honor and *Point of Honor* by Robert N. Macomber. In this series of historical novels of the naval Civil War, Captain Peter Wake, born and bred in the North, joins the U.S. Navy and arrives in Florida for duty with the East Coast Blockading Squadron. ***At the Edge of Honor*** won the 2003 Patrick Smith Award for Best Florida Fiction from the Florida Historical Society. ISBN 1-56164-252-5 (hb); 1-56164-272X (pb). ***Point of Honor*** won the 2003 Cooke Fiction Award from the Military Order of the Stars and Bars. ISBN 1-56164-270-3

Bansemer's Book of the Southern Shores by Roger Bansemer. The author shows us the Southern shores of the United States as only an artist can. His brush finds beauty in the simplicity of a sandbur, in the intricacy of ship skeletons, and in the weathered faces of ship captains. Full color. ISBN 1-56164-294-0 (hb)

Guardians of the Lights by Elinor De Wire. Stories of the men and women of the U.S. Lighthouse Service. In a charming blend of history and human interest, this book paints a colorful portrait of the lives of a vanished breed. ISBN 1-56164-077-8 (hb); 1-56164-119-7 (pb)

Guide to Florida Lighthouses (Second Edition) by Elinor De Wire. Its lighthouses are some of Florida's oldest and most historic structures, with diverse styles of architecture and daymark designs. ISBN 1-56164-216-9 (pb)

Lighthouses of the Carolinas by Terrance Zepke. Eighteen lighthouses aid mariners traveling the coasts of North and South Carolina. Here is the story of each, from origin to current status, along with visiting information and photographs. ISBN 1-56164-148-0 (pb)

The Spanish Treasure Fleets by Timothy R. Walton. The story of how the struggle to control precious metals from Spain's colonies in Latin America helped to shape the modern world. ISBN 1-56164-049-2 (hb)

Thirty Florida Shipwrecks by Kevin M. McCarthy with paintings by William L. Trotter. Sunken treasure, prison ships, Nazi submarines, and the Bermuda Triangle make what the *Florida Historical Quarterly* calls "exciting history." ISBN 1-56164-007-7 (pb)

Twenty Florida Pirates by Kevin M. McCarthy with paintings by William L. Trotter. Notorious Florida pirates from the 1500s to the present include Sir Francis Drake, Black Caesar, Blackbeard, and José Gaspar—not to mention present-day drug smugglers. ISBN 1-56164-050-6 (pb)